The Crescent in the West

The Crescent in the West
The Invasions of Europe by the Ottoman Turkish Empire 1250-1699

Edward S. Creasy

The Crescent in the West
The Invasions of Europe by the Ottoman Turkish Empire 1250-1699
by Edward S. Creasy

FIRST EDITION

Leonaur is an imprint
of Oakpast Ltd

Copyright in this form © 2016 Oakpast Ltd

ISBN: 978-1-78282-535-7 (hardcover)
ISBN: 978-1-78282-536-4 (softcover)

http://www.leonaur.com

Publisher's Notes

The views expressed in this book are not necessarily those of the publisher.

Contents

Preface to Popular Edition	7
First Appearance and Exploits of the Ottoman Turks	9
Descent on Europe	23
Battle of the Marizza	35
The Battle of Nicopolis	49
Tamberlaine & the Tartars	60
Battle of Varna	68
The Siege of Constantinople	91
Turkish Government	115
First War with Egypt	136
War with Persia	150
First Siege of Vienna	181
The Great Siege of Malta	198
The Siege of Malta Continued	219
Battle of Lepanto	246
War with Austria	259
Military Revolts	282
War with the Cossacks	295

War with Russia and Poland 311
The Second Siege of Vienna 329
Negotiations for Peace 344

Preface to Popular Edition

Having been requested to prepare a Second Edition of this work, which has long been out of print, I have made in it many corrections, and some curtailments.

The book (as I stated when it first appeared) is chiefly founded on Von Hammer. I have also carefully sought information from Knolles, Rycaut, Montecuculi, Roe, Hanway, Manstein, D'Ohsson, Thornton, Eton, Ubicini, Porter, Marmont, Sir F. Smith, Col. Chesney, Urquhart, Moltke, Hamel, Sismondi, Ranke, Finlay, Tricoupi, Campbell, Bosworth Smith, and others. I have also availed myself of the fragmentary wealth that lies heaped up in the back numbers of our periodical literature. The indices to both the *Quarterly* and the *Edinburgh* point out several articles on Turkish subjects, from which I have repeatedly gained intelligence and warnings.

Von Hammer's *History of the Ottoman Empire* will always be the standard European book on this subject. That history was the result of the labours of thirty years, during which Von Hammer explored, in addition to the authorities which his predecessors had made use of, the numerous works of the Turkish and other Oriental writers on the Ottoman history, and other rich sources of intelligence which are to be found in the archives of Venice, Austria, and other states, that have been involved in relations of hostility or amity with the Sublime Porte. Von Hammer's long residence in the East, and his familiarity with the institutions and habits, as well as with the language and the literature of the Turks, give an additional attractiveness and value to his volumes. His learning is as accurate as it is varied; his honesty and candour are unquestioned; and his history is certainly one of the best productions of the first half of our century.

This great work has never been translated into English. Its length has probably caused it to be thus neglected, while the historical productions of other German writers, though of less merit, have been eagerly translated and extensively read in this country. The first edition of Von Hammer (published at Pesth) consists of ten thick closely-printed volumes. The second and smaller edition occupies four. This second edition omits the notes and observations, many of which are highly instructive and valuable. And Von Hammer does not bring the Turkish history lower down than to the treaty of Kainardji, 1774. A translation of his entire work, with a continuation of equal copiousness, would make up at least twenty octavo volumes, such as are usually printed in this country. Both writers and publishers have evidently feared that such a work would lack readers among our busy and practical population.

I have not made a mere abridgment of Von Hammer; but I have sought to write an independent work, for which his volumes have supplied me with the largest store of materials. In using them I have arranged, and amplified, and omitted, and added at discretion, so as to assume general responsibility for comments and opinions. Where I have adopted those of Von Hammer, I have generally referred to him as their author. My intention was always to do so, but there may be instances where this has been omitted.

E. S. Creasy.

Athenaeum Club,
March 10th, 1877.

Leonaur Publisher's Note

Whilst Mr. Creasy's preface holds good for the edition you are now holding, this book, of course, confines itself to those periods of the history of the Ottoman Turkish Empire that directly concerns its attempts to spread its domains across the continent of Europe.

Chapter 1

First Appearance and Exploits of the Ottoman Turks

About six centuries ago, a pastoral band of four hundred Turkish families was journeying westward from the upper streams of the river Euphrates. Their armed force consisted of four hundred and forty-four horsemen; and their leader's name was Ertoghrul, which means "The Right-Hearted Man." As they travelled through Asia Minor, they came in sight of a field of battle, on which two armies of unequal numbers were striving for the mastery. Without knowing who the combatants were, The Right-Hearted Man took instantly the chivalrous resolution to aid the weaker party: and charging desperately and victoriously with his warriors upon the larger host, he decided the fortune of the day. Such, according to the Oriental historian Neschri, is the first recorded exploit of that branch of the Turkish race, which from Ertoghrul's son, Othman, has been called the nation of the Ottoman Turks.

★★★★★★

Neschri states this on the authority of Mewlana Ayas, who had heard the battle narrated by the stirrup-holder of Ertoghrul's grandson Orchan, who had heard it from Ertoghrul himself, and had told it to his followers. See Von Hammer's first volume.

"Osman" is the real Oriental name of the Eponymus hero, and the descendants of his subjects style themselves "Osmanlis." But the corrupted forms "Othman" and "Ottoman" have become so fixed in our language and literature, that it would be pedantry to write the correct originals. I follow the same principle in retaining "Amurath" for "Murad," "Bajazet" for "Bayezid," "*Spahi*" for "*Sipahi*," &c., &c.

★★★★★★

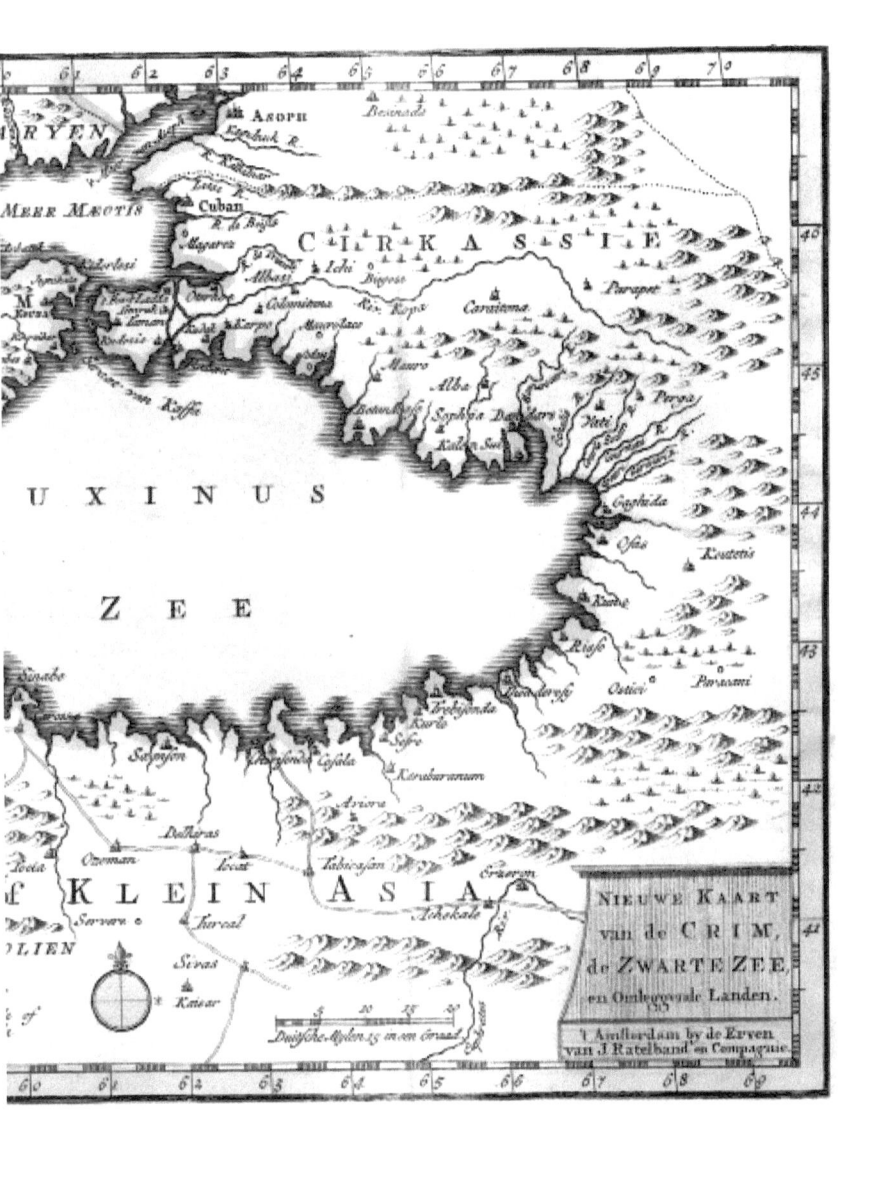

The little band of Ertoghrul was a fragment of a tribe of Oghouz Turks, which, under Ertoghrul's father, Solyman Shah, had left their settlements in Khorassan, and sojourned for a time in Armenia. After a few years, they left this country also; and were following the course of the Euphrates towards Syria, when their leader was accidentally drowned in that river. The greater part of the tribe then dispersed; but a little remnant of it followed two of Solyman's sons, Ertoghrul and Dundar, who determined to seek a dwelling-place in Asia Minor, under the Seljukian Turk, Alaeddin, the Sultan of Iconium. It so happened, that it was Alaeddin himself who commanded the army, to which Ertoghrul and his warriors brought such opportune succour on the battlefield, whither their march in quest of Alaeddin had casually led them. The adversaries, from whose superior force they delivered him, were a host of Mongols, the deadliest enemies of the Turkish race. Alaeddin, in gratitude for this eminent service, bestowed on Ertoghrul a principality in Asia Minor, near the frontiers of the Bithynian province of the Byzantine Emperors.

The rich plains of Saguta along the left bank of the River Sakaria, and the higher districts on the slopes of the Ermeni mountains, became now the pasture-grounds of the father of Othman. The town of Saguta, or Saegud, was his also. Here he, and the shepherd-warriors who had marched with him from Khorassan and Armenia, dwelt as denizens of the land. Ertoghrul's force of fighting men was largely recruited by the best and bravest of the old inhabitants, who became his subjects; and, still more advantageously, by numerous volunteers of kindred origin to his own. The Turkish race, had been extensively spread through Lower Asia long before the time of Ertoghrul. (According to Dr. Latham, all the early great Asiatic conquerors from the parts north of the Oxus have been of Turkish race, except Zenghis Khan and his descendants, and except the Mantchoo conquerors of China).

Quitting their primitive abodes on the upper *steppes* of the Asiatic continent, tribe after tribe of that martial family of nations had poured down upon the rich lands and tempting wealth of the southern and western regions, when the power of the early *khalifs* had decayed, like that of the Greek Emperors. One branch of the Turks, called the Seljukian, from their traditional patriarch Seljuk Khan, had acquired and consolidated a mighty empire, more than two centuries before the name of the Ottomans was heard. The Seljukian Turks were once masters of nearly all Asia Minor, of Syria, of Mesopotamia, Armenia, part of Persia, and Western Turkestan: and their great Sultans, Toghrul Beg, Alp Arslan, and Melek Shah, are among the most renowned conquerors that stand forth in Oriental and in Byzantine history.

But, by the middle of the thirteenth century of the Christian era, when Ertoghrul appeared on the battlefield in Asia Minor, the great fabric of Seljukian dominion had been broken up by the assaults of the conquering Mongols, aided by internal corruption and civil strife. The Seljukian Sultan Alaeddin reigned in ancient pomp at Koniah, the old Iconium; but his effective supremacy extended over a narrow compass, compared with the ample sphere throughout which his predecessors had exacted obedience. The Mongols had rent away the southern and eastern acquisitions of his race.

In the centre and south of Asia Minor other Seljukian chiefs ruled various territories as independent princes; and the Greek Emperors of Constantinople had recovered a considerable portion of the old Roman provinces in the north and east of that peninsula. Amid the general tumult of border warfare, and of ever-recurring peril from roving armies of Mongols, which pressed upon Alaeddin, the settlement in his dominions of a loyal chieftain and hardy clan, such as Ertoghrul and his followers, was a welcome accession of strength; especially as the new comers were, like the Seljukian Turks, zealous adherents of the Mahometan faith. The Crescent was the device that Alaeddin bore on his banners; Ertoghrul, as Alaeddin's vicegerent, assumed the same standard; and it was by Ertoghrul's race that the Crescent was made for centuries the terror of Christendom, as the sign of aggressive Islam, and as the chosen emblem of the conquering Ottoman power.

There was little peace in Ertoghrul's days on the frontier near which he had obtained his first grants of land. Ertoghrul had speedy and frequent opportunities for augmenting his military renown, and for gratifying his followers with the spoils of successful forays and assaults. The boldest Turkish adventurers flocked eagerly to the banner of the new and successful chieftain of their race; and Alaeddin gladly recognised the value of his feudatory's services by fresh honours and marks of confidence, and by increased donations of territory.

In a battle which Ertoghrul, as Alaeddin's lieutenant, fought against a mixed army of Greeks and Mongols, between Brusa and Yenischeer, he drew up his troops so as to throw forward upon the enemy a cloud of light cavalry, called Akindji; thus completely masking the centre of the main army, which, as the post of honour, was termed the Sultan's station. Ertoghrul held the centre himself, at the head of the four hun-

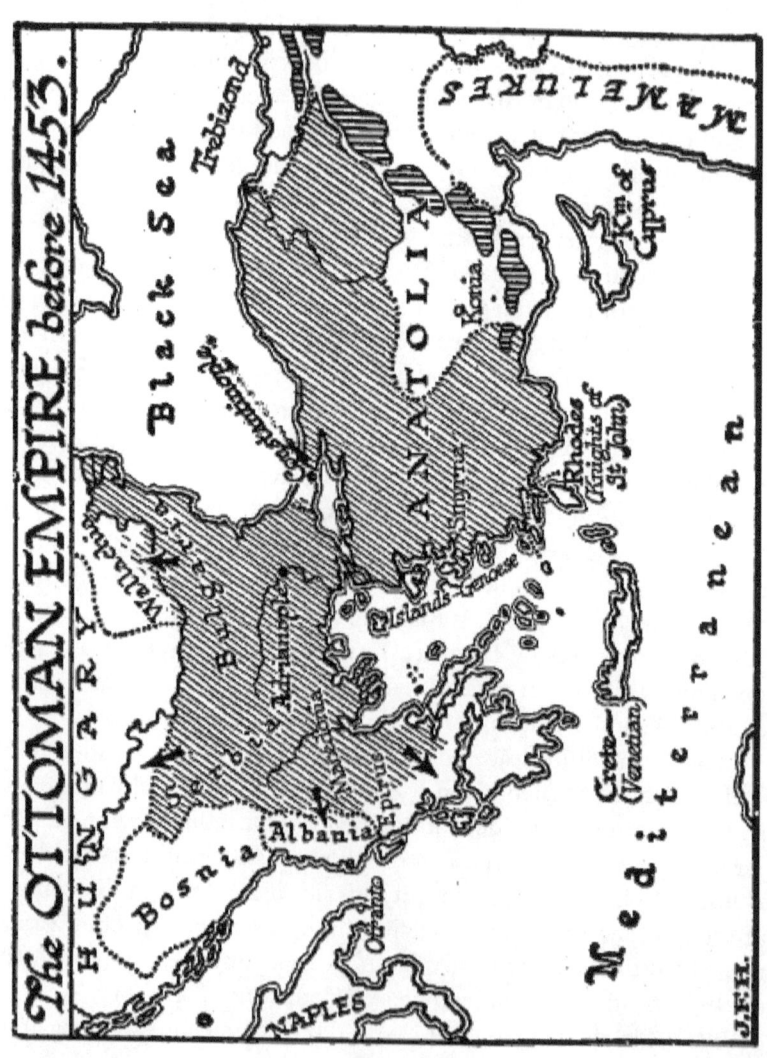

dred and forty-four horsemen, who were his own original followers, and whose *scimetars* had won the day for Alaeddin, when they first charged unconsciously in his cause.

The system now adopted by Ertoghrul of wearying the enemy by collision with a mass of irregular troops, and then pressing him with a reserve of the best soldiers, was for centuries the favourite tactic of his descendants. The battle in which he now employed it was long and obstinate; but in the end the Turkish chief won a complete victory. Alaeddin, on being informed of this achievement of his gallant and skilful vassal, bestowed on him the additional territory of Eskischeer, and in memory of the mode in which Ertoghrul had arrayed his army, Alaeddin gave to his principality the name of Sultan-Œni, which means "Sultan's Front."

The territory which received that name, and still bears it, as one of the *Sanjaks*, or minor governments of the Ottoman Empire, is nearly identical with the ancient Phrygia Epictetos. It was rich in pasturage, both in its alluvial meadows and along its mountain slopes. It contained also many fertile cornlands and vineyards; and the romantic beauty of every part of its thickly wooded and well-watered highlands still attracts the traveller's admiration, (Anadol).

Besides numerous villages, it contained, in Ertoghrul's time, the strongholds of Karadjahissar, Biledjik, Inaeni, and others; and the cities or towns of Eskischeer (so celebrated in the history of the crusades under its old name of Dorylaeum), Seid-e-ghari, Lefke, and Saegud, near which is the domed tomb of Ertoghrul, an object still of the deepest veneration to frequent pilgrims from all parts of the Ottoman Empire. Many of the places that have been mentioned were, at the time when Alaeddin, as their titular sovereign, made grant of them to Ertoghrul, held by chieftains, who were practically independent, and who little heeded the sovereign's transfer of their lands and towns. It was only after long years of warfare carried on by Ertoghrul and his more renowned son, Othman, that Sultan-Œni became the settled possession of their house.

Othman, or, according to the Oriental orthography, Osman, is regarded as the founder of the Ottoman Empire; and it is from him that the Turks, who inhabit it, call themselves Osmanlis, the only national appellation which they recognise. (They consider that the name of Turk implies rudeness and barbarism). Ertoghrul never professed to act save as the vassal and lieutenant of the Sultan of Iconium. But Othman, after the death of the last Alaeddin in 1307, waged wars and accumulated dominions as an independent potentate. He had become chief of his race twelve years before, on Ertoghrul's death, in 1288. Othman, at his succession, was twenty-four years of age, and was already of proved skill as a leader, and of tried prowess as a combatant. His early fortunes and exploits are favourite subjects with the Oriental writers, especially his love adventures in wooing and winning the fair Malkhatoon. These legends have probably been coloured by the poetical pens, that have recorded them in later years; but it is less improbable that they should be founded on fact, than that no similar traditions should have been handed down by the children and followers of so renowned a chief, as the founder of the Ottoman Empire.

The Scheikh Edebali, celebrated for his piety and learning, had come, while Othman was very young, to Itbourouni, a village near Eskischeer. Othman used often to visit the holy man, out of respect for his sanctity and learning; and the young prince's visits became still more frequent, after he had one evening accidentally obtained a view of the *scheikh's* fair daughter, Malkhatoon, a name which means "Treasure of a Woman." Othman confessed his love; but the old man thought that the disparity of station made a marriage imprudent, and refused his consent. Othman sought consolation for his disappointment in the society of his friends and neighbours, to whom he described with a lover's inspiration, the beauty of Malkhatoon. He discoursed so eloquently on this theme to the young chief of Eskischeer, that the listener fell in love with Malkhatoon upon hearsay; and, going to her father, demanded her hand for himself Edebali refused him also; but fearing his vengeance more than that of Othman, the old man removed from the neighbourhood of Eskischeer to a dwelling close to that of Ertoghrul.

The chief of Eskischeer now hated Othman as his rival. One day when Othman and his brother Goundonroulp were at the castle of their neighbour, the lord of Inaeni, an armed force suddenly appeared at the gate, led by the chieftain of Eskischeer and his ally, Michael of the Peaked Beard, the Greek lord of Khirenkia, a fortified city at the foot of the Phrygian Olympus. They demanded that Othman should be given up to them; but the lord of Inaeni refused to commit such a breach of hospitality. While the enemy lingered irresolutely round the castle wall, Othman and his brother seized an advantageous moment for a sudden sally at the head of a few companions. They chased the chief of Eskischeer off the field in disgrace, and took Michael of the Peaked Beard prisoner. The captive an the captors became staunch friends; and in after times, when Othman reigned as an independent prince, Michael left the Christian for the Mussulman creed to join him, and was thenceforth one of the strongest supporters of the Ottoman power, (Von Hammer, vol. i.).

Othman had by this encounter at Inaeni, triumphed over his rival, and acquired a valuable friend; but he could not yet gain the maiden of his heart. For two more years the course of his true love ran through refusal and anxiety, until at length, old Edebali was touched by the young prince's constancy, and he interpreted a dream as a declaration of Heaven in favour of the long-sought marriage.

One night, when Othman was resting at Edebali's house (for the shelter of hospitality could never be denied even to the suitor whose addresses were rejected), the young prince, after long and melancholy musing on her whom he loved, composed his soul in that patient resignation to sorrow, which, according to the Arabs, is the key to all happiness. In this mood he fell asleep, and he dreamed a dream.

He saw himself and his host reposing near each other. From the bosom of Edebali rose the full moon (emblem of the beauteous Malkhatoon), and inclining towards the bosom of Othman, it sank upon it, and was lost to sight. Thence sprang forth a goodly tree, which grew in beauty and in strength ever greater and greater. Still did the embracing verdure of its boughs and branches cast an ampler and an ampler shade, until they canopied the extreme horizon of the three parts of the world. Under the tree stood four mountains, which he knew to be Caucasus, Atlas, Taurus, and Haemus. These mountains were the four columns, that seemed to support the dome of the foliage of the sacred tree, with which the earth was now pavilioned. From the roots of the tree gushed forth four rivers, the Tigris, the Euphrates, the Danube, and the Nile. Tall ships and barks innumerable were on the waters.

The fields were heavy with harvest. The mountain sides were clothed with forests. Thence in exulting and fertilising abundance sprang fountains and rivulets, that gurgled through thickets of the cypress and the rose. In the valleys glittered stately cities, with domes and cupolas, with pyramids and obelisks, with minarets and towers. The Crescent shone on their summits: from their galleries sounded the *muezzin's* call to prayer. That sound was mingled with the sweet voices of a thousand nightingales, and with the prattling of countless parrots of every hue. Every kind of singing bird was there. The winged multitude warbled and flitted round beneath the fresh living roof of the interlacing branches of the all-overarching tree; and every leaf of that tree was in shape like unto a *scimetar*. Suddenly there arose a mighty wind, and turned the points of the sword-leaves towards the various cities of the world, but especially towards Constantinople. That city, placed at the junction of two seas and two continents, seemed like a diamond set between two sapphires and two emeralds, to form the most precious stone in a ring of universal empire. Othman thought that he was in the act of placing that visioned ring on his finger, when he awoke.

******

See Von Hammer, vol. i. The author of *Anadol* recounts this dream, and remarks on the part of it respecting Constantinople:—

> That link, Constantinople, fell into the hands of Osman Bey's descendant, Sultan Mohammed II., and the Turkish Empire was constituted. It is, indeed, an aggregation of many nations, and the prophetic allegory of the multitudes of foreign birds gathering under the Ottoman tent has been fully realised. For in a population of thirty-five millions, upwards of seven are Sclavonians, four claim Roman origin, two assert their Greek descent, the Arabs number nearly five, and there are two millions and a half of Armenians, fifteen hundred thousand Albanians, and a million of Kurds.

******

Othman related this dream to his host; and the vision seemed to Edebali so clearly to presage honour, and power, and glory, to the posterity of Othman and Malkhatoon, (some of the Ottoman historians call her "Kameriyé"' which means "Beautiful Moon."—Von Hammer, vol. i.), that the old *scheikh* no longer opposed their union. They were married by the saintly Dervise Touroud, a disciple of Edebali. Othman promised to give the officiating minister a dwelling-place near a mosque, and on the bank of a river. When Othman became an independent prince, he built for the *dervise* a convent, which he endowed richly with villages and lands, and which remained for centuries in the possession of the family of Touroud.

The Ottoman writers attach great importance to this dream of the founder of their empire. They dwell also on the prophetic significance of his name, signifying the resistless energy with which he and his descendants were to smite the nations of the earth. "Othman" means the "Bone-breaker." It is also a name given to a large species of vulture, commonly called the royal vulture, and which is, in the East, the emblem of sovereignty and warlike power, as the eagle is with the nations of the West

Othman is celebrated by the Oriental writers for his personal beauty, and for "his wondrous length and strength of arm." Like Artaxerxes Longimanus, of the old dynasty of Persian kings, and like the Highland chieftain of whom Wordsworth sang, Othman could touch his knees with his hands when he stood upright. He was unsurpassed in his skill and graceful carriage as a horseman; and the jet black colour of his hair, his beard, and eyebrows, gained him in youth the title of "Kara," that is to say, "Black" Othman. The epithet "Kara," which we shall often find in Turkish history, is, when applied to a person, considered to imply the highest degree of manly beauty. (*E. g.* Kara-dhissar, "The Black Castle;" Kara-Denis, "The Black Sea;" Kara Mustapha, "Black Mustapha;" Kara-dagh, "Black Mountain;" Kara-Su, "Black Water"). His costume was simple as that of the first warriors of Islam. Like them he wore a turban of ample white linen, wreathed round a red centre. His loose flowing *kaftan* was of one colour, and had long open hanging sleeves. Such in outward appearance was the successful lover of the fair Malkhatoon, whose lineal descendant still, (1877), rules the Ottoman Empire.

Othman's conquests were soon extended beyond the limits of Sultan-Œni, partly at the expense of rival Turkish chieftains, but principally by wresting fortress after fortress, and region after region from the Greek Empire. At the close of the thirteenth century of our era, the Ottoman head-quarters of empire were advanced as far northwestward as the city of Yenischeer, within a short march of the important Greek cities of Brusa and Nicaea, which were now the special objects of Turkish ambition.

It would, however, be unjust to represent Othman as merely an ambitious military adventurer, or to suppose that his whole career was marked by restless rapacity and aggressive violence against the neighbouring states. From 1291 *A.D.* to 1298, he was at peace; and the war that next followed was, at its commencement, a defensive one on his part, caused by the jealous aggressions of other Turkish Emirs, who envied his prosperity, and who were aided by some of the Greek commandants in the vicinity. Thus roused into action, Othman showed that his power had been strengthened, not corrupted by repose, and he smote his enemies in every direction.

The effect of his arms in winning new subjects to his sway was materially aided by the reputation which he had honourably acquired, as a just lawgiver and judge, in whose dominions Greek and Turk, Christian and Mahometan, enjoyed equal protection for property and person. It was about this time, A.D. 1299, that he coined money with his own effigy, and caused the public prayers to be said in his name. These among the Oriental nations are regarded as the distinctive marks of royalty. (Von Hammer discusses the question, whether these marks of sovereignty were assumed by Othman or his son Orchan, he comes to a different conclusion).

The last prince of the family of Alaeddin, to which that of Othman had been indebted for its first foundation in Asia Minor, was now dead. There was no other among the various *emirs* of that country who could compete with Othman for the headship of the whole Turkish population, and dominion over the whole peninsula, save only the Emir of Caramania, (Von Hammer). A long and fierce struggle between the Ottoman and Caramanian princes for the ascendency, commenced in Othman's lifetime, and was protracted during the reigns of many of his successors. Othman himself had gained some advantages over his Caramanian rival; but the weak and wealthy possessions of the Byzantine Emperor in the north-east of Asia Minor were more tempting marks for his ambition than the Caramanian plains: and it was over Greek cities and armies that the chief triumphs of the last twenty-six years of Othman's life were achieved.

Some of Othman's counsellors hesitated at the entrance of the bold path of conquest on which their chief strode so firmly; but Othman silenced all remonstrance, and quelled all risk of dissension and mutiny by an act of prompt ferocity, which shows that the great ancestor of the Ottoman Sultans had, besides the traits of chivalrous and noble feelings which we have recorded, a full share of the ruthless cruelty, that has been the dark characteristic of the Turkish Royal House. Othman's uncle, the aged Dundar,. who had marched with Ertoghrul from the Euphrates, seventy years before, was still alive, when Othman, in 1299, summoned a council of his principal followers, and announced to them his intention to attack the lord of the important Greek fortress of Koeprihissar.

The old uncle opposed the enterprise; and urged the danger of provoking by such ambitious aggrandisement all the neighbouring princes, Turkish as well as Greek, to league against them for the destruction of their tribe. Enraged at the chilling caution of the grey-headed man, and, observing probably that others were beginning to share in it, Othman met the arrows of the tongue by the arrows of the bow. He spake not a word in reply, but he shot his old uncle dead upon the spot—a bloody lesson to all who should harbour thoughts of contradiction to the fixed will of so stern a lord. The modern German historian, who recounts this scene, well observes that:

> This uncle's murder marks with terror the commencement of the Ottoman dominion, as the brother's murder that of Rome; only the former rests on better historical evidence. Edris, justly esteemed the most valuable historian of the Turks, who, at the beginning of his work, openly declares that, passing over in silence all that is reprehensible, he will only hand down to posterity the glorious deeds of the royal race of Othman, relates among the latter the murder of Dundar, with all the circumstances detailed above. If then such murderous slaughter of their kindred be reckoned by the panegyrists of the Osmanlies among their praiseworthy acts, what are we to think of those which cannot be praised, and of which their history is therefore silent?—Von Hammer i.

Koeprihissar was attacked, and fell; and numerous other strongholds in the vicinity of Nice soon shared the same fate. In 1301, Othman encountered for the first time a regular Greek Army, which was led against him by Muzaros, the commander of the guards of the Byzantine Emperor. This important battle took place at Koyounhissar (called Baphoeum by the Greeks) in the vicinity of Nicomedia. Othman gained a complete victory; and in the successful campaigns of the six following years, he carried his arms as far as the coast of the Black Sea, securing fortress after fortress, and hemming in the strong cities of Brusa, Nice, and Nicomedia (which yet were retained by the Greeks), with a chain of fortified posts, where his garrisons, under bold and skilful chiefs, were ever on the watch for the chance of a surprise or the material for a foray. It was in vain that the Byzantine court sought to avert the pressure of this ever-active enemy, by procuring a Mongol army to attack Othman's southern dominions. Othman sent his son Orchan against the invaders, and the young prince utterly defeated them.

Age and infirmity began now to press upon Othman, but his gallant son filled his place at the head of the troops with undiminished energy and success. In 1326, the great city of Brusa surrendered to the Ottomans. Othman was on his deathbed, at Saegud, the first town that his father Ertoghrul had possessed, when his son effected this important conquest; but he lived long enough to hear the glad tidings, and to welcome the young hero. The Oriental writers narrate the last scene of Othman's life, and profess to record his dying advice to his successor. The fair Malkhatoon had gone before him to the grave; but the two brave sons whom she had borne him, Orchan and Alaeddin, and a few of his veteran captains and sages, were at the monarch's death-bed Othman said to Orchan:

> My son, I am dying; and I die without regret, because I leave such a successor as thou art. Be just; love goodness, and show mercy. Give equal protection to all thy subjects, and extend the law of the Prophet. Such are the duties of princes upon earth; and it is thus that they bring on them the blessings of Heaven.

Then, as if he wished to take actual seisin of Brusa, and to associate himself with his son's glory, he directed that he should be buried there; and advised his son to make that city the seat of empire, (Von Hammer i.). His last wishes were loyally complied with; and a stately mausoleum, which stood at Brusa until its destruction by fire in the present age, marked the last resting-place of Othman, and proved the pious reverence of his descendants. His banner and his sabre are still preserved in the treasury of the empire: and the martial ceremony of girding on that sabre is the solemn right, analogous to the coronations of Christendom, by which the Turkish *Sultans* are formally invested with sovereign power.

Othman is commonly termed the first *Sultan* of his race; but neither he nor his two immediate successors assumed more than the title of *Emir*. He had, at the time of his death, reigned as an independent *emir* twenty-seven years, and had been chief of his tribe for thirty-nine years of his life of sixty-eight. His career fully displays the buoyant courage, the subtle watchfulness, the resolute decision, the strong common-sense, and the power of winning and wielding the affections and energies of other men, which are the usual attributes of the founders of empires. And, notwithstanding his blood-guiltiness in his uncle's death, we must believe him to have been eminently mild and gracious for an Oriental sovereign, from the traditional attachment with which his memory is still cherished by his nation, and which is expressed at the accession of each new *Sultan* by the formula of the people's prayer:

> May he be as good as Othman.

CHAPTER 2

Descent on Europe

Emir Othman now slept at Brusa, and Emir Orchan reigned in his stead. Fratricide was not yet regarded as the necessary safeguard of the throne; and Orchan earnestly besought his brother Alaeddin to share with him his sovereignty and his wealth. Alaeddin firmly refused to consent to any division of the empire, and so contravene the will of their father, who had addressed Orchan only as his successor. Nor would Alaeddin accept more of the paternal property than the revenues of a single village, near Brusa. Orchan then said to him:

> Since, my brother, thou wilt not take the flocks and the herds that I offer thee, be thou the shepherd of my people; be my *Vizier*.

The word "*Vizier*," in the Ottoman language, means the bearer of a burden; and Alaeddin, in accepting the office, took on him, according to the Oriental historians, his brother's burden of power. Alaeddin did not, like many of his successors in that office, often command in person the armies of his race; but he occupied himself most efficiently with the foundation and management of the civil and military institutions of his country.

According to some authorities, it was in his time, and by his advice, that the semblance of vassalage to the ruler of Koniah, by stamping money with his effigy, and using his name in the public prayers, was discontinued by the Ottomans. These changes are more correctly referred by others to Othman himself; but all the Oriental writers concur in attributing to Alaeddin the introduction of laws, which endured for centuries, respecting the costume of the various subjects of the empire, and of laws which created a standing army of regular troops, and provided funds for its support. It was, above all, by his advice and that of a contemporary Turkish statesman, that the celebrated corps of Janissaries was formed, an institution which European writers erroneously fix at a later date, and ascribe to Amurath I.

Alaeddin, by his military legislation, may be truly said to have organised victory for the Ottoman race. He originated for the Turks a standing army of regularly paid and disciplined infantry and horse, a fill century before Charles VII. of France established his fifteen permanent companies of men-at-arms, which are generally regarded as the first standing army known in modern history. Orchan's predecessors, Ertoghrul and Othman, had made war at the head of the armed vassals and volunteers, who thronged on horseback to their prince's banner, when summoned for each expedition, and who were disbanded as soon as the campaign was over. Alaeddin determined to ensure and improve future successes, by forming a corps of paid infantry, which should be kept in constant readiness for service.

These troops were called *Yaya*, or *Piadé*: and they were divided into tens, hundreds, and thousands, under their respective *decurions, centurions*, and colonels. Their pay was high; and their pride soon made them objects of anxiety to their sovereign. Orchan wished to provide a check to them, and he took counsel for this purpose with his brother Alaeddin and Kara Khalil Tschendereli, who was connected with the royal house by marriage. Tschendereli laid before his master and the *vizier* a project, out of which arose the renowned corps of the *Janissaries*, so long the scourge of Christendom; so long, also, the terror of their own sovereigns; and which was finally extirpated by the Sultan himself, in our own age. Tschendereli proposed to Orchan to create an army entirely composed of Christian children, who should be forced to adopt the Mahometan religion. Black Khalil argued thus:

> The conquered are the property of the conqueror, who is the lawful master of them, of their lands, of their goods, of their wives, and of their children. We have a right to do what we will with our own; and the treatment which I propose is not only lawful, but benevolent. By enforcing the conversion of these captive children to the true faith, and enrolling them in the ranks of the army of the true believers, we consult both their temporal and eternal interests; for, is it not written in the *Koran* that all children are, at their birth, naturally disposed to Islam?

He also alleged that the formation of a Mahometan Army out of Christian children would induce other Christians to adopt the creed of the Prophet; so that the new force would be recruited, not only out of the children of the conquered nations, but out of a crowd of their Christian friends and relations, who would come as volunteers to join the Ottoman ranks.

Acting on this advice, Orchan selected out of the families of the Christians whom he had conquered, a thousand of the finest boys. In the next year a thousand more were taken; and this annual enrolment of a thousand Christian children was continued for three centuries, until the reign of Sultan Mahomet IV., in 1648. When the prisoners made in the campaign of the year did not supply a thousand serviceable boys, the number was completed by a levy on the families of the Christian subjects of the *Sultan*. This was changed in the time of Mahomet IV., and the corps was thenceforth recruited from among the children of *Janissaries* and native Turks; but during the conquering period of the Ottoman power, the institution of the *Janissaries*, as designed by Alaeddin and Tschendereli, was maintained in full vigour.

The name of *Yeni Tscheri*, which means "new troops," and which European writers have turned into *Janissaries*, was given to Orchan's young corps by the Dervish Hadji Beytarch. This *dervish* was renowned for sanctity; and Orchan, soon after he had enrolled his first band of involuntary boyish proselytes, led them to the dwelling-place of the saint, and asked him to give them his blessing and a name. The *dervish* drew the sleeve of his mantle over the head of one in the first rank, and then said to the *Sultan*:

> The troop which thou hast created shall be called *Yeni Tscheri*. Their faces shall be white and shining, their right arms shall be strong, their sabres shall be keen, and their arrows sharp. They shall be fortunate in fight, and they shall never leave the battlefield save as conquerors.

In memory of that benediction, the *Janissaries* ever wore, as part of their uniform, a cap of white felt, like that of the *dervish*, with a strip of woollen hanging down behind, to represent the sleeve of the holy man's mantle, that had been laid on their comrade's neck.

The Christian children, who were to be trained as *Janissaries*, were usually chosen at a tender age. They were torn from their parents, trained to renounce the faith in which they were born and baptised, and to profess the creed of Mahomet. They were then carefully educated for a soldier's life. The discipline to which they were subjected was severe. They were taught the most implicit obedience; and they were accustomed to bear without repining fatigue, pain, and hunger. But liberal honours and prompt promotion were the sure rewards of docility and courage. Cut off from all ties of country, kith, and kin, but with high pay and privileges, with ample opportunities for military advancement, and for the gratification of the violent, the sensual, and the sordid passions of their animal natures amid the customary atrocities of successful warfare, this military brotherhood grew up to be the strongest and fiercest instrument of imperial ambition, which remorseless fanaticism, prompted by the most subtle statecraft, ever devised upon earth.

The Ottoman historians eulogise with one accord the sagacity and piety of the founders of this institution. They reckon the number of conquerors whom it gave to earth, and of heirs of paradise whom it gave to heaven, on the hypothesis that, during three centuries, the stated number of a thousand Christian children, neither more nor less, was levied, converted, and enlisted. They boast, accordingly, that three hundred thousand children were delivered from the torments of hell by being made *Janissaries*. But Von Hammer calculates, from the increase in the number of these troops under later *Sultans*, that at least half a million of young Christians must have been thus made, first the helpless victims, and then the cruel ministers of Mahometan power.

After the organisation of the *Janissaries*, Alaeddin regulated that of the other corps of the army. In order that the soldier should have an interest, not only in making, but in preserving conquests, it was determined that the troops should receive allotments of land in the subjugated territories. The regular infantry, the *Piadé*, had at first received pay in money; but they now had lands given to them on tenure of military service, and they were also under the obligation of keeping in good repair the public roads that led near their grounds. The irregular infantry, which had neither pay like the *Janissaries*, nor lands like the *Piadé*, was called *Azab*, which means "light." The lives of these undisciplined bands were held of little value; and the *Azabs* were thrown forward to perish in multitudes at the commencement of a battle or a siege. It was over their bodies that the *Janissaries* usually marched to the decisive charge or the final assault.

The cavalry was distributed by Alaeddin, like the infantry, into regular and irregular troops. The permanent corps of paid cavalry was divided into four squadrons, organised like those which the Caliph Omar instituted for the guard of the Sacred Standard. The whole corps at first consisted of only 2400 horsemen; but under Solyman the

Great the number was raised to 4000. They marched on the right and left of the *Sultan;* they camped round his tent at night, and they were his body-guard in battle. One of these regiments of Royal Horseguards was called the Turkish *Spahis,* a term applied to cavalry soldiers generally, but also specially denoting these select horse-guards. Another regiment was called the *Silihdars,* meaning the " vassal cavalry." A third was called the *Ouloufedji,* meaning the "paid horsemen;" and the fourth was called *Ghoureba,* meaning "the foreign horse." Besides this permanently embodied corps of paid cavalry, Alaeddin formed a force of horsemen, who received grants of land like the *Piadé.* As they paid no taxes for the lands which they thus held, they were termed *Moselliman,* which means "tax-free." They were commanded by *Sandjak Beys* (princes of standards), by *Binbaschi* (chiefs of thousands), and *Soubaschi* (chiefs of hundreds). There were other holders of the grand and petty fiefs which were called *Ziamets* and *Timars.*

These terms will be adverted to hereafter, when we reach the period at which the Turkish feudal system was more fully developed and defined. But in the earliest times, their holders were bound to render military service on horseback, when summoned by their sovereign; and they were arrayed under banners, in thousands and in hundreds, like the *Mosellimans.* In addition to the regular and feudal cavalry, there were the *Akindji,* or irregular light horse, receiving neither pay nor lands, but dependent on plunder, who were still called together in multitudes, whenever an Ottoman Army was on the march; and the terror which these active and ferocious marauders spread far and wide beyond the regular line of operations, made the name of the *Akindji* as much known and dreaded in Christendom, as that of the *Janissaries* and *Spahis.*

Orchan had captured the city of Nicomedia in the first year of his reign (1326); and with the new resources for warfare which the administrative genius of his brother placed at his command, he speedily signalised his reign by conquests still more important. The great city of Nice (second to Constantinople only in the Greek Empire) surrendered to him in 1330. Orchan gave the command of it to his eldest son, Solyman Pacha, who had directed the operations of the siege. Numerous other advantages were gained over the Greeks: and the Turkish prince of Karasi (the ancient Mysia), who had taken up arms against the Ottomans, was defeated; and his capital city, Berghama (the ancient Pergamus), and his territory, annexed to Orchan's dominions. On the conquest of Karasi, in the year 1336 of our era, nearly the whole of the north-west of Asia Minor was included in the Ottoman Empire; and the four great cities of Brusa, Nicomedia, Nice, and Pergamus had become strongholds of its power.

A period of twenty years, without further conquests, and without war, followed the acquisition of Karasi. During this time the Ottoman sovereign was actively occupied in perfecting the civil and military institutions which his brother had introduced; in securing internal order, in founding and endowing mosques and schools, and in the construction of vast public edifices, which yet attest the magnificence and piety of Orchan. It is indeed a remarkable trait in the characters of the first princes of the Ottoman dynasty, that, unlike the generality of conquerors, especially of Asiatic conquerors, they did not hurry on from one war to another in ceaseless avidity for fresh victories and new dominions; but, on the contrary, they were not more eager to seize, than they were cautious and earnest to consolidate.

They paused over each subdued province, till, by assimilation of civil and military institutions, it was fully blended into the general nationality of their empire. They thus gradually moulded, in Asia Minor, an homogeneous and a stable power; instead of precipitately heaping together a motley mass of ill-arranged provinces and discordant populations. To this policy the long endurance of the Ottoman Empire, compared with other Oriental empires of both ancient and modern times, is greatly to be ascribed. And the extent to which this policy was followed in Asia Minor, compared with their subsequent practice in European Turkey, in Syria, and in Egypt, may have conduced in giving to the Ottomans a firmer hold on the first-named country, than they possess on their territories westward of the Hellespont and southward of Mount Taurus.

Every traveller notes the difference; the Ottomans themselves acknowledge it; and Anatolia (a name generally though not accurately used as co-extensive with that of Asia Minor) is regarded by the modern Turks as their stronghold in the event of further national disasters. They call it emphatically, "The last Home of the Faithful," (*Anadol*; and Ubicini, vol. ii.). The facts (which have been already mentioned) of the general diffusion of Turkish populations over Asia Minor, before Othman's time, must unquestionably have greatly promoted the solidity as well as the extent of the dominion which he and his successor there established; but the far-sighted policy, with which they tempered their ambition, was also an efficient cause of permanent strength; and their remote descendants still experience its advantageous operation.

The friendly relations which Orchan formed with the Emperor Andronicus, and maintained (though not uninterruptedly) with that prince and some of his successors, contributed to give a long period of twenty years general repose to the Ottoman power. But in the civil wars which distracted the last ages and wasted the last resources of the Greek Empire, the auxiliary arms of the Turkish princes were frequently called over and employed in Europe. The Emperor Cantacuzene, in the year 1346, recognised in Orchan the most powerful sovereign of the Turks; and he hoped to attach the Ottoman forces permanently to his interests by giving his daughter in marriage to their ruler, notwithstanding the difference of creed, and the disparity of years between the young princess and the old Turk, who was now a widower of the age of sixty.

The pomp of the nuptials between Orchan and Theodora is elaborately described by the Byzantine writers; but in the next year, during which the Ottoman bridegroom visited his imperial father-in-law at Scutari, the suburb of Constantinople on the Asiatic side of the Bosphorus, scenes of a less pleasing character to the Greeks ensued. Orchan's presence protected the Greek emperor and his subjects during the display of festive splendour which Scutari exhibited at the meeting of the sovereigns; but when Orchan had returned to his Bithynian capital, some Ottoman bands crossed the Hellespont, and pillaged several towns in Thrace; but they were at last, after a series of sanguinary encounters, all killed or taken by the superior forces sent against them.

Not long afterwards, the war that raged between the two great maritime republics of Venice and Genoa along almost every coast of the Mediterranean and its connected seas, was the immediate cause of hostilities between the troops of Orchan and those of his father-in-law; and led to the settlement of the Ottomans in Europe. The Genoese possessed the European suburb of Constantinople, called Galata; and the Bosphorus was one of the scenes on which the most obstinate contests were maintained between their fleets and those of their rivals. Orchan hated the Venetians, whose fleets had insulted his seaward provinces, and who had met his diplomatic overtures with contempt, as if coming from an insignificant barbarous chieftain.

The Venetians were allies of Cantacuzene; but Orchan sent an auxiliary force across the straits to Galata, which there co-operated with the Genoese. Orchan also aided the emperor's other son-in-law, John Palaeologus, in the civil war that was kept up between him and the Greek emperor. In the midst of the distress and confusion with which

II The Byzantine Empire a[nd...]

- Byzantine Empire
- Greek Empire of Trebizond
- Kingdom of Armenia
- Ottoman (Osmanli) Turks
- Other Turks
- Kingdom of S
- Kingdom of B
- States under
- Venetian poss
- Genoese poss

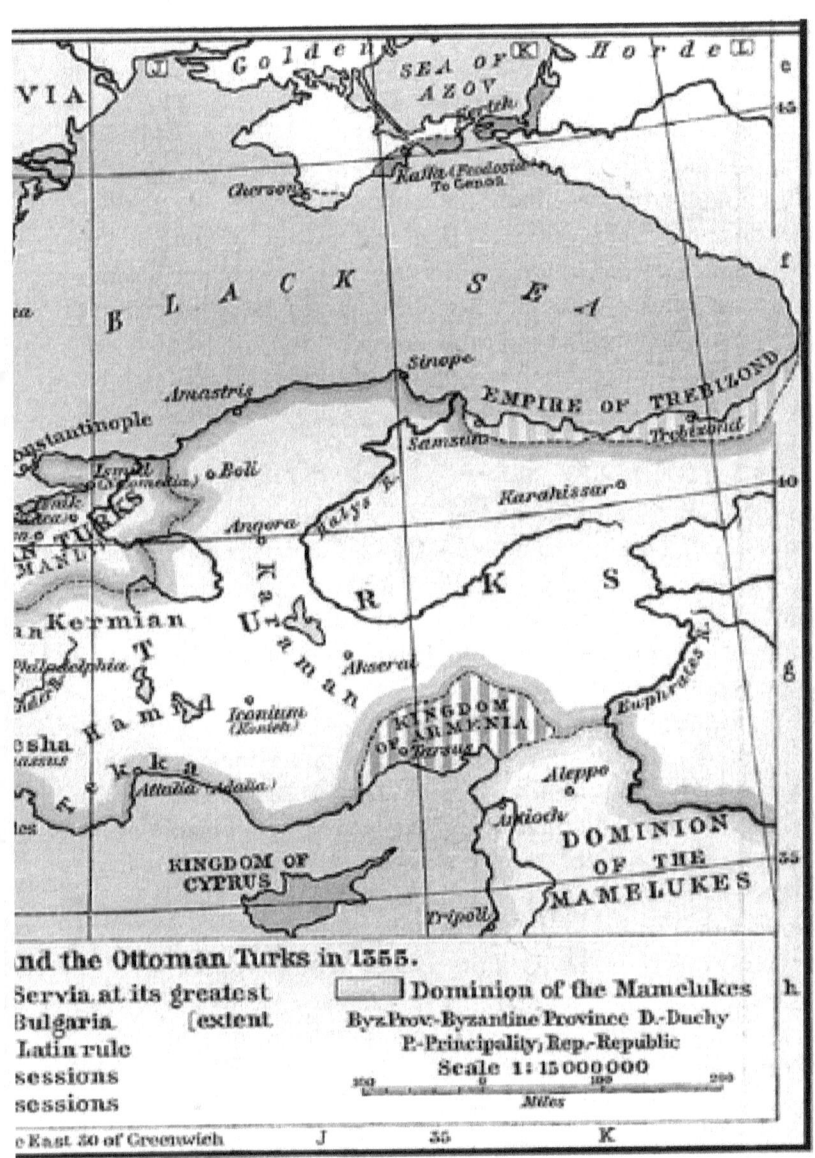

the Byzantine Empire was now oppressed, Orchan's eldest son, Solyman Pacha, struck a bold blow in behalf of his own race, which gave the Turks a permanent establishment on the European side of the Hellespont.

This important event in the world's history took place in 1366. The Ottoman writers pass over in silence the previous incursions of the Turks into Europe, which gained no conquest and led to no definite advantage; but they dwell fully on this expedition of Solyman, and adorn it with poetic legends of the vision that appeared to the young chieftain as he mused on the sea-shore near the ruins of Cyzicus. They tell how the crescent of the moon rose before him as the emblem of his race, and united the continents of Europe and Asia with a chain of silver light, while temples and palaces floated up out of the great deep, and mysterious voices blended with the sounding sea, exciting in his heart a yearning for predestined enterprise, and a sense of supernatural summons, (Von Hammer).

The dream may have been both the effect of previous schemings, and the immediate stimulant that made Solyman put his scheming into act. With but thirty-nine of his chosen warriors, he embarked at night in a Genoese bark on the Asiatic side of the Hellespont, and surprised the Castle of Tzympe, on the opposite coast. Reinforcements soon pushed across to the adventurers; and in three days Tzympe was garrisoned by three thousand Ottoman troops.

At this crisis, Cantacuzene was so severely pressed by his rival John Palaeologus, that, instead of trying to dislodge the invaders from Tzympe, or even remonstrating against their occupation of that fortress, he implored the help of Orchan against his domestic enemy. Orchan gave up his brother-in-law's cause, and provided assistance to the old emperor. But he ordered that assistance to be administered by Solyman, the conqueror of Tzympe, an auxiliary the most formidable to those with whom he was to cooperate. Ten thousand more Turks were sent across to Solyman, who defeated the Sclavonic forces which Palaeologus had brought into the empire: but the victors never left the continent on which they had conquered.

Cantacuzene offered Solyman ten thousand *ducats* to retire from Tzympe. The sum was agreed on; but before the ransom was paid, a terrible earthquake shook the whole district of Thrace, and threw down the walls of its fenced cities. The Greeks trembled at this visitation of Providence; and the Turks saw in it the interposition of Heaven in their favour, and thought that the hand of God was smoothing the path for their conquest of the Promised Land. Two of Solyman's captains, Adjé Bey, and Ghasi Fasil, instantly occupied the important town of Gallipoli, marching in over the walls which the earthquake had shattered, and unresisted by the awe-struck inhabitants. The fields in the neighbourhood still are called after Adjé; and the tombs of these two captains of the Ottoman host are yet to be seen in Gallipoli. They were buried on the scene of their great exploit; and Turkish pilgrims throng hither in veneration of the warriors, who gave to their race the strong city, the key of the Hellespont, the gate of easy passage into Europe.

Solyman, on hearing that his troops had occupied Gallipoli, refused to give up Tzympe; and threw large colonies of Turks and Arabs across the straits, which he planted in the territory which had been thus acquired. The fortifications of Gallipoli were repaired, and that important post was strongly garrisoned. Solyman took possession of other places in the Thracian Chersonese, which he strengthened with new walls and secured with detachments of his best troops. The Greek Emperor made a formal complaint of these aggressions to Orchan, who replied that it was not the force of arms that had opened the Greek cities to his son, but the will of God, manifested in the earthquake. The emperor rejoined that the question was not how the Turks had marched into the cities, but whether they had any right to retain them.

Orchan asked time to consider the subject; and afterwards made some proposals for negotiating the restoration of the cities; but he had firmly resolved to take full advantage of the opportunities for aggrandising the Ottoman power, which now were afforded by the basis for operations in Europe which had been acquired, and by the perpetual dissensions that raged between Cantacuzene and his son-in-law Palaeologus; each of whom was continually soliciting Orchan's aid against the other, and obtaining that aid according to what seemed best for the interests of the Turkish sovereign—the real enemy of them both.

Orchan only lived three years after the capture of Tzympe and Gallipoli: his son Solyman, to whom he owed those conquests, and in whom he had hoped to leave a successor who should surpass all the glories hitherto won by the house of Othman, had died before him. An accidental fall from his horse, while he was engaged in the favourite Turkish sport of falconry, caused the young conqueror's death. Solyman was not buried at Brusa; but, by Orchan's order, a tomb was built for him on the shore of the Hellespont, over which he had led his race to a second empire.

Orchan died in the year 1359 of our era, at the age of seventy-five, after a reign of thirty-three years, during which the most important civil and military institutions of his nation were founded, and the Crescent was not only advanced over many of the fairest provinces of Asia, but was also planted on the European continent, whence its enemies have hitherto vainly sought to dislodge it during five centuries.

CHAPTER 3

Battle of the Marizza

The death of Solyman Pacha had opened to his younger brother Amurath (or, as the Orientals name him, Murad), the inheritance of the Ottoman throne. Amurath was forty years of age when he succeeded his father, Orchan; and he reigned thirty years over the Ottomans in prosperity and glory. His first projects after his accession were to extend the European conquests of his father and brother; but he was checked for a time by the enmity of the Prince of Caramania, who stirred up a revolt in the Ottoman dominions in the centre of Asia Minor.

Amurath marched an army rapidly to the scene of the insurrection, which he completely quelled. He then (in 1360) led his troops to the passage of the Hellespont; and commenced a series of victories in Europe, which wore only terminated by his death on the field of battle at Kossova in 1389. Besides wresting from the Greeks numerous places of secondary value, Amurath captured, in 1361, the great city of Adrianople, which thenceforth became the capital of the Ottoman dominions in Europe, until Constantinople fell before Mahomet II. Pushing his conquests towards Macedonia and the Haemus, Amurath next took Sagrae and Philippopolis.

The Turkish armies, like the ancient Roman *legions*, found a principal part of their booty in the prisoners they made, and who were all destined for sale as slaves. The number of prisoners had increased to such a multitude during these campaigns of Amurath, that one of his statesmen pointed out to him the importance of steadily enforcing the royal prerogative (neglected by his predecessors) of taking a fifth part of the spoil This was thenceforth exercised by the *Sultans*, who sometimes took their double tithe in kind; but more frequently received a stated sum per head, as the fifth of the value of each slave. In after ages, when a Christian nation remonstrated against this practice, a formal stipulation; excepting prisoners of war of that nation from such liability, was usually established by express treaty.

Hitherto the Turkish victories in Europe had been won over the feeble Greeks; but the Ottomans now came in contact with the far more warlike Sclavonic tribes, which had founded kingdoms and principalities in Servia and Bosnia. Amurath also menaced the frontiers of Wallachia and Hungary. The Roman See, once so energetic in exciting the early crusades, had disregarded the progress of the new Mahometan power, so long as the heretical Greeks were the only sufferers beneath its arms. But Hungary, a country that professed spiritual obedience to the Pope, a branch of Latin Christendom, was now in peril; and Pope Urban V. preached up a crusade against the *infidel* Turks.

The King of Hungary, the princes of Servia, of Bosnia and Wallachia, leagued together to drive the Ottomans out of Europe; and their forces marched towards Adrianople until they crossed the River Marizza at a point not more than two days' journey from that city. Lalaschahin, who then was in command of the Ottoman forces in Europe, was unable to assemble an army equal in numbers to that of the confederate chieftains, who mustered more than twenty thousand men. But the Christians, in the pride of assured victory, neglected all military precautions against their enemy; and suddenly, while they were all engaged in a nightly revel, the sound of the Turkish drums and fifes, (all the European nations have borrowed their military music from the Turks, Von Hammer, supplement), and the shouts of *"Allah"* were heard amid the darkness. Their active enemy was on them; and they fled in panic rout. Seadeddin, the Oriental historian says:

> They were caught, even as wild beasts in their lair. They were driven before us as flames are driven before the wind, till plunging into the Marizza they perished in its waters.

Such was the issue of the first encounter of the Hungarians and Servians with the Turks; and centuries of further disaster and suffering to the Christians were to follow.

A long list of battles won, and towns taken by Amurath or his generals between the year of the Battle of Marizza, in 1363, and the year 1376, may be found in the Turkish historians. In the last-mentioned year, the capture of the strong city of Nissa by the Ottomans, forced the Prince of Servia to beg peace, which was granted to him on the condition of supplying a tribute of a thousand pounds of silver, and a thousand horse-soldiers every year. Sisvan, the King of the Bulgarians, had also taken part in the hostilities waged by the European Christians against Amurath, and he also was compelled to sue for mercy. Sisvan disliked paying money, and preferred to obtain peace by giving up his daughter in marriage to the conqueror.

Amurath now rested from warfare for six years, during which time he employed himself unremittingly in the internal affairs of his state. He improved the organisation of his military force, and completed the feudal system by which grants of land in each conquered country were made to Mahometans, on condition that each district so granted should supply one or more *Spahis* or armed horsemen in time of war. These granted districts, or *fiefs* (as we may term them by applying the phraseology of mediaeval Europe) were classified into minor, *fiefs*, called *Timars*; and grand *fiefs*, called *Ziamets*.

We shall reverb hereafter to the consideration of the effect of these feudal institutions both on the conquering and the conquered races. Amurath also formed out of the Christian subjects of his dominions a corps of camp-followers called *Woinaks*; on whom devolved all the humble and laborious duties of the barracks, the encampment, and the march; such as cleaning the stables and attending to the baggage-wagons. The red colour was now chosen for the banner of the *Spahis*, and became the national colour of the Ottoman armies.

During this season of peace Amurath was still solicitous to extend his dominions; and he used for that purpose his political and diplomatic skill in forming such matrimonial alliances for members of his family, as seemed to promise the future acquisition of new provinces. He married his eldest son Bajazet to the daughter of the Prince of Kermian, a Turkish state in Asia Minor, that adjoined the Ottoman territories in that country. The bride brought as her dowry a new kingdom to the throne of Othman. Amurath's own daughter Nifisay was given in marriage to the powerful Turkish Prince of Caramania. Amurath himself, and two of his sons, at a later period, permitted each a Byzantine princess to be added to their list of wives.

Ever since the capture of Adrianople the Greek emperor had cringed to the Ottoman sovereign, and sought eagerly to keep up such treaties with his *infidel* neighbour, as would promise him a quiet reign, though upon mere sufferance, at Constantinople. But Palaeologus hated him whom he feared; and the Greek emperor vainly, in 1380, underwent the expense and ignominy of a voyage from Constantinople to Rome, where he sought, by the most abject submissions to the papacy, to obtain a new crusade by the Frankish kings of Christendom against the Mahometan invaders of its eastern regions.

In terror at the wrath which this attempt was likely to excite in Amurath, Palaeologus sent his third son Theodoras to the Ottoman court, with a humble request that he might be allowed to serve in the ranks of the Turkish Army. This servile humility allayed the anger of Amurath. Andronicus, another son of the Greek emperor, formed about the same time a friendship with Prince Saoudji, Amurath's eldest son, which led to fatal results. The two young princes persuaded each other, and themselves, that they were neglected by their fathers, and that their brethren were unduly preferred to them. They seized an opportunity for insurrection, given by the absence of Amurath from Adrianople, whence he had been summoned by the tidings of disturbances in Asia, and during which he had left Saoudji in command of all the Ottoman dominions in Europe. They openly revolted, and established their joint camp near Constantinople, where Palaeologus lay trembling at their threats.

Amurath, on hearing of the insurrection, instantly hurried back across the straits, and summoned the Greek emperor to appear before him to answer for his son's conduct. Palaeologus earnestly disavowed all participation in his schemes; and, that he might completely allay the suspicions of Amurath, he promised to join him in acting against their sons, and agreed that the rebels should lose their eyes for their crime. The Ottoman Army then advanced to a little stream near Apicidion, behind which the insurgent princes had taken post. At nightfall, without any escort, Amurath spurred his horse across the water, and called out to the soldiery in the rebel camp to return to their duty upon promise of pardon.

At the sound of the well-known voice of their old sovereign, which had so often cheered them to victory, the troops of Saoudji deserted the two princes, and flocking round Amurath, implored forgiveness for the treason which they had been led into by his viceroy. Saoudji and Andronicus escaped into the town of Didymoticha with a small band of Turks and of young Greek nobles, who had taken part in their plot. They were besieged, and starved into surrender. Amurath had his own son led before him; and after the prince's eyes had been put out, so that the agreement between the imperial sires might be kept, Saoudji was beheaded in his father's presence. The young Greek nobles were tied together in knots of two or three at a time, and flung into the River Marizza, while Amurath sat by, and smiled with grim satisfaction at the rapidity with which they sank beneath the waves.

Having found the fathers of some of the youthful rebels, he made them kill their children with their own hands. Two parents refused the horrible office, and were themselves slain for their disobedience. When his vengeance had been satiated by these spectacles, Amurath sent young Andronicus in chains to his father, and bade Palaeologus deal with him as he himself had dealt with Saoudji. The Greek emperor, dreading his stern ally, caused his child's eyes to be scalded with burning vinegar. Amurath was pleased to consider this a sufficient obedience to his behest; and did not take notice that Andronicus's life was spared, or that the horrid punishment of blinding was so imperfectly performed, as to leave the wretched prisoner some faint power of vision.

Notwithstanding the Ottoman ruler's policy in forming a bond of marriage between his house and that of the Turkish ruler of Caramania, a war broke out in 1387 between these two powerful rivals for the headship of the Turkish race in Asia Minor. A great battle was fought between them at Iconium, in which the valour of Prince Bajazet on the side of the Ottomans was particularly signalised. He is said, by the lightning-like rapidity and violence of his charge upon the enemy on that day, to have acquired the surname of Yilderim, or "the Lightning," by which he is known in history. It is an appellation that will remind the classical reader of the Ptolemy Ceraunus of the Graeco-Macedonian era; and still more appropriately of Hamilcar Barcas, the father of the great Hannibal

The Caramanian prince was utterly defeated at Iconium, and owed the preservation of his life and kingdom to the interposition of his wife, who succeeded in calming the anger of her victorious father, and induced him to be satisfied with his defeated rival acknowledging his superiority, and kissing his hand in token of submission. Amurath dismissed his army and repaired to Brusa, where he hoped to enjoy a period of repose. He refused to be roused again by the temptation of conquering and annexing the little independent territory of Tekké, that lay near his Asiatic dominions. One of his generals advised an expedition against that place; but Amurath rejected the proposal with disdain, said he:

> The Prince of Tekké is too poor and feeble. I should feel ashamed in making war on him. A lion does not hunt flies.

But the old lion was soon roused from his rest, to encounter far more formidable foes, who were leagued together to tear his European conquests from his grasp.

The Ottoman dominions in Europe at this time (1388) comprised nearly the whole of ancient Thrace and modern Roumelia. Some important acquisitions beyond the boundary of this province had also been effected; and the conquerors pursued the system of planting colonies of Turks and Arabs from Asia in the conquered districts, while they removed large portions of the old population. By this, and by their custom of recruiting their *Janissaries* from the flower of the Christian children, they excited the alarm of the neighbouring Christian states, who saw a fierce race, alien to them in blood and in creed, thus taking root on their frontier, and organising the resources of the subdued country for future military enterprises.

The Bulgarians, the Servians, the Bosnians, all of Sclavonic blood, (Latham's *Ethnology of Europe*), now united in one great national effort against the intrusive Turks. Servia was chief of the movement. She could not forget her proud position, which she had held before the Ottomans had come into Europe, when her great King Stephen Dushan ruled victoriously, from Belgrade to the Marizza, from the Black Sea to the Adriatic, and assumed the high title of "Emperor of the Roumelians, the Macedonian Christ-loving *Czar*," (Ranke's *History of Servia*). Beside these Sclavonic nations, the Skipetars, (Latham), of Albania now armed against the common enemy from Asia.

The powers thus allied against Amurath expected also and received assistance from the semi-Roman population of Wallachia and from the Magyars of Hungary, who, like their kinsmen the Ottoman Turks, had won by force a settlement in Europe; but who, unlike the Turks, adopted the creed and the civilisation of European Christendom, and became for ages its chivalrous defenders. (For the connection between the Magyars, the Huns of Attila, and the Ottoman Turks, see Latham).

Sclavonic Poland also sent aid to her sister Sclavonic kingdom of the south. No further succour was obtainable. The other great kingdom of that family of nations, Russia, lay at this time in wretched slavery under the Mongols. The great kingdoms of western Christendom heard with indifference the sufferings and the perils, to which its eastern portions were exposed by the new Mahometan power. The old crusading enthusiasm had faded away; nor could, indeed, the immediate stimulant of a cry to the rescue of the Holy Land be employed against the Ottomans, who had not yet approached the Syrian territory. The internal condition, at the latter part of the fourteenth century, of each of the great European states, which had supplied the heroes of the early crusades, was peculiarly unfavourable for the efforts of those who strove to arouse their descendants to a similar expedition.

And the personal character of the sovereigns of England, France, and Germany, in 1388, forbade all hopes of seeing the examples of Richard Coeur de Lion, of Edward I., of Philip Augustus, of St Louis, of Conrad, and Frederick II., imitated by their successors. The weak and worthless Richard II. was sovereign of England; the imbecile Charles VI. was enthroned at Paris. Both countries were the scenes of perpetual strife between powerful nobles, and of general confusion and lawlessness. The German Empire, under the coarse and dissolute Wenceslaus, was in a still more wretched condition: and the great civil war between the confederations of brigand knights and the burghers of the free cities was raging from the Danube to the Rhine. The Christian princes of Spain were still fully occupied with their long struggles against their own Moorish invaders.

The difficulty of uniting the powers of the West in any enterprise against the common foe of their religion was augmented tenfold by the schism in the Papacy, which divided the whole of Western Christendom. Consciences were perplexed, zeal was distracted and chilled, scepticism and indifference were created by the conflicting pretensions and behests of two Popes, one at Avignon, and one at Rome; each of whom anathematised the other and his adherents with assiduity and animosity at least equal to any that could be displayed against the Ottomans.

But although the great powers of Western Christendom stood aloof from the struggle made by the Christian nations, of the East to free themselves from the pressure of the Ottoman conquests, Amurath saw that the league which the ruler of Servia had succeeded in organising against him, was one which it would tax his utmost energies to encounter. He made full and cautious arrangements for the military protection and civil government of the Asiatic states, and then recrossed the Hellespont, with the design of baffling the superior resources of his enemies by the celerity of his operations. The Bulgarians and Servians had commenced the war by falling upon an Ottoman Army which was moving through Bosnia. They destroyed fifteen out of twenty thousand Turks by the impetuous suddenness of their attack, and the great superiority of their numbers.

After this vigorous blow, the Christians relaxed in their exertions.

The vacillations and delays, which usually mark the movements of a confederacy, kept the forces of the greater number of the allies inactive during several months of the year 1389; while their vigorous and resolute adversary was pouring his forces into Bulgaria, and completing the conquest of that important member of their league. Amurath was especially incensed against Sisvan, the Bulgarian king, who had kept up the appearance of submissive devotion to the Turkish interests, until he suddenly joined the Servians in the attack upon his son-in-law's forces in Bosnia.

The necessity of making regulations for the defence and internal government of Roumelia during the war, and of calling into active service and arranging the full military force of the province, detained Amurath himself for a short time in Adrianople; but he sent his general, Ali Pacha, forward into Bulgaria with an army of thirty thousand men. The Turks now (1389) marched northward to conquest across that mountain chain of the Balkan, which their descendants in the present century trust to so earnestly, as a barrier against attacks upon themselves. Ali Pacha advanced with the main army through the passes of Nadir Derbend upon Schumla, so celebrated in modern Russian wars.

Schumla surrendered to the Turks, nor has it yet ever been retaken from them. Tirnova and Pravadi were also captured by Ali Pacha and his lieutenant, Yakshibey; and the Bulgarian king took refuge in Nicopolis on the Danube. Ali Pacha besieged him there, and Sisvan begged for peace. Amurath granted it, on condition that Silistria should be ceded to him, and that the conquered Sisvan should pay him a regular tribute. But disputes broke out as to the fulfilment of the terms of peace; the war was recommenced, and the Turks stormed the string places of Dridja and Hirschova. Besieged again in Nicopolis, the Bulgarian king surrendered at discretion. His life was spared; but Bulgaria was now annexed to the Ottoman Empire, which thus advanced its northern frontier to the Danube.

The Servian King Lazarus, alarmed at the destruction of his confederate, now earnestly collected the forces of the remaining members of the anti-Turkish league, and prepared for a resolute struggle. So large was the force which he drew around him, that in the pride and confidence of his heart he sent Amurath a formal challenge to a decisive battle. Amurath had now taken in person the command of the Turkish Army, and continued his policy of acting on the offensive, and making his enemy's territory the seat of war. He marched westward from Bulgaria through a difficult and mountainous country to the neighbourhood of Kossova, on the frontiers of Servia and Bosnia, where his enemies had collected their troops. The plain of Kossova, on which the fate of Servia was decided on the 27th of August, 1389, is traversed by the little stream of the Schinitza.

On the north side of this rivulet the combined levies of Servia, Bosnia, and Albania, with their auxiliaries from Poland, Hungary, and Wallachia, were arrayed, in numbers far exceeding those of the troops which Amurath had in hand for battle. According to the Ottoman historians, Amurath summoned a council of war to deliberate whether he should attack the enemy that seemed so superior in force. Several of the Turkish chiefs advised that he should draw up all the camels of their baggage-train in a line before the army, so as to serve as a living rampart, and to disorder the enemy's horse by the sight and smell of those animals.(Cyrus employed this very stratagem against the Lydian cavalry at the Battle of Sardis, B.C. 546—Herodotus, Clio).

Amurath's eldest son. Prince Bajazet, opposed this project: he fiercely urged that Heaven had ever manifestly favoured the arms of the house of Othman, and that to employ such artifices would show a distrust of Providence, said he:

> The honour of our flag requires that those who march beneath the Crescent, should meet their enemy face to face, let that enemy be who he will.

The *grand vizier* gave his vote also for open fighting, on the authority of what he believed to be a supernatural warning. He had opened the *Koran* at random, and had fallen upon the verse:

> *Prophet, fight the unbelievers and the hypocrites.*

He had tried these *sortes Koranicas* again, and the verse which then presented itself was:

> *Verily a large host is often beaten by a weaker one.*

Another officer, the *Beylerbey* (lord of lords) *Timourtash*, also opposed the scheme of the camels, on reasons not of religion, but of common sense. He said that it was probable that the camels themselves would take fright at the sight and sound of the hostile cavalry, and that then they would rush back on the Turkish ranks, and create there the confusion which it was wished to cause amid the enemy. Night put an end to the deliberations of the council, without any settled plan being formed. Amurath had observed that the wind blew from the side of the enemy, wafting clouds of dust, which threatened to cause serious disadvantage to his troops in the action. He spent the whole night in earnest prayer for the aid of Heaven, and asked that it might be vouchsafed him to close his life in fighting for the true faith;— the only death that ensures the martyr's prize of eternal felicity. (Von Hammer, vol. i., cites the Turkish historians who narrate the council of war, Amurath's prayer, &c.)

In the other camp the discussions of the confederate princes were equally long and uncertain. Some advised an attack on the Turks by night, in revenge probably for the disaster of the Marizza, twenty-six years before. Others opposed this plan as full of risk and confusion, and also because the enemy would have a better chance of escaping in the night, than if they waited for daylight for the victory which they deemed secure. The morning at last broke upon the two camps; and with the dawn there came a heavy fall of rain, which completely laid the dust, and seemed to Amurath and his followers to be an express sign that God was with them.

The rain ceased after a while, and the two armies came forth from their tents on a fair and open field, and drew themselves up for battle. The Turks were arranged in their customary order. As the battle was in Europe, the European feudatory troops were on the right wing; and those of Asia on the left. Prince Bajazet commanded on the right; the other wing was led by Amurath's other surviving son. Prince Yacoub. Amurath himself was in the centre with the *Janissaries*, and the cavalry regiments of his guard. The irregulars, horse and foot, the *Akindji*, and the *Azabs*, skirmished in the van. On the Christian side. King Lazarus commanded the centre.

His nephew, Vuk Brankowich, led the right, and the King of Bosnia the left wing. Both armies advanced resolutely to the charge, encountered each other fiercely, stood their ground firmly; and the event of the day was long doubtful. The Asiatic troops in the left wing of the Mahometan Army began at last to give way before the warriors of Servia and Albania, who pressed them on the Christians' right. Prince Bajazet brought succour from the right wing of the Ottomans, and restored the fight. Armed with a heavy mace of iron, he fought in person in the thick of the battle, and smote down all who dared to cross his path.

While the two armies thus strove together, and the field was heaped thickly with carnage, a Servian nobleman, Milosch Kabilovitsch, rode to the Ottoman centre, pretending that he was a deserter, and had important secrets to reveal to Amurath in person. He was led before the Turkish sovereign; he knelt as if in homage before him, and then stabbed Amurath with a sudden and mortal stroke of his dagger. Milosch sprang up from his knees, and, gifted with surprising strength and activity, he thrice cleared himself from the vengeful throng of the Ottomans who assailed him, and fought his way to the spot where his horse had been left; but ere he could remount, the *Janissaries* overpowered him, and hewed him into pieces. Amurath knew that his wound was mortal; but he had presence of mind sufficient to give the orders for a charge of his reserve, which decided the victory in his favour. His rival, the Servian king, was brought captive into his presence, and Amurath died in the act of pronouncing the death-doom of his foe.

The execution of King Lazarus was not the only one of which the royal Ottoman tent was the scene before the close of that day. Prince Bajazet, when the victory over the Christians was secure, returned to the Turkish camp, and was acknowledged by his father's generals as their sovereign. Forthwith, and in the very presence of his father's lifeless remains, Bajazet ordered his brother Yacoub, who had fought valiantly through the battle, to be seized and put to death. This fratricide (according to the historian of the empire, Seadeddin), was committed in pursuance of the maxim of the *Koran:*

Disquiet is worse than putting to death.

It was, according to the same authority, rendered particularly proper by the evil example of revolt which their brother Saoudji had given in Amurath's lifetime, which proved the necessity of cutting off those, who were likely to imitate such conduct. The death of Yacoub was also, according to Seadeddin, justifiable, because the *Sultan*, the shadow of God upon earth, and the Lord of all true believers, ought to reign in conformity with the ever-to-be-imitated example of God, alone upon the throne, and without the possibility of any one revolting against him.

According to some authorities it was from Bajazet's deadly rapidity in securing his accession by his brother's death that he acquired the surname of "Yilderim;" but his energy in war may well have been the more honourable cause of his obtaining this designation. His reign commenced in the camp, and he followed up the war against the Servians with vigour and success, that showed him to be the heir of his father's valour as well as of his throne. Stephen Lasarevich, the new

King of Servia, found that it was hopeless to continue the struggle, and entered into a treaty by which Servia became the vassal state of the Ottomans. Lasarevich gave the *Sultan* his sister to wife, and agreed to pay as tribute-money a certain portion of the produce of all the silver mines in his dominions.

He undertook also to render, in person, military service to the *Sultan* in all his campaigns; and throughout his life he honourably performed his portion of the compact. In the great battles of Nicopolis and Angora, Lasarevich fought by the side of his brother-in-law. He was (says the modern historian of Servia) apparently bound to this house by an oath, and with the zeal of a kinsman he exerted himself in the adjustment of quarrels that broke out in the Ottoman family. (Ranke's *History of Servia*).

Having successfully concluded the Servian war, Bajazet passed over to his Asiatic dominions, which he increased by fresh conquests over the neighbouring states. In 1390 the Turkish "Lightning" was again in Europe, waging war on Wallachia, Bosnia, Hungary, and the wretched remnants of the Byzantine Empire. Myrtchè, the Prince of Wallachia, submitted to Bajazet in 1391, and thenceforth Wallachia was for centuries in the list of the tributary states of the Ottoman Porte. The Bosnians, aided by the Hungarians, offered a more obstinate resistance. In 1392 the Hungarian King, Sigismund, advanced into Bulgaria and gained several advantages, but was at last overpowered by the superior forces of the Turks, and driven in utter rout back into his own kingdom. It was while King Sigismund in the course of his retreat from the campaign traversed the county of Huniadé, that he saw and became enamoured of the fair Elizabeth Morsiney. It is said and sung that monarchs seldom sigh in vain; and from this love-passage of the fugitive Sigismund ensued the birth of Hunyades the Great, the conqueror of the Turks in many a well-fought field.

Bajazet's European enemies obtained a seasonable relief from the pressure of his arms, by the sudden attack which the Prince of Caramania made in 1392 upon the Ottoman possessions in Asia. The Caramanian armies were at first so far successful that the Ottoman troops suffered a complete overthrow between Angora and Brusa; and Timourtash, Bajazet's viceroy in Asia, was taken prisoner. But on the arrival of Bajazet himself in Asia, the fortune of the war was speedily changed. The Caramanian prince was defeated and captured, and placed in the custody of his own former prisoner, Timourtash. Without waiting for orders from Bajazet, Timourtash put the unhappy

Caramanian to death. Bajazet was at first angry at such an act having been done on the general's own authority, but he excused it on consideration of high state policy, and justified it by the maxim that "*The death of a prince is not so bad as the loss of a province.*" That maxim was afterwards regularly quoted by the Turkish rulers when they ordered the execution of any prince.

Caramania now submitted to the Ottomans, and all the south of Asia Minor acknowledged Bajazet as sovereign. He then sent his armies into the east and north of that country, and annexed Sivas (the ancient Sebaste) Kastemouni, Samsoun and Amassia, with their territories to his dominions. Bajazet disdained the title of *Emir*, which his three predecessors had borne; and obtained from the successor of the *caliphs* (who was maintained in empty state by the Mameluke sovereign of Egypt, but still recognised as the religious chief of the Mahometan world) the superior title of *Sultan*.

Proud of his numerous victories and rapidly augmented power, Bajazet now gave himself up for a time to luxurious ease and to sensual excesses of the foulest description. He is the first of the Ottoman princes who infringed the law of the Prophet which forbids the use of wine. His favourite general, Ali Pasha, had set his master the example of drunkenness; and Bajazet debased himself by sharing and imitating his subject's orgies. The infamy with which their names are sullied even in the pages of Oriental writers does not end here: they introduced among the Ottoman *grandees* (and the loathsome habit soon spread far and wide) the open and notorious practice of those unutterable deeds of vice and crime, which the natural judgment of mankind in every age and among every race has branded as the most horrible of all offences against God and man.

The *Koran* is explicit in its denunciation of such acts; but the Turks, though in other respects faithful observers of the law of the Prophet, on this point compromised with their consciences and their creed. The pen recoils from this detestable subject; and it is indeed one of the shameful peculiarities of such vice, that its very enormity secures to a great extent its oblivion. But it is the stern duty of History not to flinch from the facts, which prove how fearful a curse the Ottoman power was to the lands which it overran during the period of its ascendency. It became a Turkish practice to procure by treaty, by purchase, by force, or by fraud, bands of the fairest children of the conquered Christians, who were placed in the palaces of the *Sultan*, his *viziers*, and his *pachas*, under the title of pages, but too often really to serve as the helpless materials of abomination.

Frequently wars were undertaken and marauding inroads made into other states to collect this most miserable human spoil for purposes at which humanity shudders. Sufficiently appalling is the institution of the *Janissaries*, by which the Christian boy was taken from his home, and trained to deadly service against his father's race and his father's faith. It might seem worthy of having been suggested by the fiend, whom Milton describes as—

> *The strongest and the fiercest spirit*
> *That fought in heaven.*
>
> *Moloch, horrid king, besmear'd with blood*
> *Of human sacrifice and parents' tears*:

... but infinitely more detestable is the Belial spirit that prompted these other ineffable atrocities of Turkish rule. We find an aggravation, not a mitigation of such crimes, when we read that the wretched beings, the promise of whose youth was thus turned into infamy, were frequently, when they grew to manhood, placed by their masters in posts of importance; and that the Ottoman Empire has owed many of her ablest generals and statesmen to this foul source. Pity must be blended with the loathing with which we regard the dishonest splendours of these involuntary apostates; but as unmixed as inexpressible is our abhorrence of the authors of their guilt and shame.

CHAPTER 4

The Battle of Nicopolis

Bajazet was startled from his flagitious revels by a crusade of the Christian chivalry of Frankistan (*A.D.* 1396). Sigismund the King of Hungary felt deeply after the day of Kossova and the fall of Servia, the imminence of the peril to which his own country was exposed; and he succeeded in moving the sympathies of other members of the Latin Church into active enterprise on his behalf. Pope Boniface IX., in the year 1394, proclaimed a crusade against the Ottomans, with plenary indulgence to all Christians who should forthwith repair to the rescue of Hungary and the neighbouring kingdoms. Sigismund was especially earnest in his endeavours to move the Court of France to send troops to his assistance. The cessation of hostilities between France and England, about this time, favoured the grant of the Hungarian request; and many of the martial youth of France and Burgundy were now eager for new adventures and fresh scenes of distinction.

It was resolved that the Count de Nevers, the son of the Duke of Burgundy, should lead a body of men-at-arms to the aid of the Hungarian king, and that he should be commander-in-chief of the French and other chivalry, who in the words of the contemporary chronicler, Froissart:

> ...were to break the force of Bajazet in Hungary, and when this was done, were to advance to Constantinople, cross the Hellespont, enter Syria, gain the Holy Land, and deliver Jerusalem and the holy sepulchre from the hands of the *infidels.*

Knights and squires began now to gather together, with other gentlemen who were desirous of renown. The chief commanders, under the Count de Nevers, were the Count de la Manche and the three cousins of the French king, James of Bourbon, and Henri and Philippe de Bar. Among other chiefs who joined this crusade, were Philippe of Artois, Count of Eu, prince of the blood royal, and Constable of France; the Lord de Courcy, Sir Guy de la Tremouille, Sir John de Vienne, Admiral of France, Boucicault, Marshal of France, Sir Reginald de Roye, the Lords of St. Pol, de Montmorel, and Sampi, and many more, the very flower of the French chivalry.

They marched from France in companies, about the middle of March, 1396; and as they traversed Germany, they were joined by Frederic, Count of Hohenzollern, Grand Prince of the Teutonic Order, and the Grand Master Philibert de Naillac, who came from Rhodes at the head of a strong body of the Knights of St. John of Jerusalem. Besides this splendid auxiliary force, the King of Hungary had obtained the services of a body of Bavarian knights, commanded by the Elector Palatine and the Count of Munspelgarde; and he had also been joined by a band of the chivalry of Styria, headed by Herman, second Count de Cilly.

Altogether, the crusaders of Western Christendom who marched to the Danube against the Ottomans in 1396, appear to have been from ten to twelve thousand in number, (Von Hammer collects careful and full data for this enumeration, which differs from that of Gibbon), all men "of tried courage and enterprise," as the old chronicler calls them, full of confidence in their cause and in their own valour, and who boasted in the pride of their hearts that "if the sky were to fall, they would uphold it on the points of their lances." Sigismund had collected the full strength of his own kingdom, and had also prevailed on Myrtché, the Prince or Voivode of Wallachia, to join him in this grand combined attack on the Ottoman power, although Wallachia had some time before obtained peace from the Turks on condition of paying a stipulated tribute.

The confederate Christian Army marched in divisions, partly through Transylvania and Wallachia, and partly through Servia, against the Ottoman dominions. The Servian prince remained faithful to his alliance with Bajazet, and his subjects were therefore visited with merciless pillage and devastation by the army of fellow-Christians who marched through their land. The first Turkish town that Sigismund attacked was Widdin, which surrendered immediately. Orsova yielded after five days' resistance. Raco was taken by assault, and the garrison put to the sword, though they laid down their arms and asked for quarter. The practice of refusing mercy to a fallen enemy was by no means confined to the Turkish side: and, indeed, even in the hostilities of one Christian nation against another, no law or custom of war against butchering defeated and unresisting enemies was yet recognised.

When lives were spared, it was generally from the hope of obtaining ransom, or from sheer weariness and satiety of slaughter. The Christian Army marched next against Nicopolis, which was closely invested. The commander of the Turkish garrison, Yoglan Bey, made a gallant and obstinate resistance, in the full hope that Bajazet would not suffer so important a city to fall without making an effort for its relief. The *Sultan* had indeed now crossed the Bosphorus from Asia, and was leading the best troops of his empire to encounter these new foes from the Far West. The stubborn valour of the commander of Nicopolis was of the utmost value to his sovereign, by giving him time to concentrate and bring up his forces to the scene of action. Bajazet's generalship was far superior to the military conduct on the side of the Christians. They, and especially the French, in arrogant confidence of their invincibility, gave themselves up to riotous carousals, and neglected the most ordinary precautions to ascertain whether any enemy was advancing.

"Bajazet would not dare to come across the Bosphorus." Such was their boast, at the very time when Bajazet was swiftly and silently approaching with his well-appointed and well-disciplined army within six leagues of their camp. The Count de Nevers and his French chivalry were at table on the 24th of September, 1396, when messengers hurried in with the tidings that some marauders from the camp had come upon a great army of Turks, which was even then close at hand. The young *paladins* of France rose hot and flushed at the tidings, and ran to arms, demanding that. they should be led instantly to battle.

The Turkish irregular troops, the *Azabs* and the *Akindji*, were now seen hovering near; and the Count de Nevers, while his French cavalry was forming hastily in line, required of King Sigismund that they should be the van of the Christian Army, and fill the post of honour in the battle. Sigismund, who knew well the Turkish tactics, urged on the count that it would be wiser to send some light troops against the half-armed and undisciplined hordes, which they saw before them, and to reserve the French chivalry, as the flower of the Christian Army, to meet the *Janissaries* and *Spahis*, the best troops on the other side. The Sire de Courcy and the admiral advised compliance with the king's advice, but the constable and the Maréchal Boucicault opposed it, out of a spirit of rivalry, and insisted that the French cavalry should not suffer any Hungarians to precede them to battle. The young knights all applauded these proud words; and in ferocious insolence of spirit, they massacred some Turkish prisoners, whom they had in their power, and who had surrendered on promise of quarter—an act of useless perfidy and cruelty, which was soon to receive its chastisement.

Bajazet had halted his main army in a plain at a short distance from the Christian camp. There was some rising ground in the interval, which screened the Turks from the enemy's observation. The *Sultan* sent his irregular troops forward and supported them by a body of *Janissaries*, and by a large division of his cavalry; but he reserved forty thousand of his best troops, and kept them under arms, and drawn up in perfect order on the plain. On the other side the French cavalry, about six thousand strong, galloped impetuously onward, disdaining to wait for the co-operation of the main Hungarian Army, with which King Sigismund moved forward more slowly. The French rode the Turkish irregulars down like reeds, and then with levelled spears they charged the advanced division of the *Janissaries*. They broke this redoubtable infantry; and next encountered with equal success the foremost squadrons of the Turkish regular cavalry that attempted to covet the retreat of their comrades.

The triple success which the fiery valour of the young French nobles had thus achieved was splendid, and might have led to a complete victory, had they listened to the sage advice of the Sire de Courcy and the admiral, who earnestly implored the Count de Nevers to order a halt, and wait for the Hungarians to come up; or at least to give time enough for the horses to recover their wind, and for rearranging their disordered ranks. But carried away by the excitement of the strife, and the intoxication of their partial triumph, the French knights and their young commander continued to chase the flying *Spahis*, till, on gaining the summit of the high ground, they saw before them, not as they expected, a scared remnant of the defeated Turks, but a steady forest of hostile spears, and the Sultan himself at the head of his chosen troops, which soon began to extend, and wheel their enclosing lines round the scanty band of the rash assailants.

The Turkish troops, which they had defeated in the first part of their advance, had now rallied, and formed in the rear of the French knights, cutting off all hope of retreat. In this extremity, charged furiously in every quarter by superior numbers, obliged to combat in confusion and disorder, and with their own strength and that of their horses exhausted by their previous efforts, the Christian chevaliers fought on heroically till they were nearly all cut down or made prisoners. A few only made their way back to the main army of the confederates, into which they carried the disheartening tidings of defeat. Bajazet, after the French were overpowered, restored the regular formation of his troops, and then moved forward against King Sigismund. The two wings of the Christian main army fled at once without striking a blow.

The central division of Hungarians, which the king himself commanded, and the Bavarians and the Styrians, who also were posted in the centre, stood firm. They repulsed the Turkish charge, and advanced in turn against the *Janissaries* and *Spahis*, forcing these chosen troops of the Ottomans to recoil, when they were themselves fiercely charged by the Servians, who, under their king, Stephen Lasarevich, fought as allies of Bajazet in this battle. The overthrow of the Christian Army was now complete. Sigismund's Hungarian division was almost destroyed; all the Bavarian knights and many of the Styrians died gloriously around their standards. King Sigismund and a few more of the leaders escaped with difficulty from the field; but nearly all the best and bravest of the gallant army which had marched on that crusade, lay stark on the bloody field of Nicopolis, or were helplessly waiting for the doom which it might please the triumphant *Sultan* to pass upon his captive foes.

After the conflict, Bajazet fixed his camp in front of the rescued city of Nicopolis, and then rode over the field of battle. He was enraged to find from the number of his men who lay dead, how dear the victory had cost him. He said:

> This has been a cruel battle for our people: the Christians have defended themselves desperately; but I will have this slaughter well avenged on those who are prisoners.

Accordingly on the next morning the whole Turkish Army was drawn up in the form of a crescent, the *Sultan* being in the centre. He commanded the Christian prisoners to be brought before him, and they were led out to the number of ten thousand, with their hands bound behind them, and with halters round their necks. Among them was a youth of Munich, named Schildberger, who had gone to that campaign as attendant on a Bavarian nobleman who fell in the battle. Schildberger, more fortunate than his lord, escaped death in the conflict and in the massacre that followed. He lived to witness and to share the captivity of his first captors; and, after thirty-four years of slavery, returned to his home and wrote there a memoir of his own life, which is the most interesting and most trustworthy narrative that we possess of the campaign of Nicopolis, and of many of the subsequent scenes of Turkish history.

The commander of the French chivalry, the Count de Nevers, had been taken in the battle. Bajazet ordered that he should be spared, and permitted him to select twenty-four more of the Christian nobles from among the prisoners, whose lives were also granted. The *Sultan* then gave the signal for the slaughter of the rest to commence; and the unhappy captives were led in detachments before the royal tent, at the entrance of which Bajazet stood with the Count de Nevers and the twenty-four other Christian nobles who had been spared, but who were forced to witness the fate of their comrades and fellow-Christians. The contemporaneous chronicler of chivalry, old Froissart, tells the fate of the martyred chevaliers with natural sympathy:

> Many excellent knights and squires of France and other nations, who had been taken in battle or in the pursuit, were now brought forth in their shirts, one after another, before Bajazet, who eyeing them a little, they were led on; and as he made a signal were instantly cut to pieces by those waiting for them with drawn swords. Such was the cruel justice of Bajazet this day, when upwards of three hundred gentlemen of different nations were thus pitilessly murdered. It was a cruel case for them to suffer for the love of our Saviour Jesus Christ, and may he receive their souls!
> Among the murdered of that day was the gallant knight Sir Henry d'Antoing: may God show gracious merit to his soul! The Lord Boucicault, Marshal of France, was led naked like the others, before Bajazet, and would have suffered the same cruel death, had not the Count de Nevers left his companions, who were motionless at the sad sight, and flung himself on his knees to the *Sultan*, entreating him to spare the Lord Boucicault, who was much beloved by the King of France, and well able to pay a considerable ransom; and the count made signs, as paying from one hand to the other, that he would give a large sum of money, to soften the anger of the *Sultan*.
> Bajazet consented to the request of the Count de Nevers, and the Lord Boucicault was put aside with those who were not to be killed. Others were brought forward, until the number

I have mentioned was completed; such was the cruel revenge the *infidels* had on the Christians. It seems, according to what I heard, that Bajazet took delight that the victory he had gained over the Christians, and the capture of the Count de Nevers, should be known in France, and carried thither by a French knight. Three knights, of whom Sir James de Helly was one, were brought before Bajazet and the Count de Nevers, who was asked which of the three he wished should go to the King of France and to his father the Duke of Burgundy.

Sir James de Helly had the good fortune to be made choice of, because the Count de Nevers was before acquainted with him: he therefore said to the *Sultan*—'Sir, I wish that this person may go to France from you and from me.' This was accepted by Bajazet, and Sir James de Helly remained with him and the other French lords; but the two unsuccessful knights were delivered over to the soldiery, who massacred them without pity.

It is truly characteristic of Froissart and his age, that while he thus bewails the slaughter which befell the three hundred captives of gentle birth, he says not a word respecting the thousands of the common soldiery of the Christian Army, who were massacred at the same time. It is from the lowly-born Bavarian that we learn the extent and the cruelty of the carnage of that day. Schildberger saw his comrades cut down in heaps by the *scimetars* of the Turkish executioners, or battered to death by the maces of the *Janissaries*, who were called forward to join in the bloody work. He himself was saved by the intercession of Bajazet's son, who was moved to pity by the evident youth of the captive.

The *Sultan* sate there from daybreak till four in the afternoon enjoying with inexorable eye the death-pangs of his foes, when at last the pity or the avarice of his *grandees* made them venture to come between him and his prey, and implore that the Christians who yet remained alive might be made slaves of, instead of being slain. Bajazet assented, and the surviving captives, after the *Sultan* had chosen his fifth part from among them, were given up, each to the Mahometan who had taken him in battle. The Count de Nevers and the other lords were ransomed after a long captivity, during which Bajazet carried them about his dominions as trophies of his power and glory, little thinking that he himself was soon to drink still deeper of the same bitter cup of defeat and shame, and to furnish a still more memorable spectacle of baffled ambition and fallen pride.

Bajazet and his captives were at Brusa, in 1397, when the money for their ransom arrived. Before he dismissed them, he gave them an opportunity of witnessing both his barbaric magnificence and his barbaric justice. Froissart thus relates the two scenes, and the haughty leave-taking which the *Sultan* accorded to the Christian lords:

> The *Sultan* had at this time seven thousand falconers, and as many huntsmen: you may suppose from this the grandeur of his establishments. One day, in the presence of the Count de Nevers, he flew a falcon at some eagles; the flight did not please him; and he was so wroth, that, for this fault he was on the point of beheading two thousand of his falconers, scolding them exceedingly for want of diligence in their care of his hawks, when the one he was fond of behaved so ill. Another time, when the Count de Nevers and the French barons were with the *Sultan*, a poor woman came to him in tears, to demand justice against one of his servants, and said—
>
> '*Sultan*, I address myself to thee, as. my sovereign, and complain of one of thy servants, who is, I understand, attached to thy person. He, this morning, entered my house, and seized by force the goat's milk I had provided for myself and children, and drank it against my will. I told him that I should complain to thee of this outrage, but I had no sooner uttered the words, than he gave me two great cuffs, and would not leave me, though I ordered him in thy name. *Sultan*, do me justice, as thou hast sworn to thy people thou wouldest, that I may be satisfied, this injury be punished, and that everyone may know thou wilt see the meanest of thy subjects righted.'
>
> The *Sultan* was very rigidly determined that all crimes committed within his dominions should be severely punished: he therefore listened to her attentively, and said he would do her justice. He then ordered the varlet to be brought, and confronted with the woman, who repeated her complaint. The varlet, who dreaded Bajazet, began to make excuses, saying it was all false. The woman told a plain tale, and persisted in its truth. The *Sultan* stopped her, and said—'Woman, consider well thy accusation; for, if I find thou hast told me a lie, thou shalt suffer death.' 'Sir,' replied the woman, 'I consent to it; for were it not true, I could have no reason to come before thee, and I only

ask for justice.' 'I will do it,' answered the *Sultan*, 'for I have so sworn, and indiscriminately to every man or woman within my dominions.'

He then ordered the varlet to be seized, and to have his belly opened, for otherwise he would not have known if he had drank the milk or not. It was there found, for it had not had time to be digested; and the *Sultan*, on seeing it, said to the woman, 'Thou hadst just cause of complaint: now go thy way, for the injury done thee has been punished.' She was likewise paid for her loss. This judgment of Bajazet was witnessed by the French lords, who were at the time in his company.

When the Count de Nevers and the lords of France who were made prisoners at the Battle of Nicopolis (excepting the Count d'Eu and the Lord de Courcy, who had died), had been some time entertained by the Sultan, and had seen great part of his state, he consented they should depart, which was told them by those who had been ordered to attend to their personal wants. The count and his companions waited on the *Sultan* in consequence, to thank him for his kindness and courtesy. On taking his leave, the *Sultan* addressed him, by means of an interpreter, as follows:—

'John, I am well informed that in thy country thou art a great lord, and son to a powerful prince. Thou art young, and hast many years, to look forward to; and, as thou mayest be blamed for the ill success of thy first attempt in arms, thou mayest perchance, to shake off this imputation and regain thine honour, collect a powerful army to lead against me, and offer battle. If I feared thee, I would make thee swear, and likewise thy companions, on thy faith and honour, that neither thou nor they would ever bear arms against me. But no: I will not demand such an oath: on the contrary, I shall be glad that when thou art returned to thy country, it please thee to assemble an army, and lead it hither. Thou wilt always find me prepared, and ready to meet thee in the field of battle. What I now say, do thou repeat to any person, to whom it may please thee to repeat it; for I am ever ready for, and desirous of deeds of arms, as well as to extend my conquests.'

These high words the Count de Nevers and his companions understood well, and never forgot them as long as they lived.

Nothing indeed could surpass the arrogant confidence in the strength of his arms with which Bajazet was inspired by this victory over the chosen warriors of the Christian nations. It was his common boast, that he would conquer Italy, and that his horse should eat his oats on the high altar of St. Peter's. From his capital at Brusa, he sent vaunting messages to the princes of Asia and Egypt, announcing his victory at Nicopolis; and the messengers to each Mahometan court took with them a chosen band of the Christians who had been taken in the battle, as presents from the conqueror, and as attesting witnesses of his exploits. Nor was it in words only that Bajazet showed his unceasing energy against the yet unsubdued nations of the West.

His generals overran and devastated Styria, and the south of Hungary; and the *Sultan* himself led the Turkish armies to the conquest of Greece. He marched through Thessaly, as Xerxes had marched nearly nineteen centuries before. But no modern Leonidas guarded Thermopylae; and Locris, Phocis, and Boeotia fell almost without resistance into the Turkish power. Bajazet's lieutenants passed with equal celerity across the isthmus of Corinth, and subdued the whole Peloponnesus. Thirty thousand Greeks were removed thence by Bajazet's order, and transported into Asia; and Turcoman and Tartar colonies were settled in their stead in the classic regions of Laconia, Messenia, Achaia, Argolis, and Elis. Athens was taken in 1397, and the Turkish Crescent waved over "The City of the Wise," as she is termed by the Oriental historians who narrate the triumphs of Bajazet.

Constantinople had more than once been menaced, and had been pressed with actual siege by Bajazet, from which the Greek emperor obtained a temporary respite by turning one of the churches of Constantinople into a mosque, and by binding himself to pay the *Sultan* an annual tribute of 10,000 *ducats*. But, in 1400, Bajazet, no longer sated in his ambition with such concessions, commanded the Greek emperor to surrender his crown to him, threatening extermination to all the inhabitants of the city in case of refusal. The Byzantines nobly replied—

> We know our weakness, but we trust in the God of justice, who protects the weak and lowly, and puts down the mighty from on high."

Bajazet was preparing to execute his threats, when the desolater was laid desolate and the victor overthrown, not by any efforts of European statesmanship or violence, but by the superior might of another Asiatic conqueror, before whom the spirit of the Ottoman power, high and unmatchable where Timour's was not, "*became a Fear as being overpowered.*"

Chapter 5

Tamberlaine & the Tartars

Timour the Tartar, as he is usually termed in history, was called by his countrymen Timourlenk, that is, Timour the Lame, from the effects of an early wound; a name which some European writers have converted into Tamerlane, or Tamberlaine. He was of Mongol origin, and a direct descendant, by the mother's side, of Zenghis Khan. He was born at Sebzar, a town near Samarcand, in Transoxiana, in 1336, and was consequently nearly seventy years of age, when his conquests clashed with those of Bajazet, and the Ottoman power was struck by him to the dust. Timour's early youth was passed in struggles for ascendency with the petty chiefs of rival tribes, but at the age of thirty-five, he had fought his way to undisputed pre-eminence, and was proclaimed Khan of *Zagatai* by the *couroultai*, or general assembly of the warriors of his race.

He chose Samarcand as the capital of his dominion, and openly announced that he would make that dominion comprise the whole habitable earth. When he took possession of the throne of Samarcand, he assumed, in addition to his name of Timour (which means "Iron," and which typified, in the eyes of the Orientals, the resistless might with which he subdued all things), the titles of the Great Wolf (*Gurgan*), the Lord of the Age (*Sahet Kiwan*), and Conqueror of the World (*Jehargyr*). The boastful appellations of Eastern sovereigns are frequently as ridiculous as they are pompous; but those which Timour bore were emblems of fearful truths; for in the thirty-six years of his reign he raged over the world from the great wall of China to the centre of Russia on the north; and the Mediterranean and the Nile were the western limits of his career, which was pressed eastward as far as the sources of Ganges. He united in his own person the sovereignties of twenty-seven countries, and he stood in the place of nine several dynasties of kings. He was often heard to quote a passage of an Eastern poet, which declares that as there is but one God in heaven, so there ought to be but one lord on earth, and that all the kingdoms of the universe could not satiate the ambition of one great sovereign.

The career of Timour as a conqueror, is unparalleled in history; for neither Cyrus, nor Alexander, nor Caesar, nor Attila, nor Zenghis Khan, nor Charlemagne, nor Napoleon, ever won by the sword so large a portion of the globe, or ruled over so many myriads of subjugated fellow-creatures. Timour's triumphs were owing not only to personal valour and to high military genius, but to his eminent skill as a politician and a ruler. His code of laws, which he drew up for the regulation of his army, for. the administration of justice, and for the finances of his empire, shows keen observation, and deep and sound reflection. The chief force of his art of government, and of his foreign policy, was derived from the admirable system, which he established of gaining accurate and full intelligence from the reports of emissaries, who were sent by him to travel in all directions, under various disguises, and especially as pilgrims or *dervises*.

He thus knew the strength and the weakness of his enemies in each place, and at each crisis. Whatever information he obtained from his agents was by his orders carefully collected in registers and delineated on maps, which were kept ready for immediate reference. Thoughtful and provident in balancing probabilities, and guarding well against each contingency before he undertook an enterprise, he was unshaken in his resolution when his plans were matured. He countermanded no order which had once been issued; and it was a maxim with him never to repent, and never to regret. He had such an ascendency over his soldiers, that they not only underwent the severest privations, and lavished their lives at his bidding, but would, if Timour ordered, abstain from plunder in the hour of victory, and give up the spoils of war without a murmur. He was a generous master; but his cruelty to those who ventured to resist him surpasses all the similar horrors with which military history is so rife. Timour evidently employed terror as one of his principal instruments of conquest; and the punishments which he inflicted on whole populations often show the cold calculating subtlety of a practised tormentor, rather than the mere savage ferocity of an irritated despot.

Bajazet had, by his generals, extended the frontier of his empire in the east of Asia Minor during the three years that followed the Battle of Nicopolis. Timour's dominions were already spread over Georgia, and other countries west of the Caspian Sea, so that a collision between these two great potentates of the Mahometan world became inevitable. Each sheltered the princes whom the other had dethroned, and a series of angry complaints and threats followed, which soon led to open insult and actual war. The strong city of Sivas (the ancient Sebaste in Cappadocia) near the Armenian frontier, which had submitted to Bajazet, was the first place in the Ottoman dominions which Timour assailed; and it was by the tidings of the fall of Sivas that Bajazet was recalled from the siege of Constantinople.

Bajazet had sent Ertoghrul, the bravest of his sons, with a chosen force to protect Sivas; and the strength of the fortifications, the number and spirit of the population, and the military skill with which they were directed, had seemed to set the threats of its Tartar assailants at defiance. But Timour employed thousands of miners in digging huge cavities beneath the foundations of the city walls, taking care to prop up the walls with timber planking and piles until the excavations were complete. When this was done, the miners set fire to the timber, and the walls sank down by their own weight. The defenders of Sivas saw their town and ramparts thus swallowed up by the earth before their eyes, and implored in despair the mercy of the conqueror. Never had Timour shown himself so merciless.

Four thousand Christian warriors from Armenia, who had formed part of the garrison, were buried alive by his orders. Their heads were tied down by cords lashed tightly round the neck and under the thighs, so as to bring the face between the legs. Bound in this agonising posture, they were flung into graves, which were planked over before the earth was thrown back, so as to prolong the torture of the wretched victims as long as possible. Prince Ertoghrul, and the Turkish part of the garrison were put to the sword. The fall of Sivas delayed that of Constantinople. Bajazet proceeded to Asia Minor in bitterness of heart for the blow that had been struck at his empire, and in deep affliction for the loss of the best beloved of his sons. One day, on his march, he passed near where a shepherd was singing merrily, and he exclaimed, "Sing me this burden:

Leave not Sivas to be taken,
And thy son to die forsaken.

Before Bajazet had reached the eastern provinces of his dominions, Timour had marched southward from Sivas, spreading devastation far and wide through the southern regions of Asia Minor. An insult from the Sultan of Egypt had drawn the wrath of the Tartar conqueror in a southern direction, and Syria experienced for two years the terror and the cruelty of his arms. In the spring of 1402 Timour marched again against the Ottomans. A new interchange of letters and embassies had taken place between him and Bajazet, which had only incensed still more each of these haughty conquerors against the other. But though professing the utmost scorn for his adversary, Timour knew well how formidable were the Turkish arms, and he carefully drew together for this campaign the best-appointed, as well as the most numerous army, that his vast dominions could supply. He practised also the subtle policy of weakening his enemy by sowing discontent and treachery among Bajazet's troops. Timour's secret agents were sent to the Ottoman camp, and urged on the numerous soldiers of Tartar race who served there, that they ought not to fight against Timour, who was the true chief of all Tartar warriors, and that Bajazet was unworthy to command such brave men.

The efforts of these spies and emissaries were greatly aided by the dissatisfaction which Bajazet's ill-judged parsimony and excessive severity in discipline had already created in his army. His best generals observed the bad spirit which was spreading among the men, and implored their *Sultan* not to risk a decisive encounter with the superior forces of Timour, or at least to regain the good-will of his soldiers by judicious liberality. Bajazet was both arrogant and avaricious; he determined to attack his enemy, but to keep back his treasures; reserving them, as one of his generals bitterly remarked, as certainly for Timour's use, as if the Turkish bullion was already stamped with Tartar coinage. Bajazet advanced with about 120,000 men against the far superior forces of Timour, which were posted near Sivas.

The Mongol emperor did not immediately encounter the Ottomans; but manoeuvred so as to ensure that the battle should take place on ground most advantageous for the action of cavalry, and on which he could avail himself most fully of his numerical superiority. By an able forced march through Kaisyraiah and Kirschehr he evaded Bajazet, and reached the city and plain of Angora. He immediately formed the siege of the city, knowing that Bajazet would not suffer the shame of letting so important a place fall without an effort to relieve it As he expected, the Ottoman *Sultan* hurried to the rescue of Angora, and Timour then took up an advantageous position on the broad plain of Tchibukabad, to the north-west of the town.

Notwithstanding the immense preponderance of numbers which

he possessed, the Mongol sovereign observed all military precautions. One of his flanks was protected by the little River Tchibukabad, which supplies Angora with water; on the other he had secured himself by a ditch and strong palisade. Bajazet, blinded by his former successes, seemed to have lost all the generalship which he usually exhibited, and to have been seized at Angora by the same spirit of rashness which possessed the Frankish chivalry whom he overthrew five years before at Nicopolis. He camped first to the north of Timour's position; and then, to show his contempt for his enemy, he marched his whole army away to the high grounds in the neighbourhood, and employed them in a grand hunting. The troops were drawn out, according to the Asiatic custom, in a vast circle, enclosing many miles; and they then moved in towards the centre, so as to drive the game to where the *Sultan* and his officers were posted.

Unfortunately the districts in which Bajazet made this, his last chase, were destitute of water, and the sufferings of his troops whom he thus devoted to the image of war, equalled those which an army ordinarily endures in war's stern reality. Five thousand of the Ottoman soldiers perished with thirst and fatigue to promote their *Sultan's* fatal sport. After this imperial folly, Bajazet marched back to his enemy; but he found that the camp which he had left was now occupied by the Tartars, and that the only stream of water to which the Ottoman Army could gain access, had been turned and filled up by Timour's orders, so as to be almost unserviceable.

Bajazet was thus obliged to seek a battle, nor would he have declined it even if he had the choice, such was his pride and confidence in his power. On the 20th of July, 1402, the decisive conflict took place. The Mongol Army is said to have exceeded 800,000 men, and it certainly was far more numerous than that led by Bajazet, who could not have brought more than 100,000 into the field; and not only in numbers, but in equipment, in zeal, and in the skill with which they were directed, the superiority was on the side of the Mongols. Except the corps of *Janissaries*, who were under the *Sultan's* immediate orders, and the Servian auxiliaries who fought gallantly for the Ottomans under their king, Stephen Lasarevich, Bajazet's troops showed little prowess or soldiership at Angora.

The arts of Timour's emissaries had been effective; and, when the action commenced, large numbers of the Tartars who were in Bajazet's service, passed over to the ranks of his enemies. The contingents of several of the Asiatic tributary princes took the same course; and it was only in the Ottoman centre, where Bajazet and his *Janissaries* stood, and in the left centre, where the Servians fought, that any effective resistance was made to the fierce and frequent charges of the Mongol cavalry. Bajazet saw that the day was irreparably lost, but he rejected the entreaties of his officers to fly while escape was yet practicable. He led his yet unbroken veterans to some rising ground, which he occupied with them, and there beat off all the attacks of the enemy throughout the day.

But his brave *Janissaries* were sinking beneath thirst, fatigue, and wounds; and it was evident that the morning would see them a helpless prey to the myriad enemies who swarmed around them. At nightfall Bajazet attempted to escape from the field, but he was marked and pursued; his horse stumbled and fell with him; and Mahmoud, the Titular Khan of Jagetai, who served in Timour's army, had the glory of taking the great *Sultan* of the Ottomans prisoner. Of his five sons who had been in the battle, three had been more fortunate than their father. Prince Solyman had escaped towards the Ægean Sea, Prince Mahomet to Amassia, and Prince Issa towards Caramania. Prince Musa was taken prisoner; and the fifth, Prince Mustapha, disappeared in the battle, nor was his fate ever certainly known.

Bajazet was at first treated by Timour with respect and kindness; but an ineffectual attempt to escape incensed the conqueror, and increased the rigour of the *Sultan's* captivity. Thenceforth Bajazet was strictly watched by a numerous guard, and was placed in fetters every night. When the Mongol Army moved from place to place, Timour took his captive with him; but, in order to avoid the hateful sight of his enemies, Bajazet travelled in a covered litter with iron lattice-work. The similarity of sound between two Turkish words caused the well-known story that the Tartar king carried the captive *Sultan* about in an iron cage.

★★★★★★

In Marlowe's play of *Tamburlaine*, Bajazet and "the Turkess," his wife, brain themselves against the bars of the cage on the stage. Though he stoops to much bombast and extravagance, Marlowe breathes nobly the full spirit of the ferocious energy and fiery pride of the great Oriental conquerors. His *Tamburlaine* is immeasurably superior to the benevolent Tamerlane of Rowe, both as a dramatic character, and as an image of historic truth.

★★★★★★

The real ignominy which Bajazet underwent was sufficient to break a proud heart, and he died in March, 1403, eight months after the battle of Angora. Timour had sufficient magnanimity to set at liberty Prince Musa, Bajazet's son, and to permit him to take the dead body to Brusa for honourable interment in the burial-place of the Ottoman sovereigns. He himself did not long survive his fallen rival. He died at Otrar, on the 1st of February, 1405, while on his march to conquer China. In the brief interval between his victory at Angora and his death, he had poured his desolating armies throughout the Ottoman dominions into Asia Minor, sacking the Turkish cities of Brusa, Nice, Khemlik, Akshehr, Karahissar, and many more, and then assailing the great city of Smyrna, which had escaped the Ottoman power, and had been for half a century held by the Christian Knights of St. John of Jerusalem.

Timour directed the siege of Smyrna in person. In fifteen days a mole had been thrown across the harbour, which deprived the besieged of all succour, and brought the Mongol troops close to the seaward parts of the city; large portions of the landward walls had been undermined; huge movable towers had been constructed, from which the besiegers boarded the city's battlements, and Smyrna was taken by storm, notwithstanding the heroic defence of the Christian knights. Timour ordered a general massacre of the inhabitants without mercy to either age or sex.

It was the custom of the Tartar Conqueror to rear a vast pyramid of human heads, when any great city had been captured by his troops. The garrison and population of Smyrna proved insufficient to supply materials for one of these monuments on his accustomed scale of hideous grandeur. But Timour was resolved not to leave the site of Smyrna without his wonted trophy; and he ordered that the supply of heads should be economised, by placing alternate layers of mud between the rows of heads in the pyramid. After other similar acts of gigantic cruelty in Asia Minor, he marched into Georgia to punish the prince of that country for not having come in person when required to the Tartar camp. The unhappy Georgians perished by thousands for the imputed fault of their sovereign, and seven hundred towns and villages were destroyed by the troops of Timour.

In 1404, the Conqueror rested for a short time from blood-shedding, and displayed his magnificence in his capital city of Samarkand, which he had not seen for seven years. But the unslaked thirst of conquest and slaughter urged him onward to the attack of the Chinese

Empire before the year was closed; and that wealthy and populous realm must have been swept by his destroying hordes, had it not been saved by the fever which seized him at Otrar, after his passage of the River Sihoon on the ice in February, 1405. Timour died in that city, at the age of seventy-one, having reigned thirty-six years, during which he shed more blood and caused more misery than any other human being that ever was born upon the earth.

Chapter 6

Battle of Varna

The Ottoman Empire, which during the fourteenth century had acquired such dimensions and vigour, lay at the beginning of the fifteenth century in apparently irretrievable ruin. Besides the fatal day at Angora, when its veteran army was destroyed, and its long-victorious sovereign taken captive, calamity after calamity had poured fast upon the house of Othman. Their ancient rivals in Asia Minor, the Seljukian princes of Caramania, Aidian, Kermian, and other territories which the three first Ottoman sovereigns had conquered, were reinstated by Timour in their dominions. In Europe the Greek Empire accomplished another partial revival, and regained some of its lost provinces. But the heaviest and seemingly the most fatal of afflictions was the civil war which broke out among the sons of Bajazet, and which threatened the utter disintegration and destruction of the relics of their ancestral dominions.

At the time of Bajazet's death, his eldest son, Solyman, ruled at Adrianople. The second son, Prince Issa, established himself as an independent ruler at Brusa, after the Mongols retired from Asia Minor. Mahomet, the youngest and the ablest of the brothers, formed a petty kingdom at Amassia. War soon broke out between Mahomet and Issa, in which Mahomet was completely successful. Issa fled to Europe, where he sought protection and aid from Solyman, who forthwith attacked Mahomet, so that European Turkey and Asiatic Turkey were now arrayed against each other. At first Solyman was successful.

He invaded Asia, and captured Brusa and Angora. Meanwhile the other surviving son of Bajazet, Prince Musa, had, after his liberation by Timour, been detained in custody by the Seljukian Prince of Kermian, through whose territories he was passing with the remains of Bajazet, which he was to bury at Brusa. The interposition of Mahomet had put an end to this detention, and Prince Musa fought on Mahomet's side against Solyman in Asia. After some reverses which they sustained from Solyman in the first campaign, Musa persuaded Mahomet to let him cross over to Europe with a small force, and effect a diversion in Mahomet's favour by attacking the enemy in his own territories. This manoeuvre soon recalled Solyman to Europe, where a short but sanguinary contest between him and Musa ensued. At first Solyman had the advantage; but the better qualities of this prince were now obscured by the debasing effects of habits of debauchery. He treated his troops with savage cruelty, and heaped the grossest insults on his best generals. The result was that his army passed over to the side of Musa, and Solyman was killed while endeavouring to escape to Constantinople (1410).

Musa was now master of the Ottoman dominions in Europe, and speedily showed that he inherited a fall proportion both of the energy and of the ferocity of his father Bajazet. In an expedition which he undertook against the Servian prince, whom he accused of having treacherously aided Solyman in the civil war, he is said to have not only practised the customary barbarities of ravaging the country, carrying off the male youth as captives, and slaughtering the rest of the population; but according to the Byzantine writer Ducas, Musa caused the carcasses of three Servian garrisons to be arranged as tables, and a feast to be spread on them, at which he entertained the generals and chief captains of the Ottoman Army.

The Greek emperor, Manuel Palaeologus, had been the ally of Solyman; Musa therefore attacked him, and besieged his capital Palaeologus called over Mahomet to protect him, and the Asiatic Ottomans now garrisoned Constantinople against the Ottomans of Europe. Mahomet made several gallant but unsuccessful sallies against his brother's troops, and was obliged to recross the Bosphorus, to quell a revolt that had broken out in his own territories. Musa now pressed the siege of the Greek capital; but Mahomet speedily returned to Europe, and obtained the assistance of Stephen, the Servian King. The armies of the rival Ottoman brethren were at last arrayed for a decisive conflict on the plain of Chamurli, near the southern Servian frontier.

But Musa had alienated the loyalty of his soldiers by conduct similar to that by which Solyman's desertion and destruction had been caused, while Mahomet was as eminent for justice and kindness towards those who obeyed him, as for valour and skill against those who were his opponents. When the two armies were about to close in battle, Hassan, the Aga of the *Janissaries* on the side of Mahomet, stepped out before the ranks, and exhorted his old comrades, who were on the part of Musa, to leave the cause of a madman from whom they met with constant outrage and humiliation, and to range themselves among the followers of the most just and virtuous of the princes of the house of Othman.

Enraged at hearing his troops thus addressed, Musa rushed against Hassan, and cut him down with his own hand, but was himself wounded by an officer who had accompanied Hassan. Musa reeled back bleeding towards his own soldiers, who were seized with a panic, and broke their ranks, and fled in all directions. Musa endeavoured to escape, but was found by the pursuers lying dead in a marsh near the field where the armies had met. His death ended the war of succession in the Ottoman Empire, for Prince Issa had disappeared some years before, during the hostilities between Solyman and Mahomet in Asia; and Mahomet was now, after Musa's death, the sole known surviving son of Bajazet.

Sultan Mahomet I. was surnamed by his subjects Pehlevan, which means the Champion, on account of his personal activity and prowess. His graciousness of disposition and manner, his magnanimity, his love of justice and truth, and his eminence as a discerning patron of literature and art, obtained for him also the still more honourable title of Tschelebi, which, according to Von Hammer, expresses precisely the same idea which is conveyed by the English word "gentleman." Other Turkish sovereigns have acquired more celebrity; but Mahomet, the Champion and the Gentleman, deserves to be cited as one of the noblest types of the Ottoman race. His humanity and his justice are attested by Greek as well as by Oriental historians. He was through life the honourable and firm ally of the Byzantine Emperor; the dreaded foe of the rebellious Turcomans; the glorious bulwark of the throne of Othman; and, as his country's histories term him, "The Noah who preserved the ark of the empire, when menaced by the deluge of Tartar invasions."

After the fall of Musa, Mahomet received at Adrianople the ready homage of the European subjects of the Ottoman Empire, and the felicitations of the neighbouring rulers. The Emperor Palaeologus and Mahomet had reciprocally aided each other against Musa; and Mahomet honourably showed his gratitude and good faith by restoring according to promise to the Greek Empire the strong places on the Black Sea and the Propontis, and the Thessalian fortresses which had been previously wrested from it by the Turks. A treaty of amity was also concluded between the *Sultan* and the Venetians. The little republic of Ragusa had in the reign of Mahomet's grandfather placed itself by treaty under the protection of the Turks, and that treaty was now renewed with Sultan Mahomet. The ambassadors of the princes of Servia, of Wallachia, of the Albanian prince who reigned at Yanina, of the petty sovereigns or despots of the Morea, who after Bajazet's ruin had established themselves at Lacedaemon and in Achaia, came also before Mahomet at Adrianople. The *Sultan* received them all with friendly courtesy; and on their departure he said to them:

> Forget not to tell your masters that peace I grant to all, peace I accept from all. May the God of peace be against the breakers of peace!

A brief season of unusual calm was thus obtained for the countries westward of the Bosphorus and the Hellespont; but Asia was seething with insurrection and war, and Mahomet was speedily obliged to quit his feast of peace at Adrianople to reconquer and secure the ancient possessions of his house. The important city of Smyrna and the adjacent territory were at this period commanded by an Ottoman governor of the name of Djouneid, who had resumed possession of them after the Mongols had withdrawn from Asia Minor, and who had succeeded afterwards in making himself also master of the principality of Aidin. Djouneid had submitted first to Solyman, and afterwards to Mahomet, as his *Sultan*; but during the last civil war he had openly revolted against Mahomet and he now aspired to make himself an independent sovereign.

At the same time the Prince of Caramania had taken advantage of the absence of Mahomet and his best troops from Asia to attack the very heart of the Ottoman Asiatic dominions, and had laid siege to Brusa. The city was well garrisoned, and held out firmly against him; but he burnt to the ground the mosques and other public buildings of the suburbs; and, in the rage of his heart against the race of Othman, he ordered the tomb of Bajazet, which was outside the city walls, to be opened, and the remains of that Sultan to be given to the flames. While the Caramanians were thus engaged in profaning the sanctuaries of their own creed, and in violating the repose of the dead, they suddenly saw approaching them from the west the funeral procession of Prince Musa, whose body had been borne by Mahomet's orders from Europe to Asia for burial in the mosque of Amurath at Brusa.

The besiegers were panic-stricken at this unexpected spectacle: and the Caramanian Prince, thinking possibly that Sultan Mahomet with an army was close at hand, or perhaps seized with remorse and ghostly terror at the sepulchral apparition, fled from Brusa, unchecked by the bitter reproach of one of his own followers, who said to him:

> If thou fliest before the dead Ottoman, how wilt thou stand against the living one?

The *Sultan*, when he had crossed over from Europe to Asia with his forces, marched first against his rebellious vassal. He besieged Smyrna, and compelled it to surrender; and Djouneid was soon reduced to beg for mercy, which Mahomet, moved by the tears of the fallen rebel's family, accorded him. He then marched against the Caramanians. He captured many towns in person: but was obliged to leave his army by a sudden and severe malady, which baffled the skill of all his physicians save one, the celebrated Sinan, who prescribed the news of a victory as the best medicine that the *Sultan* could receive. His favourite general, Bajezid Pacha, soon supplied the desired remedy by completely defeating the Caramanians, and taking their prince, Moustapha Bey, prisoner. Mahomet recovered his health at the joyous intelligence of this success. The Caramanians now sued for peace, which the Ottoman *Sultan* generously granted. The captive Caramanian prince in Mahomet's presence placed his right hand within the robe on his own bosom, and solemnly pronounced the oath:

> I swear that so long as there is breath in this body I will never attack or covet the *Sultan's* possessions.

Mahomet set him at liberty with every mark of honour; but while he was yet in sight of the conqueror's camp, the prince, who held that between the Caramanians and the Ottomans war ought to reign from the cradle to the grave, commenced marauding on some of the herds that were grazing on the plain round him. His officers reminded him of the oath which he had just taken; but he drew from his bosom a dead pigeon squeezed tightly in his right hand, and sarcastically repeated the words of his oath:

> So long as there shall be breath in *this* body.

Incensed at this perfidy, Mahomet renewed the war, and gained great advantages; but he again was generous enough to grant peace on the reiterated entreaties of the Caramanians. They had received such severe blows in the last war, that terror now kept them quiet for several years, and the Asiatic dominions of the *Sultan* enjoyed peace and tranquillity; which Mahomet further secured by entering into friendly diplomatic relations with the various princes of Upper Asia, so as to avert further invasions like those of Timour.

On his return to Europe, in 1416, Mahomet became involved in a war with the Venetians. The petty lords of many of the islands of the Ægean Sea were nominal vassals of the Republic of Venice; but, in disregard of the treaty between that power and the *Sultan*, they continued to capture the Turkish shipping and to plunder the Turkish coasts. Mahomet fitted out a squadron of galleys to retaliate for their injuries, and this led to an encounter with the Venetian fleet, which, under their admiral, Loredano, completely defeated the Turks off Gallipoli, on the 29th May, 1416. Peace was soon restored; and a Turkish ambassador appeared at Venice in the same year, with a new treaty between his master and the Republic.

Mahomet's troops sustained some severe reverses in expeditions undertaken against Styria and Hungary between 1416 and 1420; but no very important hostilities were waged between him and his neighbours in European Christendom. A far more serious peril to the *Sultan* was a revolt of the *dervishes*, which broke out both in Europe and Asia; and was only quelled by the Sultan's troops after several sanguinary battles. This insurrection was organised by the judge of the army, Bedreddin, aided by an apostate Jew, named Tirlak. The nominal chief of the fanatics was a Turk of low birth, named Baerekludye Mustapha, whom they proclaimed as their spiritual lord and father. All these three perished either in battle or by the executioner, and their sect was extinguished with them. Their revolt is remarkable, as being, with the exception of the Wahabite rebellion in the last and present centuries, the only religious war by which the Ottoman Empire has ever been troubled.

After this formidable peril had passed away, Mahomet was called on to defend his throne from another domestic enemy. It has been mentioned, that one of Bajazet's sons. Prince Mustapha, who was present on the day of Angora, disappeared after the defeat of the Turks in that battle. His body was not found among the slain, though Timour caused diligent search to be made for it; nor was the mode of his escape (if he escaped) ever ascertained. Certain it is, that, in 1420, a claimant to the Ottoman sovereignty appeared in Europe, who asserted that he was Mustapha, the son of Sultan Bajazet, and who was recognised as such by many of the Turks. Supported by the Prince of Wallachia, and by Djouneid, the old rebel against Mahomet, the pretender penetrated into Thessaly with a large army. Mahomet met him with his customary vigour, and a pitched battle was fought near Salonica, in which the claimant was utterly defeated, and fled for protection to the Greek commandant of that city. The Byzantine emperor refused to surrender the suppliant fugitive, but consented to keep him in strict custody on condition of Mahomet paying annually a large sum of money, ostensibly for the captive's maintenance, but in reality as the wages for his imprisonment.

There was one other son of Sultan Bajazet, who figures little in history, but whose melancholy lot must not be passed over for the sake of uniformly preserving the bright colour, in which we would gladly represent the character of Mahomet I. Prince Kasimir does not appear to have fought at Angora, like his five brethren, or to have taken any part in the subsequent civil wars between them. He came into Mahomet's power; and though he was not put to death in conformity with the precedent which Bajazet had established, he was deprived of sight by his brother's order. The blinded prince received the grant of a domain near Brusa, where he resided; and Turkish historians praise the good-nature of Sultan Mahomet, who, whenever he visited his Asiatic capital, sent for his sightless brother to the palace and treated him with benevolence truly fraternal.

Another stain on the memory of Mahomet the Gentleman is his guilty weakness in seeking to strengthen his sovereignty by the death of the son of his brother Solyman. But in this case, as in his conduct towards Prince Kasimir, Mahomet recoiled from following out to its full extent the stern principle of extinguishing in the blood of those nearest to the throne all risk of their rivalry with its occupant. He spared a daughter whom Solyman had also left; and when that daughter was married, and bore a son, Mahomet conferred ample wealth on the child, so that it should be maintained in a manner worthy of its rank. Mahomet indeed showed on his death-bed, that no sophistry or statecraft could blind his natural sense to the heinous guilt of fratricide.

He was stricken with apoplexy near the close of the year 1421; and though he partially recovered, he knew that his end was approaching, and earnestly implored his favourite general, Bajezid Pacha, to place his two infant sons under the protection of the Greek emperor, lest their elder brother, Prince Amurath, on becoming *Sultan*, should imitate the crimes of his grandfather and his father, and study his own security by their destruction. Mahomet did not long survive the shock which his system had received; but his death was concealed from the public by his general and chief officers of state for more than forty days, while intelligence of the event was sent to Prince Amurath, who, at the time of his father's mortal illness, held a command on the frontiers of Asia Minor.

Mahomet I. was but forty-seven years of age at the time of his death; and his reign, as *Sultan* of the re-united empire, had lasted only eight years. But he had been an independent prince for nearly the whole preceding period of eleven years that passed between his father's captivity at Angora and his own final victory over his brother Musa at Chamurli. For nineteen years, therefore, he was a ruler over his people; and his memory is still deservedly cherished and honoured among them. He was buried at Brusa, in a mausoleum erected by himself near the celebrated mosque which he built there, and which, from its decorations of green porcelain, is called the Green Mosque. This edifice is said to be the most beautiful specimen of Saracenic architecture and carving that is in existence. Mahomet I. also completed the vast and magnificent mosque at Brusa, which his grandfather Amurath I. had commenced, but which had been neglected during the reign of Bajazet.

It is deserving of mention that Mahomet founded in the vicinity of his own mosque and mausoleum two characteristic institutions, one a school, and one a refectory for the poor, both of which he endowed with royal munificence. The reign of this *Sultan* is cited by Von Hammer as the period when a taste for literature and fondness for poetry first prevailed among the Ottomans. He was a liberal patron of intellectual merit; and the name of an early literary Turkish politician, Sehiri, is preserved in honourable reputation for having, while Mahomet was Governor of Amassia, and Sehiri his *Defterdar* or Chancellor of the Exchequer, inspired the young prince with an enduring zeal for the advancement of literature and art, and for the generous patronage of their professors.

Amurath II., when called from his vice-royalty in Asia Minor to become the sovereign of the Turkish Empire, was only eighteen years of age. He was solemnly recognised as Sultan, and girt with the sabre of Othman, at Brusa; and the troops and officers of state paid willing homage to him as their sovereign. But his reign was soon troubled by insurrection. The Greek Emperor, despising the youth of Amurath, released the pretender Mustapha from confinement, and acknowledged him as the legitimate heir to the throne of Bajazet; having first stipulated with him that he should, if successful, repay the Greek emperor for his liberation by the cession of a large number of important cities. The pretender was landed by the Byzantine galleys in the European dominions of the *Sultan*, and for a time made rapid progress.

Large bodies of the Turkish soldiery joined him, and he defeated and killed the veteran general Bajezid Pacha, whom Amurath first sent against him. He then crossed the Dardanelles to Asia, with a large army; but the young *Sultan* showed in this emergency that he possessed military and political abilities worthy of the best of his ancestors. Mustapha was out-manoeuvred in the field; and his troops, whose affection to his person and confidence in his cause he had lost by his violence and incapacity, passed over in large numbers to Amurath. Mustapha took refuge in the strong city of Gallipoli; but the *Sultan*, who was greatly aided by a Genoese commandant named Adorno, besieged him there, and stormed the place. Mustapha was taken and put to death; and the *Sultan* then turned his arms against the Greek emperor, and declared his resolution to punish the unprovoked enmity of Palaeologus by the capture of Constantinople.

The embassies, charged with abject apology, by which the Greeks now sought to appease the Sultan's wrath, were dismissed with contempt; and in the beginning of June, 1422, Amurath was before the trembling capital with twenty thousand of his best troops. Ten thousand of the dreaded Akindji, under their hereditary commander, Michael Bey, had previously been let loose by the *Sultan* upon the lands which the Greek emperor yet retained beyond the city walls, and had spread fire and desolation through the doomed territory, without any attempt being made by the Byzantines to check or to avenge their ravages. Amurath's own army seemed still more irresistible; and the *Sultan* carried on the siege with a degree of skill as well as vigour, rarely to be found in the military operations of that age. He formed a line of embankment only a bowshot from the city wall, and extended it from the sea to the Golden Horn, so as to face the whole landward side of the city.

This rampart was formed of strong timber, with a thick mound of earth heaped up along its front; and it received uninjured the discharges of firearms and the shocks of the heaviest stones that the *balistas* of the Greeks could hurl against it Under cover of this line, Amurath's army urged on the work of attack. Movable towers were built to convey storming parties to the summits of the city wall; mines were laboriously pushed forward; and breaching cannon were now for the first time employed by the Ottomans, but with little effect. Wishing to increase the zeal and the number of the assailants, Amurath proclaimed that the city and all its treasures should be given up to the true believers who would storm it; and crowds of fanatic volunteers flocked to the camp to share in the harvest of piety and plunder.

Among the recruits were a large number of *dervishes*, headed by a renowned saint named Seid Bokhari, who announced the day and the hour at which it was fated for him to lead the Mahometans to the capture of Constantinople. Accordingly, at the appointed time, one hour after noon on Monday, the 25th of August, 1422, Seid Bokhari led on the Ottoman Army to the assault. 500 *dervishes*, who had stipulated that the Christian nuns of Constantinople should be assigned as their particular share of the booty, formed the forlorn hope of the stormers. The Ottomans attacked vehemently, and the Greeks resisted steadily along the whole length of the city wall; but it was near the gate of St. Romanus that the combat raged most fiercely.

The Christians as well as the Mahometans were animated by religious enthusiasm, and by the assurance that their arms were aided by the interposition of supernatural power. At last some said that they beheld, and all believed that there was seen on the outer bastions a bright apparition of a virgin robed in garments of violet hue and dazzling lustre, whose looks darted panic amid the assailing columns. This was the Panagia, the Holy Virgin, who had descended for the special protection of the sacred maids of the Christian city from the boastful impiety of the monks of Mahomet. The besiegers themselves (not unwilling perhaps to find some pretext for their defeat, besides the strength of the fortifications and the bravery of the defenders) gave credit and confirmation to this legend.

It is certain that the attack failed, and that the siege was soon afterwards raised. But it is little consonant with the character of Amurath, that a single repulse, in which the loss of life was inconsiderable, should have made him abandon a siege for which he had made such ample and scientific preparations. The intrigues of the Byzantine emperor had lit up a new civil war in his enemy's Asiatic dominions; and Amurath, like his grandfather Bajazet, was obliged to relinquish Constantinople, when the prize seemed to be within his grasp, and to fight for safety as well as for empire on the eastern side of the Bosphorus.

Besides the two infant brothers, of whom mention has already been made, Amurath had another brother named Mustapha, who was in Asia Minor at the time of their father's death. Prince Mustapha was of the age of thirteen when that event occurred; and his attendants, ignorant of the character of Amurath, fled with their princely charge into Caramania. He had grown up to manhood there without Amurath making any attempt against his life or liberty; but after the overthrow of the pretender, Mustapha, his supposed uncle, he listened to the suggestions and promises of the emissaries whom the Greek emperor now sent to him; and being supported with some troops by the Princes of Caramania and Kermian, he suddenly invaded his brother's dominions, made himself master of several places of importance, and laid siege to Brusa.

The rapidity with which Amurath marched a veteran and well-appointed army to the rescue, disconcerted all young Mustapha's projects. The Ottomans who had joined him after his first successes deserted him; his Greek allies were far too feeble to encounter Amurath's forces; and the unfortunate prince fled for his life, but was pursued, overtaken, and captured by some of his brothers officers, who instantly hanged their prisoner on the nearest tree, without giving an opportunity to their master either to exercise a perilous clemency, or to become an actual participator in taking away his brother's life.

The civil war was thus promptly extinguished; and in 1424 Amurath returned to Europe, having re-established perfect order in his Asiatic provinces, and chastised the neighbouring sovereigns who had promoted the late hostilities against him. Amurath did not renew the siege of Constantinople, but accepted a treaty by which the Greek emperor bound himself to pay an annual tribute of 30,000 *ducats* to the *Sultan*, and surrendered the city of Zeitoun (Lysimachia) and all the other remaining Greek cities on the River Strania (Strymon) and the Black Sea, except Selymbria and Derkos.

In 1430 Amurath besieged and captured the important city of Thessalonica, which had thrown off its allegiance to the emperor, and placed itself under the protection of the Venetians, who were at that time in enmity with the *Sultan*. Other accessions of power in the same quarter, and successful hostilities with various Asiatic princes, are recorded in the detailed narratives of the acts of Amurath; but the main feature of the reign of this great *Sultan* is his long contest with the warlike nations on the northern and western frontiers of his European dominions; a struggle marked by many vicissitudes, and which called forth into energetic action the high qualities of Amurath himself, and also of his renowned opponents, Hunyades, the hero of Hungary, and

Scanderbeg, the champion of Albania.

We have seen how valuable to the Turkish Empire, in its season of disaster, after the overthrow of Sultan Bajazet, was the steady fidelity and friendship with which the Lord of Servia, Stephen Lasarevitch, adhered to his engagements with the house of Othman. That prince died in 1427; and his successor, George Brankovich, who was bound by no personal ties, like those of his predecessor, to the interest of the Ottomans, resolved to check their further progress. The Hungarians also, whom the recollection of dreadful defeat at Nicopolis had kept inactive during the temporary dismemberment and feebleness of the power which had smitten them, now felt their martial confidence in their own prowess revive; and their jealousy of the growth of the Turkish dominion was reawakened.

Moreover, the Bosnians, who saw their country gradually overrun from the military frontier on which the Ottomans had established themselves at Scupi, and the Albanians, who beheld their strong places, Argyrocastrum and Croia, in Amurath's possession, were conscious that their national independence was in danger, and were favourably disposed for action against the common foe, (Ranke's *Servia*). Wallachia was eager for liberation; and the unsleeping hatred of the Caramanians to the Ottomans made it easy for the Christian antagonists of the *Sultan* in Europe to distract his arms by raising war and insurrection against him in Asia. Yet there was for several years no general and vigorous confederation against the *Sultan*; and a chequered series of partial hostilities and negotiations filled nearly twenty years, during which the different Christian neighbours of the *Sultan* were sometimes his antagonists and sometimes his allies against each other.

At last the accession of Ladislaus, the third King of Lithuania and Poland, to the crown of Hungary, brought fresh strength and enterprise to the *Sultan's* foes; and a severe struggle followed, which after threatening the utter expulsion of the house of Othman from Europe, confirmed for centuries its dominion in that continent, and wrought the heavier subjugation of those who were then seeking to release themselves from its superiority.

In 1442 Amurath was repulsed from Belgrade; and his generals, who were besieging Hermanstadt, in Transylvania, met with a still more disastrous reverse. It was at Hermanstadt that the renowned Hunyades first appeared in the wars between the Hungarians and the Turks. He was the illegitimate son of Sigismond, King of Hungary, and the fair Elizabeth Morsiney. In his early youth he gained distinction in the wars of Italy; and Comines, in his memoirs, celebrates him under the name of the White Knight of Wallachia. After some campaigns in Western Christendom, Hunyades returned to protect his native country against the Ottomans; and in 1442 he led a small but chosen force to the relief of Hermanstadt. He planned his movements ably; and aided by an opportune sally of the garrison, he completely defeated Mezid Bey, the Turkish general, killing 20,000 of his troops, and taking prisoner Mezid Bey himself, his son, and many more. Hunyades was no whit inferior to the fiercest Turkish generals in cruelty. Mezid Bey and his son were hewn to pieces in his presence; and one of the chief entertainments at the triumphal feast of the victorious Hungarians was to see captive Turks slaughtered during the banquet

Amurath sent Schehadeddin Pacha with an army of 80,000 men against Hunyades to avenge this disgrace. But the "White Knight," as the Christians called Hunyades, from the colour of his armour, met Schehadeddin at Vasag, and, though his numbers were far inferior, utterly routed the Turks with even heavier loss than they had sustained before Hermanstadt The next year, 1443, is the most illustrious in the career of Hunyades, and brought the Ottoman power to the very brink of ruin. The Servian, the Bosnian, and the Wallachian princes were now actively co-operating with King Ladislaus against the Sultan; and an attack of the Caramanians on the Ottoman dominions in Asia compelled Amurath to pass over to that continent and carry on the war there in person, while he left to his generals the defence of his empire in Europe against the Hungarians and their allies.

The Christian Army that invaded European Turkey in the remarkable campaign of this year, was the most splendid that had been assembled since the French chivalry and the Hungarians advanced against Bajazet at Nicopolis; and it was guided by the ablest general that Christendom had yet produced against the house of Othman. The fame of Hunyades had brought volunteers from all the nations of the West to serve under him in the holy war against the Mahometans; and the most energetic efforts of Pope Eugenius and his legate. Cardinal Julian, had been devoted to give to these champions of their faith the enthusiasm as well as the name of crusaders. The main body of the confederates, consisting chiefly of Hungarian, Servian, Wallachian, and German troops, crossed the Danube near Semendra. Hunyades, at the head of 12,000 chosen cavalry, then pushed forward nearly to the walls of Nissa.

King Ladislaus and the Cardinal Julian followed him with the Polish, and part of the Hungarian troops, and with the crusaders from Italy. On the 3rd of November Hunyades won the first battle of the campaign on the banks of the Morava, near Nissa. The grand army of the Turks was beaten, and fled beyond the Balkan, with the loss of nine standards, 4000 prisoners, and many thousand slain. Hunyades followed close upon the foe, captured the city of Sophia, and then prepared to cross the Balkan, and advance upon Philippopolis.

The passage of the Balkan is an exploit almost as rare in military history as those passages of the Alps that have conferred so much lustre on Hannibal, Charlemagne, and Napoleon.

******

The operations of the Persian Darius Hystaspis (B.C. 506), and of the Russian Svatoslaus (*A.D.* 907), in the regions of the Haemus, cannot be satisfactorily traced or verified.

******

Alexander forced the barrier of the Balkan in 335 B.C., probably through the same pass which Hunyades penetrated from the opposite direction, in *A.D.* 1443. Amurath I. crossed the Balkan in 1390; and the Russian general, Diebitsch, forced this renowned mountain chain near its eastern extremity in 1827. Hunyades and Diebitsch are the only two commanders who have crossed it from north to south, in spite of armed opposition; and the fact of their accomplishing that exploit against the same enemy (though with an interval of nearly four centuries), and the splendour of the success which each thereby obtained over the Ottoman power, make the similitude between their achievements more remarkable.

If the Balkan campaign of Hunyades presents nothing equal to the noble audacity, with which Diebitsch threw a numerically feeble army across the mountain to Adrianople, trusting to the moral effect of such a blow at the crisis when it was dealt, the actual passage which the Hungarian leader effected in the December of 1443 was a more brilliant scene of mountain-warfare, than that of the Russian marshal in 1829, both on account of the enormous increase in the natural difficulties of the transit, caused by the difference of season, and by reason of the superior preparation on the part of the Turks, which Hunyades encountered and overcame.

Two defiles, the openings of which on the northern side are near each other, one to the west named the defile of Soulourderbend, the other to the east that of Isladi, or Slatiza, lead through the Balkan on the road from Sophia to Philippopolis. The Turks, who defended the passage against Hunyades, had barricaded both these defiles with heaps of rocks; and when they found the Hungarian vanguard approach, they poured water throughout the night down the mountain slope, which froze as it fell, and formed at morning a wall of ice against the Christians. Undaunted by these obstacles and the weapons of the enemy, Hunyades encouraged his men by voice and example to clamber onward and through the western defile, until they reached a part where the old Roman works of Trajan completely barred the way. The Hungarians retreated; but it was only to advance up the eastern defile, which was less perfectly fortified.

There, through the rest of the winter's day, Hunyades and his chivalry fought their gallant upward battle against Turkish arrow and *scimetar*, amid the still more formidable perils of the precipice, the avalanche, the whelming snowdrift, and the bitter paralysing cold. They triumphed over all; and the Christmas-day of 1443 was celebrated by the exulting Hungarians on the snow-plains of the southern slopes of the conquered Balkan.

The Turks, who had rallied and received reinforcements at the foot of Mount Cunobizza, again fought with Hunyades and were again defeated. It surprises us to read that after this last victory, the Christian Army, instead of pushing forward to Adrianople, returned to Buda, where Hunyades displayed his trophies and his prisoners, before his rejoicing fellow-countrymen. There is little sign here of such high spirit as afterwards animated Diebitsch, or even of common generalship or policy. But we may be acting unjustly if we throw on the hero of mediaeval Hungary the blame of this infirmity of purpose. Such an army, as he led, was very different in subordination and discipline to the regular troops of modern times, or even to the Turkish troops who were its contemporaries and opponents.

Amurath had been personally successful in Asia; but the defeats which his forces had sustained in Europe, and the strength of the confederacy there formed against him filled him with grave alarm. He sought by the sacrifice of the more remote conquests of his House to secure for the rest of his European dominions the same tranquillity which he had re-established in the Asiatic. After a long negotiation a treaty of peace for ten years was concluded at Szegeddin on the 12th of July, 1444, by which the *Sultan* resigned all claims upon Servia, and recognised George Brankovich as its independent sovereign. Wallachia was given up to Hungary; and the *Sultan* paid 60,000 *ducats* for the ransom of Mahmoud Tchelebi, his son-in-law, who had commanded against Hunyades, and had been taken prisoner in the late campaign. The treaty was written both in the Hungarian and in the Turkish languages; King Ladislaus swore upon the Gospels, and the *Sultan* swore upon the *Koran*, that it should be truly and religiously observed.

Amurath now thought that his realm was at peace, and that he himself, after so many years of anxiety and toil, might hope to taste the blessings of repose. We have watched him hitherto as a man of action, and we have found ample reason to admire his capacity and vigour in council and in the field. But Amurath had also other virtues of a softer order, which are not often to be found in the occupant of an Oriental throne. He was gentle and affectionate in all the relations of domestic life. Instead of seeking to assure his safety by the death of the two younger brothers, for whose fate their father had been so anxious, Amurath treated them with kindness and honour while they lived, and bitterly lamented their loss when they died of the plague in their palace at Brusa.

The other brother, who took up arms against him, was killed without his orders. He forgave, for the sake of a sister who was married to the Prince of Kermian, the treasonable hostility with which that vassal of the House of Othman assailed him; and the tears of another sister for the captivity of her husband Mahmoud Tchelebi, and her entreaties that he might be rescued from the power of the terrible Hunyades, were believed to have prevailed much in causing Amurath to seek the pacification of Szegeddin. When that treaty was concluded, Amurath passed over to Asia, where he met the deep affliction of learning the death of his eldest son Prince Alaeddin, who had shared with him the command of the Ottoman forces in Asia during the operations of the preceding year.

The bitterness of this bereavement increased the distaste which Amurath had already acquired for the pomp and turmoil of sovereignty. He determined to abdicate the throne in favour of his second son, Prince Mahomet, and to pass the rest of his life in retirement at Magnesia. But it was not in austere privation, or in the fanatic exercises of Mahometan monasticism, that Amurath designed his private life to be wasted. He was no contemner of the pleasures of sense; and the scene of his retreat was amply furnished with all the ministry of every delight. The tidings of warfare renewed by the Christian powers soon roused the bold Paynim, like Spenser's Cymochles, from his Bower of Bliss.

The King of Hungary and his confederates had recommenced

hostilities in a spirit of treachery that quickly received its just reward. Within a month from the signature of the treaty of Szegeddin the Pope and the Greek emperor had persuaded the King of Hungary and his councillors to take an oath to break the oath which had been pledged to the *Sultan*. They represented that the confessed weakness of the Ottomans, and the retirement of Amurath to Asia, gave an opportunity for eradicating the Turks from Europe, which ought to be fully employed. The Cardinal Julian pacified the conscientious misgivings, which young King Ladislaus expressed, by his spiritual authority in giving dispensation and absolution in the Pope's name, and by his eloquence in maintaining the infamously celebrated thesis, that no faith is to be kept with misbelievers.

Hunyades long resisted such persuasions to break the treaty; but his conscience was appeased by the promise that he should be made independent King of Bulgaria, when that province was conquered from the Turks. He only stipulated that the breach of the treaty should be delayed till the 1st of September; not out of any lingering reluctance to violate it, but in order that the confederates might first reap all possible benefit from it by securely establishing their forces in the strongholds of Servia, which the Ottomans were then evacuating in honest compliance with their engagements.

On the 1st of September the king, the legate, and Hunyades, marched against the surprised and unprepared Turks with an army of 10,000 Poles and Hungarians. The temerity which made them expect to destroy the Turkish power in Europe with so slight a force was equal to the dishonesty of their enterprise. They advanced into Wallachia, where Drakul, the prince of that country, joined them with his levies. That sagacious chieftain saw the inadequacy of King Ladislaus's means for the task which he had undertaken, and remonstrated against advancing farther. This brought on a personal difference between him and Hunyades, in the course of which Drakul drew his sabre against the Hungarian general, and was punished by an imprisonment, from which he was only released on promising fresh supplies of troops, and a large contribution of money.

The Christian Army, in full confidence of success, crossed the Danube, and marched through Bulgaria to the Black Sea. They then moved southward along the coast, destroying a Turkish flotilla at Kaundjik, receiving the surrender of many fortresses, and storming the strongholds of Sunnium and Pezech. The Turkish garrisons of these places were put to the sword, or thrown over precipices. Kavarna was next attacked and taken, and finally the Christians formed the siege of the celebrated city of Varna.

The possession of Varna was then, as now, considered essential for the further advance of an invading army against the Turkish European Empire. Hunyades was still successful; Varna surrendered to his arms: the triumphant Christians were encamped near it, when they suddenly received the startling tidings, that it was no longer the boy Mahomet that was their adversary, but that Sultan Amurath was himself again. They heard that the best warriors of Asiatic Turkey had thronged together at the summons of their veteran sovereign—that the false Genoese had been bribed to carry Amurath and his army, 40,000 strong, across the Bosphorus, by a *ducat* for each soldier's freight, thus baffling the papal fleet that cruised idly in the Hellespont Other messengers soon hurried into the Christian camp, who announced that the unresting *Sultan* had come on against them by forced marches, and that the imperial Turkish Army was posted within four miles of Varna.

A battle was inevitable; but the mode, in which Hunyades prepared for it, showed that his confidence was unabated. He rejected the advice which some gave in a council of war to form entrenchments and barricades round their camp, and there await the *Sultan's* attack. He was for an advance against the advancing foe, and for a fair stricken field. The young king caught the enthusiastic daring of his favourite general, and the Christian Army broke up from their lines, and marched down into the level ground northward, of the city, to attack the *Sultan*, who had carefully strengthened his encampment there by a deep ditch and palisades.

★★★★★★

Amurath had probably crossed the Balkan by the pass that leads from Aides to Pravadi, and had then marched eastward upon Varna. This would bring him to the rear of Hunyades.

★★★★★★

On the eve of the feast of St. Mathurin, the 10th of November, 1444, the two armies were arrayed for battle. The left wing of the Christian Army consisted chiefly of Wallachian troops. The best part of the Hungarian soldiery was in the right wing, where also stood the Frankish crusaders under the Cardinal Julian. The king was in the centre with the royal guard and the young nobility of his realms. The rear-guard of Polish troops was under the Bishop of Peterwaradin. Hunyades acted as commander-in-chief of the whole army. On the Turkish side the two first lines were composed of cavalry and irregular infantry, the Beyler-Bey of Roumelia commanding on the right, and the Beyler-Bey of Anatolia on the left. In the centre, behind their lines, the *Sultan* took his post with his *Janissaries* and the regular cavalry of his bodyguard. A copy of the violated treaty was placed on a lance-head, and raised on high among the Turkish ranks as a standard in the battle, and as a visible appeal to the God of Truth, who punishes perjury among mankind. At the very instant when the armies were about to encounter, an evil omen troubled the Christians. A strong and sudden blast of wind swept through their ranks, and blew all their banners to the ground, save only that of the king.

Yet, the commencement of the battle seemed to promise them a complete and glorious victory. Hunyades placed himself at the head of the right wing, and charged the Asiatic troops with such vigour that he broke them and chased them from the field. On the other wing, the Wallachians were equally successful against the cavalry and *Azabs* of Roumelia. King Ladislaus advanced boldly with the Christian centre; and Amurath seeing the rout of his two first lines, and the disorder that was spreading itself in the ranks round him, despaired of the fate of the day, and turned his horse for flight.

Fortunately for the House of Othman, Karadja, the Beyler-Bey of Anatolia, who had fallen back on the centre with the remnant of his defeated wing, was near the *Sultan* at this critical moment. He seized his master's bridle, and implored him to fight the battle out. The commandant of the *Janissaries*, Yazidzi-Toghan, indignant at such a breach of etiquette, raised his sword to smite the unceremonious Beyler-Bey, when he was himself cut down by an Hungarian sabre. Amurath's presence of mind had failed him only for a moment; and he now encouraged his *Janissaries* to stand firm against the Christian charge.

Young King Ladislaus, on the other side, fought gallantly in the thickest of the strife; but his horse was killed under him, and he was then surrounded and overpowered. He wished to yield himself up prisoner, but the Ottomans, indignant at the breach of the treaty, had sworn to give no quarter. An old *janissary*, Khodja Khiri cut off the Christian king's head, and placed it on a pike, a fearful companion to the lance, on which the violated treaty was still reared on high. The Hungarian nobles were appalled at the sight, and their centre fled in utter dismay from the field. Hunyades, on returning with his victorious right wing, vainly charged the *Janissaries*, and strove at least to rescue from them the ghastly trophy of their victory. At last he fled in despair with the wreck of the troops that he had personally commanded, and with the Wallachians who collected round him.

The Hungarian rearguard, abandoned by their commanders, was attacked by the Turks the next morning and massacred almost to a man. Besides the Hungarian King, Cardinal Julian, the author of the breach of the treaty and the cause of this calamitous campaign, perished at Varna beneath the Turkish *scimetar*, together with Stephen Bahory, and the Bishops of Eilau and Grosswardein. This overthrow did not bring immediate ruin upon Hungary, but it was fatal to the Sclavonic neighbours of the Ottomans, who had joined the Hungarian king against them. Servia and Bosnia were thoroughly reconquered by the Mahometans; and the ruin of these Christian nations, which adhered to the Greek Church, was accelerated by the religious intolerance with which they were treated by their fellow Christians of Hungary and Poland, who obeyed the Pope, and hated the Greek Church as heretical.

A Servian tradition relates that George Brankovich once inquired of Hunyades what he intended to do with respect to religion, if he proved victorious. Hunyades answered that he would compel the country to become Roman Catholic. Brankovich thereupon asked the same question of the *Sultan*, who replied that he would build a church near every mosque, and leave the people at liberty to bow in the mosques or to cross themselves in the churches, according to their respective creeds. The Servians, who heard this, thought it better to submit to the Turks and retain their ancient faith, than to accept the Latin rites, (Ranke's *Servia*).

The tradition expresses a fact, for which ample historical evidence might be cited. So also in Bosnia, the bigotry of the Church of Rome in preaching up a crusade against the sect of the Patarenes, which was extensively spread in that country, caused the speedy and complete annexation of an important frontier province to the Ottoman Empire. Seventy Bosnian fortresses are said to have opened their gates to the Turks within eight days. The royal House of Bosnia was annihilated, and many of her chief nobles embraced Mahometanism to avoid a similar doom.

******

The complete degradation of Servia and Bosnia was not effected until the reign of Mahomet II., Amurath's successor. But Ranke's *History of Servia* rightly treats this as the result of the Battle of Varna,

******

Amurath's projects for retirement had been disappointed by the necessity of his resuming the sovereign power to save the Ottoman Empire from the Hungarians and their confederates. After the decisive blow which he had dealt at Varna to the enemies of his race, the *Sultan* again sought to obtain the calm of private life, and was again compelled to resume the cares of state. Early in 1445 he abdicated a second time in favour of his son, and went back to his Epicurean retreat at Magnesia. But the young hand of Mahomet was too feeble to curb the fierce Turkish soldiery; and the *Janissaries* showed their insubordinate violence in acts of pillage and murder, and in arrogant demands for increased pay, which threatened open mutiny and civil war. The veteran statesmen, whom Amurath had placed as councillors round his son, saw the necessity of recalling their old master to the helm of the empire.

Amurath yielded to their entreaties, and hastened to Adrianople, where he showed himself once more to the people and the army, as their sovereign. He was rapturously welcomed. The ringleaders in the late disorders were promptly punished, and the masses were judiciously pardoned. Order was thoroughly restored in court and camp. Young Prince Mahomet, who had twice during twelve months tasted supreme power, and twice been compelled to resign it, was sent to Magnesia, to remain there till more advanced age should make him more capable of reigning. Amurath did not venture a third time on the experiment of abdication. He has been highly eulogised as the only sovereign who had ever abdicated *twice*, and descended into private life after having learned by experience the contrast between it and the possession of a throne.

The remaining six years of Amurath's life and reign were signalised by successful enterprises against the Peloponnesus, the petty despots of which became tributary vassals of the Ottomans, and by a great defeat which he gave his old antagonist, Hunyades, at Kossova, after a three days' battle in October, 1448. In Albania his arms were less fortunate; and during the latter part of Amurath's reign his power was defied, and his pride repeatedly humbled by the celebrated George Castriot, called by the Turks Scanderbeg, or Lord Alexander, the name by which he is best known in history.

The father of this champion, John Castriot, Lord of Emalthia (the modern district of Moghlene), had submitted, like the other petty despots of those regions, to Amurath early in his reign, and had placed his four sons in the *Sultan's* hands as hostages for his fidelity. Three of them died young. The fourth, whose name was George, pleased the *Sultan* by his beauty, strength, and intelligence. Amurath caused him to be brought up in the Mahometan creed; and, when he was only eighteen, conferred on him the government of one of the *Sanjaks* of the empire. The young Albanian proved his courage and skill in many exploits under Amurath's eye, and received from him the name of Iskanderbeg, the Lord Alexander.

When John Castriot died, Amurath took possession of his principalities, and kept the son constantly employed in distant wars. Scanderbeg brooded over this injury; and when the Turkish armies were routed by Hunyades in the campaign of 1443, Scanderbeg determined to escape from their side, and assume forcible possession of his patrimony. He suddenly entered the tent of the *Sultan's* chief-secretary, and forced that functionary, with the poniard at his throat, to write and seal a formal order to the Turkish commander of the strong city of Croia, in Albania, to deliver that place and the adjacent territory to Scanderbeg, as the *Sultan's* viceroy. He then stabbed the secretary, and hastened to Croia, where his stratagem gained him instant admittance and submission. He now publicly abjured the Mahometan faith, and declared his intention of defending the creed of his forefathers, and restoring the independence of his native land.

The Christian population flocked readily to his banner, and the Turks were massacred without mercy. For nearly twenty-five years Scanderbeg contended against all the power of the Ottomans, though directed by the skill of Amurath and his successor Mahomet, the conqueror of Constantinople. The difficult nature of the wild and mountainous country, which he occupied, aided Scanderbeg materially in the long resistance which he thus opposed to the elsewhere triumphant Turks. But his military genius must have been high: and without crediting all the legends of his personal prowess, we may well believe that the favourite chief of the Albanian mountaineers, in the guerilla warfare by which he chiefly baffled the Turks, must have displayed no ordinary skill and daring, and may have possessed strength and activity such as rarely fall to the lot of man.

******

According to the authorities that were used and decorated by Knolles, Scanderbeg "ever fought against the Turks with his arm bare, and that with such fierceness, that the blood did oftentimes burst out of his lips. It is written that he, with his own hand, slew three thousand Turks in the time of his wars against them." One of the best of the numerous harangues which Knolles introduces in his history, is the speech which, at p. 198 of his first volume, he puts in the mouth of a Turkish soldier, "a rough, bold-spirited fellow," at Sfetigrade, in defiance of the threats of Scanderbeg. The Turk bids Scanderbeg's messengers tell their master, that "If he seeks to impose those conditions on us, let him once more have that arm of his which men of courage fear not so much as he thinketh." Byron, when a boy, was (like Johnson) fond of reading Knolles, and he must have had this picture of Scanderbeg in his mind when he described Alp in the *Siege of Corinth*.

******

The strongest proof of his valour is the superstitious homage which they paid to him when they occupied Lissa in the Venetian territories, whither Scanderbeg had at last retired from Albania, and where he died in 1567. The Turkish soldiers forced open his tomb, and eagerly sought portions of his bones to wear as amulets, thinking that they would communicate a spirit of valour similar to that of the hero to whose mortal fabric they had once belonged.

The *Sultan*, under whom Scanderbeg fought in youth, died long before the bold Albanian, who once had been his favourite pupil in the art of war, and afterwards his most obstinate adversary. Amurath expired at Adrianople in 1451, after having governed his people with justice and in honour for thirty years. His noble qualities are attested by the Greek as well as by Turkish historians. He was buried at Brusa. Our own old historian, Knolles, who wrote in 1610, says of his sepulchre:

> Here he now lieth in a chapel without any roof, his grave nothing differing from that of the common Turks, which they say he commanded to be done in his last will, that the mercy and blessing of God might come unto him by the shining of the sun and moon, and the falling of the rain and dew of heaven upon his grave."

CHAPTER 7

The Siege of Constantinople

Mahomet II., surnamed by his countrymen "the Conqueror," was aged twenty-one years when his father died. He heard of that event at Magnesia, whither the *grand vizier* had despatched a courier to him from Adrianople. He instantly sprang on an Arab horse, and exclaiming, "Let those who love me, follow me," galloped off towards the shore of the Hellespont. In a few days he was solemnly enthroned. His first act of sovereign authority showed that a different spirit to that of the generous Amurath would now wield the Ottoman power. Amurath had left a little son, a babe still at the breast, by his second wife, a princess of Servia. Mahomet ordered his infant brother to be drowned in a bath; and the merciless command was executed at the very time when the unhappy mother, in ignorance of her child's doom, was offering her congratulations to the murderer on his accession.

Mahomet perceived the horror which the atrocity of this deed caused among his subjects; and he sought to avert it from himself by asserting that the officer who had drowned the infant prince had acted without orders, and by putting him to death for the pretended treason. But Mahomet himself, when in after years he declared the practice of royal fratricide to be a necessary law of the state, confessed clearly his own share in this the first murder of his deeply-purpled reign.

He had now fully outgrown the boyish feebleness of mind, which had unfitted him for the throne when twice placed on it by his father six years before. For craft, capacity, and courage, he ranks among the highest of the Ottoman *Sultans*. His merits also as a far-sighted statesman, and his power of mind as a legislator, are as undeniable as are his military talents. He was also keenly sensible to all intellectual gratifications, and he was himself possessed of unusually high literary abilities and attainments. Yet with all these qualities we find combined in him

an amount of cruelty, perfidy, and revolting sensuality, such as seldom stain human nature in the same individual.

Three years before Mahomet II. was girt with the *scimetar* of Othman, Constantine XI. was crowned Emperor of Constantinople —a prince whose heroism throws a sunset glory on the close of the long-clouded series of the Byzantine annals. The Roman Empire of the East was now shrunk to a few towns and a scanty district beyond the walls of the capital city; but that city was itself a prize of sufficient splendour to tempt the ambition and excite the hostility of a less aspiring and unscrupulous spirit than that of the son of Amurath. The Ottomans felt that Constantinople was the true natural capital of their empire. While it was in the hands of others, the communication between their European and their Asiatic provinces could never be secure. Its acquisition by themselves would consolidate their power, and invest them with the majesty that still lingered round those walls, which had encircled the chosen seat of Roman Empire for nearly eleven hundred years.

The imprudence of Constantine, who seems to have judged the character of Mahomet from the inability to reign which he had shown at the premature age of fourteen, hastened the hostility of the young *Sultan*. Constantine sent an embassy, demanding the augmentation of a stipend which was paid to the Byzantine Court for the maintenance of a descendant of Solyman, Sultan Bajazet's eldest son. This personage, who was named Orkhan, had long been in apparent retirement, but real custody at Constantinople, and the ambassadors hinted that if their demands were not complied with, the Greek emperor would immediately set him loose, to compete with Mahomet for the Turkish throne.

Mahomet, who at this time was engaged in quelling some disturbances in Asia Minor, answered with simulated courtesy; but the old *grand vizier*, Khalil, warned the Byzantines, with indignant vehemence, of the folly of their conduct, and of the difference which they would soon experience between the fierce ambition of the young *Sultan* and the mild forbearance of his predecessor. Mahomet had indeed bent all his energies on effecting the conquest of the Greek capital, and he resolved to secure himself against any interruption or division of his forces while engaged in that great enterprise He provided for the full security of his territories in Asia; he made a truce of three years with Hunyades, which guaranteed him from all attack from the north in Europe; and he then contemptuously drove away the imperial agents who received the revenues of the lands allotted for the maintenance of Orkhan, and began to construct a fortress on the European side of the Bosphorus, about five miles above Constantinople, at a place where the channel is narrowest, and immediately opposite one that had been built by Bajazet Yilderim on the Asiatic shore.

Constantine remonstrated in vain against these evident preparations for the blockade of his city; and the Ottomans employed in the work were encouraged to commit acts of violence against the Greek peasantry, which soon led to conflicts between armed bands on. either side Constantine closed the gates of his city in alarm, and sent another embassy of remonstrance to the *Sultan*, who replied by a declaration of war, and it was evident that the death-struggle of the Greek Empire was now fast approaching.

Each party employed the autumn and winter of 1462 in earnest preparations for the siege, which was to be urged by the one and resisted by the other in the coming spring. Mahomet collected the best troops of his empire at Adrianople; but much more than mere numbers of soldiery, however well disciplined and armed for the skirmish or the battlefield, was requisite for the capture of the great and strong city of Constantinople. Artillery had for some time previously been employed both by Turkish and Christian Armies; but Mahomet now prepared a more numerous and formidable park of cannon than had ever before been seen in warfare.

A Hungarian engineer, named Urban, had abandoned the thankless service and scanty pay of the Greeks for the rich rewards and honours with which the *Sultan* rewarded all who aided him in his conquest. Urban cast a monster cannon for the Turks, which was the object both of their admiration and terror. Other guns of less imposing magnitude, but probably of greater efficiency, were prepared; and ammunition and military stores of every description, and the means of transport, were collected on an equally ample scale.

But Mahomet did not merely heap together the materials of war with the ostentatious profusion so common in Oriental rulers. He arranged all, he provided for the right use of all, in the keen spirit of skilful combination, which we admire in the campaigns of Caesar and Napoleon. He was almost incessantly occupied in tracing and discussing with his officers plans of the city, of his intended fines, of the best positions for his batteries and magazines, of the spots where mines might be driven with most effect, and of the posts which each division of his troops should occupy.

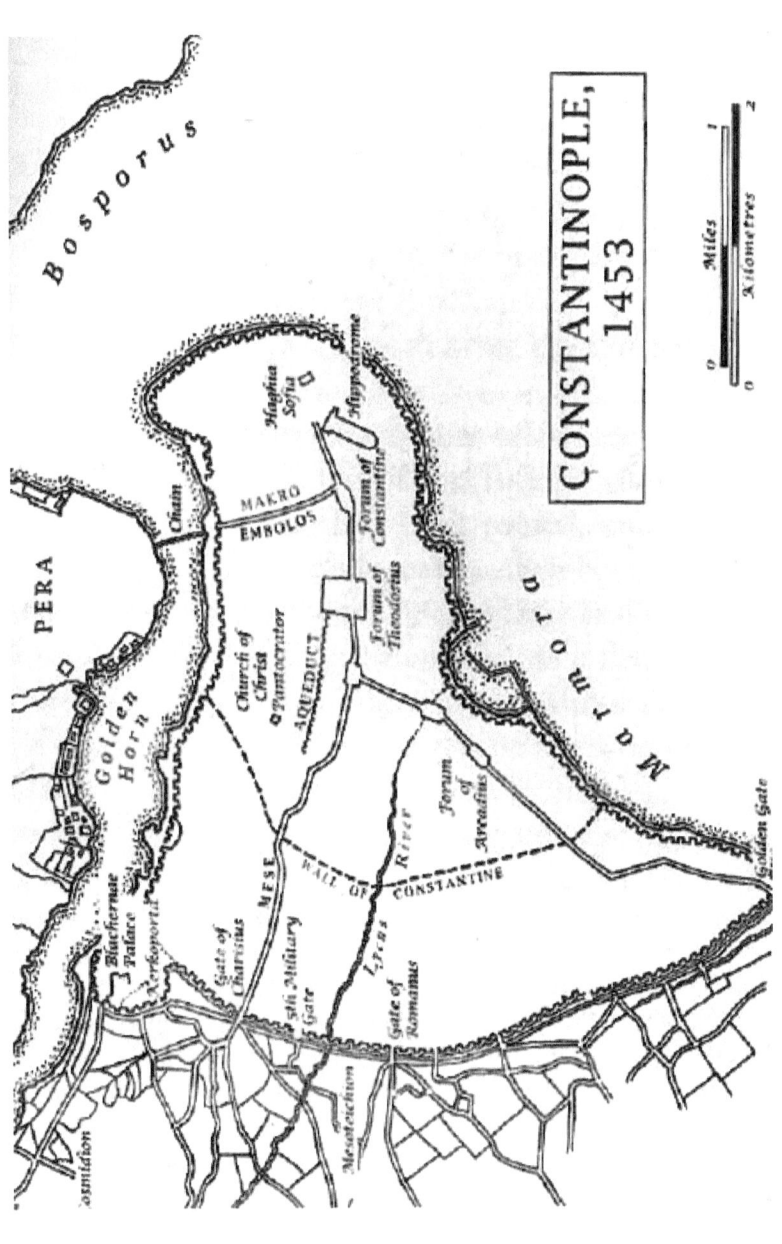

In the devoted city, the emperor, with equal ability, but far different feelings, collected the poor resources of his own remnant of empire, and the scanty succours of the Western nations for the defence. The efforts which he had made to bring the Greek Church into communion with the Church of Rome, as the price of cordial and effectual support against the Mahometans, had alienated his own subjects from him; and the bigoted priests of Byzantium, when called on by the emperor to contribute their treasures, and to arm in the defence of their national independence, replied by reviling him as a heretic. The lay leader of the orthodox Greeks, the Grand Duke Notaras, openly avowed that he would rather see the turban of the *Sultan* than the tiara of the Pope in Constantinople, (Ducas, Finlay, vol. ii.). Only six thousand Greeks, out of a population of one hundred thousand, (Finlay), took any part in the defence of the city; and the emperor was obliged to leave even these under the command of the factious Notaras, whose ecclesiastical zeal showed itself in violent dissensions, instead of cordial military co-operation with the chiefs of the Latin auxiliaries.

These auxiliaries were partly contributed by the Pope, who sent Cardinal Isidore with a small body of veteran troops, and some pecuniary aid, to the Greek Emperor. The Italian and Spanish commercial cities that traded with Constantinople, showed their interest in her fate, by sending contingents to her defence. Bands of Aragonese, of Catalans, and of Venetians, gave assistance to Constantine, which their skill and bravery made of great value, though their numbers were but small. His most important auxiliary was the Genoese commander, John Giustiniani, who arrived with two galleys and three hundred chosen men, a little before the commencement of the siege.

Altogether, Constantine had a garrison of about 9000 troops to defend walls of fourteen miles in extent, the whole landward part of which, for a space of five' miles, was certain to be attacked by the Turkish troops. The fortifications, built in ancient times, and for other systems of warfare, were ill adapted to have heavy cannon placed and worked on them; and many places had been suffered to become dilapidated. Still, amid all this difficulty and distress, Constantine did his duty to his country and his creed. No means of restoring or improving the defences were neglected, which his own military skill and that of his Latin allies could suggest, and which his ill-supplied treasury, and his disloyal subjects, would enable him to supply. But the patriotism, and even the genius, of a single ruler are vain to save the people that will not save themselves. The Greeks had long been ripe for slavery, nor could their fall be further delayed.

In the spring of 1453, the Turks were for the last time before the city, so often besieged by them and others, and so often besieged in vain.

★★★★★★

Von Hammer enumerates twenty-nine sieges of the city since its foundation by the Megarians, 658 B.C., under the name of Byzantium. It was besieged, 477 B.C., by Pausanias, Generalissimo of the Greeks, after the campaign of Plataea; in 410 B.C., by Alcibiades; in 347 B.C., by Leon, General of Philip of Macedon; in 197 A.D., by the Emperor Severus; in 313, by the Caesar Maximius; in 315, by Constantine the Great; in 616, by Khosroes, King of Persia; in 626, by the Chagan of the Avars; in 654, by the Arabs under Moawya; in 667, by Yezid, the Arab; in 672, by Sofien Ben Aouf, the Arab; in 715, by Moslema and Omar Abdul-Aziz, the Arabs; in 739, by Solyman, son of the Caliph Abdul Melek; in 764, by Paganos, Kral of the Bulgarians; in 780, by Haroun-al-Rashid: in 798, by Abdul-Melek, Haroun's general; in 811, by Kramus, Despot of the Sclavi; in 820, by the Sclavian Thomas; in 866, by the Russians, under Oswald and Dir; in 914, by Simeon, Kral of the Bulgarians; in 1048, by the rebel Thornicius; in 1081, by Alexius Comnenus; in 1204, by the Crusaders; in 1261, by Michael Palaeologus; in 1356, by Bajazet Yilderim, for the first time; in 1402, by the same, for the second time; in 1414, by Musa, Bajazet's son; in 1422, by Amurath II.; and in 1453, by Mahomet II. Since then it has been unbesieged for four centuries. Of the numerous commanders who have attacked the city, eight only have captured it:—Pausanias, Alcibiades, Severus, Constantine, Alexius Comnenus, Dandolo, Michael Palaeologus, and Mahomet.

★★★★★★

Mahomet formed his lines, as Amurath had done, from the harbour to the sea, and they were strengthened with a similar embankment. Fourteen batteries were formed opposite those parts of the landward wall of the city that appeared to be the feeblest. The chief attack was directed against the gate of St. Romanus, near the centre of the wall. Besides the Turkish cannon, *balistas* were planted along the lines, which hurled large stones upon the battlements. The Turkish archers kept up a shower of arrows on any part of the walls where the defenders showed themselves; and a body of miners, whom the *Sultan* had brought from the mines of Novoberda, in Servia, carried on their subterranean works as far as the city wall, and forced large openings in the outer of the two walls. The aggregate of the Turkish troops is variously estimated at from 70,000 to 250,000. The smaller number must have been sufficient for all the military operations of the siege; nor is it probable that Mahomet would have increased the difficulty of finding sufficient provisions for his army by uselessly crowding its ranks.

Besides the land forces, the *Sultan* had collected a fleet of 320 vessels, of various sizes, but all inferior to the large galleons of the Greeks and their allies. But the Christian ships were only fourteen in number. These were moored in the Golden Horn, or Great Harbour, the entrance of which was secured by a strong chain. The siege commenced on the 6th of April, and was prolonged by the bravery and skill of Constantine, Giustiniani, and their Latin troops until the 29th of May. Many gallant deeds were performed during this time.

The ability with which Giustiniani taught the defenders to work their artillery, and to use the important arm of war which they still exclusively possessed in the Greek fire, excited the regretful eulogies of the *Sultan* himself. A general assault, which the Turks hazarded before the walls were completely breached, and in which they employed the old machinery of movable towers, was repulsed; and the besiegers' engines were destroyed A squadron of four Genoese ships, and one Greek ship from Chios, forced their way through the Turkish flotilla, and brought seasonable supplies of com and ammunition to the city.

This action, which took place in the middle of April, was the most brilliant episode of the siege. Mahomet had ordered out a division of his galleys, 150 strong, to intercept the five ships of the Christians, that were seen running swiftly and steadily through the Propontis, before a full and favourable wind. The Greeks thronged the walls, and the Turks crowded down to the beach to watch the issue of this encounter. The *Sultan* himself rode down to the water's edge, in full expectation of witnessing a triumph of his marine force, and the destruction or capture of his enemies. On came the Christian ships, well-armed, well-manned, and well-manoeuvred. They crashed through the foremost of their brave but unpractised assailants. Their superior height made it impossible for their enemies to grapple or board them, and the very number and eagerness of the Turks increased the disorder in which their vessels soon were heaped confusedly together.

Shouts of joy rose from the city walls; while Mahomet, furious at

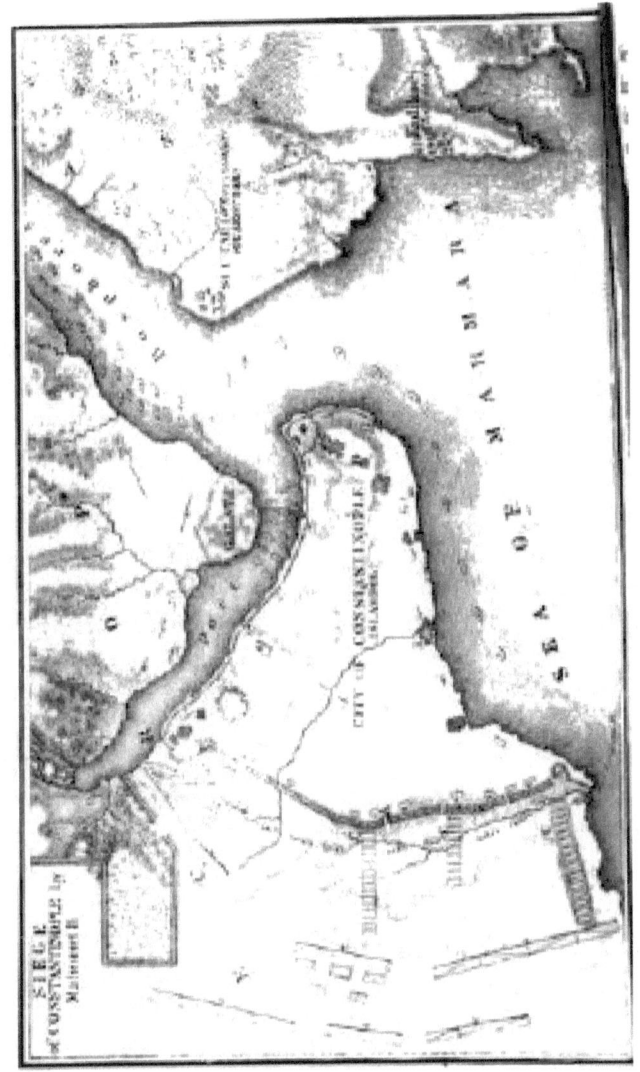

the sight, spurred his horse into the very surf, as if with his own hand he would tear the victory from the Greeks. Still onward came the exulting Christian seamen. From their tall decks, they hurled large stones, and poured incessant volleys of the inextinguishable Greek fire upon the Turkish *barks* beneath and around them. Onward they came to the harbour's mouth; the guard-chain was lowered to receive them; and the welcome reinforcement rode securely in the Golden Horn, while the shattered remnant of the Turkish squadron crept back to the shore, where their sorrowing comrades of the land force, and their indignant *Sultan* awaited them.

Mahomet, in his wrath at the loss, and still more at the humiliation which he had sustained, ordered his defeated admiral, Baltaoghli, to be impaled on the spot. The murmurs and entreaties of the *Janissaries* made him recall the atrocious command; but he partly wreaked his wrath by inflicting personal chastisement on his brave but unsuccessful officer. Four slaves stretched the admiral prostrate on the ground, and Mahomet dealt him one hundred blows with his heavy battle-mace. This reverse of the first Turkish admiral is said to have given rise to a national opinion among the Ottomans, that God had given them the empire of the earth, but had reserved that of the sea for the unbelievers. If such an opinion did really exist among the Turks before their late centuries of defeat and disaster, it must have been largely modified by the exploits of Barbarossa, Dragut, Pialé, Piri Reis, Sidi-Ali, Kilig-Ali, and their other naval commanders, who have shed such splendour over the history of the Turkish Navy.

The victory which the five relieving galleys obtained, did more even than the material succour which they conveyed, to re-animate the defenders of Constantinople. But it was a solitary reinforcement. Constantine and Giustiniani never again "saw the horizon whiten with sails" that bore hope and succour on their wings. And Mahomet was no Xerxes, (who witnessed the defeat of his armament at Salamis), to be disheartened by a single defeat, or to turn back from an enterprise because its difficulties surpassed expectation. Unable to gain the entrance of the harbour, he determined by a bold engineering manoeuvre to transport part of his fleet across the land, and launch it at the upper part of the Golden Horn, where in the narrow smooth water, and with aid ready from either shore, his galleys would have the mastery over the far less numerous though larger vessels of the Greeks.

A smooth road of planks was accordingly made along the five miles of land which intervene between the Bosphorus and the Golden

Horn; and a large division of the Turkish galleys was hauled along it, and safely launched in the harbour. As it was necessary to overcome a considerable inclination of the ground, this engineering achievement reflects great credit on Sultan Mahomet; though the transport of war-galleys over broad spaces of land was no novelty either in classical or mediaeval warfare; and a remarkable instance had lately occurred in Italy, where the Venetians, in 1437, had moved a fleet overland from the Adige to the Lake of Garda.

Thus master of the upper part of the port, Mahomet formed a pontoon bridge across it, the western end of which was so near to the angle of the landward and the harbour walls, that cannon placed on the pontoon bridge could play upon the harbour side of the city. Giustiniani in vain attempted, with the Genoese and Greek galleys, to destroy this bridge and burn the Turkish flotilla. The Venetians renewed the attempt with equally bad success.

Although no serious effect was produced on the fortifications from the additional line of attack along which the Ottomans now established their cannonade, the labours of the scanty garrison were made more severe; and it became necessary to weaken the defence on the landward side, by detaching men and guns to the wall along the harbour. Meanwhile, the exertions of the besiegers on the original and chief line of the siege were unremitting. The fire of their batteries, though slow and feeble in comparison with the artillery practice of modern times, was kept up for seven weeks, and its effects were at last visible in the overthrow of four large towers, and the yawning of a broad chasm in the city walls, near the gate of St. Romanus.

The ditch was nearly filled up by the ruins of the defences, and the path into Constantinople was at last open. Mahomet now sent a last summons to surrender, to which Constantine nobly replied, that if the *Sultan* would grant him peace he would accept it, with thanks to Heaven, that he would pay the *Sultan* tribute if demanded, but that he would not surrender the city which he had sworn to defend to the last moment of his life.

The capitulation was demanded and refused on the 24th May, and the *Sultan* gave orders for a general assault on the 29th. He announced to his army that all the plunder of the city should be theirs; and that he only reserved the land and the buildings. The Ottoman soldiery received the announcement with shouts of joy. The chiefs of the *Janissaries* pledged themselves that victory was certain, and a general illumination of the Turkish camp and fleet at night showed to the besieged the number, the purpose, and the exulting confidence of their foes.

Within the city, the Greek population passed alternately from terror at the coming storm to turbulent confidence in certain superstitious legends, which promised the help of saints and angels to men who would not help themselves. Only a small proportion of his subjects listened to the expostulations and entreaties, by which their noble-minded emperor urged them to deserve the further favour of Heaven by using to the utmost those resources which Heaven had already placed in their hands. Even among those who bore arms as part of the garrison, the meanest jealousy of their Latin auxiliaries prevailed.

On the very eve of the final assault, when Giustiniani, who was charged with the defence of the great breach, required some additional guns, the Grand Duke Notaras, who had the general control of the ordnance, refused the supply, saying that it was unnecessary. The Latins did their duty nobly. Of the twelve chief posts in the defence, ten were held by them. Giustiniani in particular distinguished himself by his valour and skill. He formed new works in rear of the demolished towers and gate of St. Romanus; and extorted the admiration of the *Sultan*, who watched his preparations, and exclaimed, " What would I not give to gain that man to my service!" But the chief hero of the defence was Constantine himself. He knew that his hour was come; and prepared to die in the discharge of duty with the earnest piety of a true Christian and the calm courage of a brave soldier.

On the night before the assault, he received the Holy Sacrament in the church of St. Sophia. He then proceeded to the great palace, and lingered for a short time in the halls where his predecessors had reigned for so many centuries, but which neither he nor any prince sprung from his race was ever to see again. When he had passed forth from the palace to take his station at the great breach, and there await his martyrdom, all thoughts of earthly grandeur were forgotten; and turning to those around him, many of whom had been his companions from youth, Constantine asked of them, as fellow-Christians, their forgiveness for any offence that he had ever committed towards them. Amid the tears and prayers of all who beheld him, the last of the Caesars then went forth to die.

In the Ottoman camp all was ready for the work of death. Each column had its specified point of attack; and the *Sultan* had so arranged the vast masses of men at his command, that he was prepared to send fresh troops successively forward against the city, even if its defenders were to hold their ground against him from daybreak to noon. At sunrise, on the 29th May, 1453, the Turkish drums and trumpets sounded for the assault, and the leading divisions of the *Sultan's* army rushed forward. Prodigal of lives, and reckoning upon wearing down the resistance of the garrison by sending wave upon wave of stormers against them, Mahomet placed his least valued soldiers in the van, to receive the first steady volleys of the Greek guns, and dull the edge of the Christian sword.

The better troops were to follow. The main body of the *Janissaries*, under the *Sultan's* own eye, was to assault the principal breach. Detachments of those chosen warriors were also directed against other weakened points of the defence. At the same time that the attack commenced from the camp, the Turkish flotilla moved against the fortifications along the harbour; and the assault soon raged by sea and by land along two sides of the Greek city. For two hours the Christians resisted skilfully and steadily; and though the *Sultan* in person, by promises, by threats, and by blows, urged his columns forward to the great breach, neither there nor elsewhere along the line could they bear back the stubborn courage of the defenders; nor could a living Mahometan come into Constantinople.

At last Giustiniani, who, side by side with the emperor, conducted the defence of the great breach, received a severe wound, and left his post to die on board his galley in the harbour. The garrison was dispirited at the loss; and the chiefs of the assailing *Janissaries* observing that the resistance had slackened, redoubled their efforts to force a passage. One of them, named Hassan of Ulubad, conspicuous by his stature and daring, rushed with thirty comrades up the barricaded ruins of one of the overthrown towers that flanked the breach. They gained the summit; and though Hassan and eighteen of his forlorn hope were struck down, others rapidly followed, and carried the Greek defences by the overwhelming weight of their numbers. Nearly at the same time, another Ottoman corps effected an entrance at a slightly-protected part of the long line of walls, and wheeling round, took the garrison in the rear. Constantine saw now that all was lost, save honour, and exclaiming, "I would rather die than live!" the last of the Romans rushed amid the advancing foe, and fell stretched by two sabre wounds among the undistinguished dead.

Torrent after torrent of the conquerors now raged through the captured city. At first they slew all whom they met or overtook; but when they found that all resistance had ceased, the love of plunder

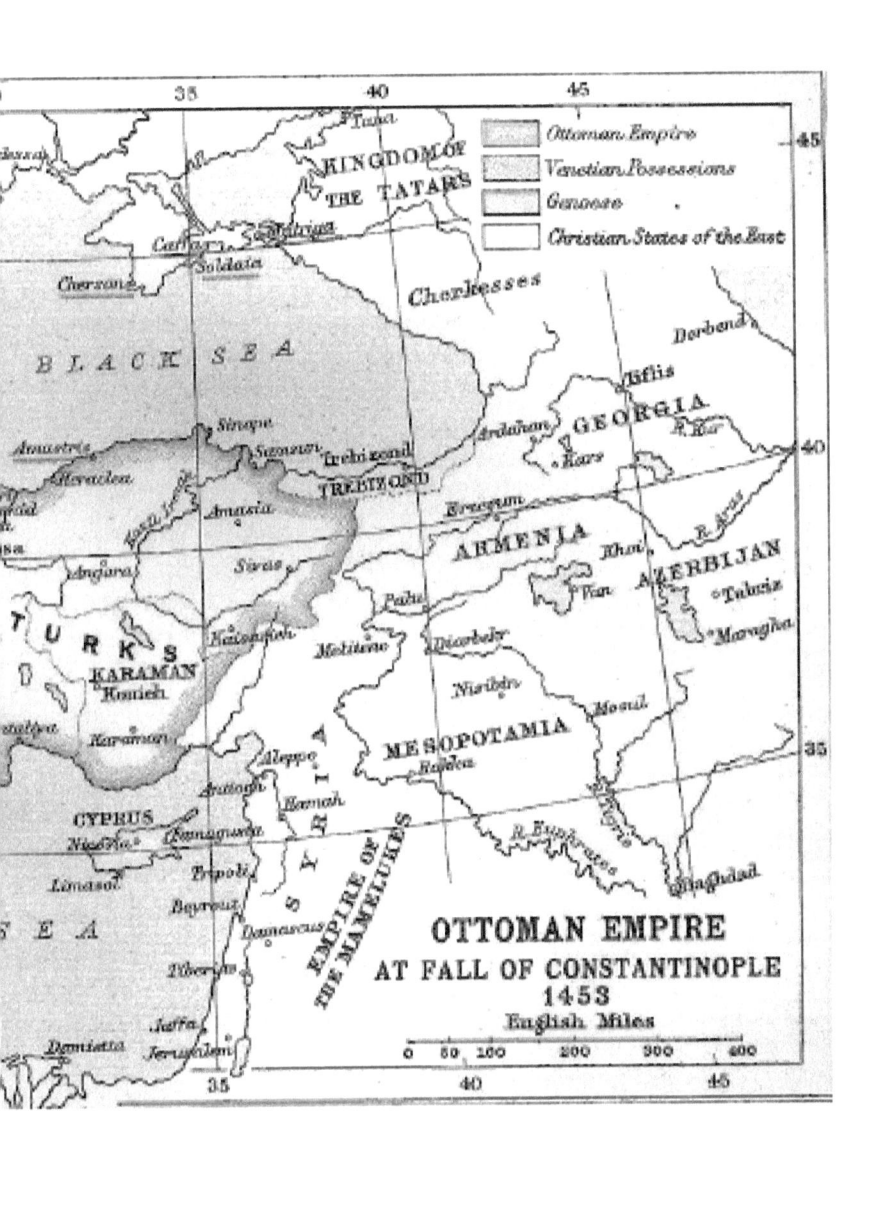

predominated over the thirst for blood, and they strove to secure the fairest and strongest of the helpless thousands that cowered before them, for service or for sale as slaves. About the hour of noon, Sultan Mahomet, surrounded by his *viziers*, his *pachas*, and his guards, rode through the breach at the gate of St. Romanus into the city which he had conquered. He alighted at the church of St Sophia, and entering the splendid edifice, he ordered one of the *muezzins* who accompanied him to summon the true believers to prayer. He then himself mounted the high altar, and prayed.

Having thus solemnly established the creed of the Prophet in the shrine where his fallen adversary had on the preceding eve celebrated the holiest Christian rite, and where so many generations of Christians had worshipped, Mahomet ordered search to be made for Constantine's body. It was found under a heap of slain in the great breach, and was identified, beyond all possibility of dispute, by the golden eagles that were embroidered upon the emperor's *buskins*. The head was cut off, and exhibited for a time between the feet of the bronze horse of the equestrian statue of Justinian in the place called the Augustan. The ghastly trophy of Mahomet's conquest was subsequently embalmed, and sent round to the chief cities of Asia.

The greater number of the emperor's Latin auxiliaries had shared his noble death. Some few had made their way to the harbour, and escaped through the Ottoman fleet. Others came as captives into Mahomet's power, and were either put to death or required to pay heavy ransoms. The Genoese inhabitants of the suburb of Galata obtained terms of capitulation, by which they were protected from pillage. The Grand Duke Notaras was brought prisoner before Mahomet, who made a show of treating him with favour, and obtained from him a list of the principal Greek dignitaries and officers of state. The *Sultan* instantly proclaimed their names to his soldiers, and offered 1000 *sequins* for each of their heads.

******

The general accuracy of Gibbon's splendid description of the taking of Constantinople is not impeached by the minute diligence of Von Hammer or Finlay, though they supply us with some not unimportant connections and additions. I think that Mr. Finlay's vindication of the Genoese commander Giustiniani from the heavy censures of Gibbon is successful, and have gladly followed it.

******

On the day after the capture of the city, Mahomet continued his survey of his conquest, and took possession of the imperial palace. Struck by the solitude of its spacious halls, and the image of desolation which it presented, Mahomet repeated two lines of the Persian poet Firdousi:—

> *The spider's web is the royal curtain in the palace of Caesar; the owl is the sentinel on the watch-tower of Afrasiab.*

The quotation showed the well-read and elegant scholar, and the subsequent deeds of the *Sultan* on that day exemplified the truth that intellectual eminence is no sure guarantee against the co-existence of the vilest depravity. On leaving the palace, Mahomet repaired to a sumptuous banquet which had been prepared for him in the vicinity. He there drank deeply of wine; and he ordered the chief of his eunuchs to bring to him the youngest child of the Grand Duke Notaras, a boy aged fourteen years of age. Notaras during the siege had only displayed the qualities of a factious bigot; but he now acted as became a Christian, a father, and a man. He told the messenger that his child should never minister to the *Sultan's* brutality, and that he would rather see him under the executioner's axe. Furious at hearing this reply, Mahomet ordered Notaras and his whole family to be seized and put to death.

Notaras met his fate with dignity, and exhorted his children to die as fitted Christians. He saw their heads fall one by one before him; and then, after having asked a few moments for prayer, he gave himself up to the executioner, acknowledging with his last breath the justice of God. The bloody heads were brought to Mahomet, and placed by his order in a row before him on the banquet table. Many more executions of noble Christians followed on that day, to please the tyrant's savage mood; and it was said that the natural ferocity of Mahomet was goaded on by the malevolent suggestions of a French renegade, whose daughter was in the *Sultan's harem*, and was at that time the object of his passionate fondness.

But though thus merciless in his lust and wrath, Mahomet knew well that for Constantinople to become such a seat of empire as his ambition desired, it was necessary that the mass of the Greek population which had escaped death and captivity during the sack of the city, should be encouraged to remain there, and to be orderly and industrious subjects of their new master. The measures taken by him with this design attest the clear-sighted statesmanship which he possessed.

Constantine had alienated his subjects from him by conforming to the Latin Church. Mahomet now gratified the Greeks, who loved their orthodoxy far more than their liberty, by installing a new patriarch at the head of the Greek Church, and proclaiming himself its protector. This was on the 1st of June, only ten days after the storm. He then by solemn proclamation invited all the fugitives to return to their homes, assuring them of safety, and encouraging them to resume their former occupations.

A formal charter was afterwards granted by him, which declared the person of the Greek patriarch inviolable, and exempted him and the other dignitaries of his Church from all public burdens. The same document assured to the Greeks the use of their churches, and the free exercise of their religious rites according to their own usages. (The contents of this charter—which had been destroyed in a fire—were solemnly proved in the reign of Selim I. by an old *janissary*, who had been at the taking of Constantinople.—Von Hammer).

But the Greek population of Constantinople had been long declining, and even before its sufferings in the fatal siege, had been far inadequate for the vast space occupied by the buildings. Mahomet therefore sought other modes of replenishing the city. Thousands of families were transplanted to the capital from various parts of his empire; and throughout his reign, at every accession of territory that he made, he colonised his capital with portions of his new subjects. Before the close of his reign, Constantinople was again teeming with life and activity; but the Greek character of the city was merged amid the motley crowds of Turkomans, Albanians, Bulgarians, Servians, and others, who had repaired thither at the *Sultan's* bidding.

The vision of Othman was now accomplished, and Constantinople had become the centre jewel in the ring of Turkish Empire. The capture of that city closes the first of the seven periods into which Von Hammer, (Supplement), divides the Ottoman history. The first period consists of 150 years of rapid growth, from the assumption of independent sovereignty by Othman to the consolidation of the European and Asiatic conquests of his house by the taking of Constantinople. The second is the period of its further growth by conquest until the accession of Solyman I. in 1520. The third is its period of meridian ascendency under Solyman and Selim II., (from 1520 to 1574).

The fourth is the commencement of its decline under Amurath III. (1574) to the epoch when the sanguinary vigour of Amurath IV. (from 1623 to 1640) restored for a time its former splendour. The fifth is the period of anarchy and insurrection, between the death of Amurath IV. (1640) and the ministry of the first Kiuprili (1656). The sixth is the period of new energy given to the empire by men of the family of Kiuprili, from 1656 to the calamitous war with Austria, which was closed by the treaty of Carlowitz in 1688. Then comes the seventh period, one of accelerated disaster and downfall, to 1763, when the treaty of Kainardji with Russia confirmed its humiliation.

Mahomet II. was but twenty-three years of age when he took Constantinople; being one year older than Alexander was when he fought the battle of the Granicus, and three years less than the age of Napoleon when he commanded at Lodi. The succession of wars and victories which filled the thirty years of Mahomet's reign might perhaps bear comparison with the exploits of the other two imperial conquerors whom we have mentioned. The fragments of the Greek Empire, which had lingered for a while unconnected with the central power of the emperor, were speedily subdued by the new ruler of Constantinople.

The Peloponnesus was conquered in 1454, and Trebizond in the following year. Servia and Bosnia were completely reduced into Turkish provinces. The last Bosnian king and his sons surrendered to Mahomet on a capitulation which guaranteed their lives, and which the *Sultan* swore to observe. Mahomet obtained a decision from the *mufti* Ali-Bestami, which declared that the *Sultan's* treaty and oath were not binding on him, as being made with unbelievers, and that he was at liberty to put his prisoners to death. The *mufti* begged as a favour that he might carry his own opinion into effect by acting as executioner. The captive Bosnian King was ordered into the *Sultan's* presence, and came with the treaty of capitulation in his hand. The *mufti* exclaimed, "It is a good deed to slay such *infidels*," and cut the king down with his own sabre. The princes were put to death in the interior of the tent. The elder and better spirited of the Ottomans, who witnessed this treacherous murder, must have thought with shame how completely Mahometan and Christian had changed characters since the days of Amurath and of Cardinal Julian.

In Albania, Scanderbeg held out gallantly against the power of the *Sultan*, who, in 1461, was even forced to accede to a temporary treaty which acknowledged Scanderbeg as Lord of Albania and Epirus. Hostilities were soon renewed, and the Turks gradually gained ground by the lavish sacrifice of life and treasure, and by the continued pressure of superior numbers. But the breakwater which Scanderbeg long formed against the flood of Mahometan conquest, and the glorious resistance which Hunyades accomplished at Belgrade, were invaluable to Western Christendom. They delayed for many years the cherished projects of Mahomet against Italy; and the victory of Hunyades barred the principal path into the German states.

It was in 1456 that the *Sultan* besieged Belgrade, then regarded as the key of Hungary. Hunyades exerted in its defence all the fiery valour that had marked him from his youth up, and the skill and caution which he had acquired during maturer years. He was powerfully aided by the bands of Crusaders, whom the efforts of Pope Calixtus II., and the celebrated preacher, St. John Capistran, brought to his assistance. The tidings of the fall of Constantinople had filled Western Christendom with shame, indignation, and alarm. Formal vows of warfare for the rescue of the fallen city from the *infidel* were made by many of the chief princes, but evaporated in idle pageants and unexecuted decrees. But when another great Christian city was assailed, and when it was evident that, if Belgrade fell, Vienna, and other Western capitals would soon be in jeopardy, religious zeal and patriotic caution were for a time active; and a large and efficient auxiliary force was led by Capistran in person to fight under the banner of Hunyades.

Mahomet had been made over-confident by his success at Constantinople, and boasted that Belgrade would be an easy prize. His powerful artillery soon shattered the walls; and in a general assault on the 21st July, 1456, the *Janissaries* carried the trenches, and forced their way into the lower part of the town. But the Christians at Belgrade were numerous, were brave, and ably commanded. Capistran rallied the garrison; the Turks were repulsed from the upper town; and after six hours' hard fighting they were driven out of the portion which they had occupied. At this critical moment the martial saint, with the discernment of a great general, and the fiery energy of a devotee, sallied with a thousand Crusaders upon the enemy's batteries. Calling on the name of Jesus, while their panic-stricken enemies fled with cries of "*Allah*," the Christians fought their way into the Ottoman camp, and captured the whole of the besiegers' artillery.

Mahomet, indignant at the flight of his troops, strove in vain to stem the tide, and fought desperately in person against the advancing foes. With a blow of his sabre he struck off the head of one of the leading Crusaders, but received at the same instant a wound in the thigh, and was obliged to be carried off by his attendants. Furious at his defeat and disgrace, he saw, as they bore him away, Hassan, the general of the *Janissaries*, and overwhelmed him with reproaches and threats. Hassan replied that many of his men were slain, and that the rest would no longer obey the word of command. He then, before his sovereign's eyes, threw himself among the advancing Hungarians, and met a soldier's death. The *Sultan's* horse-guards checked the further pursuit of the Christians, and secured the retreat of their wounded master.

But three hundred cannons, and the whole of the Turkish military stores, were captured; and 25,000 of Mahomet's best troops had fallen. Hunyades did not long survive this crowning triumph of his gallant though chequered career. He died at Belgrade twenty days after the flight of Mahomet from before the walls; and the other hero of the defence, to whom even more than to Hunyades the Christian victory was due, died also in the October following. John Capistran was canonised by the Pope; and there are few saints in the long Romish calendar whose names Christendom has worthier cause to venerate.

In Asia Mahomet's arms were more uniformly successful. He conquered and annexed to his empire Sinope and Trebizond, and he finally subdued the princes of Caramania) those long and rancorous enemies of the House of Othman. The most important of all his conquests, after that of Constantinople, was the subjugation of the Crimea in 1475, by one of the most celebrated of the Turkish captains, Ahmed, surnamed Kedük, or Broken-mouth, who was Mahomet's *grand vizier* from 1473 to 1477. The immediate causes of the expedition to the Crimea were the *Sultan's* hostility with the Genoese, who possessed the strong city of Kaffa in that country, and the entreaties which the deposed *khan* of the Crim Tartars addressed to Mahomet for aid against his revolted brothers. But it cannot be doubted that a prince of Mahomet's genius discerned the immense value of the Crimea to the occupiers of Constantinople, and the necessity of securing his dominions by its annexation.

Ahmed Kedük attacked Kaffa with a powerful fleet, and an army of 40,000 men. That city, then called Little Constantinople from its wealth and strength, surrendered in four days. The booty which the conqueror seized there was immense; 40,000 of the inhabitants were transplanted to Constantinople; and 1500 young Genoese nobles were compelled to enter into the corps of *Janissaries*. The whole of the Peninsula was speedily occupied by the Turkish troops; and the Crimean Khans were thenceforth for three centuries the vassals of the Ottoman Sultans.

Mahomet was frequently engaged in hostilities with the Venetians as well as with the Genoese. The Archipelago and the coasts of Greece were generally the scenes of these wars; in the course of which the *Sultan* obtained possession of Euboea, Lesbos, Lemnos, Cephalonia, and other islands. The conquest of the Euboea was marked by base treachery and cruelty on the part of the *Sultan*, and signalised by the pure courage of a Christian heroine. The Venetian commander, Paul Erizzo, after a long and brave defence, surrendered the citadel on condition of the *Sultan* pledging his word for the safety of all within it

Mahomet signed the capitulation; and when the garrison had marched out, and laid down their arms, he put all of them, except the Greeks, to death with the cruellest tortures. Paul Erizzo was sawn in two by his orders. The daughter of the Venetian general, the young and fair Anne Erizzo, was dragged to the *Sultan's* tent: but the Christian maiden preferred death to dishonour; and, unmoved by either promise or threat, she was killed by the slaves of the angry tyrant.

Towards the end of Mahomet's reign, Scanderbeg was completely overpowered by the Ottoman forces; and Albania and the district of Herzegovinia were united with the *Sultan's* dominions. These conquests brought the Turkish arms into more extensive contact with the possessions of Venice along the eastern coasts of the Adriatic. In 1477, a powerful Turkish Army marched into the territory of Friuli at the northern extremity of that sea, and menaced Venice itself. The Venetians formed fortified camps at Gradina and Fogliania, and carried a line of entrenchments from the mouth of the Isonzo to Gaerz. But the Turks in the October of that year passed their lines, and defeated their army. Omar Pacha, the Ottoman general, next passed the Tagliamento, a stream destined to become illustrious in after warfare.

The Turkish troops spread themselves without resistance over all the rich level country as far as the banks of the Piave; and the trembling senators of Venice saw from their palace-roofs the northern horizon glow with the light of burning towns and villages. The Turks retired in November, loaded with booty. Venice eagerly concluded a treaty of peace with the *Sultan*, which (according to one Italian historian) contained a stipulation, by which the republic was to aid the *Sultan*, if attacked, with a fleet of 100 galleys, and the *Sultan* was, in case of like necessity, to send 100,000 Turkish cavalry against the enemies of Venice.

The subjugation of Italy was a project which Mahomet, though often obliged to delay, had never abandoned. In 1480 he prepared to carry it into execution on a scale of military and naval preparation equal to the grandeur of the enterprise; and at the same time he resolved to quell the sole formidable enemy that yet remained near the heart of his dominions. The strong island of Rhodes was still in the possession of the Knights of St. John of Jerusalem, who had established themselves there in 1311, and gallantly maintained their sovereignty of the island as an independent power for upwards of a century and a half. Three renegades from the order had incited the *Sultan* to attack Rhodes, by giving him plans of its fortifications, and promising that it would be easily captured by forces which the Turks could employ against it.

Mesih Pacha was sent to capture Rhodes in the April of 1480, with a fleet of 160 galleys, a powerful army, and a large park of the heaviest artillery. The Ottoman *pacha* effected a landing on the island; and after capturing some inferior posts, he formed his lines of siege against the city itself, which is built on the northern extremity of the isle. The Grand Master of the Knights, Peter d'Aubusson, defended the city with indomitable fortitude and consummate skill; but it must have fallen, had it not been for the ill-timed avarice or military rigour of the Turkish commander.

After a long siege and many severe encounters, the Turks made a general assault on the 28th July, 1480. Their artillery had opened a wide rent in the walls; their numbers were ample; their zeal was never more conspicuous. In spite of the gallantry of the Christian knights, the attacking columns had gained the crest of the breach; and the Ottoman standard was actually planted on the walls, when Mesih Pacha ordered a proclamation to be made that pillage was forbidden, and that all the plunder of the place must be reserved for the *Sultan*.

This announcement filled the Turkish Army with disgust and disaffection. The soldiery yet outside the town refused to march in to support their comrades who had won the breach, and these were borne back and driven in disorder from the city by a last desperate charge of the chevaliers, who had marked the sudden wavering of their assailants. The siege was raised, and Rhodes rescued for half a century.

On the same day that the Turks advanced to their unsuccessful assault on Rhodes, the leader of their other great expedition, Ahmed Kedük, the conqueror of the Crimea, effected his disembarkation on the southern coast of Italy, where no Ottoman before him had placed his foot. He landed on the Apulian shore, and marched against Otranto, which was then considered the key of Italy. His fleet cast anchor in the roads; and the city was promptly and fiercely assailed both by sea and by land. The resistance of Otranto, though spirited, was brief. The place was stormed on the 11th August, 1480. Out of a population of 22,000, the greater number were massacred without mercy, and the wretched survivors subjected to the worst atrocities of Turkish warfare.

Mahomet was now master of a strong city and harbour, which secured an entrance for his armies into Italy. His arms had met reverses at Rhodes when he was absent; but he resolved to conduct the next enterprise in person. Early in the spring of 1481 the horsetails were planted on the Asiatic shore of the Bosphorus, as signals for a new campaign; but no one, save the *Sultan* himself, knew against which quarter the power of Turkey was now to be directed. His maxim was that secrecy in design and celerity in execution are the great elements of success in war.

Once, when at the commencement of a campaign one of his chief officers asked him what were the main objects of his operations, Mahomet answered sharply, "If a hair of my beard knew them, I would pluck it out and cast it into the fire." No one could tell what throne was menaced by the host that now gathered at the *Sultan's* bidding; but while the musters were yet incomplete, the expedition was arrested by the death of the *Sultan*, who expired suddenly in the midst of his army on the 3rd May, 1481.

CHAPTER 8

Turkish Government

The personal character of Mahomet II. has been already discussed; nor would we willingly turn again to a repulsive subject. What he accomplished as a conqueror for the advancement of the Ottoman power has been made apparent in the narrative of his reign, but it would be injustice to pass over his political institutions; and we may conveniently take this occasion of surveying generally the internal organisation of the Turkish Empire.

From the time when Othman first killed his uncle in full council for contradicting his schemes, to the self-imposed limitations of the *Sultans* during the last few years, there is no trace in Turkish history of any civil constitutional restraint upon the will of the ruling sovereign. There is indeed a popular tradition among the Turks that the *Sultan* has a right to put to death seven men, and no more, in each day without any cause, save that it is his pleasure so to do, (Von Hammer).

★★★★★★

In Thornton, *Account of the Turkish Empire*, the number that the *Sultan* is privileged to slay is fifteen. Rycaut (cited by Thornton), in his *State of the Ottoman Empire*, written at the close of the 17th century, says: "The *Grand Signior* can never be deposed or made accountable to any for his crimes, while he destroys causelessly of his subjects under the number of a thousand a day." The same writer states that death by the *Sultan's* hand, or by his order, was, if submitted to without resistance or murmur, considered to give a title to eternal felicity.

★★★★★★

But even the limitation of arbitrary homicide which this tradition imports, has never been real; and abundant instances may be found in the reigns of Selim I., of Amurath IV., Mahomet IV., and of Mahomet the Conqueror himself, where far greater numbers have been sacrificed without form of trial, at the royal command The title of "*Hunkiar,*" the "Manslayer," is (or till lately has been) one most commonly used by the subjects of the *Sultan* in speaking of their sovereign, not as conveying any censure or imputation of tyranny, but in simple acknowledgment of his absolute power of life or death. Only the person of the *mufti*, the chief of the men of law, has been supposed to be inviolable; an exception doubtful even in theory, and unimportant in practice, as the *Sultan* could depose a refractory *mufti* whenever he pleased, and the inviolability of the individual must cease with the loss of office.

The sovereign's power is absolute over property as well as over person; but the *Sultans* have ever refrained from seizing property that has been consecrated to pious uses. Such an act would have been regarded as sacrilegious by zealous Mahometans, and have been probably followed by an insurrection. Nor, in practice, has private property suffered in Turkey from royal rapacity, except in the case of officers in the service of the government, whose wealth has always been subject to confiscation. All honours, commands, and dignities have been in the *Sultan's* absolute disposal to give or to take away as he pleases; and all his Mahometan subjects are equal before him, none having any privilege of birth, either from family or from place of nativity, one over the other.

But though free from the barriers of civil law, and unchecked by the existence of any privileged aristocracy, no Turkish *Sultan* could openly disregard with impunity the obligations and restraints of the religious law of the Mahometans. He combines legislative with executive power; but his *khatti-cherifs,* or imperial edicts, are regarded as subordinate to the three primary sources of law, which are, the *Koran* itself the written word of God, the *Sounna* or traditional sayings of the Prophet, and the sentences or decisions of the four first great *Imams,* or Patriarchs, of the Mahometan religion. The edicts of princes are called *Ourfi,* which means supplemental. The collection of the edicts, which successive *Sultans* pronounce on each ecclesiastical or temporal emergency not provided for in the first three sources of Mahometan law, is called *Kanounnamé* (the book or the code of canons) from the Greek word *Kanon,* which has been applied by the Turkish jurists to political as well as to ecclesiastical legislation.

By ancient and long-continued custom, the *Sultan,* before the execution of any important political act, obtains its sanction by a solemn declaration, or *Fetva*, of the chief *mufti* in its favour. Instances occur in Turkish history, where the refusal of the *mufti* has caused the sovereign to abandon his project; and some writers have represented this officer as exercising an effective constitutional check on the royal prerogative, and possessing a *veto* like that of the old Yeoman *tribunes*, or the Polish nobles. But the fact of the *mufti* being removable from office at the royal will (like our judges before 1714) shows how erroneous are such theories, (Thornton).

When a resolute and not unpopular *Sultan* is on the throne, the *mufti* is a mere passive instrument in his hands; though sagacious rulers in Turkey, as elsewhere, have understood the policy of sometimes showing a seeming deference to judicial rebuke; and the deep devotion of most of the *Sultans* to their religion must have made them to some extent really value the solemn opinions of the highest interpreters of their law, which is based upon their religion. When indeed the reigning sovereign is feeble and unsuccessful, the opposition of the *mufti*, seconded by "the hoarse voice of insurrection" round the palace walls, may be truly formidable; and his declaration that the *Sultan* is a breaker of the divine law, a tyrant, and unfit to govern, forms a sentence of deposition which popular violence has often carried into effect

In truth, with a martial and high-spirited people, earnestly attached to the national religion, and keenly sensitive as to their national honour, such as the Ottoman Turks have ever been, the worst practices of despotic sovereignty are, and ever must be, curbed by the practice of armed resistance and popular vengeance. As we proceed in this history, we shall often see the heads of the sovereigns' ministers fall at the people's bidding, and we shall become familiar with scenes of dethronement and regicide. These wild and terrible remedies of the evils of absolute monarchy have often in Turkey, as elsewhere, been cruelly misapplied. They have often degenerated into mere military mutinies, or into the sordid and anarchical riotings of a city rabble. But they have preserved the Ottoman race from utter prostration; and they are less odious than the series of domestic and oligarchical assassinations, by which despotism has been tempered in the rival empire of the *Czar*.

The implicit and religious loyalty of the Ottoman nation to the House of Othman (however roughly they may have dealt with individual members of it) has been uniform and undiminished. It is from that family alone that the *padishah* (the emperor), the *Zil-Ullah* (the shadow of God as the *Sultan* is styled), can be supplied. Governors of provinces have frequently revolted against the sovereign authority. They have made themselves locally independent, and carried on wars on their own account, even against the sovereign himself. But they have always professed titular allegiance to the royal house; nor has any adventurous *seraskier* or *pacha* ever attempted to seat a new dynasty on the throne of Constantinople. The certain continuity with which *Sultans* of the race of Othman, in lineal male descent from their great founder, have for four centuries held that throne, offers a marked contrast to the rapid vicissitudes with which imperial families rose and fell during the ages of the Greek Empire. Nor can the annals of any of the royal houses of Western Christendom show us, like the Turkish, an unbroken succession of thirty sovereigns, without the sceptre ever lapsing to the spindle, and without the accession of a collateral branch.

The will of the *Sultan* has been, from the earliest period of Turkish history, to the reign of Abdul Medjid, the mainspring of the Ottoman Government; and in demonstrating its plenary importance, we have been led far beyond the times of the conqueror of Constantinople. In continuing our examination of the Turkish institutions as organised by the legislation of that prince, there will be less need to deviate from chronological regularity.

The figurative language of the institutes of Mahomet II., still employed by his successors, describes the state under the martial metaphor of a tent, (Othman's dream). The Lofty Gate of the Royal Tent (where Oriental rulers of old sate to administer justice) denotes the chief seat of government. The Italian translation of the phrase, "*La Porta Sublima*," has been adopted by Western nations with slight modifications to suit their respective languages; and by "The Sublime Porte" we commonly mean the Imperial Ottoman Government The Turkish legists and historians depict the details of their government by imagery drawn from the same metaphor of a royal tent.

The dome of the state is supported by four pillars. These are formed by, 1st, the *viziers*; 2nd, the *kadiaskers* (judges); 3rd, the *defterdars* (treasurers); and 4th, the *nis-chandyis* (the secretaries of state). Besides these, there are the Outer *Agas*, that is to say, the military rulers; and the Inner *Agas*, that is to say, the rulers employed in the court There is also the order of the *Ulema*, or men learned in the law.

The *viziers* were regarded as constituting the most important pillar that upheld the fabric of the state. In Mahomet II's time the *viziers* were four in number. Their chief, the *grand vizier*, is the highest of all officers, both of the dignitaries of the sword and of the pen. The legal order supplied the second pillar of the state. The chiefs of the legal order were, in the time of Mahomet II., the two *kadiaskers*, who respectively presided over the judicial establishments of Europe and Asia. The other high legal dignitaries (who were at that time next in rank to the *kadiaskers*) were, 1st, the *kho-dya*, who was the tutor of the *Sultan* and the Princes Royal;. 2nd, the *mufti*, the authoritative expounder of the law; and, 3rdly, the Judge of Constantinople. As has been mentioned, the third and fourth state pillars consisted of the officers of the Exchequer, who were called *defterdars*, and of the secretaries, who were termed *nis-chandyis*.

The great council of state was named the *divan*; and, in the absence of the *Sultan*, the *grand vizier* was its president The other *viziers* and the *kadiaskers* took their stations on his right; the *defterdars* and the *nis-chandyis* on his left. The *teskeredyis* (or officers charged to present reports on the condition of each department of the state) stood in front of the *grand vizier*. The *divan* was also attended by the *reis-effendi*, a general secretary, whose power afterwards became more important than that of the *nis-chandyis*; by the grand chamberlain, and the grand marshal, and a train of other officers of the court. The *grand vizier* had the power of convoking a special divan at his own palace when he judged it necessary; and to him was entrusted the custody of the imperial seal.

Besides the military *agas*, who were very numerous, many officers in the civil departments held the rank of *aga*, which means ruler. The administration of the provinces was in the time of Mahomet II. principally entrusted to the *beys* and *beylerbeys*. These were the natural chiefs of the class of feudatories, whom their tenure of office obliged to serve on horseback in time of war. They mustered under the *sanjak*, the banner of the chief of their district, and the districts themselves were thence called *sanjaks*, and their rulers *sanjak-beys*. The title of *pacha*, so familiar to us when speaking of a Turkish provincial ruler, is not strictly a term implying territorial jurisdiction, or even military authority. It is a title of honour, meaning literally the *shah's* or sovereign's foot, and implying that the person to whom that title was given was one whom the sovereign employed. The classical reader will remember that among the ancient Persians the king's officers were called the king's eyes and the king's hands.

The title of *pacha* was not at first applied among the Ottomans exclusively to those officers who commanded armies, or ruled provinces or cities. Of the five first *pachas*, that are mentioned by Ottoman writers, three were literary men, (Von Hammer). By degrees this honorary title was appropriated to those whom the *Sultan* employed in war, and set over districts and important towns; so that the word *pacha* became almost synonymous with the word governor. The title *padishah*, which the *Sultan* himself bears, and which the Turkish diplomatists have been very jealous in allowing to Christian sovereigns, is an entirely different word, and means the great, the imperial *schah* or sovereign, (Ubicini, vol. i.).

In the time of Mahomet II. the Ottoman Empire contained in Europe alone thirty-six *sanjaks* or banners, round each of which assembled about 400 cavaliers. The entire military horse and foot of the empire in both continents was more than 100,000, without reckoning the irregular bands of the *Akindji* and *Azabs*. The ordinary revenues of the state amounted to more than 2,000,000 *ducats*.

The *Janissaries* were still the main strength of the Turkish armies, Mahomet increased their number, yet he had never more than 12,000 under arms. But when we remember to how great a degree the other nations of that age relied on their cavalry, and neglected the composition and equipment of their infantry, we can well understand the advantage which the presence of a chosen body of perfectly trained foot soldiers in the Turkish armies must have given them in pitched battles, and still more in sieges and other elaborate operations of warfare.

The English and the Swiss were the only two Christian nations of that period which sent into the field a well-armed infantry, not raised from the mere rabble, but from the valuable classes of the population; and the Turkish sabre never clashed with the English bills and bows, or with the heavy halberds of Helvetia.

The pay and the privileges of the *Janissaries* were largely augmented by the conqueror of Constantinople: and, as the Turkish power was extended in Europe, care was taken to recruit that chosen corps from children who were natives of that continent rather than among the Asiatics. The levies for that purpose were generally made in Albania, Bosnia, and Bulgaria. It is said that there was seldom need to employ force in collecting the requisite number of suitable children, and that the parents were eager to obtain the enrolment of their boys in the list of *Janissary* recruits. (D'Ohsson, *Constitution et Administration de l'Empire Ottoman*, vol. viii.).

This, if true, is rather a proof of the moral depravity of the Christian population, which the Ottomans subdued, than of any mildness of the Ottomans in enforcing the institutions of Khalil Tchendereli. It is also stated that no compulsion was used to induce the young recruits to leave the Christian and adopt the Mahometan faith: but this was a mere pretext of forbearance; as, from the early age at which the children were selected, it would be absurd to suppose that they were free agents in following the new religious rites, and repeating the new prayers, which were taught them as soon as they entered the training schools of the *Janissaries*. It is certain that the compulsory enrolment and conversion of youths taken in war was often practised; as in the instance of the young Genoese nobles, who became the captives of Mahomet at the conquest of Kaffa.

The attention which the Ottomans paid to their artillery, and to the adoption of every improvement in military engineering, must have been another great cause of their superiority to the nations, whose brave but tumultuous and ill-provided armies they encountered. Nor is the care, which their *Sultans* and *pachas* bestowed upon what in modern military language would be termed the ordnance and commissariat departments, less remarkable. The Greek Chalcondylas, the contemporary of Amurath II., in his account of the Ottoman armies, after describing their number, the excellence of their organisation, and the strictness of their discipline, mentions the corps that were especially employed in keeping the roads on the line of march in available condition; he speaks of the abundant supply of provisions that was always to be found in their well-arranged and symmetrical camps; and he notices the large number of beasts of burden which always accompanied a Turkish Army, and the employment of a special corps to ensure the proper transport of provisions and military stores, (Von Hammer).

There was certainly no state of Christendom during the fifteenth or sixteenth century, which cared for the well-being of its soldiers, on such seemingly generous but truly economical principles. The campaigns of Mahomet himself, especially that against Constantinople, and those of his grandson Sultan Selim, furnish many instances of the enlightened liberality and forethought, with which the mediaeval Turks provided their soldiery with those material instruments and adjuncts of warfare, the importance of which, in order to enable an army "to go anywhere and do anything," our own great captain of the present age has so fully taught us.

In examining the political and military institutions of the Ottomans, we have been repeatedly led to notice the *Ziamets* and *Timars*, the lands granted to individual subjects of the *Sultan* on condition of military service. The phraseology of the feudalism of mediaeval Christendom has generally been adopted by writers who have treated of these parts of the Turkish system; and the real resemblance between these institutions of the East and of the West is in many respects so remarkable, that the historical inquirer may at first feel surprised at feudalism failing to produce in Turkey those important effects on the progress of civilisation, (Guizot's *Lectures on European Civilisation*), and constitutional development, which he knows to have been wrought by it in the west and centre of Christian Europe. The problem offered by this variance between the results of apparently like causes, is complicated and difficult. It cannot be dealt with so fully in these pages as it deserves; but even the partial investigation of it, which can be undertaken here, may be of service towards acquiring a clearer discernment of many important points in the Turkish laws and usages, and in the national character of the Turks themselves. The tenures of land in Turkey will first require consideration, (Ubicini).

When the Ottomans conquered a country, the territory was divided into three portions. Part became ecclesiastical property, and was devoted to pious and charitable purposes, to the maintenance of the mosques, the public schools, the hospitals, and other institutions of a similar character. The lands appropriated to these purposes were called *Vaks* or *Vakoufs*. A second part became full private property, resembling the allodial lands in mediaeval Christendom. This property was subject to different liabilities, according to the creed of its owner. If held by a Mussulman, it was called *Aschriie,* that is to say, tithable, and the holder was obliged to pay a tithe of its produce to the state.

This was the only burden attached to it. If left in the possession of a Christian, its holder paid tribute (*kharadj*) to the state, which consisted of a capitation tax, and also of a tax levied on the estate, which was sometimes a fixed sum according to its extent, and was sometimes an impost on its proceeds varying from an eighth to one half The remaining part of the conquered country, became domainland, including, 1st, those of which the revenues were appropriated to the state treasury or *miri*; 2nd, unoccupied and waste lands (of which the amount is large in Turkey); 3rd, the private domain of the *Sultan*; 4th, escheated and forfeited lands; 5th, the appanages of the *Sultan's* mother, and other members of the blood royal; 6th, lands assigned to the offices filled by *viziers*; 7th, lands assigned to *pachas* of the second rank; 8th, lands assigned to the ministers and officers of the palace;

and, 9th, the military *fiefs*, the *ziamets* and *timars*. These last formed the largest class of the domain-lands, and are the objects of most interest to the student of comparative history.

The smallest *fief* or portion of conquered land granted out to a distinguished soldier was called a *timar*, and generally contained from three to five hundred acre, (Thornton's *Turkey*). Each *fief* was to furnish in time of war an armed horseman for each 3000 *aspres* of its revenue; like the knight's fee, which was the integer of our own feudal array. The larger *fiefs* or *ziamets* comprehended upwards of five hundred acres; (*Ibid*), and there was a still higher class of *fiefs*, called *beyliks* or lordships. The general name for the holders of military *fiefe* was *Spahi*, a *cavalier*, a title which exactly answers to those which we find in the feudal countries of Christian Europe. The *ziamets* and *timars* appear to have been generally hereditary in the male line.

When any became vacant by failure of heirs or by forfeiture for misconduct, the *beylerbey* of the district filled up the vacancy, his nomination being subject to approval by the Porte, (report presented to Sultan Ahmed III., cited by Ubicini). The higher rank of *bey*, and the still higher rank of *beylerbey*, were not at first hereditary, but were conferred by the *Sultan* on individuals selected by him. It was, however, usual to let the rank and estate of a *bey* pass from father to son, and in later times the custom of hereditary descent grew often into a right; there being a considerable difference in this respect among the various provinces of the empire.

We seem to have here before us the essential elements of feudalism; and we might naturally expect to find a feudal aristocracy developing itself in Turkey, and aggrandising itself, as in mediaeval Christendom, at the expense both of the monarchy and commonalty. We shall, in fact, find such an aristocracy growing up in the Ottoman Empire; but not until we come to the recent century and a half of decline and corruption, which preceded the reforms of Sultan Mahmoud II. and of the late Sultan Abdul Medjid. Such an aristocracy did not exist during the ages of Ottoman progress and splendour.

The causes of its non-existence during that period are, I believe, to be principally found, 1st, in the high personal energies and abilities of the *Sultans*, under whom the Turkish conquests were effected, and the Turkish Empire consolidated; 2ndly, in the existence of the *Janissary* force; 3rdly, in the effects of the religion of the Turks, both in elevating the authority of the sovereign, and in maintaining a feeling of equality among all his Mahometan subjects; (Ubicini vol. i.), and, 4thly, in the absence of that habitual aptitude for public assemblies, which is the characteristic of nations that contain a considerable element of Germanic or Scandinavian race.

It is to be remembered that the feudal system of mediaeval Europe was principally fashioned and matured during the reign of feeble and unsuccessful princes, who were engaged in repeated and calamitous contests not only with barbarous invaders and domestic temporal rebels, but with the bishops and the Popes of their church. But let us suppose a succession of princes, such as Charlemagne and his father, to have continued among the Franks, and we shall readily understand that the haughty peers and insubordinate noblesse of the eleventh and twelfth centuries, with their rights of private warfare, of subinfeudation, and territorial jurisdiction, would never have arisen in France. We shall still more fully realise to our minds the difference; if we suppose the Frankish sovereigns to have been, like the Turkish *Sultans*, the heads both of the church and state, and to have combined in their own persons the claims of both Pope and Emperor. And if we look to the history of our own country, we shall clearly see that a feudal system of baronial reforms, as well as of baronial aggrandisements, never could have grown up under successive rulers of the stamp of our Henry VIII.

The fact is indisputable (to whatever cause we assign it), that the Ottoman Empire employed the military spirit of feudalism for national defence and for conquest; but kept clear (during its flourishing ages) of the social and political influences both for good and for bad, which feudalism produced in the west of Europe. No feudal nobility existed among the Turks until the period of the decline of the empire, when the *Dereh Beys*, or lords of the valleys, as the mutinous feudatories termed themselves, made themselves hereditary chiefs; and, fortified in their strongholds and surrounded by their armed vassals, defied their sovereign, and oppressed their dependents. But except this period (which the new reforms have terminated), the Ottomans have never had a nobility or noblesse, or a caste or class of any kind, that was privileged by reason of birth. All the Mahometan subjects of the *Sultan* (who are not in a state of domestic slavery) are on a level beneath him. Equality in the eye of the law among the Turks themselves is a social fact, as well as a legal theory, (Ubicini, vol. i.)

Neither law nor popular opinion ever recognised in Turkey any superior claim of one part of the nation to the enjoyment of civil or military offices, such as the *noblesse* of France possessed over the *roturiers*. No surprise or indignation was ever felt if the *Sultan* elevated the poorest Osmanli from the toils of a common artisan or labourer to the highest dignity; and, on the other hand, the deposed *Vizier* or *Seraskier* descends to an inferior employment, or into the mass of the Moslem population, without loss of caste, or any change in his future civil rights and capabilities. With a few exceptions (such as that of the remarkable House of the Kiuprilis), family names are unknown in Turkey. There could not be a stronger proof of the entire absence of aristocracy from her institutions.

There is another element of European civilisation, the analogue of which appears among the Ottomans. This is the municipal, or the principle of local self-government in local matters. Each trade or craft has its guild (*esnaf*), (Ubicini, vol. i.), and every village has its municipality. The inhabitants choose their own elders or head-men, who assess and collect the amount of public contributions imposed upon the community, manage the municipal funds, which are in some cases considerable, act as arbitrators in minor disputes, attest important contracts, and are the customary organs of remonstrance against official oppression. This excellent system is not confined to the Ottomans themselves, but it flourishes among the Greeks, the Armenians, and the Christian Bulgarians under their sway.

It is believed, (Urquhart *Turkey and its Resources;* Ubicini), that these nations acquired it from the Turkish conquest, and the boon may be thought to outbalance much of the misery that has fallen upon the Rayas from the same quarter.

The *Ulema*, the order of men learned in the law, has been mentioned as supplying, according to the institutes of Mahomet II., one of the four pillars of the Turkish state. The predecessors of Mahomet II., especially Orkhan, had been zealous in the foundation of schools and colleges; but Mahomet surpassed them all, and it was by him that the "Chain of *Ulema*" was organised, and the regular line of education and promotion for the legists and judges of the state was determined. The conqueror of Constantinople knew well that something beyond mere animal courage and military skill was requisite in order to maintain as well as to create a great empire.

Eminent himself for learning and in the acquirements of general science, Mahomet provided liberally for the encouragement of learning and science among his people. He knew also well that to secure the due administration of justice it is necessary that the ministers of justice should be respected; and that in order for them to be respected, it is necessary that they should not only have learning and integrity, but rank and honour in the state; and that they should be raised above the temptations and anxieties of indigence.

Mahomet established and endowed numerous public schools of the higher order, or colleges, called *Medresses*, in addition to the elementary schools, the *Mektebs*, that are to be found in every quarter of every town, and in almost every large village in Turkey, (Von Hammer, book xviii.; Ubicini, vol. i.). The students at the *Medresses* went through ten regular courses of grammar, syntax, logic, metaphysics, philology, the science of tropes, the science of style, rhetoric, geometry, and astronomy. This is a curriculum which will certainly bear comparison with those of Paris and Oxford in the middle of the fifteenth century. The Turkish collegian, who had mastered these ten subjects, received the title of *Danis-chmend* (gifted with knowledge), and in that capacity, like the Western masters of arts, instructed the younger students.

A *Danis-chmend* might claim the headship of one of the minor public schools, without further study; but in that case he renounced the prospect of becoming a member of the *Ulema*, and of all the higher educational appointments. To become a member of the *Ulema*, it was necessary to commence and complete an elaborate course of study of the law, to pass repeated examinations, and to take several successive degrees. While care was thus taken to make the *Ulema* consist of men of the highest learning and abilities, great outward honour, liberal endowments, and many important privileges were conferred on those who attained that rank. The *Ulema* supplies all the professors in the high schools, who are called *Muderris*; and from this order also are chosen all the ministers of justice, including the Cadis, or judges of the smaller towns and rural districts; the *Mollas*, or judges of the principal cities; the *Istambol Effendi*, the judge and inspector-general over the city of Constantinople; the *Cadiaskers*, or supreme judges of Roumelia and Anatolia; and the *Mufti*, the importance of whose office has been already considered.

It is to be carefully remembered that the *Ulema* is not an ecclesiastical body, except so far as law in Mahometan countries is based on the *Koran*. The actual ministers of public worship, such as the *Imans*, who pronounce the public prayers, the *scheiks* or preachers, and others, form a very subordinate part of the *Ulema*. There is no country in which the clergy, properly so called, have less authority than in Turkey, or where the legal profession has more.

******

The influence exercised over the multitude by the fanatic *dervishes*, who are the monks and friars of Mahometanism, is quite unconnected with any state authority. See, on this subject, the fifth letter in Ubicini's first volume.

******

It ought also to be recorded to the honour of the Ottomans, that more respect is shown among them than in any Christian nation to the schoolmaster, and to all who are eminent for possessing intellectual endowments themselves, or for their skill in guiding others to acquire them, (Ubicini and Von Hammer).

Hitherto we have been examining the institutions of the Turkish Empire with reference chiefly to the dominant Mahometans. They are yet to be regarded with reference to the conquered but unconverted races, the Rayas, who have always formed the large majority of the population in European Turkey, and a very considerable proportion of the inhabitants of the Asiatic provinces. We must also consider the position of the slaves.

The *Koran*, while it enjoins war against unbelievers, requires the Mahometan to spare the peoples of the Books (a term including the Christians and the Jews), on their submission to pay tribute. "*The bended head is not to be stricken off*," such is the maxim of the Turkish law. It was once asked of the *mufti*:

> If eleven Mussulmans without just cause kill an *infidel*, who is a subject of the *Padischah* and pays tribute, what is to be done?

The judicial reply was:

> Though the Mussulmans should be a thousand and one, let them all die.

The Rayas (as the tributary Christians are called in Turkey) were entitled to protection for property as well as for person, and to the free exercise of their religion, (Thornton; Ubicini, vol. ii.). It is written in the *Koran*, saith the prophet:

> My mission is to combat the unbelievers until they say 'there is no God but God.' When they have uttered these words, they have preserved their blood and their goods from all attack from me. Of their own belief, they must give account to God. (Ubicini ii.).

The earliest capitulation between Mussulmans and Christians, being the capitulation granted by the Caliph Omar to the Christians of Jerusalem in 637, *A.D.*, and the charter given by Mahomet II. to the Greeks of Constantinople, were alike framed in the spirit of this text. The Christian subjects of Mahometan power were bound to pay tribute; they were forbidden the use of arms and horses; they were required to wear a particular costume to distinguish them from the true believers, and to obey other social and political regulations, all tending to mark their inferior position. In Turkey, the terrible tribute of children was an additional impost on the Rayas.

This last most cruel liability (which was discontinued two centuries ago) must be remembered; and so must the sufferings and the shames caused by the horrible practices, which we have been compelled to notice, when speaking of the reign and character of Bajazet Yilderim. Otherwise, it is correctly said that the lot of the Christian subjects of the Ottomans was less severe than that of the Jews in the various states of mediaeval Christendom. During the later ages of corruption and anarchy in the Turkish Empire, the Rayas were unquestionably made the victims of numberless acts of lawless cruelty and brutal oppression; but these were the results of the decay of the Ottoman government, and not the effects of its institutions as ordained in the ages of its vigour. ("It is not the Turkish laws, but a corrupt administration of them, that brings opprobrium on the Empire."—Sir James Porter.)

Domestic slavery has always existed among the Turks, as among other Oriental nations, but in a milder form, and with brighter hopes for those who undergo it, than the history of servitude among the various races and in the various ages of the world usually exhibits, (Ubicini, vol. i.). The Turkish law protects the slave from arbitrary cruelty and brutal or excessive chastisement; and the general kindness of the Turkish character (when not excited by war or religious fanaticism), has been a still more effectual safeguard. The *Koran* inculcates the duty of treating a faithful servant with generosity; and teaches that the man, who sets free his fellow-creature from slavery, does much to set himself free from the infirmities of human nature and from the torments of hell fire.

The emancipated slave, if a true believer, becomes at once the equal in civil rights of all the other Mahometan subjects of the *Sultan*. Many of the ablest officers, both in war and in peace, of the Sublime Porte, have been originally slaves: and a wide field has thus ever been open to her rulers for choosing men of tried ability and devotion, for the highest and most confidential employments.

Another important source, whence the Ottoman ranks have been recruited, has been the long stream of voluntary deserters from the Cross. The Turkish court and camp, where no heed was taken of a man's pedigree or birthplace, but where distinction, wealth, and power were open to all the bold and brave, who would profess the creed of the Prophet, presented irresistible attractions to many of the Rayas, and also to those strong and daring spirits from abroad, for whom, either through their own faults, or the fault of their fellow-countrymen, all similar careers in Christendom were closed.

We may observe the working of this attraction even in the recent times of Turkish adversity. It was far more effective when the Crescent was the symbol of victory and conquest. If we look to the period when the Turkish power was at its height, the period of the reign of Solyman I. and Selim II., we shall find that out of ten *grand viziers* of this epoch eight were renegades. Of the other high dignitaries of the Porte during the same period, we shall find that at least twelve of her best generals, and four of the most renowned admirals, were supplied to her by Christian Croatia, Albania, Bosnia, Greece, Hungary, Calabria, and Russia. There was no fear of these apostates from the Christian faith ever halting in zeal for their new masters. Their sincerity as to their adopted creed might be doubtful, but not so their animosity against that faith which they had deserted; and Christendom for ages supplied her foes with the ablest, the most unscrupulous, and the most deadly leaders against herself.

All the circumstances of the settlement of the Turks in Europe tended to keep up in them the spirit of war and the capacity as well as the zeal for future victories. By enrolling the flower of the children of the subjugated European provinces as *Janissaries*, by the impost of tribute money, by the sale of captives, and the acquisition of other plunder, by parcelling out the conquered lands into *fiefs*, wherein the best soldiers of the victorious army were planted as military colonists—each conquest was made to supply the means for further conquests, and Turkish war grew by what it fed on. The Moslem occupants of the rich and beautiful lands east of the Adriatic felt their pride in their own prowess daily confirmed, and their fervour for the faith of the Prophet daily rekindled by the sight of the Christian Rayas around them, on whom fell the chief burdens of taxation and manual toil, "a weaponless herd, whose duty was obedience and subjection."

✶✶✶✶✶✶

Ranke's *Servia*. "The Turks in the country—not only those of distinction, but others of lower rank who had gradually assembled around them—considered themselves the masters of the Raya. Not only did the Turks reserve for themselves the exercise of arms, but also the right of carrying on such trades as were in any way connected with war. like our northern ancestors, or their own Oriental forefathers, amongst whom the son of a smith once founded a dynasty, many a Turk has been seen to turn back his silken sleeve, and shoe a horse; still he regarded himself as a kind of gentleman. Other occupations the Mussulmans left with contempt to Christian mechanics: for instance, no Turk would have condescended to be a furrier. Everything that they thought suitable and becoming—beautiful arms, rich dresses, magnificent houses—they claimed exclusively for themselves." In Constantinople and other large cities the proportionate number of Moslems engaged in trade and labour, and the variety of their occupations, was far greater than in the country.

✶✶✶✶✶✶

This long-continued position of unquestionable and unquestioned superiority, "with nothing to provoke the strong to needless cruelty," may have conduced to develop in the Turkish character that dignity of manner, that honourable self-respect, that truthfulness, honesty, and sense of justice, that gentleness and humanity even towards the brute creation, which the bitterest enemies of the Ottomans confess, and which is the theme of uniform admiration with foreigners who have been dwellers in. the Ottoman Empire. Lying and theft are the vices of weakness; and a morbid fondness for practising petty tyranny over creatures weaker than themselves is the special sin of those who have been subject to oppression. But it would be eminently unjust to attribute the characteristic virtues of the Turks solely to the circumstance of their having long been a conquering people settled among a subject population, though such a fact must have had its influence.

Those virtues are found among the Ottoman Turks of Asia, where the number of Rayas is far less than westward of the Dardanelles, as well as among the sparse Moslems of European Turkey: nor have those virtues been found to decay with the declining fortunes of their empire. Much is due to the moral precepts of their creed, which ensures sobriety and cleanliness, as well as benevolence, integrity, and charity, among its true disciples. But the Turks are also distinguished above other Mahometan nations for their high personal qualities, though these are alloyed with many evil traits, which, however, are to a great extent the peculiar vices of their men in power. Among no people are the injurious effects of court intrigue, and of elevation to high authority and wealth upon individual character, so marked as among the Ottomans. Modem observers have been repeatedly struck by the metamorphosis of the high-minded and generous country gentleman of Anatolia or Roumelia, exemplary in all the relations of domestic life, into a sordid grasping tyrant and a selfish voluptuary of the worst description, when invested with the power and exposed to the temptations of a *pacha*.

And it must be confessed that the renegades from Christendom, of whom so large a portion of the Turkish officials has been composed, have generally set the worst example in all respects to the rulers of native origin. The ferocious cruelty, which has too often marked the Turks in warfare, and their ruthless fanaticism, when roused by the cry that their religion is in danger, are seeming contradictions to the general benevolence and gentleness of character, which have been ascribed to them as a people; but they are seeming contradictions only. The Turk is, in ordinary life, calm, mild, and indulgent, not because he is void of the fiercer passions, but because he is self-trained to control them. When the occasions come, on which it seems to him to be a duty to withdraw that strong curb of self-control, all those passions—Wrath, Revenge, and—

The blind wild beast of force.
Whose home is in the sinews of a man,—Tennyson

—stir in him to strike, with a wild unchained delirium such as is unknown in bosoms, where no similar restraint has been practised. It is like what we often witness in private life, when the man, who habitually rules his temper the best, is, if it once gets the mastery of him, hurried into excesses, from which others, more frequently prone to anger, would have been able to stop short.

The *Sultan's* summons to war still meets a ready response from the inherent bravery of every Turk: and Europe has of late years justly admired the gallantry with which the Ottomans have risen to defend their land and their faith from almost overwhelming enemies, and amid every circumstance of difficulty and discouragement. If such is the martial spirit of the people, now that they advance to the campaign "with no fear and little hope," what must it have been in the olden time, when almost unvarying victory crowned their arms, and when honour and wealth were the prompt rewards of distinguished valour? We may imagine the excitement and the exultation, which the announcement of a new war and the summons to a fresh enterprise, must have created throughout the Moslem world on either side of the Dardanelles, from the Euphrates to the Danube, from the Crimea to the Peloponnesus, in the days of Mahomet the Conqueror, or Solyman the Magnificent

The feudal chivalry left their *ziamets* and *timars*, and mustered beneath the banner of the neighbouring *bey* or *pacha*, each vying with the other in the condition and magnificence of his horse and accoutrements, and in the display of his band of aimed and mounted retainers. The *ziam*, who signalised his prowess, might hope for elevation to the rank of *bey*; and the *timariot*, who brought in ten prisoners, or ten enemies' heads, was entitled to have his minor *fief* enlarged into a *ziamet*. (Report to Sultan Achmet III., already cited from Ubicini). The Moslem, who did not yet possess either *ziamet* or *timar*, and was not enrolled in the regular paid troops, still served as a zealous volunteer on horse or foot according to his means; and, besides the prospect of enriching himself by the plunder of the province that was to be invaded, or the city that was to be besieged, he looked forward to win by daring deeds performed among the *Akindji* or *Azabs* one of the *timars*, that at the end of the war would be formed out of the newly-conquered territory, or which the casualties of the campaign would leave vacant.

The regular troops, the *Janissaries*, and the royal horse-guards, who fought immediately under the *Sultan's* eye, and whose trade was war, were even more eager for the opportunities of booty and promotion. Above all, religious enthusiasm roused the Moslem of every class to share in the Holy War against the misbelievers. The *Koran* teaches, indeed, that war is in itself an evil, and pronounces that "Man is the work of God. Cursed be he who dares to destroy God's workmanship," (D'Ohsson, vol. ii.). But it teaches also that, when there is war between the true believers and the enemies of Islam, it is the duty of every Mussulman to devote to such a war his property, his person, and his life. The *Koran* divides the world into two portions, the House of Islam, *Dar-ul-Islam*, and the House of War, *Dar-ul-harb*.

It has generally been represented by Western writers on the institutes of Mahometanism, and on the habits of Mahometan nations, that the *Dar-ul-harb*, the House of War, comprises all lands of the misbelievers; so that there is, or ought to be, perpetual hostility on the part of the true believers against the dwellers in *Dar-ul-harb*, although actual warfare may be suspended by treaty.

There is even a widely-spread idea among superficial talkers and writers that the holy hostility, the *Jehadm* (sometimes written *Dhihad*), of Mussulmans against non-Mussulmans is not limited to warfare between nation and nation; but that "it is a part of the religion of every Mahometan to kill as many Christians as possible, and that by counting up a certain number killed, they think themselves secure of heaven." But careful historical investigators, and statesmen long practically conversant with Mahometan populations have exposed the fallacy of such charges against those who hold the creed of Islam. (G. Campbell *Handy-Book on the Eastern Question*; Bosworth Smith *Mohammed and Mohammedanism*).

"The craving of the Mahometans, as such, for Christian blood is purely a myth," (G. Campbell). Their Prophet was certainly a stern iconoclast, and taught the duty of unremitting warfare against idolaters. In the *Koran* he bids his disciples "Fight on till there be no temptation to idolatry, and the religion becomes God's alone," (G. Campbell). But the Prophet also taught them with regard to Jews and Christians:

> Dispute not except with gentleness; but say unto them. We believe in the revelation which has been sent down to us, and also in that which hath been sent down to you, and our God and your God are one.—Bosworth Smith

A country which is under Christian rulers, but in which Mahometans are allowed free profession of their faith, and peaceable exercise of their ritual, is not portion of the House of War, of the *Dar-ul-harb*; and there is no religious duty of warfare, no "*Jehad*" on the part of true Mussulmans against such a state. This has been of late years formally determined by the chief authorities in Mahometan law with respect to British India, and the principle is practically acknowledged by our sovereign being publicly prayed for in every mosque throughout her Indian dominions, which contain a population of not less than 40,000,000 of Mahometans.

★★★★★★

Not long ago, in India, a question was raised and discussed by various Moslem lawyers, which might have had a tremendous result for ourselves. It was nothing less than the question whether Hindustan was a *Dar-ul harb* or enemies' country, that is whether the *Jehad* was in active or potential existence there, and consequently whether or no Moslems could consistently with their faith, preserve their allegiance to their Christian rulers. The decision was given almost unanimously in favour of peace and submission to the existing rulers: and the chief argument adduced in support of this view is a convincing proof of the truth of Mr. Bosworth Smith's theory that not only is the spirit of Islam favourable to peace and progress, but that such spirit really actuates its professors now.

The practice of Mohammed himself was adduced, namely, that when he laid siege to a town, or declared war against a tribe or people, he invariably delayed his operations till sunset, that he might ascertain whether the '*izan*' or call to prayers was heard amongst them. If it were, he refrained from the attack, maintaining that where the practice of his religion was allowed by the rulers of the place he had no grievance against them. This one argument, and the fact that the name of our most gracious sovereign is now inserted in the '*Khotbah*' or Friday 'bidding-prayer' in all mosques throughout India, is a sufficient proof that Islam is not antagonistic either to religious or political toleration, and that the doctrine of *Jehad*, a holy war, is not so dangerous or barbarous as is generally imagined.—*Quarterly Review, January,* 1877.

******

But, unquestionably, Mahometans of all ages have believed and have acted on the belief that when there is actual warfare between a state that holds the faith of Islam, and enemies who are of a different creed, it is a holy war on the part of the Moslems. Certain pacific texts of the *Koran* may be cited, that appear to some extent to qualify the fierce spirit of others, but the general tone of the Mahometan Sacred Book is eminently warlike, and must in the palmy days of Islam have stirred the bold blood of the Turks, like the sound of a trumpet, to wrest fresh cities and provinces for *Allah* from the Giaour. The Turkish military code breathes the full inspiration of the words of the Prophet, "In the shade of the crossing *scimetars*, there is Paradise."

Every Mahometan is required to be a soldier, (D'Ohsson). Every soldier killed in battle, for the defence of the faith, is styled *schedid* or martyr. (D'Ohsson. By a somewhat strange limitation the crown of martyrdom is denied to those who die on the field of battle by the effects of their wounds received on it). And the Moslem who deserts his post, or flies before the foe, is held to sin against both God and man: his punishment is death in this world, and hell-fire in the next.

No enemy with arms in his hands is entitled to quarter; and war is held to make all modes of destruction lawful captives, women, and children, and all that can do Mahometans no harm, are ordered to be spared; but those among the enemy, who from their abilities, station, or other causes, may hereafter become dangerous to the true believers, may be slain, though they have ceased to resist. All cruelty and mutilation are forbidden, and all breach of faith. Capitulations must be observed, and promises to an enemy kept by whomsoever they were given. If the sovereign disapprove of the terms, he must punish his Mahometan officer who made them. The Turk is never to make a disadvantageous treaty unless when every mode of warfare has been tried, and under pressure of the direst necessity. But such a treaty, if once made, is to be kept strictly.

******

> D'Ohsson, vol. ii. D'Ohsson collected the Turkish military (and other) laws from the great Ottoman Code, that was compiled and published by the celebrated Turkish jurist Ibrahim Halebey, who died in 1549. See D'Ohsson's Introduction. But now that Turkey is formally admitted to the public law and system of Europe (see Treaty of Paris, article vii.) she must be considered, even more decidedly than before, bound to observe the laws of war as generally recognised by civilised nations. I have discussed these laws in the *First Platform of International Law*.

******

In the general view which we have been taking of the Turkish institutions, we have lost sight of the individual Mahomet the Conqueror. But our attention is forcibly recalled to him when we cite one of the canons of the Turkish system of government, without notice of which our survey would be incomplete. It is the legislation of imperial fratricide. Mahomet II. ordained it by the following part of his institutes:

> The majority of my jurists have pronounced, that those of my illustrious descendants who ascend the throne, may put their brothers to death, in order to secure the repose of the world. It will be their duty to act accordingly.—Von Hammer, book xviii.

CHAPTER 9

First War with Egypt

On the death of Sultan Mahomet II., a struggle for the sovereignty ensued between his two sons, Prince Bajazet and Prince Djem, in which success rested with the eldest but not the bravest or ablest of the brothers. Both the princes were absent from Constantinople at the time of their father's decease. Prince Bajazet, then aged thirty-five, was at Amassia, the capital of the province which he ruled: and Prince Djem, who was twenty-two years old, was in Caramania, of which his father had made him governor. Bajazet was of a contemplative, melancholy disposition, simple in his habits, austere in his devotions, fond of poetry and speculative philosophy; whence came the surname of Sofi (the Mystic), which is given to him by many of the Ottoman historians. Djem had the energy, the ambition, the love of pomp and the voluptuousness, which had marked his father the Conqueror; and, without sharing his brother's fondness for metaphysics and abstruse learning, Djem was more eminent even than the other members of his highly-gifted family for his love of poetry; and his own poems are ranked among the most beautiful in Turkish literature.

On the death of Sultan Mahomet being known in the camp and capital, the *Janissaries* rose in open anarchy, plundered the houses of the rich Jews and other wealthy inhabitants, and put to death the *grand vizier*, who had vainly endeavoured to disguise from them the fact of the *Sultan's* death. As this minister was known to be a supporter of the interests of Prince Djem, the *Janissaries* were easily led by the adherents of the elder brother to pronounce in favour of Prince Bajazet; and the rest of the army followed their example. Messengers had been despatched to each prince by their respective partisans in the capital; but the bearer of the important tidings to Prince Djem was waylaid and slain on the road; and Bajazet obtained the inestimable advantage over his competitor of first learning that the throne was vacant, and first reaching Constantinople to claim it.

The *Janissaries* appeared before him on his arrival at the capital, and asked forgiveness for their late acts of violence; but these formidable suppliants asked it in battle array, and accompanied their petition by a demand for an increase of pay, and for a donative on their new sovereign's accession. Bajazet obeyed all their requests; and thenceforth the distribution of large sums of money at the commencement of each reign among these Mahometan praetorians became a regular custom in Turkey, alike burdensome to the treasury and disgraceful to the *Sultan*, until it was abolished by the Sultan Abdul-Hamid, during the war with Russia, 300 years after the time of the second Bajazet.

Djem was not of a disposition to resign the sovereignty to his brother without a struggle; and, remembering the bloody law by which their father had made imperial fratricide a state maxim, the young Ottoman prince may be said to have armed as much for life as for empire. A civil war followed, in which the abilities of the veteran Ahmed-Kedük, the conqueror of Kaffa and Otranto, and the treachery of some of Djem's principal followers gave the victory to Bajazet A proposition had been made before the battle by Djem to his brother to divide the empire, Bajazet taking the European and Djem the Asiatic provinces. Bajazet refused to listen to such a scheme; and when the aged Sultana, Seldjoukatoun, who was the daughter of Mahomet I., and the great aunt of the two rivals, came to his camp and endeavoured to move his fraternal feelings in Djem's favour, Bajazet answered with stern brevity, by citing the Arab proverb, "*There is no relationship among princes.*"

Nevertheless, the Mystic *Sultan*, though resolute to maintain his rights, and to suffer no dismemberment of the Ottoman Empire, showed no remorseless eagerness for his brother's death, till after Djem had proved that, so long as life was in him, he would strive for a kingly crown at Bajazet's expense. After his first defeat (20th June, 1481), and the dispersion of his army, Djem fled to the dominions of the *Sultan* of Egypt and Syria, where he was favourably received and sheltered for a year, during which time he visited the holy cities of Medina and Mecca. He and a daughter of Mahomet I. are the only members of the Turkish royal family that have made that pilgrimage.

In 1482, Djem, assisted by the Egyptian sovereign, and some of the malcontent Ottoman commanders in Asia Minor, renewed the war, but was again defeated and forced to seek safety in foreign lands.

He did not return to his former protector, but sought the means of passing to the Ottoman dominions in Europe, in the hopes of reviving the civil war with effect in that continent, though unsuccessful in the Asiatic, as Prince Musa had done during the interregnum after the defeat of the first Bajazet. With this view, he requested the Grand Master of Rhodes to grant him a temporary shelter, and the means of passing into Europe.

The Knights of St. John assembled in solemn chapter to discuss Prince Djem's requisition; and it was finally resolved that it was consonant with the dignity and policy of the Order to receive the Ottoman prince. (*Senatus-consultum,* "*Regem excipiendum, alendum, fovendum,*" Caoursin, cited in Von Hammer). Accordingly on the 23rd of July, 1482, Djem, with thirty attendants, landed at Rhodes, and entered on a long period of captivity most discreditable to the Christian potentates by whom he was nominally protected, but who in reality made him the subject of barter and sale, of long imprisonment, and ultimately of treacherous murder.

He was received at Rhodes by the Grand Master and his Knights with ostentatious pomp, and every semblance of hospitable generosity. But it was soon thought desirable to remove him from Rhodes to one of the commanderies which the Order possessed in France. It was considered by D'Aubusson and his comrades that by removing the Ottoman prince from their island they would be better able to evade the demands which Sultan Bajazet was sure to make for the surrender of his brother to him, and that there would be less risk of losing their prisoner by assassination. Before Djem left Rhodes, D'Aubusson took the precaution of obtaining his signature to a treaty which Djem bound himself, in the event of his ever becoming *Sultan,* to conditions highly favourable to the Order.

D'Aubusson, whose skill as an unscrupulous diplomatist was at least equal to his gallantry as a soldier (which we have had occasion to admire while tracing the times of Mahomet II.), next sent an embassy to the reigning *Sultan,* in order to secure all possible advantages from having the Pretender in the power of the Knights. It was agreed that there should be peace and free trade between the Order and the Porte, and that the *Sultan* should pay a yearly sum of 45,000 *ducats,* ostensibly for the maintenance of his brother, but in reality as the price of his compulsory detention in some of the possessions of the Knights.

Before Djem had thrown himself into the hands of the Christians, Bajazet had offered him the revenues of the province which he had formerly governed, on condition of his living quietly at Jerusalem. Djem refused this offer, and demanded the cession of certain provinces to him in full sovereignty. Bajazet replied, that "Empire is a bride whose favours cannot be shared." On Djem's persisting in his resolution to seek through Christian help the means of renewing the civil war, Bajazet endeavoured unremittingly to compass his death, or at least to purchase his imprisonment.

The high-spirited but unhappy prince (whose adventures and poetical talents have made him a favourite character in Frankish as well as Turkish history) was landed by a galley of the Knights at Nice in November, 1482. Djem expressed his gratification with the beautiful scenery of the Frankish city, but was urgent to commence his journey to Hungary, whence he designed to pass into Roumelia. His conductors informed him that as he was on French territory, he ought not to depart without the formal permission of the king of the country. Djem accordingly sent one of his suite to Paris, and was assured by the chevaliers that his messenger might easily travel thither, and return in twelve days. But care was taken to arrest the Turkish envoy on the road; and Djem lingered for many months at Nice, closely watched, though treated with apparent respect, and in vain expectation of a messenger from the French court.

At last the plague broke out in that city, which gave the Knights a plausible excuse for conveying their prisoner to a commandery in the interior of the kingdom. The greater number of the Ottoman prince's native followers were now forcibly removed from him; and Djem was confined, first at Roussillon, then at Puy, and afterwards at Sassenage, where he inspired the fair Phillippine Helena, the daughter of the lord of the castle, with an ardent passion, which was not unreturned; and love for a time lightened the weary hours of the captive prince. At last the Knights took Prince Djem to a tower which they had caused to be built expressly for his safe custody. It was seven stories high. The kitchens were on the first storey; the chambers of the domestics on the second and third. The fourth and fifth were for the apartments of the prince; and his jailors, the Knights, themselves occupied the two highest.

For seven years the Ottoman prince was detained in France. The remonstrances against such treatment which he addressed to the Knights, and to the Christian princes and chiefs by whom he was visited, and his repeated attempts to escape, were fruitless; though he was an object of interest to all Christendom; and many kings negotiated with the Grand Master D'Aubusson, for the purpose of obtaining possession of the claimant to the Ottoman throne. D'Aubusson purposely protracted the discussion of terms, and was unwilling to put an end to a custody, which although little creditable, was eminently lucrative to the Knights of St. John. Djem's family, consisting of his mother, his wife, and his infant children, were at Cairo. D'Aubusson had the unknightly craft to obtain 20,000 *ducats* from the wife and mother of his victim, under pretence that the prince was immediately to be set at liberty, and that the money was necessary for the expenses of his voyage. This was in addition to the 45,000 *ducats*, which Sultan Bajazet paid annually as the price of his brother's captivity.

At last Charles VIII. of France interposed, not to set Prince Djem free, but to transfer him from the hands of the Knights of Rhodes, to the custody of the Pope. A guard of fifty French knights was appointed to attend the Turkish prince; and it was agreed that in the event of the Pope giving him up to any other Christian sovereign without leave from the French court, a sum of 10,000 *ducats* should be paid as forfeit money to Charles. The court of Rome undertook to indemnify the Knights of Rhodes; and a variety of privileges were accordingly granted to them by the sovereign pontiff; and D'Aubusson himself received the honour of being made a cardinal

In 1489, Prince Djem made his entry into Rome, with the empty pageantry of honours like those amid which he had eight years previously been conducted into Rhodes. He was lodged in the Vatican, and formerly presented to Pope Innocent VIII., by the Grand Prior of Auvergne and the ambassador of France. It was in vain that the chamberlains and other papal officers urged on Djem the necessity of paying the accustomed homage to the spiritual head of the Church and temporal sovereign of Rome. The son of Mahomet the Conqueror would neither vail the turban, nor bend the knee; but walking straight up to the Pope, Djem saluted him as the Cardinals do, by a kiss on the shoulder.

Then in a few words, full of manly feeling and princely spirit, Djem asked the pontiff's protection, and requested a private interview. It was granted; and Djem then narrated the hopes deferred, the deceits and the hardships, which he had undergone during his captivity. He spoke of the cruelty of his separation from his mother, his wife, and his children, and of his earnest desire to behold them again, and to sail to Egypt for that purpose. The tears flowed fast down the cheeks of the unhappy Turkish prince, while he told his wrongs; and even the Pope was moved and wept as he listened. But Innocent said that for Djem to sail for Egypt was incompatible with his project for winning his father's throne; that the King of Hungary required his presence on the frontiers of that kingdom; and that, above all, he ought to think seriously of embracing the Christian faith. Djem replied that such an act of apostasy would irretrievably ruin him in the opinion of his fellow-countrymen; and he proudly stated that he would not be false to his religion for the sake of the Ottoman Empire, or for the sake of the empire of the world. Innocent did not press the work of conversion further, and closed the interview with hollow words of consolation and encouragement.

At this time there happened to be at Rome an ambassador from the Sultan of Egypt; and soon afterwards there arrived an ambassador from Sultan Bajazet The Egyptian ambassador sought out Prince Djem, and prostrated himself before him as before the lawful sovereign of Turkey. Djem learned from him that the Rhodian Grand Master had extorted the 20,000 *ducats* from Djem's mother and sister, under the false pretence of their being required for the voyage from France. Djem and the Egyptian envoy complained loudly at the Papal court against the Rhodian Knights for this fraud, and demanded the restitution of the money. The Pope and Sultan Bajazet's ambassador interceded in favour of the Knights, and by their means the Order was discharged from the debt for 6000 *ducats* paid down immediately.

The ambassador from the Turkish court was charged with the ostensible mission of presenting to the Pope certain holy relics of the Crucifixion, but he was also commissioned to arrange the price for which Innocent VIII. would pledge himself to keep Djem within the Papal States. 40,000 *ducats* a year was the sum agreed on between the rulers of Rome and Constantinople for this purpose; and Djem was accordingly detained at the court of Innocent for three years; and on the death of that pontiff, the Turkish prince was safely guarded in the Vatican until the successor to Innocent was elected.

The new Pope was the infamous Alexander Borgia. He forthwith sent an ambassador to Bajazet, and bargained for the continuation of the payment of the 40;000 *ducats* for continuing the detention of Djem. But Borgia also stipulated that he was to have the option of receiving 300,000 *ducats* paid down at once, if he took the shortest and most effectual means of securing Djem from invading Turkey, by putting him to death. Borgia is said to have been the only Pope that sent an ambassador to an Ottoman *Sultan*. His envoy was George

Bocciardo, his Master of the Ceremonies. Bajazet was so pleased with the ambassador, and thought so much of the assurances which were conveyed to him of the Pope's high esteem and friendly regard for him, that he requested the Pope, as a personal favour to himself, to make Bocciardo a cardinal.

✶✶✶✶✶✶

Von Hammer, in his note, says, that about the middle of the last century, a Dalmatian monk relied on this precedent of Mahometan interest with the Holy See, and begged the then reigning *Sultan* to aid him in obtaining a cardinal's hat. But, in order to save the officers of the Porte the trouble of sending a formal letter of recommendation, he framed himself a laconic note, which he addressed in duplicate to both the *Sultan* and the Pope. It was as follows: "Most Holy Father,—The poor friar, N. W., is to be made a cardinal, or all the friars in Jerusalem are to be impaled."

✶✶✶✶✶✶

While the *Sultan* and the Pope's ambassador at Constantinople were trafficking for Djem's bondage and blood, Charles VIII. invaded Italy, and on the last day of 1495 entered Rome. Pope Alexander sought refuge in the Castle of St. Angelo, taking Djem with him as one of the most valuable of the papal treasures. Eleven days after the entry of the French Army, there was an interview between Pope Alexander and King Charles for the purpose of arranging a treaty of peace. One of the chief conditions was the transfer of Prince Djem into Charles's hands. A meeting of the Pope, the king and Djem, subsequently took place, in which the Pope gave Djem for the first time the title of prince, and asked him if he was willing to follow the King of France, who desired his presence. Djem answered with dignity:

> I am not treated as a prince, but as a prisoner; and it matters little whether the king takes me with him, or whether I remain here in captivity.

Djem was transferred to the French king, who entrusted him to his *grand mareschal*. He accompanied the French Army from Rome to Naples, and witnessed the slaughters of Monte Fortino and Monte San Giovanni The Pope had now given up all chance of making any profit by the custody of Djem; but there yet remained the still more lucrative venture of procuring his assassination. This was accordingly done; though the Italian and Turkish historians differ as to the mode in which Borgia effected the crime. According to the first, Djem was poisoned by a bribed attendant, who mixed in the sugar, of which the Turkish prince ordinarily partook, some of the white powder, by means of which the Pope was wont to rid himself of obnoxious or over-wealthy cardinals, and with which he at last accidentally poisoned himself.

According to the Oriental writers, Djem's barber, a Greek renegade, named Mustafa, inoculated his master with deadly venom, by slightly wounding him with a poisoned razor. They add, that Mustafa, though it was for the sake of the Pope's money that he did the deed, acquired favour afterwards with Bajazet for this service, and was raised by degrees to the dignity of Grand Vizier. All agree that Djem was murdered by the Pope, and that he died by a slowly wasting poison. A letter, which his mother had written from Egypt, reached Naples before his death, but the unhappy prince was too weak to be able to read it. His last prayer was—

> Oh, my God, if the enemies of the true faith are to make use of me to farther their destructive projects against the followers of Islam, let me not outlive this day, but take at once my soul unto Thyself.

Djem died in the thirty-sixth year of his age, after thirteen years of captivity. Sultan Bajazet sent a formal embassy to reclaim his remains from Christendom, and Prince Djem was buried with royal pomp at Brusa.

Sultan Bajazet, though victorious in civil war, gained little glory in the encounters of the Ottoman power with foreign enemies during his reign. Immediately on his accession, the veteran conqueror Ahmed Kedük was recalled from Otranto to aid Bajazet against domestic foes; and Ahmed's successor, Khaireddin, unsupported from Turkey, was obliged to capitulate to the Duke of Calabria, after a long and gallant defence. Thus, Italy was relieved from the grasp which the dreaded Ottomans had laid on her; nor was any lodgement of the Turks within her peninsula again effected. Bajazet was engaged in frequent wars against the Venetians and the Hungarians, and also against the Poles, which brought little increase to the empire, except the acquisition of the cities of Lepanto, Modon, and Coron.

There is small interest in tracing the details of the campaigns of the Ottoman troops in Europe during this reign, marked, as they are, by a degree of ferocity and cruelty on the Christian as well as on the

Turkish side, which is repulsively striking, even in the history of mediaeval warfare.

******

One specimen may suffice. The Hungarian commander, Demetrius Yaxich (a Servian by birth), had taken prisoner the Turkish general, Ghazi Mustafa, and his brother. Yaxich broke all Mustafa's teeth in his head, and then forced him to turn the spit on which his own brother was roasted alive at a slow fire. It is not surprising to read that Mustafa, some years afterwards, when Yaxich was sent on an embassy to Constantinople, waylaid him and slew him.

******

The epoch of Bajazet II. is brighter in the history of the Turkish Navy than in that of the Ottoman armies. Kemal-Reis, the first great admiral of the Turks, signalised himself under this prince, and became the terror of the Christian fleets. He was originally a slave, and had been presented to the *Sultan* by the Capitan-Pacha Sinan. His remarkable beauty caused Bajazet to name him "*Kemal*," which means "Perfection," and he was in youth one of the royal pages.

The first mention of him as a sea-captain is in 1483, where he was placed in command of the fleet which Bajazet sent to ravage the coasts of Spain, in consequence of an earnest entreaty which the Moors of Granada had sent to the Sultan of Constantinople, as "lord of the two seas and the two continents," for succour against the overwhelming power of the Spanish Christians. Kemal-Reis afterwards, in 1499, won a desperate battle over the Venetians off the island of Sapienza, and materially assisted in the reduction of the city of Lepanto. We find him also, in 1500, contending skilfully and boldly against the far superior fleets of the Pope, of Spain, and of Venice. The Ottoman marine had not yet acquired such an ascendency in the Mediterranean as it afterwards held under Bajazet's grandson, Sultan Solyman.

Bajazet's melancholy and dreamy disposition made him indifferent to the excitements of strife and conquest; and though, as A zealous devotee, he looked on warfare against the *infidels* as meritorious; and though sometimes, as an act of religious duty, he shared in the campaigns of his troops, his general policy was to seek peace at almost any sacrifice. As is usually the case with over-pacific princes, he was unfortunate enough to be entangled against his will in many wars, from which his empire acquired little advantage, and he himself less credit. Besides his hostilities with Christian powers, he was obliged to oppose by armed force the encroachments which the Mameluke *Sultan* of Egypt and Syria continually made on the Ottoman territory on the south-eastern confines of Asia Minor.

The first war between the Ottoman sovereigns of Constantinople and the rulers of Egypt began in 1485, and was eminently disastrous for the Turks. Their armies were repeatedly beaten by the Mamelukes; and the spirit of revolt which had so long smouldered in Caramania, broke out and menaced open war. The Ottoman generals succeeded in reducing the Caramanians to subjection; but Bajazet, after five years of defeats by the Egyptians, concluded a peace with them, which left in their hands three fortresses which they had conquered. The wounded pride of the Sublime Porte was soothed by the pretext that the three fortresses were to be considered as given to endow the holy cities of Mecca and Medina, of which the Egyptian *Sultan* was protector.

As Bajazet advanced in years, the empire was again troubled with domestic dissension and civil war. He had made his sons and grandsons governors over provinces; and as the *Sultan's* infirmities increased, his three surviving sons, Korkoud, Ahmed, and Selim, began to intrigue against each other with a view to secure the succession. Selim was the youngest of the three, but the ablest, and the least likely to be deterred by any scruples of remorse from cutting his way to the throne by the readiest path. He was governor of Trebisond. His martial habits and bold readiness with tongue and hand had made him the favourite of the troops; and he sought to aggrandise his influence by making incursions into the Circassian territory on his own account.

When the old and pacific *Sultan* remonstrated against these proceedings, Selim replied by demanding a *Sanjak* in Europe, so as to place him nearer to the central seat of government. He next asked permission to visit his father at Adrianople, to pay his filial respects; and, on this being refused, he crossed the Black Sea, and advanced to Adrianople with a retinue so numerous and well appointed, that it deserved the name of an army. The old *Sultan*, who was suffering under severe illness, joined the forces which some of his faithful followers had collected for his defence; but he wept bitterly on seeing the standards of Selim's troops, and at the prospect of encountering his own child in battle.

In this mood, he was easily persuaded to negotiate by the *Beylerbey* of Roumelia, who strove to avert the unnatural conflict, and acted as mediator between father and son. Selim received the European government of Semendra; and the *Sultan* promised not to abdicate in favour of his brother Ahmed, who was known to be the old man's favourite child. While these events were passing in Europe, Asia Minor was troubled by the machinations of the other two princes, Korkoud and Ahmed, and still more by the hordes of brigands who, under the feeble sovereignty of Bajazet, long infested the kingdom, and at last formed a regular army in conjunction with the numerous devotees of the Shia sect, who at that time abounded in Asia Minor. They professed unbounded veneration for the great Shia Prince, the Persian ruler.

Shah Ismail: and the leader of this mixed force of ruffians and fanatics, took the name of *Schah-Kouli*, which means "Slave of the Schah;" but the Ottomans called him *Scheytan-Kouli,* which means "Slave of the Devil." He defeated several detachments of the Sultan's troops; and at last it was thought necessary to send the *grand vizier* against him. The Devil's Slave resisted skilfully and desperately, and both he and the *vizier* at last perished in an obstinate battle which was fought near Sarimschaklik in August, 1511.

Selim took advantage of these disturbances as pretexts for his keeping an army together, to be ready for any emergencies of the State. At last he forcibly entered Adrianople, and assumed the rights of an independent sovereign. Some, however, of the Ottoman soldiery were yet averse to the dethronement of their old sovereign, and Bajazet marched upon Adrianople with a true though small army. Selim came out with his troops to meet him; and the old *Sultan* was with difficulty persuaded to give the order to engage his rebellious son.

At length Bajazet raised himself on the cushions of his litter, and called out to his army, " My slaves, you who eat my bread, attack those traitors." Ten thousand loyal soldiers at once raised the battle-cry of " God is great," and rushed upon the rebel ranks. Selim's troops were broken by the charge, and fled in disorder; and Selim was indebted for his safety to the fleetness of his horse, called Karaboulut (the Black Cloud), and to the devotion of his friend Ferhad, who threw himself in a narrow pass between the flying prince and the foremost cavaliers of the pursuers. Selim fled to Akhioli on the Black Sea, where he embarked for the Crimea. The Khan of that peninsula was his father-in-law, and Selim was soon at the head of a new army of Tartar allies and Turkish malcontents, and in readiness to strike another blow for the throne.

Bajazet anxiously wished to make his second son, Ahmed, his successor; but neither this prince nor his elder brother Prince Korkoud, was popular with the *Janissaries*, who looked on Selim as the fit Padischah of the warlike House of Othman, and who considered the impiety of his attacks upon his own father to be far outweighed by the warlike energy and relentless vigour which he displayed Bajazet had secretly encouraged some warlike preparations of Ahmed in Asia; but the indignation of the soldiery of the capital against that prince compelled the old Sultan to disown his acts, and even to send a messenger to the Crimea to Selim, requiring him to march to the protection of the capital from Ahmed.

It was winter when Selim received the welcome summons; but he instantly assembled 3000 horsemen, half of whom were Tartars, and hastened round the north-western coast of the Euxine. Many of his followers perished by the severity of the cold, and the length and rapidity of their marches; but the indomitable Selim still pressed forward. He crossed the Dniester on the ice near Akerman, and, disregarding an injunction which the terrified Bajazet sent him to repair to his government at Semendra, he continued his progress towards the capital. When he was yet thirty miles from Constantinople, the *aga* of the *Janissaries* came to meet him; and he made his entry into the capital in almost royal state, with the *viziers* and other dignitaries of state in his train.

The old *Sultan* had amassed a large treasure during his reign; and he now sought to bribe his rebellious son back to obedience by an immediate donation of 300,000 *ducats*, and the promise of a yearly payment of 200,000 more. Selim regarded the offered treasure as an additional inducement to seize the throne, and refused all terms of compromise. Bajazet still occupied the royal palace, the *serail*; but on the 25th of April, 1612, the *Janissaries*, the *Spahis*, and the turbulent population of Constantinople assembled before the palace-gates, and demanded to see the *Sultan*. The gates of the *serail* were thrown open; and Bajazet received them, seated on his throne. He asked them what it was they desired, and the populace cried with one voice, "Our *padishah* is old and sickly, and we will that Selim shall be the *Sultan*."

Twelve thousand *Janissaries* followed up the popular demand by shouting their formidable battle-cry; and the old *Sultan*, seeing the people and the army against him, yielded, and uttered the words:

I abdicate in favour of my son Selim. May God grant him a prosperous reign!

Shouts of joy pealed round the palace and through the city at this announcement. Selim now came forward and kissed his father's hand with every semblance of respect. The old *Sultan* laid aside the emblems of sovereignty with the calm indifference of a philosopher, and asked his successor the favour of being allowed to retire to the city of Demotika, where he had been born. Selim escorted him to the gate of the capital, walking on foot by his father's litter, and listening with apparent deference to the counsels which the old man gave him. But the dethroned *Sultan* never reached Demotika: he died at a little village on the road on the third day of his journey. His age, and his sufferings both of mind and body, sufficiently accounted for his death: but a rumour was widely spread that he had been poisoned by an emissary of his son. The savage character of Selim may be thought justly to have exposed him to suspicion; but there seems to have been no clear evidence of the horrible charge.

Bajazet's feeble and inglorious reign was clouded by insurrection and military mutiny at its commencement and at its close. Nor were these the only scenes in which the insolent power of the soldiery, and the infirmity of Bajazet's government were displayed. At one period during his reign the vice of drunkenness had become so common in Constantinople, that Bajazet published an edict threatening the punishment of death to all who were detected in using wine, and ordering all the public places, at which it had been sold, to be closed. But the *Janissaries* assembled, and breaking the taverns and wine stores open, forced their proprietors to resume their trade; and Bajazet, alarmed at the anger and threats of these perilous guardians of his throne, withdrew the obnoxious edict four days after it had been pronounced.

Had Bajazet been succeeded on the Turkish throne by princes of a character like his own, there seems little doubt that the decline of the Ottoman power would have been accelerated by many years. But the stern energy of Selim I., and the imperial genius of the great Solyman, not only gave to the Turkish Empire half a century of further conquest and augmented glory, but reinvigorated the whole system of government, so as long to delay the workings of corruption.

It is in the reign of Bajazet II. that the ominous name of Russia first appears in Turkish history. In 1492 the *Czar*, Ivan III., wrote a letter to Bajazet on the subject of certain exactions which had recently been practised on Russian merchants in Turkey, and proposing a diplomatic intercourse between the two empires. Three years afterwards, Michael Plettscheieff, the first Russian ambassador, appeared at Constantinople. He was strictly enjoined by his master not to bow the knee to the

Sultan, and not to allow precedence to any other ambassador at the Ottoman court. Plettscheieff appears to have displayed such arrogance as justly to offend the *Sultan*. Bajazet stated in a letter on the subject to the *Khan* of the Crimea (who had exerted himself to promote friendship between the empires), that:

> ... he was accustomed to receive respect from the powers of the East and the West, and blushed at the thought of submitting to such rudeness."

Had Bajazet's father or son been on the Turkish throne, the haughty Muscovite would probably have received a sharper chastisement than the mild mark of offended dignity which Bajazet displayed by sending no ambassador to Russia in return. No one at Bajazet's court could foresee that in the rude power of the far North, whose emissaries then excited the contemptuous indignation of the proud and polished Osmanlis, was reared the deadliest foe that the House of Othman was ever to encounter.

Chapter 10

War with Persia

Sultan Selim I. was forty-seven years of age when he dethroned his father. He reigned only eight years, and in that brief period he nearly doubled the extent of the Ottoman Empire. The splendour of his conquests, the high abilities which he displayed in literature and in politics, as well as in war, and the imperious vigour of his character, have found panegyrists among European as well as Asiatic writers; but his unsparing cruelty to those who served, as well as to those who opposed him, has justly brought down on his memory the indignant reprobation of mankind, as expressed by the general sentence of the great majority both of Oriental and Western historians. In his own reign the wish "Mayst thou be the *vizier* of Sultan Selim," had become a common formula of cursing among the Ottomans. Selim's *viziers* seldom survived their promotion more than a month. They whom he raised to this perilous post, knew that they were destined for the executioner's sabre, and carried their last wills and testaments with them, whenever they entered the *Sultan's* presence.

One of these officers, the Grand Vizier Piri Pacha, ventured to say to Selim, in a tone half in earnest and half sportive:

My *padishah*, I know that sooner or later thou wilt find some pretext for putting me, thy faithful slave, to death; vouchsafe me, therefore, a short interval, during which I may arrange my affairs in this world, and make ready for being sent by thee to the next.

Selim laughed loud in savage glee at the frank request, and answered:

I have been thinking for some time of having thee killed; but I have at present no one fit to take thy place; otherwise I would willingly oblige thee.

Unsparing of the blood of his relations, his subjects, and his ablest servants, Selim was certain to be fond of war; and his reign was one of almost ceaseless carnage. Vigorous in body and mind, and indifferent to sensual pleasures, he pursued with keenness the martial pastime of the chase. He devoted all his days to military duties or to hunting. He slept but little; and employed the greater part of the night in literary studies. His favourite volumes were books of history, or of Persian poetry. He left a collection of odes written by himself in that language, for which he showed a marked preference. An Italian writer has asserted that Selim, like his grandfather, Mahomet II., loved to study the exploits of Caesar and Alexander; but the classical histories of those conquerors were unknown in the East, and the Turkish *Sultan* only possessed the Oriental romances on their exploits, which are of the same character with the chivalrous legends current in the West respecting Charlemagne and the Knights of the Round Table.

Selim showed especial favour and honour to men of learning, and promoted many of them to posts of high dignity and importance. He entrusted to the historian Idris the task of organising the newly-conquered province of Kurdistan; and the jurist Kemel Paschazadé accompanied him on his Egyptian expedition as historiographer. Selim was tall in stature, with long body though short limbs. Contrary to the example of his predecessors he kept his chin close shaved, but he wore enormously large black *moustachios*, which, with his dense and dark eyebrows, contributed to give him the fierce aspect which impressed with awe all who beheld him. His eyes were large and fiery; and his red complexion showed (according to the report of the Venetian ambassador Foscolo) a sanguinary disposition. His pride met with a sharp trial on the very first day of his reign.

The *Janissaries* resolved to force from their new *Sultan* a donative, and drew up in double lines along the street through which he was expected to pass. They were to clash their arms together when he arrived, as an impressive hint of the means which had given him the throne, and of the means which might force him from it. Selim was apprised of their gathering; and, indignant at the prospect of thus passing publicly under the yoke of his own soldiers on the first day of his reign, he avoided the humiliation by riding round in another direction. He dared not however refuse the donative; and a distribution larger than had been made on any similar occasion, nearly exhausted the treasury. Emboldened by this concession, one of the governors of the smaller departments, a *sanjak-bey*, approached the *Sultan*, and asked for an increase of revenue. Selim answered by drawing his sabre and striking the bold petitioner's head off on the spot

Selim had acquired the throne by successful rebellion against his father; and he had good reason to dread the jealousy of his brothers, who were in command of some of the best provinces of the empire, and were little likely to give up the imperial heritage without a struggle. Five of the eight sons of Bajazet had died in their father's lifetime, Abdallah, Mahomet, Schehinshah, Alemshah, and Mahmoud. Schehinshah left a son named Mahomet; and Alemshah, one named Osman. Mahmoud left three, Musa, Orchan, and Emin. Of the two surviving brothers of Selim, the eldest. Prince Korkoud was childless; the second. Prince Ahmed, had four sons. Selim himself had but a single son, Prince Solyman. Thus there were twelve princes of the blood of Bajazet alive.

At first, Selim's brothers appeared willing to acknowledge him as *Sultan*, and accepted the confirmation in their respective governments which he offered. But Prince Ahmed, who ruled at Amassia, soon showed his design of striving for the throne, by occupying the great city of Brusa, and levying heavy taxes on the inhabitants. Selim marched instantly into Asia Minor at the head of a powerful army, and sent a fleet to cruise along the coasts. Ahmed fled before him, and despatched two of his sons to implore assistance from the Persian prince. Shah Ismail. Selim took possession of Brusa, and sent the greater part of his army into winter quarters. Encouraged by some of Selim's officers, whom he had gained over, Ahmed renewed the war, and gained several slight advantages. Selim instantly caused his *grand vizier, who* was one of the traitors against him, to be strangled; and proceeded to further executions of a more atrocious character.

Five of the young princes, his nephews, were in honourable detention in the houses of some of the chief men of Brusa. The eldest of them, Osman, son of Prince Alemshah, was twenty years old; the youngest, Mahomet, son of Prince Schehinshah, was only seven. Selim sent *Janissaries* to apprehend them, and they were shut up by his orders in one apartment of the palace. On the next morning the *Sultan's* mutes entered to put them to death. A fearful scene ensued, which Selim witnessed from an adjoining chamber. The youngest of the captive princes fell on their knees before the grim executioners, and with tears and childish prayers and promises begged hard for mercy.

The little Prince Mahomet implored that his uncle would spare him, and offered to serve him all the days of his life for an *aspre* (the lowest of all coins) a day. The elder of the victims, Prince Osman, who knew that there was no hope of mercy, rushed fiercely upon the murderers, and fought hard for a time against them. One of the mutes was struck dead, and another had his arm broken. Selim ordered his personal attendants to run in and assist in the execution; and at length the unhappy princes were overpowered by numbers, and strangled. Their bodies were deposited with all display of royal pomp near the sepulchre of Amurath II.

At the tidings of this massacre. Prince Korkoud, who had hitherto been quiet in his government of Saroukhan, saw clearly what doom was designed for himself He endeavoured to win over the *Janissaries*, and prepared for a struggle for life or death with Selim. Selim detected his brother's plans; and without giving any intimation of his discovery or his purpose, he left Brusa, under pretence of a great hunting; and then suddenly advanced with 10,000 cavalry into Korkoud's province. Korkoud fled with a single attendant of the name of Pialé. They were pursued and captured.

Selim sent an officer named Sinan to announce to his brother that he must die. Sinan arrived in the night at the place where the royal captive was detained; and, waking Prince Korkoud from sleep, he bade him come forth to death. Korkoud demanded a respite of an hour, and employed it in writing a letter in verse to his brother, in which he reproached him with his cruelty. He then gave up his neck to the fatal bowstring. Selim wept abundantly when he read his brother's elegy. He carried his real or pretended grief so far as to order a general mourning for three days; and he put to death some Turkomans who had guided the pursuers of Korkoud to his hiding-place, and who came to Brusa to ask a reward for that service.

In the meanwhile. Prince Ahmed had collected a considerable force; and had gained further advantages over Selim's forces, which, if vigorously followed up, might have given him the throne. But Ahmed, though personally brave, was far inferior to his brother in energy and perseverance. Selim reinforced his army, and on the 24th of April, 1513, a pitched battle was fought, in which Ahmed was completely defeated and taken prisoner. His doom was the same as that of Korkoud, and was executed by the same officer, Sinan.

Before death, Ahmed had begged to see the Sultan; but the request was refused; and Selim remarked that he would give his brother such a domain as fitted an Ottoman prince. Ahmed understood the words; and when Sinan entered, gave himself up to death without resistance. Before he was bowstrung, he drew from his finger a jewel said to equal in value a year's revenue of Roumelia, and charged Sinan to convey it to Selim as his brother's parting gift, with a hope that the *Sultan* would excuse the smallness of its worth. Ahmed was buried with the five murdered young princes at Brusa.

Selim now thought himself secure on the throne; and prepared for foreign warfare. Fortunately for Christendom, it was against other Mahometan powers that his energies were directed; and he willingly arranged or renewed a series of treaties with the different states of Europe, which secured tranquillity along the western frontiers of the Ottoman Empire. Selim had not fallen off from his ancestors in zeal for the faith of Islam. He was indeed the most bigoted of all the Turkish *Sultans*, But it was the very vehemence of his bigotry, that made him hate the heretics of Islam even more than the Giaours of Christendom.

The schism of the Sunnites and the Schiis (the first of whom acknowledge, and the last of whom repudiate the three immediate successors of the Prophet, the Caliphs Abubeker, Omar, and Othman) had distracted the Mahometan world from the earliest times. The Ottoman Turks have been Sunnites. The contrary tenets have prevailed in Persia: and the great founder of the Saffide dynasty in that country, Shah Ishmail, was as eminent for his zeal for the Schii tenets, as for his ability in the council, and his valour in the field.

The doctrine of the Schiis had begun to spread among the subjects of the Sublime Porte before Selim came to the throne; and, though the *Sultan*, the *Ulema*, and by far the larger portion of the Ottomans, held strictly to the orthodoxy of Sunnism, the Schiis were numerous in every province, and they seemed to be rapidly gaining proselytes. Selim determined to crush heresy at home before he went forth to combat it abroad; and in a deliberate spirit of fanatic cruelty he planned and executed a general slaughter of all his subjects, who were supposed to have fallen away from what their sovereign considered to be the only true faith. This is a deed to which the massacre of St. Bartholomew in the same century offers too sad a parallel; and indeed the treachery, by which that crime of Christendom was accomplished, makes it the more detestable of the two.

Selim did not allure his victims by false professions of esteem, or by profaning the rights of hospitality, but he organised a system of secret police throughout his dominions, which contemporary writers term admirable; and he thus obtained a complete list of all the Mahometans in European and in Asiatic Turkey, who were suspected of belonging to the sect of the Schiis. The number of the proscribed, including men, women, and children, amounted to 70,000. Selim distributed troops throughout the empire, and stationed them in each city and district, in strength proportioned to the number of Schiis that it contained. He then suddenly went forth the messengers of death, and the whole of those unhappy beings were arrested. 40,000 of them were slain; the Test were condemned to perpetual imprisonment.

The contemporaneous Ottoman historians give Selim the title of "The Just," for this act of atrocity. The modern German historian well remarks that it is still more revolting to read that the Christian ambassadors at the *Sultan's* court adopted the surname, and that it is found applied to Selim in the reports of the massacre which they sent to their respective countries. Indeed, at a later time, and when Selim had shown by many more ferocious deeds, how deeply his soul was incarnadined with cruelty, the Venetian Mocenigo, who had been accredited to his court, and had known him well, declared that he never met a man who was Sultan Selim's equal in virtue, justice, *humanity*, and greatness of mind.

★★★★★★

Giovio, in a letter written to Charles V., in 1541, says: "*Mi diceva il clarissimo Messa Luigi Mocenigo quel fù uno dei ambasciadori di Venetia appresso V. M. in Bologna, che essendo lui al Cairo ambasciadore appresso a Sultan Selim e se havendo molto ben prattichato, nullo huomo era par ed esso in virtu, justizia, humanita, e grandezza d'animo.*" It is difficult to imagine among what human creatures humanity existed in that age.

★★★★★★

The slaughter of his co-religionists increased the animosity with which Shah Ismail already regarded Selim; and the two sovereigns prepared for an encounter with equal rancour and resolution. Many grounds of quarrel, besides that of religious difference, existed between them. Shah Ismail had humbled the Ottoman arms in some encounters with the troops of the governors of the Turkish provinces near his frontier in Bajazet's reign; he had also sheltered the fugitive Prince Amurath, son of Selim's brother Ahmed; and he now assembled his troops, with the avowed intention of deposing and punishing

Selim, and of placing young Amurath on the Turkish throne. Selim, on his part, made his preparations for an aggressive campaign with his accustomed vigour and determination. The renown of the Persian arms, and of the skill and good fortune of Shah Ismail, was widely spread throughout the East; and when Selim announced his intention of attacking Persia, the members of his council were ominously mute, Thrice the *Sultan* told them that he would lead them to war, and thrice they spake not, till at last a common *janissary*, named Abdullah, who stood by on guard, broke the silence, and throwing himself on his knees before the *Sultan*, told him that he and his comrades would rejoice in marching under him to fight the Shah of Persia. Selim made him *bey* of the Sanjak of Selnik on the spot.

The Turkish Army mustered in the plain of Yenischeer. Selim began his march on the 20th of April, 1614, on a Thursday, a day of the week thought fortunate by the Ottomans. On the 27th a Persian spy was seized in the camp, and Selim sent him to Ismail with a letter containing a declaration of war. Von: Hammer, (also D'Ohsson), cites this remarkable document from the contemporary Oriental writers; and as he truly states, it admirably represents the general spirit of the age, and the especial character of Selim himself It is as follows:

> The Supreme Being, who is at the same time the Sovereign of the destiny of man, and the source of all light and all knowledge, announces in His holy scripture that the true religion is the religion of the Mussulmans; and that he who professes another religion, far from being heard and saved, will be cast out among the reprobates at the great day of the last judgment Again He saith, the God of truth, that His designs and His decrees are immutable, and all the actions of man ought to have regard to Him, and that he who abandons the good path shall be condemned to hell fire and eternal punishment. Place us. Lord, in the number of the true Believers, of those who walk in the path of salvation, and take heed to turn away from vice and unbelief! May the purest and most holy blessings be upon Mohammed-oul-Mustapha, the master of two worlds, the prince of prophets;. and blessed also be his descendants and those who follow his law!
>
> I, chief and sovereign of the Ottomans;—I, the master of the heroes of the age;—I, who combine the force and power of Feridoon, the majesty of Alexander the Great, the justice and

the clemency of Keikhosrew;—I, the exterminator of the idolators, the destroyer of the enemies of the true faith, the terror of the tyrants, and of the Pharaohs of the age;—I, before whom proud and imperious kings are abased, and the strongest sceptres shattered;—I, the glorious Sultan Selim Khan, son of the Sultan Bajazet Khan, who was the son of the Sultan Mohammed Khan, who was the son of the Sultan Murad Khan;—I graciously address my words to thee. Emir Ismail, chief of the Persian troops, who art like in tyranny to Zohak and Afrasiah, and art destined to perish like the last Dara (Darius), to make thee know that the words of the Most High are not the frail productions of caprice or foolishness, but that they contain an infinity of mysteries impenetrable by the spirit of man. The Lord Himself hath said in His holy book, 'We have not created the heaven and earth that they should be a sport.'

Man, who is the noblest of the creatures, and a compendium of the marvels of God, is consequently the living image of the Creator on earth. It is He that hath made ye, oh men, the Caliphs of the earth, because man, who unites the faculties of the soul with perfection of body, is the only being, that can comprehend the attributes of the Divinity, and adore His sublime beauties. But man does not possess that rare intelligence, nor does he arrive at that divine knowledge except in our religion, and by keeping the commandments of the prince of prophets, the caliph of caliphs, the right arm of the God of mercy. It is therefore only by the practice of the true religion that a man will prosper in this world, and deserve eternal life in the world to come.

As for thee. Emir Ismail, such a reward will never be thy lot; for thou hast deserted the path of salvation, and of the holy commandment; thou hast defiled the purity of the doctrine of Islam; thou hast dishonoured and cast down the altars of the Lord; thou hast by unlawful and tyrannical devices usurped a sceptre in the East; thou hast by base stratagem alone raised thyself—thou sprung from the dust—to a seat of splendour and glory; thou hast opened to Mussulmans the gate of tyranny and oppression; thou hast joined iniquity, perjury, and blasphemy to impiety, heresy, and schism; thou hast under the cloak of hypocrisy sown in all parts the seeds of trouble and sedition; thou hast raised the standard of ungodliness; thou hast given way to thy shameful passions, and abandoning thyself without restraint to the most disgraceful excesses; thou hast untied the band of Mussulman laws, and thou hast permitted licentiousness and rape, the massacre of the most virtuous and honourable of men, the destruction of shrines and temples, the profanation of tombs, the contempt of the *Ulema*, of teachers of the law, and of descendants of the Prophet, and the degradation of the *Koran*, and the cursing of the true and lawful *Caliphs* (Abubeker, Omar, and Othman.)

Therefore, as the first duty of a Mussulman, and above all of a pious prince, is to obey the commandment, 'Oh ye faithful, who believe, perform ye the decrees of God,' the *Ulema* and our teachers of the law have pronounced death upon thee, perjurer and blasphemer as thou art, and have laid upon every good Mussulman the sacred duty of taking arms for the defence of religion, and for the destruction of heresy and impiety in thy person and the persons of those who follow thee.

Animated by the spirit of that Fetva, in conformity with the *Koran*, the code of the divine laws, and wishing both to strengthen Islam and to deliver the countries and the peoples who are groaning under thy yoke, we have resolved to lay aside our royal robes of state, to put on the cuirass and the coat of mail, to unfurl our ever-victorious banner, to assemble our invincible armies, to draw the avenging sword from the scabbard of our wrath and indignation, to march with our soldiers, whose swords deal mortal blows, and whose arrows fly to pierce a foe even in the constellation of the Sagittary.

In fulfilment of that noble resolution we have taken the field; we have passed the channel of Constantinople, and, guided by the hand of the Most High, we trust soon to put down thy arm of tyranny, to dispel those fumes of glory and grandeur that now confuse thy head and cause thee deadly wanderings; to rescue from thy despotism thy trembling subjects; and finally to smother thee in those same fiery whirlwinds which thy infernal spirit raises wherever it passes.

So shall we fulfil upon thee the saying, 'He who sows discord must reap affliction and woe.' Nevertheless, jealous in our obedience to the spirit of the law of the Prophet, we propose, before we begin war, to place before thee the *Koran*, instead of the sword, and to exhort thee to embrace the true religion:

therefore do we address to thee this letter.

We differ in our dispositions, one man from another; and the human race is like mines of gold and silver. Among some vice is deeply rooted; they are incorrigible; and it is as impossible to lead them back to virtue as to make a negro white. With others vice has not yet become a second nature; they may return from their wanderings of the will, by seriously retiring into themselves, mortifying their senses, and repressing their passions.

The surest mode to cure evil is for a man to search deeply his conscience, to open his eyes to his own faults, and to ask pardon from the God of mercy with a true repentance and a bitter sorrow. We therefore invite thee to retire into thyself, to renounce thy errors, and walk towards that which is good, with a firm and resolute step. We further require of thee that thou give up the lands wrongfully detached from our dominions, and that thou replace our lieutenants and our officers in possession of them. If thou valuest thy safety and thy repose, thou wilt resolve to do this without delay.

But if, for thy misfortune, thou persist in conduct like thy past; if, drunk with the thoughts of thy power and foolish bravery, thou wilt pursue the course of thy iniquities, thou shalt in a few days see thy plains covered with our tents and flooded with our battalions. Then shall be performed prodigies of valour; and then shall the world witness the decrees of the Most High, who is the God of battles and the Sovereign Judge of the deeds of men. For the rest, may he fare well, who walks well in the true faith.

Much as Selim prided himself on his piety and his literary skill, he neglected no means of bringing more substantial weapons to bear upon his heretical opponent In a general review of his army at Sivas, Selim ascertained that his available forces amounted to 140,000 well-armed men; and 6000 more were employed in the commissariat department, which also was provided with 60,000 camels. He had a reserve force of 40,000 men placed in echelon, between Kaissyraia and Sivas. The great difficulty of the campaign was to keep up his line of communications and to ensure a supply of provisions; as the Persians, instead of encountering him on the frontier, retired before him, laying waste the whole country, and leaving nothing that could shelter or feed a foe.

Selim's chief magazines were at Trebizond, whither his fleets brought large supplies, and whence they were carried on mules to the army. Selim endeavoured to provoke Ismail to change his judicious tactics and risk a battle, by sending him more letters, written partly in verse and partly in prose, in which he taunted the Persian sovereign with cowardice in not playing out the royal part which he had usurped. Selim said:

> They, who by perjuries seize sceptres ought not to skulk from danger, but their breast ought, like the shield, to be held out to encounter peril; they ought, like the helm, to affront the foeman's blow. Dominion is a bride to be wooed and won by him only, whose lip blenches not at the biting kiss of the sabre's edge.

Ismail replied to the homilies and rhapsodies of the *Sultan* by a calm and dignified letter, in which he denied the existence of any reason why Selim should make war on him, and expressed his willingness to resume peaceful relations. Ismail then regretted that the *Sultan* should have assumed in his correspondence a style so unnatural and so unfitting the dignity of the nominal writer; but with polished irony Ismail asserted his firm belief that the letters must have been the hasty productions of some secretary who had taken an overdose of opium. Ismail added, that:

> Without doubt, the will of God would soon be manifested; but it would be too late to repent when that manifestation had commenced. For his part, he left the *Sultan* at liberty to do what he pleased, and was fully prepared for war if his amicable letter was ill received.

This letter was accompanied by the present of a box of opium, ostensibly for the supposed secretary who had written the letter in Selim's name; but, as Selim himself was addicted to the use of that drug, the satiric stroke was sure to be keenly felt. Enraged at the dignified scorn of his adversary, Selim vented his wrath by an outrage on the law of nations, and ordered the Persian envoy to be torn to pieces. His nephew Amurath, the refugee prince at Ismail's court, had, with Ismail's sanction, set the example of such atrocity, by mutilating and putting to death a Turkish ambassador, who had been sent to the Persian court to demand that Amurath. should be given up to Selim.

The Ottoman Army continued to advance through the north of

Diarbekir, Kourdistan, and Azerbijan, upon Tabriz, which was then the capital of Persia, and the usual royal residence of Shah Ismail The prudent system of operations, which the Persian prince continued to follow, inflicted great hardships upon the advancing Turks, as wherever they moved they found the country entirely desolate, and the difficulty of forwarding supplies increased with each march. The *Janissaries* murmured; but Selim only redoubled his vigilance in preserving strict order, and his exertions in providing as far as possible the means of reaching Tabriz. One of his generals, Hemdar Pacha, who had been brought up with Selim from infancy, was persuaded by the other officers to remonstrate with the Sultan against marching farther through those desert countries. Selim beheaded him for his interference, and still marched on.

At Sogma, Selim received an embassy from the Prince of Georgia, and a welcome supply of provisions. After a short halt he gave orders to resume the march upon Tabriz, and the *Janissaries* broke out into open tumult, and loudly demanded to be led back to their homes. Selim had pretended not to observe their murmurs on former occasions during the march, but he now rode boldly into the midst of them, he cried:

> Is this your service to your *Sultan?* Does your loyalty consist of mere boast and lip-worship? Let those among you who wish to go home, stand out from the ranks, and depart. As for me, I have not advanced thus far merely to double on my track. Let the cowards instantly stand aloof from the brave, who have devoted themselves with sword and quiver, soul and hand, to our enterprise.

He ended by quoting a passage from a Persian, poem:

> *I never flinch, or turn back from the purpose*
> *Which once has gained dominion o'er my soul.*

He then gave the word of command to form column and march, and not a *janissary* dared leave his banner.

At length the pride of Ismail overcame his prudence; and, exasperated at the devastation which the war caused to his subjects, and at the near approach of his insulting enemy to his capital, the Persian prince determined to give battle, and arrayed his forces in the valley of Calderan. Selim's joy was extreme when, on mounting the heights to the westward of that valley, on the 23rd of August, 1514, he saw the Persian Army before him. He gave command for an immediate engagement, and drew up his troops in order of battle on the heights, before marching to action in the valley. He had about 120,000 troops, of whom 80,000 were cavalry. But both men and horses were worn by the fatigues and privations of the march, and seemed to be ill-fitted to encounter the magnificent cavalry of the Persians, which was perfectly fresh and in admirable spirit and equipment. The Persian cavalry was equal in numbers to the Turkish horse, but it constituted the whole of Shah Ismail's army. He had neither infantry nor cannons; while Selim brought a powerful train of artillery into action, and a large portion of his *Janissaries* bore firearms.

Selim drew up the feudal cavalry of Anatolia on his right wing under Sinan Pacha, and the feudal cavalry of Roumelia on the left, under Hassan Pacha. He placed his batteries at the extremity of each wing, masking them by the light troops of his army, the *Azabs*, who were designed to fly at the enemy's first charge, and lure the best Persian troops under the muzzles of the Turkish guns. The *Janissaries* were a little in the rear, in the centre, protected by a barricade of baggage-waggons. Behind them were the *Sultan's* horse-guards, and there Selim took his own station.

On the other side Ismail drew up two chosen brigades of cavalry, one on each side of his line, one of which he led himself, and the other was entrusted to the command of a favourite general, Oustadluogli. Ismail designed to turn his enemy's wings with these two brigades, and, avoiding the Ottoman batteries, to take the *Janissaries* in the rear. He anticipated that Selim's light troops, the *Azabs*, would, when charged, wheel away to the extreme right and left of the Ottoman line, so as to unmask the cannons; and he therefore ordered that his two brigades should not endeavour to break through the *Azabs*, but should wheel as they wheeled, so as to keep the *Azabs* between them and the artillery, until they were clear of the guns, and then ride in on the flanks and rear of the Ottoman army.

This manoeuvre seemed the more practicable as Selim's cannons in each wing were chained together, so that it was almost impossible to change their position when the battle had once commenced. Full of confidence, the Persian cavaliers galloped forward with loud cries of " The *Shah!* the *Shah* !" and the Turks raised the cry of "*Allah!*" and stood firm to meet them. The wing which Ismail led in person was completely successful. He outflanked the wheeling *Azabs*, and then, bursting in on the left of the Ottomans, he drove them in confusion upon their rear-guard.

But, on the other side of the field, Sinan Pacha, the commander of the Turkish right wing, out-generalled his opponent Oustadluogli. Instead of wheeling his retreating *Azabs* away from the front of the batteries, Sinan called them straight back, let them pass over the chains by which the guns were fastened together, and then poured in a deadly discharge upon the dense column of Persian horse that was galloping forward in close pursuit. Oustadluogli was one of the first that fell, and the whole left of the Persians was thrown into disorder, which a charge of Sinan's *Spahis* soon turned into utter rout. Victorious in this part of the battle, Selim was able to bring succour to his defeated troops, who had been broken by Shah Ismail. He led his *Janissaries* into action, and the *Shah's* cavalry, already somewhat exhausted and dismayed by their previous efforts, were unable to break this veteran infantry, or long to endure their fusillade.

The Persians had begun to waver, when Shah Ismail himself fell from his horse, wounded in the arm and the foot. The Turks closed upon him; and he was only saved by the devoted gallantry of one of his followers, Mirza Sultan Ali, who rushed upon the Ottomans, exclaiming, "I am the *Shah*." While the enemy mastered Mirza Ali and examined his person, Ismail was raised from the ground. Another of his attendants named Khizer, gave up his own horse, on which Ismail was mounted by those around him, and hurried from the field.

The victory of Selim was complete, but it had been dearly purchased. No less than fourteen Ottoman *Sanjak Beys* ("Lords of Standards") lay dead on the field of battle; and an equal number of *khans* who had fought on the Persian side had also perished.

Selim took possession of his enemy's camp, in which were his treasures and his *harem*, including the favourite wife of the Shah Selim put all his prisoners, except the women and children, to death; and then marched upon Tabriz, and entered the Persian capital in triumph.

Selim levied on the conquered city a contribution of 1000 of its most skilful artisans. These were sent by him to Constantinople, and received houses and the means of carrying on their respective manufactures in the Ottoman capital. After a halt of only eight days at Tabriz, the *Sultan* marched northwards towards Karabagh, meaning to fix his winter quarters in the plains of Azerbijan, and resume his career of conquest in the spring. But the discontent of the troops at this prolongation of their hardships, and their desire to revisit their homes, broke out into such general and formidable murmurings, that Selim was, like

Alexander, compelled to give way, and return with his victorious, but refractory veterans towards Europe. His expedition, however, was not barren of important augmentation to his empire.

The provinces of Diarbekir and Kurdistan, through which he had marched against Ismail, were thoroughly conquered and annexed to his dominions by the military skill of the generals whom he detached for that purpose, and still more by the high administrative ability of the historian Idris, to whom Selim confided the important duty of organising the government of the large and populous territories which had been thus acquired. The pacific overtures of Shah Ismail were haughtily rejected by the *Sultan*; and throughout Selim's reign there was war between the two great Mahometan sovereigns, in which the Persian arms were generally unsuccessful against the Turkish, though Shah Ismail maintained the contest with spirit, and preserved the greater part of his territories under his sway.

Selim's hatred against the Schii heretics and his warlike energy were unchecked throughout his life; but after the campaign of Calderan he did not again bring the whole weight of the Ottoman power to bear upon Persia, nor did he himself again lead his invading armies against her. Syria and Egypt proved more tempting objects to his ambition; and the aggressive strength of the Mameluke rulers of those countries made a decisive contest between them and the Ottomans almost inevitable. The dominion of the Mamelukes is one of the most remarkable phenomena in history, especially in the history of slavery.

The word *Mameluke*, or *Memlook*, means slave; and this body of Oriental chivalry, which, for nearly six centuries, maintained itself in lordly pride in Egypt, which encountered Selim and Napoleon with such valour as to extort the admiration of those two great conquerors, and which, though often partially broken, was only destroyed by the darkest treachery in our own age;—this military aristocracy of the East consisted of men, who had been bought and sold and bred as slaves, and who recruited their own ranks, not from among the natives of the land which became their country, but from the slave markets of far distant regions.

Malek Salech, of the Eyoub dynasty of the *Sultans* of Egypt, formed in the beginning of the thirteenth century (a hundred years before the institution of the *Janissaries*), an armed corps of twelve thousand slaves, chiefly natives of the Caucasian countries. These, from their servile condition, were called *Memlooks*. Their discipline and military spirit soon made them formidable to their masters, and in 1264 they killed

Touroon Shah, the last prince of the Eyoub dynasty, and placed one of their own body on the throne of Egypt. The first Mameluke sovereigns of Egypt were called *Baharites*. They conquered Syria; a country which the Pharaohs, the Ptolemies, and all the various rulers of Egypt, down to the times of Napoleon and Mehemet Ali, have ever regarded as a necessary rampart for their dominions along the banks of the Nile.

In 1382 Berkouk, a Mameluke of Circassian race, overthrew the *Baharite* sovereign, and founded the dynasty of the Circassian Mamelukes, which continued to reign till the time of Selim's invasion. At this period the military force of the Mamelukes consisted of three classes of warriors; all cavalry superbly mounted and armed, but differing materially in rank. First, there were the Mamelukes themselves—properly so called—all of whom were of pure Circassian blood, and who had all been originally slaves. The second corps was called the Djelbans, and was formed principally of slaves brought from Abyssinia. The third, and lowest in rank, was called the Korsans, and was an assemblage of mercenaries of all nations. There were twenty-four *beys* or heads of the Mamelukes, and they elected from among themselves a *sultan*, who was called also Emirol-Kebir, or Chief of Princes. He reigned over Egypt and Syria, and was also recognised as supreme sovereign over that part of Arabia in which the holy cities of Mecca and Medina are situate.

The first war between the Mamelukes and the Ottoman Turks broke out, as we have seen, during the weak reign of Bajazet II. at Constantinople, and terminated to the disadvantage of the Sublime Porte. The Mameluke princes saw clearly that under Sultan Selim the vast resources of the Turkish Empire would be wielded in a far different spirit from that of his father, and they watched with anxious attention the conquests of the provinces of Diarbekir and Kurdistan, which Selim made from the Persians, and which brought the Ottoman frontiers more extensively in contact with those of the Egyptian possessions in Syria.

The Sultan of Egypt, Kanssou-Ghawri, assembled a strong army of observation in the north of Syria, in 1516. Sinan Pacha, the commander of the Ottoman forces in the south-east of Asia Minor, reported this to Selim, and stated that he could not with safety obey the *Sultan's* orders to march towards the Euphrates, while menaced by the Mamelukes on flank and rear. Selim assembled his divan at Constantinople, and the question of war with Egypt was earnestly deliberated. The Secretary Mohammed (who was distinguished for his scientific attainments, and whom Selim had raised to office as a mark of his regard for science) spoke strongly in favour of war, and urged that it ought to be a point of honour with the *Sultan* of the Ottomans to acquire by conquest the protectorate of the Holy Cities.

Selim was so delighted with the warlike speech of his favourite philosopher, that he gave him the rank of *vizier* on the spot. Mohammed at first declined the promotion, but Selim took a summary method of curing his scruples. With his own royal hands he applied the bastinado to the man whom he delighted to honour, till the diffident follower of science accepted the proffered dignity. It was resolved to wage war in Egypt, but messengers requiring submission were first to be sent in obedience to the precepts of the *Koran*. Selim, however, did not delay his preparations for warfare until the result of the message was ascertained. He left Constantinople at the same time with his ambassadors, and placed himself at the head of the intended army of Egypt.

Kanssou-Ghawri was at Aleppo when Selim's ambassadors reached him. He committed the folly as well as the crime of treating them with insult and personal violence, though on the approach of the Turkish army he set them at liberty, and vainly endeavoured to open negotiations. The first battle, which determined the fate of Syria, was fought on the 24th August, 1516, not far from Aleppo, in a plain where, according to Mahometan tradition, is the tomb of David. The effect of the Turkish artillery, and the dissensions among the Mamelukes themselves, gave Selim an easy victory; and the aged Sultan Ghawri died while endeavouring to escape.

The Mamelukes chose as their new *Sultan*, Touman Bey, a chief eminent for his valour and the nobility and generosity of his disposition. Their defeat had not damped the spirits of the Mamelukes, who remembered their victories in the former war, and considered themselves far superior to the Ottomans in military skill and personal prowess. During the confusion caused by the defeat and death of the *Sultan*, and the retreat of the principal surviving *Beys* to Cairo for the purpose of electing his successor, Selim had been suffered to occupy Aleppo, Damascus, Jerusalem, and the other Syrian cities, without resistance; but it was resolved to defend the passage of the desert against him; and an advanced force of Mamelukes was sent to Gaza, while Touman Bey concentrated the mass of the Egyptian forces in the vicinity of Cairo.

Selim prepared for the difficult march from the inhabited portion of Syria to the Egyptian frontier with his customary forethought and energy. He purchased many thousand camels, which were laden with water for the use of his army while crossing the desert, and he distributed a liberal donative of money among his men. His *grand vizier*, Sinan Pacha, defeated the advanced force of the Mamelukes near Gaza, after an obstinate fight, which was determined in favour of the Turks by their artillery. The Turkish Army then crossed the desert in ten days, and marched upon the Egyptian capital, Cairo. Touman Bey's army was at Ridania, a little village on the road leading towards that city; and it was there that the decisive battle was fought on the 22nd January, 1517.

Two of the Egyptian *Sultan's* chief officers, Ghazali and Khair Bey, had betrayed him, and baffled the skilful tactics by which he hoped to take the Ottoman Army in flank while on the march. Though compelled to fight at disadvantage, the Mameluke chivalry never signalised their valour more than on the fatal day of Ridania.

At the very commencement of the action, a band of horsemen, armed from head to foot in steel, galloped from the Egyptian left in upon the Turkish centre, to where the *Sultan's* own banner was displayed. Touman Bey himself, and two of his best captains, Alan Bey, and Kourt Bey, led this daring charge. They had sworn to take the Ottoman *Sultan* dead or alive; and Selim was only saved by their mistaking for him Sinan Pacha, the *grand vizier*, who was at that moment in the centre of a group of the principal officers of the Turkish Army. Touman Bey speared Sinan through and through: Alan Bey, and Kourt Bey, killed each a *pacha*; and then rapidly wheeling their ready chargers, the bold Mamelukes rode back to their own army, though Alan Bey received a severe wound from a bullet. The other Mamelukes (save those whom treachery kept back) charged with valour worthy of such chiefs; but the efforts of this splendid cavalry were as vain against the batteries of Selim's artillery, as were in aftertime the charges of their successors against the rolling fire of Napoleon's squares., Touman Bey and a relic of his best cavaliers escaped to Adviyé, but 25,000 Mamelukes lay heaped on the plain of Ridania.

Selim sent a detachment of his army to occupy Cairo. They entered it without resistance, seven days after the battle; but the indomitable Touman Bey suddenly came upon the intrusive garrison, and slew them to a man. Selim sent his best troops to retake the city, which had no regular fortifications, but in which the Turks now found every street barricaded, and every house a fortress. A desperate street battle now ensued, and for three days the Mamelukes held Cairo against the assaulting columns of the *Sultan*. At the suggestion of the traitor Khair Bey, Selim now proclaimed an amnesty to such Mamelukes as would surrender. On the faith of this promise the warfare ceased, and 800 of the chief Mamelukes voluntarily became Selim's prisoners, or were given up to him by the citizens. Selim had them all beheaded, and then ordered a general massacre of the wretched inhabitants of Cairo, 50,000 human beings are said to have perished in this atrocious butchery.

Kourt Bey, who was reputed the most valiant of the Mamelukes, was for a time concealed in Cairo; but Selim, by promises of safety, induced the champion of the Circassian race to present himself before him Selim received him, seated on his throne, and with all the dignitaries of his camp around him. Selim, looking on him, said, "Thou wast a hero on horseback—where is now thy valour?"

"It is always with me," answered Kourt Bey, laconically. "Knowest thou what thou hast done to my army?"

"Right well." Selim then expressed his astonishment at the attack on his person, which Kourt Bey had, in concert with Touman Bey and Alan Bey, dared to make at Ridania, and which had proved so fatal to Sinan Pacha. Upon this, Kourt Bey, who was as renowned for his eloquence as for his courage, poured forth a brilliant eulogy on the valour of the Mamelukes, and spoke with contempt and abhorrence of guns, which, he said, killed so cowardly and so like an assassin.

******

The reader will remember *Hotspur*. Old Knolles, in relating the victory of Selim over the Persians, breathes the same spirit. He says that the Persian cavalry "had been of the Turks invincible, if it had not been overwhelmed by the cruel, cowardly, and murdering artillery, and wonderful multitude of men." See also Byron's *Island*.

With respect to the speech of Kourt Bey in the text, it is to be observed that it ought not to be considered a mere imaginary composition, like the speeches in many of the classical historians, and in many of their modern imitators. Von Hammer gives this dialogue between Kourt Bey and Selim, on the authority of, among others, the Scheik Seinel, who had held an appointment at Touman Bey's court, and who must have been an eye and ear-witness of much related in his narrative of the conquest of Egypt. See Von Hammer, book xiii.

******

He told Selim that the first time that Venetian bullets (so the Mamelukes call cannon and musket-balls—Bindikia, *i.e.* Venetian, Von Hammer says that bullets are still called so in Egypt), were brought into Egypt, was in the reign of Eschref-Kanssou, when a Mauritanian offered to arm the Mamelukes with them; but the *Sultan* and the *Beys* of the army rejected that innovation in warfare as unworthy of true valour, and as a departure from the example of the Prophet, who had consecrated the sabre and the bow as the fit weapons for his followers.

Kourt Bey said that the Mauritanian had, on this refusal, cried out, "Some of you shall live to see this empire perish by these bullets."

"Alas!" added Kourt Bey, "that prediction is accomplished: but all power is in the hands of God the Most High."

"How comes it," said Selim, " if ye place all your strength in the word of God, that we have beaten you, and driven you from your strong places, and thou thyself standest here a prisoner before me?"

"By *Allah*," answered Kourt Bey, "we were not overthrown because ye were braver in battle or better horsemen than we; but because it was our destiny. For, all that has a beginning must have an end, and the duration of empires is. limited. Where are the *caliphs*, those champions of Islam? Where are the mightiest empires of the world? And your time also, ye Ottomans, will come; and your dominion shall in turn be brought to nothing. As for myself, I am not thy prisoner, Sultan Selim, but I stand here free and secure by reason of thy promises and pledges."

Kourt Bey then turned to the traitor Khair Bey, who stood by Selim during this interview, and after heaping the most withering invectives on him, he counselled Selim to strike the betrayer's head off, lest he should drag him down to hell. Then said Selim, full of wrath, "I had thought to set thee free, and even to make thee one of my *Beys*. But thou hast loosened thy tongue in an unseemly course, and not set respect of my presence before thine eyes. He who stands before princes without reverence, is driven from them with shame."

Kourt Bey answered with spirit: "God preserve me from ever being officer of thine."

At these words Selim's rage overflowed, and he called for executioners. A hundred swords were ready at his command.

"What good will my single head do thee," continued the fearless Mameluke, "when so many brave men are on the watch for thine; and Touman Bey still trusts in God?"

Selim signed to one of his headsmen to strike. While the sabre was swung round to slay, the doomed hero turned to Khair Bey, "Take my bloody head, traitor, and place it in thy wife's lap, and may 'God make the betrayer betrayed.'"

Such were the last words of Kourt Bey, the bravest of the brave Mamelukes.

Touman Bey, after the final loss of Cairo, had sought to strengthen himself by employing Arabs in his army, contrary to the former practice of the Mamelukes. He gained some advantages over detachments of Selim's army: and Selim offered him peace on condition of his acknowledging himself to be vassal of the Ottoman Sultan. But the treacherous massacre at Cairo, and the execution of Kourt Bey, had exasperated the Mamelukes; and they put Selim's messenger and the whole of his attendants to death. Selim retorted by the slaughter of 3000 prisoners.

The war continued a little longer; but the Arabs and the Mamelukes under Touman Bey quarrelled with each other, and fought in the very presence of the Ottoman Army, which poured its cannonade upon the combatants with impartial destructiveness. At length, Touman Bey's forces were entirely dispersed; and he himself was betrayed into the hands of the Turks. When Selim was informed of his capture, he exclaimed, "God be praised; Egypt is now conquered." He at first treated his brave prisoner with merited respect; but the traitors Ghazali and Khair Bey were determined that their former sovereign should perish, and they raised Selim's suspicions that there was a plot to liberate the royal prisoner and restore him to power. Selim, on this, ordered him to be put to death; and the last Mameluke Sultan, the brave, the chivalrous, the just Touman Bey perished on the 17th of April, 1517.

Egypt was now completely subdued by the Turks; but Selim remained there some months, engaged in settling the future government of the new empire which he had acquired, and in visiting the public buildings of its capital. The mysterious monuments of the Pharaohs and the relics of the splendours of the Ptolemies had no interest for the Ottoman *Sultan*. He did not even visit the Pyramids; but all his attention was concentrated on the mosques and other religious foundations of the early Mahometan sovereigns of Egypt. He attended divine worship in the chief mosques of Cairo on the first Friday after his conquest, and gave to the assembled people an impressive example of religious humility and contrition, by causing the rich carpets which had been spread for him to be removed, and by prostrating himself with his bare forehead on the bare pavement, which he visibly moistened with his tears.

It is throwing no slur on the Mahometan religion to believe in the sincerity of Selim's devotion; though at this very time the most cruel exactions were practised on the people of Egypt by his orders. Christendom could, during that century, show many a crowned tyrant, as earnest in bigotry, and as barbarous and unprincipled towards his fellow-creatures as Sultan Selim. Some of his principal followers imitated their master in oppression and rapacity; but there were also nobler and more generous spirits among the Ottoman chiefs. The historian Idris has been already mentioned with honour for the justice and skill, with which he organised the administrative system of Diarbekir and Kurdistan, when set over those newly-conquered countries by Selim.

He had subsequently attended the *Sultan* during the Egyptian campaign; and he now risked his life by interceding with his savage master in behalf of the oppressed natives. He had been commissioned by Selim to translate from the Arabic the work of Demiri on natural history; and he added to his translation a short poem, which he wrote in Persian, and in which he gave the *Sultan* severe and salutary advice about the administration of Egypt.

The Ottoman *viziers* in whose hands he placed his book (according to the court ceremonial) for presentation to the *Sultan*, dreaded his wrath on receiving such free-spoken counsel; and they offered Idris 1000 *ducats* if he would take his poem of advice back, and suffer the *Treatise on Natural History* to be laid before their royal master without it. Idris refused the money, and insisted on his treatise and poem being presented to the *Sultan*, threatening the *viziers* that unless they did their duty he would himself bring his writings to Selim's notice, and inform him of the negligence of his court officers. Thus threatened, the *viziers* were obliged to comply, and Idris had the noble daring to subjoin to his poem a letter, in which he requested the *Sultan's* permission to leave Egypt, unless the misery and misgovernment, which he saw in all directions there, were remedied.

The heads of Selim's best generals would have fallen for half this boldness; but Selim's admiration for literary merit was strong and sincere, and he only showed the mortification which he experienced from Idris's rebuke, by sending the high-minded historian to Constantinople by the Turkish fleet, which at Selim's orders had sailed to the harbour of Alexandria, and which, on its return, menaced, but did not attack, the island of Rhodes.

Another literary favourite of Selim, Kemal Paschazadé, who held the high legal station of Cadiasker of Anatolia, ventured with impunity, about the same time, to bring to the knowledge of the *Sultan* the discontent that was gathering among the ranks of the army at their prolonged detention in Egypt. Thus cautioned, Selim abandoned the projects which, like Cambyses, he had formed of conquering the countries beyond the cataracts of the Nile, and prepared for his march back to Europe. He had respected the persons of his literary reprovers, and he abstained, as was his custom, from punishing the common soldiery for their opposition to his wishes; but he vented his wrath on his *viziers* and other high officers at every opportunity. The *grand vizier,* Younis-Pacha, was one of his victims.

As he rode with Selim on the march back to Syria, Selim said to him, "Well, our backs are now turned on Egypt, and we shall soon see Gaza."

Younis-Pacha (who had always opposed the Egyptian expedition) answered nastily, "And what has been the result of all our trouble and anxiety, except that we have left half our army on the battlefield, or in the sands of the desert, and have set up a gang of traitors as chiefs of Egypt?"

Selim instantly bade his guards put Younis to death, and the *grand vizier's* head was struck off as he sate on horseback by the *Sultan's* side.

The mode of administering the government of Egypt was a subject of deep anxiety to Selim, as it had been to all former conquerors of that wealthy and powerful country. The Persian kings, the Roman emperors, and the Syrian *caliphs,* had ever found good cause to dread that their Egyptian province would assert its independence. An ambitious *pacha,* if of daring genius and favoured by circumstances, might have raised up against the Ottomans the Arabian nation, of which Egypt (according to its last great conqueror. Napoleon) is the natural metropolis.

★★★★★★

He would not sow in a foreign soil the seeds of independence, which he was intent upon crushing nearer home. Egypt, with the sea in its fronts and a desert on either hand, was difficult of access to the Roman armies; its overflowing stores of grain might give it the command of the Italian markets, and its accumulated treasures might buy the swords of mercenary legions. Octavius made it his own. He appointed a favourite officer, Cornelius Gallus, whose humble rank as a knight, as well as his tried services, seemed to ensure his fidelity, to govern it.

In due time he persuaded the senate and people to establish it as a principle, that Egypt should never be placed under the administration of any man of superior rank to the equestrian, and that no senator should be allowed even to visit it, without express permission from the supreme authority. For the defence of this cherished province Octavius allotted three legions, besides some squadrons of cavalry, and a body of nine *cohorts* of pure Roman extraction.

One *legion* was quartered in Alexandria, the inhabitants of which, though turbulent, were incapable of steady resistance; a division of three cohorts garrisoned Syene on the Nubian frontier, and others were stationed in various localities. Under the military commander was a revenue officer, whose accounts were delivered to Octavius himself, by whom he was directly appointed.—Merivale's *History of the Romans under the Empire*, vol. iii.; see also observations of Napoleon on Egypt, vol. iv.; Montholon's *Memoirs*. Though not always accurate in his historical details, Napoleon is the best writer on the subject of Egypt that a general or a statesman can consult. He seems to have almost prophesied the rising of Mehemet Ali against the Porte. There is a sketch of the history of Egypt under the Mamelukes and under the Porte, in the first volume of Hope's *Anastasius*. amusement.

★★★★★★

Selim even feared that the division of Egypt into several *pachalics* would not be a sufficient guarantee for its subjection to the Porte; and he, therefore, resolved to divide authority among the variety of races in the country, and so to secure his imperial sovereignty. He did not extirpate the Mamelukes; nor did he provide for their gradual extinction by forbidding the *beys* to recruit their households with new slaves from Circassia. Twenty-four *beys* of the Mamelukes, chosen from those who had acted with the invaders, continued to preside over the departments of the province, and their chief, the arch-traitor Khair Bey, was styled governor of Egypt.

Selim, however, sent Khair Bey's wives and children to Europe, as securities for his good behaviour. He formed a more effectual and lasting safeguard for the Turkish supremacy, by placing a permanent force of 5000 *Spahis* and 500 *Janissaries* in the capital, under the command of the Ottoman Aga Khaireddin, who had orders never to leave the fortifications. This force was recruited from among the inhabitants of Egypt, and formed gradually a provincial militia with high privileges and importance. Selim placed the greater part of the administrative functions of law and religion in the hands of the Arab *scheiks*, who possessed the greatest influence over the mass of the population, which, like themselves, was of Arabic origin. The *scheiks* naturally attached themselves, through religious spirit and inclination, to Constantinople rather than to the Mamelukes, and drew the feelings of the other Arab inhabitants with them.

Selim took no heed of the Copts, the aboriginal natives of Egypt; but it was from among this despised class and the Jews, that the Mameluke Beys generally selected their agents and tax-gatherers, and the villages were commonly under the immediate government of Coptic local officers, (Von Hammer, Napoleon, and Hope). The Mameluke *Sultans* of Egypt, whose dynasty Selim cut short, had been the recognised *suzerains*, and protectors of the holy cities of Arabia; and Selim now acquired the same titles and rights, which were of infinite worth in the eyes of that imperial devotee, and which were, and are, of real practical value to an Ottoman *Sultan*, from the influence which they give him over the whole Mahometan world.

Another important dignity, which the Sultan Selim and his successors obtained from the conquest of Egypt, was the succession to the Caliphate, and to the spiritual power and pre-eminence of the immediate Vicars of Mahomet himself After the deaths of the four first *caliphs*, who had been personal companions of the Prophet, the spiritual sovereignty of Islam passed successively to the Ommiade *caliphs* and to the *Abbassides*, whose temporal power was overthrown by Houlogou Khan, a grandson of Zenghis Khan, in 1258.

But though the substantial authority of the *caliphs* as independent princes was then shattered, the name was perpetuated three centuries longer in eighteen descendants of the House of Abbas, who dwelt in Egypt with titular pomp, but no real power, in the capital of the Mameluke rulers, like the descendants of the Great Mogul in British India. They gave their names to the edicts of the Mameluke *Sultans* when required; and we have seen in the case of the Ottoman Bajazet I., that Mahometan princes in other countries still regarded the Egyptian *caliph* as the fountain of honour, and sought from him the stamp and sanction of sovereignty. When Selim conquered Egypt, he found there Mohammed, the twelfth *caliph* of the family of Abbas, and he induced him solemnly to transfer the *caliphate* to the Ottoman *Sultan* and his successors. At the same time Selim took possession of the visible insignia of that high office, which the *Abbassides* had retained—the sacred standard, the sword, and the mantle of the Prophet.

In a preceding chapter of this volume, attention has been drawn to the importance of the Turkish *Sultan* being at once the spiritual and the temporal chief of his Mahometan subjects—of his being both Pope and Emperor. It will readily be imagined how much the *Sultan's* authority must have been augmented by his acquiring the sacred position of *caliph*, Vicar of the Prophet of God, Commander of the Faithful, and Supreme *Imam* of Islam. It gives the Turkish *Sultan* dignity and authority (and may possibly give him practical influence), not only over his own Mahometan subjects, but over all who profess the creed of Islam, whatever be their race, and whatever be their country—except the Persians, and the few others who hold the Schiite tenets.

★★★★★★

Sir George Campbell speaks contemptuously of the idea of the Turkish *Sultan* having any influence beyond the Turkish dominions over Sunnite Mahometans, because he is *caliph*. I do not presume to compare my opportunities for observing Mahometan populations with those long possessed by Sir George Campbell, nor do I cavil at his ability in using such opportunities. But I have had practical occasion to learn much of the habits and feelings of the Moormen of Ceylon, a country never under Turkish rule, and I have conversed much with those who have long been familiar with Mahometans in other parts of the Far East.

I know as a fact that on one occasion of deep interest to the Mahometan population of Ceylon, when their principal mosque at Barberyn had been polluted by some Sinhalese, who laid a dead pig in it, on the desk of the reader of the *Koran*, and when there was great difficulty felt among the Moormen as to the lawfulness of their religious rites and liturgy being resumed there, a deputation was sent to Mecca to seek the advice of the chief doctors of the law in the Holy City, and that such advice was obtained and followed. I believe that the teachers of the law at Mecca are generally consulted on questions of religious duty by Sunnite Mahometans; and certainly the authority of the *Sultan*, as *caliph*, is fully recognised at Mecca.

I may add that there is full proof in Eastern newspapers at present, that very deep interest in the fate of Turkey is felt and expressed by Mahometans far beyond the limits of Turkish temporal power.

******

In September, 1517, Sultan Selim led back his victorious army from Egypt to Syria. A thousand camels, laden with gold and silver, carried part of the rich spoils of the war; and a more valuable portion had been sent by Selim on board the Ottoman fleet to Constantinople. This consisted of the most skilful artisans of Cairo, whom Selim selected, as he had done at Tabriz, and removed to the capital city of his empire. Selim halted his army for some months, first at Damascus . and afterwards at Aleppo. During this time he received the submission of several Arabian tribes, and arranged the division of Syria into governments, and the financial and judicial administration of that province. He returned to Constantinople in August, 1518. He had been absent but little more than two years, and in that time had conquered three nations, the Syrian, the Egyptian, and the Arabian.

Selim's attention was now earnestly directed to the development of the maritime resources of his empire. In 1519 he built 150 new ships of various dimensions, some of 700 tons; at the same time 100 new galleys, that lay ready for launching, were ordered to be rigged and fully equipped for sea. A powerful army of 60,000 men, with a large train of artillery, was collected and kept on foot in Asia Minor, ready to enter on a campaign at the first word of command. It was supposed by some that Selim designed a great attack upon Persia; but it was generally believed that the Turkish preparation would make for Rhodes.

But Selim was resolved not to strike until the blow was sure to be effective; and the armaments in the Turkish seaports, and the building of fresh dockyards and arsenals, were continued with unremitting industry in the succeeding year. From the immense naval force which was thus created, it could no longer be doubted that Rhodes was the object of attack. Selim had not forgotten the humiliating repulse from that stronghold of the Christians, which his grandfather had sustained; and he would not open the campaign until everything that could be required during the expedition had been amply provided and arranged, even in the minutest details. His *viziers* were more eager to commence the enterprise, and drew down on themselves the rebuke of their stern and thoughtful master.

One day when the *Sultan*, in company with Hasandschan, the father of the historian Seadeddin, was leaving the mosque of Eyoub, he saw one of the new first-lass galleys, which he had ordered to be fitted out and kept ready for launching, sailing along the port of Constantinople. Transported with fury, he demanded by whose order the galley had left the stocks; and it was with great difficulty that the *Grand Vizier*, Piri Pacha, saved the admiral's head, by representing to the *Sultan* that it had long been usual to launch vessels when they were completely ready. Selim called his *viziers* round him, and said to them:

> You try to hurry me to the conquest of Rhodes; but do you know what such an expedition requires? Can you tell me what quantity of gunpowder you have in store?

The *viziers*, taken by surprise, were unable to answer; but the next day they came to the *Sultan*, and said that they had ammunition sufficient for a siege of four months. Selim answered, angrily:

> What is the use of ammunition for four months, when double the amount would not be enough? Do you wish me to repeat the shame of Mahomet II.? I will not begin the war, nor will I make the voyage to Rhodes, with such scant preparations. Besides, I believe that the only voyage, which I have to make, is the voyage to the other world.

These words were uttered with a true presentiment of approaching death. He left his capital with the intention of going to Adrianople; and though symptoms of acute disease had already appeared, he rode on horseback, notwithstanding the remonstrance and entreaties of his physicians: nor could they prevail on him to discontinue the use of opium. When he reached the little village, on the road to Adrianople, where he had formerly given battle to his father, and where, according to the Venetian narrative of his death, he had received his father's curse, the agony of his disease became so violent that he was compelled to stop.

On, the seventh night after he had left Constantinople, Hasandschan, who was his inseparable companion, was sitting by the dying monarch, and reading to him from the *Koran*. The movement of Selim's lips seemed to show that he followed the words of the reader; but, suddenly, at the verse "*The word of the Almighty is salvation*," Selim clenched his hand convulsively, and ceased to live (22nd September, 1520).

This prince died in the fifty-fourth year of his age, and the ninth of his reign. The maxim which, in our great dramatist, the evil spirit gives to the northern usurper, "*Be bloody, bold, and resolute*," might seem to have been the ruling principle of Sultan Selim's life. But no one can deny his high administrative and military abilities; and in religion, though a bigot of the darkest order, he was unquestionably sincere. His personal eminence in literature, and his enlightened and liberal patronage of intellectual merit in others are matters of just eulogy with the Oriental writers.

One of the most remarkable legal characters of this reign is the Mufti Djemali. If he disgraced himself by the *fetva* with which he sanctioned, on the most frivolous pretexts, the war with Egypt, the honesty and the courage with which he often opposed the cruelty of Selim are highly honourable to his memory; nor can we refuse our praise to the monarch, who repeatedly curbed his haughty will, and abstained from the coveted blood-shedding at his subject's rebuke. On one occasion Selim had, for some slight cause of wrath, ordered 150 of the persons employed in his treasury to be put to death. Djemali stood before the *Sultan*, and said to him:

"It is the duty of the *mufti* to have a care for the weal of the *Sultan* of Islam in the life to come. I therefore ask of thee the lives of the 150 men unrighteously sentenced by thee to death."

Selim answered:

"The *Ulema* have nothing to do with affairs of state. Besides, *the masses are only to be kept in order by severity.*" (The German of Von Hammer gives this more pithily).

Djemali replied:

"It is not a question of policy of this world, but of the next, where mercy meets with everlasting reward, but unjust severity with everlasting punishment."

Selim gave way to the *mufti*; and not only spared those whom he had sentenced, but restored them to their functions.

At another period in Selim's reign he had issued an ordinance prohibiting the trade in silk with Persia, and he had seized the goods of the merchants engaged in the traffic, and ordered the merchants themselves, to the number of 400, to be put to death. Djemali interceded in their favour as he rode by the *Sultan's* side on the Adrianople road. Selim cried out, in indignation, "Is it not lawful to slay two-thirds of the inhabitants of the earth for the good of the other third?"

"Yes," answered the *mufti*, " if those two-thirds threaten to bring great wickedness upon earth."

"And can there be greater wickedness," said Selim, "than disobedience to a sovereign's command? Every country that renounces obedience to its rulers goes headlong to destruction."

"The disobedience is not proved here," rejoined the intrepid Djemali "The trade in silk was not previously prohibited."

"Keep yourself from meddling with state affairs," exclaimed Selim in fury; and the *mufti*, not seeking to conceal his indignation, left the *Sultan* without the customary reverence. Selim's surprise equalled his wrath. He checked his horse, and sate, for some time absorbed in reflection. But at last he gained the victory over himself, and on his return to Constantinople he set the condemned merchants at liberty, and restored their merchandise. He then sent a letter to Djemali, in which he announced his royal pleasure to confer on him the united highest dignities of the law, those of Judge of Roumelia and Judge of Anatolia. Djemali declined the proffered rank, but continued to retain the *Sultan's* esteem and friendship. The most memorable exercise of his salutary influence was in preserving the whole Greek population of the Ottoman Empire from the destruction with which they were menaced by Selim's bigotry.

After the massacre of the heretical Schiis, Selim formed the idea of extirpating unbelief and misbelief of every kind from his dominions; and he resolved to put all the Christians to death, and turn their churches into Mahometan mosques. Without avowing his precise purpose, he laid before his Mufti Djemali the general question, "Which is the most meritorious—to conquer the whole world, or to convert the nations to Islam?"

The *mufti* gave an answer that the conversion of the *infidels* was incontestably the more meritorious work, and the one most pleasing to God. Having obtained this *fetva*, Selim ordered his *grand vizier* forthwith to change all the churches into mosques, to forbid the practice of the Christian religion, and to put to death all who refused to become Mahometans. The *grand vizier*, alarmed at the sanguinary edict, consulted Djemali, who had unconsciously given the *fetva*, which the *Sultan* used to justify the massacre of this Christians. By Djemali's recommendation the Greek patriarch sought an audience of the *Sultan*; and although with much difficulty, was heard before the *divan* at Adrianople. He appealed to the pledges given by Mahomet II. in favour of the Christians when Constantinople was conquered; and he eloquently invoked the passages of the *Koran*, which forbid compulsory conversion, and enjoin the Mussulmans to practise religious toleration to all the people of the Books, who submit to pay tribute.

Selim yielded to the remonstrances and entreaties of the menaced

Greeks, and to the urgent advice of his best counsellors, so far as to abstain from the slaughter of the Rayas which he had intended. Still he refused to suffer the finest churches of Constantinople to be used any longer by the Christians:—they were changed into mosques; but inferior structures of wood were built in their stead, and the ruinous churches were repaired by Selim's orders, so that apparent respect might be paid to the grant of liberties from his great ancestor to the Greeks.

CHAPTER 11

First Siege of Vienna

The period comprised within the reign of Solyman I. (1520-1566), is one of the most important, not only in Ottoman history, but in the history of the world. The great monarchies of Western Christendom had now emerged from the feudal chaos. They had consolidated their resources, and matured their strength. They stood prepared for contests on a grander scale, for the exhibition of more sustained energy, and for the realisation of more systematic schemes of aggrandisement, than had been witnessed during the centuries which we term the ages of mediaeval history. At the commencement of this epoch (1520), nearly forty years had passed away since the Ottomans had been engaged in earnest conflict with the chief powers of central and western Europe. The European wars of the feeble Bajazet II. had been coldly waged, and were directed against the minor states of Christendom; and the fierce energies of his son Selim the Inflexible had been devoted to the conquest of Mahometan, nations.

During these two reigns, the great kingdoms of modern Europe had started from childhood into manhood. Spain had swept the last relics of her old Moorish conquerors from her soil, and had united the sceptres of her various Christian kingdoms under the sway of a single dynasty. France, under three warlike kings, Charles VIII., Louis XII., and Francis I., had learned to employ in brilliant schemes of foreign conquest those long-discordant energies and long-divided resources, which Louis XI. had brought beneath the sole authority of the crown. In England, and in the dominions of the House of Austria, similar developments of matured and concentrated power had taken place.

Moreover, while the arts, which enrich and adorn nations, had received in Christendom, towards the close of the fifteenth century, an almost unprecedented. and unequalled impulse, the art of war had been improved there even in a higher degree. Permanent armies, comprising large bodies of well-armed and well-trained infantry, were now employed. The manufacture and the use of firearms, especially of artillery, were better understood, and more generally practised; and a school of skilful as well as daring commanders had arisen, trained in the wars and on the model of the Great Captain Gonsalvo of Cordova. Besides the commencement of the struggle between France and Austria for the possession of Italy, many great events signalised the transition period from mediaeval to modern history, at the end of the fifteenth and the commencement of the sixteenth centuries: and those events, though not all strictly connected with warfare, were all of a nature calculated to waken a more far-reaching, and a more enduring heroism among the Christian nations, and to make them more formidable to their Mahometan rivals.

The great maritime discoveries and the conquests effected by the Portuguese and the Spaniards in the East Indies and in the New World; the revival of classical learning; the splendid dawnings of new literatures; the impulse given, by the art of printing to enlightenment, discussion, and free inquiry; all tended to multiply and to elevate the leading spirits of Christendom, to render them daring in aspiration, and patient of difficulty and of suffering in performance. There was also reason to expect that these new energies of the Franks would find their field of action in conquests over Islam; for, religious zeal had again become fervent in that age; and the advancement of the Cross was the ultimate purpose of the toils of the mariner, the philosopher, and the student, as well as of the statesman and the soldier. The hope that the treasures to be derived from his voyages would serve to rescue the Holy Land from the *infidels*, was ever present to the mind of Columbus amid his labours and his sufferings, and amid the perils of the unknown deep; even as Charles VIII., amid his marches and battlefields between the Alps and Naples, still cherished the thought of proceeding from conquered Italy to the rescue of Constantinople from the Turks.

The probability of a marked change in the balance of power between Christendom and Islamism before the middle of the sixteenth century, may seem to have been materially increased by the fact that one Christian sovereign combined many of the most powerful states under his single rule. The Emperor Charles V. reigned over an empire equal to that of Charlemagne in space, and immeasurably surpassing it in wealth and strength. He had inherited the Netherlands, the Austrian states, and the united Spanish monarchy, with the fair kingdoms of Naples and Sicily. He obtained by election the imperial throne of Germany; and Cortes and Pizarro gave him the additional transatlantic empires of Mexico and Peru, with their almost countless supplies of silver and gold. It might perhaps have been foreseen that the possessor of this immense power would be trammelled when employing it against the Ottomans, by the ambitious rivalry of France, and by the religious dissensions of Germany; but, on the other hand, the Ottoman Empire was at least in an equal degree impeded from full action against Christendom by the imperial rivalry of Persia, by the hatred of Schiite against Sunnite, and by the risk of revolt in Syria and Egypt

Yet, the House of Othman not only survived this period of peril, but was lord of the ascendant throughout the century, and saw numerous and fair provinces torn from the Christians, and heaped together to increase its already ample dominions. Much, unquestionably, of this success was due to the yet unimpaired vigour of the Turkish military institutions, to the high national spirit of the people, and to the advantageous position of their territory. But the principal cause of the Ottoman greatness throughout this epoch was the fact that the empire was ruled by a great man—great, not merely through his being called on to act amid combinations of favouring circumstances—not merely by tact in discerning and energy in carrying out the spirit of his age—but a man great in himself, an intelligent ordainer of the present, and a self-inspired moulder of the future.

Sultan Solyman I., termed by European writers "Solyman the Great," and "Solyman the Magnificent," bears in the histories written by his own countrymen the titles of "Solyman Kanouni" (Solyman the Lawgiver), and "Solyman Sahibi Kiran" (Solyman the Lord of his Age). That age was remarkably fertile in sovereigns of high ability. The Emperor Charles V., King Francis I., Pope Leo X., our Henry VIII., Vasili Ivanovitch, who laid the foundations of the future greatness of Russia, Sigismond I. of Poland, Andreas Gritti, the sage Doge of Venice, Shah Ismail, the restorer and legislator of Persia, and the Indian Akbar, the most illustrious of the dynasty of the Great Moguls, (Von Hammer, vol. i.), shone in the drama of the world at the same time that Solyman appeared there. Not one of these great historical characters is clothed with superior lustre to that of the Ottoman Sultan.

Solyman had, while very young, in the time of Bajazet II., been entrusted with the command of provinces; and in his father's reign he had, at the age of twenty, been left at Constantinople as viceroy of the

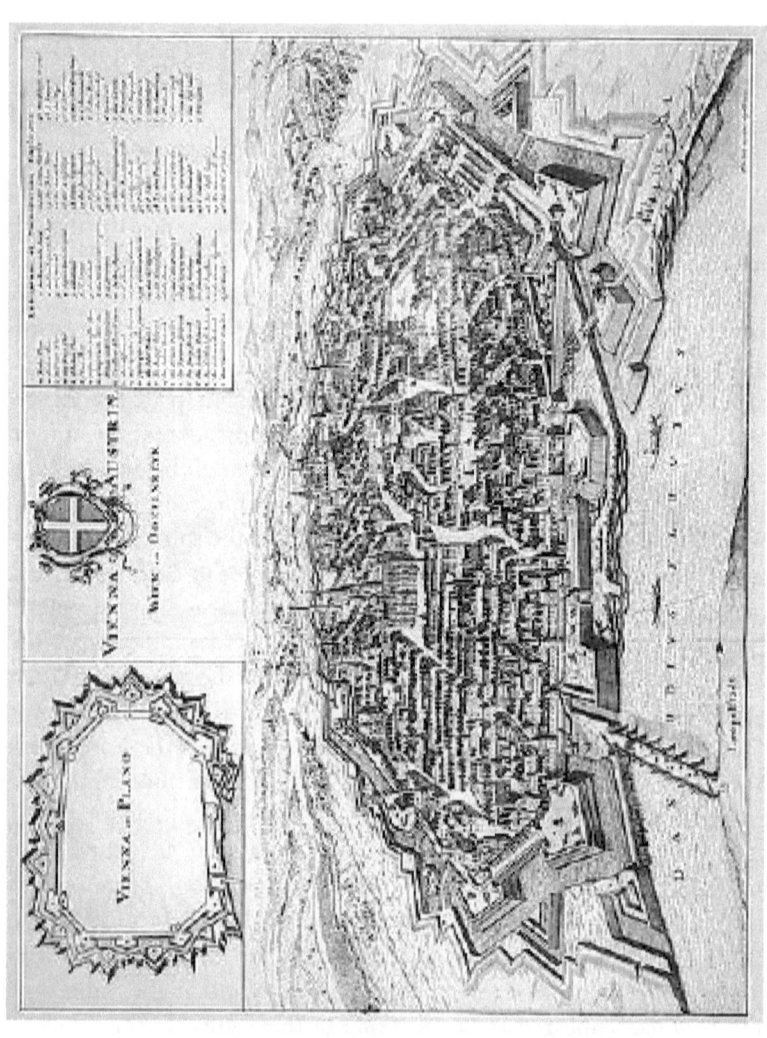

empire, when Selim marched to attack Persia. He governed at Adrianople during the Egyptian war; and during the last two years of Selim's reign he administered the province of Saroukhan. Thus, when at the age of twenty-six he became *Sultan* of the Ottoman Empire, he had already gained experience as a ruler; and he had displayed. not only high abilities, but also a noble generosity of disposition, which won for him both affection and respect The people, weary of the ferocity of Selim the Inflexible, rapturously welcomed the accession of a new ruler in the prime of youthful manhood, conspicuous by dignity and grace of person, and whose prowess, justice, clemency, and wisdom were painted by fame and hope in the brightest colours.

The first acts of Sultan Solyman announced that an earnest love of justice and generous magnanimity would be the leading principles of his reign. Six hundred Egyptians, whom Selim had forcibly transplanted to Constantinople, received permission to return to their homes. A large sum of money was distributed to merchants who had suffered by Selim's arbitrary confiscation of their property for trafficking with Persia. Several officers, high in rank, including the admiral of the fleet, who were accused of cruelty and malversation, were brought to trial, convicted and executed.

The report of these and similar deeds of the new *Sultan* spread rapidly through, the empire; and Solyman's commands to his viceroys to repress every and of disorder among rich and poor, among Moslems and Rayas, and to make the impartial dispensation of justice the great object of their lives, received universal applause and general obedience. The people felt that they were under a strong as well as a merciful government; and the *Sultan* was better loved for being also feared. It was only in Syria that any troubles followed the death of Sultan Selim. There, the double traitor, Ghazali, the Mameluke Bey, who had betrayed the Mameluke cause to the Turks, and had received the Syrian government as his reward, attempted to make himself independent; but Solyman sent an army against him without delay; and the defeat and death of the rebel not only restored tranquillity to Syria, but checked the hostile designs of Shah Ismail, who had assembled his forces on the frontier, and stood in readiness to avail himself of Ottoman weakness as Persia's opportunity.

It was not, however, long before Solyman was called on to display his military abilities in foreign warfare; and it was over the Hungarians that his first conquests were achieved. There had been disturbances and collisions on the frontiers of Hungary and Turkey in the

The Siege of Vienna

last part of Selim's reign; and the weak prince, who filled the Magyar throne, Louis II., now imprudently drew the full weight of the Ottoman power against his dominions, by insulting and putting to death the ambassador of Solyman. The young *Sultan* instantly placed himself at the head of a powerful army, which was provided with a large train of heavy artillery; and arrangements were made for the transport and regular delivery of stores and supplies, which showed that Solyman possessed the forethought and skill, as well as the courage of his lather.

The Ottoman soldiery followed him to battle with peculiar alacrity; and their military enthusiasm was augmented by their belief in his auspicious destiny, on account of his name, on account of the prosperous commencement of his reign, and still more on account of the fortunate recurrence of the mystical number Ten in all that related to him. The Orientals have ever attached great importance to numbers, and they esteem the number Ten the most fortunate of all. Solyman was the Tenth Sultan of the House of Othman; he opened the Tenth century of the Hegira; and for these and other decimal attributes he was styled by his countrymen "the Perfecter of the Perfect Number." The firm conviction which his soldiers felt that their young *Sultan* was the favourite of Heaven, made them march at his bidding as to certain victory in the cause of God. They commonly quoted, as prophetic of the fate which awaited the enemies of their sovereign, the words of the epistle from Solyman (or Solomon) to Balkis, Queen of Sheba, in the 27th chapter of the *Koran*:

> Thus saith Solyman, 'In the name of the Most Merciful God, dare not to rise up against me, but come and submit yourselves to me, and confess the true faith.'—Hulme

Such military prophecies do much to work out their own fulfilment. The first campaign of Sultan Solyman against the Giaours was eminently successful. Sabacz and other places of minor importance in Hungary were besieged and taken by his generals; but Solyman led his main force in person against Belgrade, which long had been a bulwark of Christendom against the Turks, and before which Mahomet, the captor of Constantinople, had so signally failed Belgrade was now captured (29th of August, 1521), and Solyman, after having turned the principal church into a mosque, repaired the fortifications, and provided for the maintenance of the city as a Turkish stronghold, marched back in triumph to Constantinople, after his first victorious campaign.

Under his active and skilful superintendence new buildings for ornament and use in peace and in war rose rapidly in the principal cities of the Empire. The arsenal at Constantinople was enlarged; and thousands of workmen were daily employed in framing and fitting out new squadrons, and in the preparation of naval and military stores on an unprecedented scale of grandeur. In taking Belgrade, Solyman had surmounted one of the two shoals, by which the victorious career of Mahomet II. had been checked. He now resolved to efface the shame of the other reverse; which his renowned ancestor had sustained, and to make himself master of the Isle of Rhodes, where the Christian knights of St. John of Jerusalem had so long maintained themselves near the heart of the Turkish power. Indeed, the possession of Rhodes by the Ottomans was indispensable for free communication between Constantinople and her new conquests along the Syrian coasts and in Egypt, and for the establishment of that supremacy of the Ottoman navy in the east of the Mediterranean, which Solyman was determined to effect.

On the 18th of June, 1522, the Ottoman fleet of 300 sail quitted Constantinople for Rhodes. Besides its regular crews and immense cargoes of military stores, it carried 8000 chosen soldiers and 2000 pioneers. At the same time Solyman led an army of 100,000 men along the western coast of Asia Minor. The place of rendezvous for fleet and army was the Bay of Marmarice, where, long afterwards, in 1801, the English fleet and army, under Sir Ralph Abercromby, were mustered as allies of the Turks for the re-conquest of Egypt from the French.

The Grand Master of Rhodes at the time of Solyman's attack was Villiers De Lisle Adam, a French knight of proved worth and valour. The garrison consisted of 5000 regular troops, 600 of whom were knights. Besides these, the seafaring men of the port were formed into an effective corps; the citizens were enrolled and armed; the peasantry, who crowded from the rest of the island into the city to escape the Turkish marauders, were disciplined as pioneers, and the slaves were made to work on the fortifications. The defences of the city had been much increased and improved, since the siege by Mahomet II's troops; and even if the outer walls were breached and carried, there were now inner lines of strong walls prepared to check the assailants; and several quarters of the city had their own distinct fortifications, so as to be tenable (like the quarters of ancient Syracuse) even after other parts of the city were in possession of the besiegers.

Solyman landed in the island of Rhodes on the 28th of July, 1522, and the siege began on the 1st of August It was prolonged for nearly five months by the valour of De Lisle Adam and his garrison, and by the skill of his engineer, Martinego. The war was waged almost incessantly underground by mines and countermines, as well as above ground by cannonade and bombardment, desperate sallies, and still more furious assaults. A breach was effected, and some of the bastions of the city were shattered early in September; and four murderous attempts at storming were made and repulsed during that month.

Three more assaults, one on the 12th of October, one on the 23rd, and one on the 30th of November, were fiercely given and heroically withstood, though the effect of the cannonade on the fortifications was more and more visible. The Turkish commanders at length resolved to lavish no more lives in attempts to storm the city, but to trust to their mines and artillery for its gradual destruction. Advancing along trenches according to the plan of gradual approach which since has been habitually employed, but which was previously unknown, or, at least, never used so systematically, the Turks brought their batteries to bear closer and closer upon the city; and at length established themselves within the first defences.

******

It appears that the first regular approaches against a fortress were introduced by this people.—Col. Chesney's *Turkey*.

The Turks also used shells for the first time in this siege.—Von Hammer, ii.

******

Solyman now offered terms of capitulation, and the besieged reluctantly treated for a surrender. There were yet the means of prolonging the defence; but there were no hopes of succour, and the ultimate fall of the city was certain. Honourable terms might now be obtained, the Order might be preserved, though forced to seek a home elsewhere, and the Rhodians might gain protection from the conqueror for person and property. To continue their resistance until the exasperated enemy overpowered them, would be not only to sacrifice themselves, but to expose the citizens to massacre, and their wives and daughters to the worst horrors of war. These reasons weighed with De Lisle Adam and his knights, as with truly brave men, and they laid down their good swords which they had so honourably wielded.

That they did their duty to Christendom in their surrender, as well as in their previous resistance, was proved afterwards by the effectual check which their Order gave to Solyman at Malta. How much heroism would the world have lost, if the Knights of St. John had obstinately sought in Rhodes the fate of Leonidas!

******

I have been guided in these remarks on the surrender of Rhodes by the criticisms made by Marshal Marmont on this siege (Marmont's *State of the Turkish Empire, &c.*, translated by Sir F. Smith, 2nd ed.). While giving conclusive military reasons for thinking that the defence might have been prolonged, the marshal justly terms it "honourable, and even glorious."

******

By the terms of capitulation (Dec. 25, 1522) which Solyman granted to the Knights, he did honour to unsuccessful valour; and such honour is reflected with double lustre on the generous victor. The Knights were to be at liberty to quit the island with their arms and property within twelve days in their own galleys, and they were to be supplied with transports by the Turks if they required them: the Rhodian citizens, on becoming the *Sultan's* subjects, were to be allowed the free exercise of their religion; their churches were not to be profaned; no children were to be taken from their parents; and no tribute was to be required from the island for five years. The insubordinate violence of the *Janissaries* caused some infraction of these terms; but the main provisions of the treaty were fairly carried into effect.

By Solyman's request, an interview took place between him and the Grand Master before the knights left the island. Solyman addressed, through his interpreter, words of respectful consolation to the Christian veteran; and, turning to the attendant *vizier*, the *Sultan* observed: "It is not without regret that I force this brave man from his home in his old age." Such indeed was the esteem with which the valour of the Knights had inspired the Turks, that they refrained from defacing their armorial bearings and inscriptions on the buildings. For more than three hundred years the Ottomans have treated the memory of their brave foemen with the same respect; and the escutcheons of the Knights of St John, who fought against Sultan Solyman for Rhodes, still decorate the long-captured city.

******

Three hundred and fifteen years have now elapsed, (1877), since this illustrious order was obliged to abandon its conquests, after a possession of two hundred and twelve years. The street of the knights is uninjured, and the door of each house is still ornamented with the escutcheon of the last inhabitant. The buildings have been spared, but are unoccupied; and we could almost fancy ourselves surrounded by the shades of departed heroes. The arms of France, the noble *fleur-de-lis*, are seen in all directions. I observed those of the Clermont-Tonnerres, and of other ancient and illustrious families.—Marshal Marmont.

★★★★★★

Solyman had experienced the turbulence of the *Janissaries* at Rhodes; and he received three years afterwards a more serious proof of the necessity of keeping that formidable body constantly engaged in warfare, and under strict, but judicious discipline. The years 1523 and 1524 had not been signalised by any foreign war. The necessity of quelling a revolt of Ahmed Pacha, who had succeeded Khair Bey in the government of Egypt, had occupied part of the Ottoman forces; and after the traitor had been defeated and killed, Solyman sent his favourite Grand Vizier Ibrahim, a Greek renegade, into that important province to re-settle its administration, and assure its future tranquillity. Solyman's personal attention for the first eighteen months after the campaign of Rhodes was earnestly directed to improving the internal government of his empire; but, in the autumn of 1525, he relaxed in his. devotion to the toils of state; and, quitting his capital, he repaired, for the first time, to Adrianople, and followed there with ardour the amusement of the chase.

The *Janissaries* began to murmur at their Sultan's forgetfulness of war, and at last they broke out into open brigandage, and pillaged the houses of the principal ministers. Solyman returned to Constantinople, and strove to quell the storm by his presence. He boldly confronted the mutinous troops, and cut down two of their ringleaders with his own hand; but he was obliged to pacify them by a donative, though he afterwards partly avenged himself by putting to death many of their officers, whom he suspected of having instigated or of having neglected to check the disorder.

He then recalled his Vizier Ibrahim from Egypt; and, by his advice, determined to lead his armies into Hungary, with which country he was still at war, though no important operations had taken place since the campaign of Belgrade. Solyman was at this time vehemently urged to invade Hungary by Francis I. of France, who wished to distract the arms of his rival Charles V.; (Von Hammer, vol. ii.), and, on the other hand, an ambassador had been sent from Persia, the natural foe of Turkey, to the courts of Charles and the King of Hungary, to form a defensive and offensive league against the Ottomans, (*ibid*).

In 1526, the *Sultan* invaded Hungary with an army more than

100,000 strong, and 300 pieces of artillery. Like his predecessors Selim and Mahomet II., he paid extreme attention to this important arm of war; and, throughout his reign, the artillery of the Ottomans was far superior in number, in weight of metal, in equipment, and in the skill of the gunners, to that possessed by any other nation. King Louis of Hungary rashly gave battle, with a far inferior force, to the invaders. The Hungarian chivalry charged with their wonted gallantry; and a chosen band forced their way to where Solyman had taken his station at the head of his Janissaries.

The *Sultan* owed his life to his *cuirass*, against which the lance of a Magyar knight was shivered. But the fiery valour of the "furious Hun" was vain against superior numbers, arms, and discipline. In less than two hours the fate of Hungary was decided. King Louis, eight of his bishops, the greater number of the Magyar nobles, and 24,000 Hungarians of lower rank had perished. Search was made by the victors for the body of King Louis, which was found in a stream near the field of battle. Louis had been wounded in the head, and was endeavouring to escape, but his horse was forced from the bank by the throng of the fliers, and the weight of his armour bore him down in the deep water.

The *Sultan* felt a generous sorrow on learning the fate of his rival sovereign, who was nearly his equal in years. Solyman exclaimed:

> May *Allah* be merciful to him, and punish those who misled his inexperience. I came indeed in arms against him; but it was not my wish that he should thus be cut off, while he had scarcely tasted the sweets of life and royalty.

This battle was fought at Mohacz, on the 28th August, 1526, and is still known by the terribly expressive name of "the Destruction of Mohacz."

After this decisive victory, Solyman marched along the Danube to the twin cities of Buda (or Ofen) and Pesth, on the opposite banks of that river, and the capital of Hungary at once submitted to him. The *Akindji* swept the whole country with fire and desolation; and it seemed as if it was the object of the Ottomans to make a desert rather than a province of Hungary. At last, at the end of September, Solyman began his homeward march. His soldiers were laden with the richest plunder; and they drove before them a miserable herd of 100,000 Christians, men, women, and little children, destined for sale in the Turkish slave-markets.

Disturbances in Asia Minor had hastened Solyman's departure

from Hungary, but he returned in the third year, still more menacing and more formidable. The strode was now to be with Austria; and the next campaign of Solyman, the campaign of the first siege of Vienna, is one of the most important in German and in Ottoman history.

Solyman entered Hungary in 1529 under the pretext of placing on the throne the right successor to King Louis, who fell at Mohacz. That prince died without issue; and the Archduke Ferdinand of Austria, brother of Charles V., claimed the crown as Louis's brother-in-law, and by virtue of an old treaty. But there was an ancient law of Hungary, by which none but a native prince could occupy the throne; and a powerful noble, named Zapolya, appealed to this in opposition to Ferdinand, and procured some of the surviving magnates of the land to elect him as king.

A civil war ensued, in which the adherents of Ferdinand and his Austrian forces defeated Zapolya's troops, and drove him from the kingdom. Zapolya then took the desperate step of applying for aid to the Sultan. Ferdinand, alarmed on hearing of this proceeding of his rival, sent an embassy to Constantinople to negotiate for a peace with Solyman, or at least to obtain a truce. His envoys had the ill-timed boldness to require, at the same time, the restoration of Belgrade and of the chief places which the Turks had captured in Hungary.

Nothing could exceed the arrogance shown by the Ottoman ministers to the rival claimants of the Hungarian throne. The *grand vizier* told the Polish Palatine Lasczky, who acted as ambassador for Zapolya, that every place where the hoof of the Sultan's horse once trod, became at once, and for ever, part of the *Sultan's* dominions. The *vizier* said:

> We have slain King Louis of Hungary, his kingdom is now ours, to hold, or to give to whom we list. Thy master is no king of Hungary till we make him so. It is not the crown that makes the king—it is the sword. It is the sword that brings men into subjection; and what the sword has won, the sword must keep.

He promised, however, that Zapolya should be king, and that the *Sultan* should protect him against Ferdinand of Austria and all his other enemies. Solyman himself confirmed his *vizier's* promise; and added:

> I will be a true friend to thy master. I will march in person to aid him. I swear it, by our Prophet Mahomet, the beloved of God, and by my sabre.

Ferdinand's ambassadors were dismissed with indignant scorn. They were ordered to say from Solyman to Ferdinand, that hitherto there had been little acquaintance or neighbourhood between them; but that they soon should be intimate enough. He would speedily visit Ferdinand, and drive him from the kingdom he had stolen. Solyman said:

> Tell him, that I will look for him on the field of Mohacz, or even in Pesth; and if he fail to meet me there, I will offer him battle beneath the walls of Vienna itself."

These were no idle menaces from the Lord of the Age; and the forces of the Ottoman Empire were speedily mustered for the march from Constantinople to Vienna.

Solyman left Constantinople on the 10th May, 1529, with an army of 250,000 men and 300 cannons. A season of almost incessant rain made their march to the Danube laborious and slow; and it was the 3rd of September before the *Sultan* reached Ofen, which had been occupied by the troops of Ferdinand during the preceding year. Ofen was taken in six days, and Zapolya was solemnly installed by the Turkish victors on the ancient throne of the dynasty of Arpad. The *Sultan* then continued his advance to Vienna, taking with him his vassal king, and a corps of the Hungarians who recognised Zapolya as their sovereign.

With the storms of the autumnal equinox, the first squadrons of the terrible irregular cavalry of the Turks swept round the walls of Vienna. These *Akindji*, 30,000 strong, called by the French "*Faucheurs*" and "*Ecorcheurs*"—"*mowers*" and "*flayers*"—by the Germans "*Sackmen*," were led by Michael Oglou, the descendant of Michael of the Peaked Beard, who had been the friend of the first Othman. These ferocious marauders, who received no pay, and whose cruelty exceeded even their rapacity, spread devastation and slaughter throughout all Austria, as far as the River Ems. On the eve of the feast of St. Wenceslaus (27th September), Solyman himself arrived with the main Turkish army beneath Vienna, and fixed the imperial headquarters on the high ground to the west of the village of Simmering.

12,000 *Janissaries* were posted round the *Sultan's* tent. Seven encampments were raised by the various divisions of the army, forming nearly a circle round Vienna: and the whole country west of the Danube, far as the eye could range from the highest steeple in the city, was white with the Moslem tents. The water-meadows and islands of the

Danube, and its branches near the city, were also strongly occupied; and a flotilla of 400 Turkish barks, well-manned and commanded, watched the city by water, and kept up the communication between the besieging troops.

The force that defended Vienna amounted to only 16,000 men; and, when the campaign began, the fortifications of the city consisted of little more than a continuous wall, about six feet thick, without bastions; the artillery amounted to only seventy-two guns. King Ferdinand had exerted himself earnestly to induce the other German princes to aid him; but his brother, the Emperor Charles, was occupied with his own ambitious schemes in Italy; and the princes of the empire, to whom Ferdinand had appealed at the Diet of Spires, thought more of their religious differences with each other than of the common danger of their fatherland, though warned by Ferdinand that Sultan Solyman had declared his determination to carry his arms to the Rhine. The Diet voted aid; but it was inadequate and tardy; and, while the princes deliberated, the Turk was in Austria Ferdinand himself dreaded Solyman's threats, and kept aloof from Vienna.

But some brave Christian leaders succeeded in forcing their way into the city before it was entirely beleaguered; and a body of Spanish and German veterans, under the Palgrave Philip, proved an invaluable reinforcement to the garrison. But, though the Christian defenders of Vienna were few, they were brave and well commanded. The Palgrave Philip was the nominal superior, but the veteran Count of Salm was the real director of the defence. All possible preparations were made while the Turks were yet approaching. The suburbs were destroyed.

A new earthen rampart was raised within the city; the river bank was palisadoed; provisions and stores were collected; and the women and children, and all the other inhabitants who were unable to do service as combatants or as labourers, were compelled to leave the city. Providentially for Vienna, the incessant rains, and the consequent badness of the roads, had caused the Turks to leave part of their heaviest artillery in Hungary. They were obliged to rely chiefly on the effect of mines for breaching the walls; but the numbers, and the zeal of the besiegers, made the fall of the city apparently inevitable.

Many sallies and partial assaults took place, in which great gallantry was displayed on both sides; and infinite skill and devotion were shown by the defenders in counteracting the mining operations of their enemies. But the Ottoman engineers succeeded in springing several mines, which tore open large gaps in the defences; and on three consecutive days, the 10th, 11th, and 12th of October, the Turks assaulted the city with desperation, but were repelled with heavy carnage by the steady valour of the besieged. The Ottoman forces now began to suffer severely by scarcity of provisions, and by the inclemency of the season; and the slaughter which had fallen on their best troops filled the army with discouragement.

But it was resolved to make one more attempt to carry Vienna; and, on the 14th of October, the Turkish infantry, in three huge columns, charged up to the breach, which their miners and cannoneers had rent for their road to victory and plunder. Solyman had endeavoured to stimulate their courage and emulation by a liberal distribution of money, and by the promise of high rank and wealth to the Moslem who should be first on the crest of the breach. The *grand vizier* and the highest officers of the army accompanied the stormers: and when the Christian cannons and musketry roared forth their deadly welcome, and the dispirited Mahometans reeled back from the bloodstained ruins, the Turkish chiefs were seen amid the confusion, striving, after the old Oriental custom, to force their men on again to the assault by blows with stick and whip and sword. (One of the Assyrian *bas-reliefs* discovered by Mr. Layard represents an officer with a whip in his hand, directing the passage of a river by the troops).

But even the best veterans now sullenly refused obedience, and said that they had rather be killed by the sabres of their own officers than by the long muskets of the Spaniards and the German spits, as they called the long swords of the *lanzknechts*, (*Two Sieges of Vienna by the Turks*). About three in the afternoon, the Turkish engineers sprung two new mines, which threw down much more of the wall; and under cover of a fire from all their batteries, the *Sultan's* troops were again formed into columns, and brought forward once more up to the breach. It was only to heap it again with Turkish dead.

The hero of the defence, Count Salm, received a wound on the last day of the siege that proved ultimately fatal: but though other chiefs had fallen;—though the Ottoman shot and shell had told severely among the Christian ranks:—though many brave men had perished in sorties, and in hand-to-hand conflict in the breaches;—and though many had been swept away by the bursting of the Turkish mines, the courage of the garrison grew higher and higher at each encounter with their lately boastful, but now despairing foes.

Solyman himself felt at last compelled to abandon the favourite project of his heart, and drew his troops finally back from the much-coveted city. The 14th of October, the day on which Vienna was saved from the greatest of the *Sultans*, is marked by the German historian as being made memorable in his country's history by many great events. It is the day of the fall of Brisach (1639), of the peace of Westphalia (1648), of the Battle of Hochkirken (1758), of the surrender of Jim (1805), of the Battle of Jena (1806), and of the overthrow of Napoleon at the Battle of the Nations at Leipsic in 1813. (Von Hammer, vol. ii.).

It was near midnight, after the repulse of Solyman's last assault upon Vienna that its full effect appeared. The *Janissaries* then, by the *Sultan's* order, struck their tents; and all the spoil which had been swept into the Turkish camp, and which could not be carried away, was given to the flames. At the same time, the disappointed and savage soldiery commenced a general massacre of thousands of Christian captives, whom the deadly activity of the *Akindji* had brought in during the three weeks of the siege. The fairest girls and boys were preserved to be led into slavery, but the rest were put to the sword, or thrown yet alive into the flames without mercy.

After this last act of barbarous but impotent malignity, the Turkish army retreated from Vienna. Solyman's courtiers pretended to congratulate him as victorious; and he himself assumed the tone of a conqueror, whom the fugitive Ferdinand had not dared to meet, and who had magnanimously retired after chastising, though not destroying his foes. But the reverse, which he had sustained, was felt deeply by him throughout his life; and it was said that he laid a curse upon any of his descendants who should renew the enterprise against Vienna.

There is no foundation for the charge which later writers have brought against the Grand Vizier Ibrahim, of haying been bribed to betray his master, and to baffle the operations of the besiegers, (Von Hammer, vol. ii.). The city was saved by the heroism of her defenders, aided, unquestionably, by the severity of the season, which the Asiatic troops in the Ottoman Army could ill endure, and by the insubordination of the impatient *Janissaries*. But, whatever be the cause assigned to it, the repulse of Solyman from Vienna is an epoch in the history of the world.

The tide of Turkish conquest in central Europe had now set its mark. The wave once again dashed as far; but only to be again broken, and then to recede for ever.

Chapter 12

The Great Siege of Malta

A peace was concluded between the *Sultan* and Ferdinand in 1533, by which Hungary was divided between Ferdinand and Zapolya. Solyman had, in the interval, again invaded Germany with forces even stronger than those which he led against Vienna; and as Charles V., on this occasion (1532), put himself at the head of the armies of the empire, which gathered zealously around him, a decisive conflict between the two great potentates of Christendom and Islam was anxiously expected. But Solyman was checked in his advance by the obstinate defence of the little town of Güns; and after honourable terms had been granted to the brave garrison of that place (29th August, 1532), Solyman finding that Charles did not come forward to meet him, but remained posted near Vienna, turned aside from the line of march against that city; and, after desolating Styria, returned to his own dominions.

Each, probably, of these two great sovereigns was unwilling to risk life, and empire, and the glorious fruits of so many years of toil and care, on the event of a single day; and neither was sorry that his adversary's lukewarmness for battle furnished a creditable excuse for his own. The warlike energies of the Ottomans were now for some time chiefly employed in the East, where the unremitted enmity of Persia to Turkey, and the consequent wars between these two great Mahometan powers, were a cause of relief to Christendom, which her diplomatists of that age freely acknowledged.

✴✴✴✴✴✴

Busbequius, Ferdinand's ambassador at Solyman's court, says: "'Tis only the Persian stands between us and ruin. The Turk would fain be upon us, but he keeps him back. This war with him affords us only a respite, not a deliverance."

✴✴✴✴✴✴

Solyman led his armies against the Persians in several campaigns (1533, 1534, 1535, 1548, 1553, 1554), during which the Turks often suffered severely through the difficult nature of the countries through which they traversed, as well as through the bravery and activity of the enemy. But the *Sultan* effected many important conquests. He added to the Ottoman Empire large territories in Armenia and Mesopotamia, and the strong cities of Erivan, Van, Mosul, and, above all, of Bagdad, which the Orientals call "The Mansion of Victory."

The modern Turk, who seeks consolation in remembering the glories of the Great Solyman, must dwell with peculiar satisfaction on the tokens of respectful fear, which his nation then received from the most powerful as well as from the weaker states of Christendom. And the year 1547 is made a peculiarly proud one in the annals of the House of Othman, by the humble concession which its rival, the Austrian House of Hapsburg, was then compelled to make to its superior strength and fortune.

The war in Hungary had been renewed in consequence of the death of John Zapolya, in 1539; upon which event Ferdinand claimed the whole of Hungary, while the widow of Zapolya implored the assistance of the *Sultan* in behalf of her infant son. Solyman poured his armies into that country, and in 1541, and the following years, he again commanded in person on the banks of the Danube. He professed the intention of placing the young Prince Zapolya on the throne of Hungary and Transylvania, when he should have attained the age of manhood; but Ofen and the other chief cities were now garrisoned with Turkish troops; the country was allotted into *Sanjaks*, over which Turkish governors were appointed: and the Ottoman provincial system was generally established.

The strong cities of Gran, Stuhlweissenburg, and many others, were taken by the Turks in this war; and though their success was not unvaried, the general advantage was so far on the side of the Sultan, that as early as 1544 Charles V. and Ferdinand made overtures for peace; and in 1547 a truce for five years was concluded, which left the Sultan in possession of nearly 'the whole of Hungary and Transylvania, and which bound Ferdinand to pay to the Sublime Porte 30,000 *ducats* a year—a payment which the Austrians called a present, but the Ottoman historians more correctly term a tribute.

This treaty, to which the Emperor Charles, the Pope, the King of France, and the Republic of Venice were parties, may be considered as a recognition by Christendom of the truth of Solyman's; title, "*Sa-*

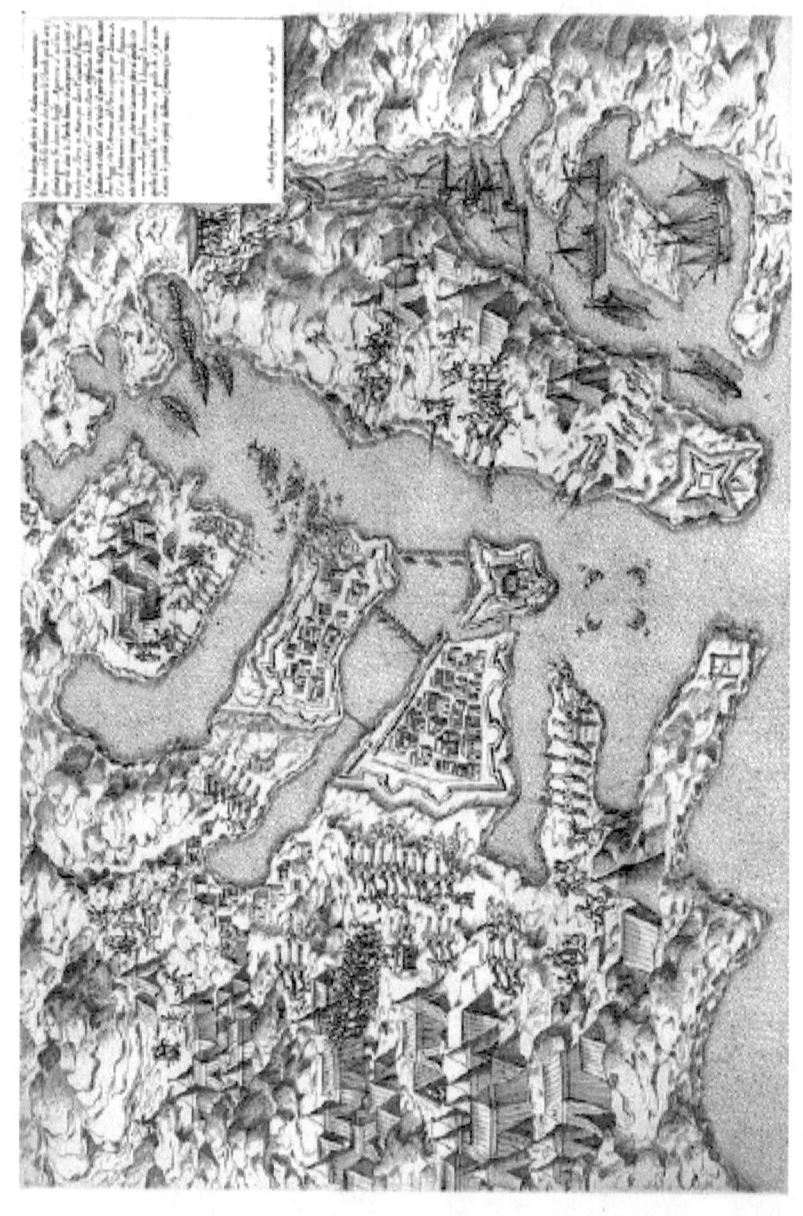

hibi Kiran," "Lord of his Age." Austrian pride, indeed, had previously stooped so low before the Sultan, that King Ferdinand, when seeking peace in 1533, consented to style himself the brother of Ibrahim, Solyman's favourite minister, and thus to place himself on the level of a Turkish *vizier*. Francis I. had repeatedly sought the aid of Solyman in the most deferential and submissive terms. That aid was more than once effectively given by the Turkish invasions of Hungary and Germany, which compelled the emperor to draw the weight of his arms from off France; and, still more directly, by the Turkish fleets which were sent into the Mediterranean to attack the enemies of the French king.

★★★★★★

As early as 1525, while Francis was a prisoner at Madrid, the aid of the young Sultan Solyman had been implored and promised in his behalf. Hellert, the French translator of Von Hammer, gives in his notes to the fifth volume of his translation, a translation of a remarkable letter of Solyman to Francis, promising him assistance, which has been discovered in the French archives. The letter is couched in the loftiest strain of haughty generosity, and bids the French monarch, now that he has laid his petition before the throne which is the refuge of the world, fear no longer the enemy who has threatened and ravaged his dominions, and made him captive. M. Hellert gives another letter of Sultan Solyman's to Francis, written in 1528, in answer to requests made by the French king in favour of the Christians of the Latin Church at Jerusalem. M. Hellert truly says that the *Sultan's* letter shows a spirit of justice, and religious toleration, as honourable as it was rare, especially in the age in which it was written.

★★★★★★

England, during the reign of Solyman, had no need of foreign help; but we shall see her in the reign of Solyman's grandson, when menaced by the power of Spain, have recourse to the Sublime Porte for aid and protection, as respectfully and earnestly as the proudest Follower of the Prophet could desire.

We have hitherto directed our chief attention to the military history of Solyman's reign; but the awe which the Ottoman Empire inspired in this age, was due not only to the successes gained by the Turkish armies, but also to the achievements of the Turkish navy, which extended the power and the renown of Sultan Solyman along all the coast of the Mediterranean, and in the more remote waters of the Red Sea and the Indian Ocean. His predecessors had devoted much care and treasure to the maritime force of their empire, but they were all surpassed in this respect by Solyman; and the skill and valour of his admirals made the Ottoman flag almost as formidable by sea as it was by land. The most celebrated of the Turkish naval commanders in this reign was Khaireddin Pacha, better known in Europe by the surname of Barbarossa. It was principally by his means that the piratical states of North Africa placed themselves under the sovereignty of the *Sultan*; and that the naval resources of the Sublime Porte were augmented by the commodious havens, the strong forts and cities, the well-built and well-found squadrons, and the daring and skilful *corsairs* of Algiers, Tripoli, and Tunis.

******

A description of the system of Mediterranean warfare of this age, and of the character of the vessels employed in it, may be found useful; and I subjoin one, which I have partly drawn from Fincham's *Naval History*, but chiefly from an admirable paper by Mr. Hulme in his *Chapters on Turkish History*.

The names commonly given to vessels of war in the Mediterranean daring this century, were *galley*, *galleon*, and *galleas*. The two last are names familiar to the student of the history of the Spanish Armada. They both were applied to vessels of considerable size, and some *galleons* and *galleases* are said to have been of from 1500 to 2000 tons burthen. They had more than one deck, and heavy cannon were used by means of portholes on the lower decks, as well as the upper.

They were very lofty at both stem and stern. Guns were mounted on the elevated poop; and also on the forecastle, a term which then was strictly accurate. These large vessels, which were also called carracks, had one or more tiers of long oars, each worked by several rowers, but they depended principally on their masts and sails for locomotion. But though large ships of this description were used in war, it was not in them but in the long, low, light galleys, that the principal force of contending navies consisted. In order to understand this, we must bear in mind the difference between the naval gunnery of those times and our own; and how much less the peril was, which small and light craft then incurred by exposing themselves to the broadside of those of far superior tonnage.

The galleys with which the sea-captains of Venice, Genoa, Barcelona, Carthagena, Malta, Algiers, and Constantinople performed their chief exploits, during the fifteenth and sixteenth centuries, were essentially rowboats; and the oars were usually pulled by slaves or prisoners of war.

The hull lay very low and close to the water, extremely sharp built and straight in the run, and of such extraordinary length in proportion to the beam or width, that the Venetian galleys of the largest class, which measured 165 feet from stem to stern, were only thirty-two feet in total breadth. The prow was furnished, as of old, with a long and sharp beak: and from this, as well as from the usually black colour of the hull, the epithet of *grab* (literally raven) was popularly applied to these vessels by the Moors. The after-part was occupied by an extensive poop or quarter-deck, which was the station of the captain and the soldiers, and which was defended on the quarter by galleries and boarding-nettings.

From this a descent of two or three steps led to a long narrow platform called in French *coursier*, and in Spanish *cruxia*, running the whole length of the vessel from the forecastle to the poop, and serving both for a gangway and a flush deck; on this the guns were mounted, usually a single long heavy piece pointed forwards in a groove near the bow, and two or four others of smaller calibre amidships. The rowing benches (to which the galley-slaves were usually chained by one foot) were arranged on a sort of sloping gallery or wide gunwale (in French *pont*), which projected over the ship's side, so that those who rowed in the highest rank were immediately below the *coursier*, and under the eye of their taskmasters, who quickened their exertions by the unsparing use of the lash.

The galley was pulled with twenty-six oars on a side—a number which seems to have been nearly invariable in all rates; but the smaller classes (*galères subtiles*, or *legères*, called *fergata* or frigate, and *khirlangitsch* by the Turks, and by the Moors *jafan* and *thelthi*) had only one or two men to each oar; the largest (*galeazza* of the Venetians, and *maona* of the Turks) had sometimes even as many as five or six; those of the ordinary rate (*galères bâtardes*, whence the Turkish *bashtarda*), which were almost exclusively employed by the Turks, had three.

The galley was provided with a main and foremast, which might

be raised or struck as required, and which carried large lateen sails; but a craft of the construction just described could only have been trusted under sail in light winds and smooth seas, as her want of heel, and deficiency in beam, must have made her at all times a bad sea-boat; while her great length must have exposed her to break her back and founder in a rough sea.

But these disadvantages were compensated by the swiftness with which vessels so navigated could be impelled, like the steamboats of modern days, over the smooth summer seas of the Mediterranean, and by the facility with which they penetrated into creeks, rivers, and inlets, which the intricacy or shallowness of their waters rendered impervious to vessels of draught, and depending only on sails.

With their masts lowered, and their long, low hulls indiscernible on the surface of the sea by the sentinels on shore, the *corsair* galleys lay during the day unsuspected in the offing, opposite to a town which they had marked for plunder; at midnight the inhabitants were roused by the flames of their dwellings, and the fierce cry of the *tecbir*, and daybreak saw the marauders again far at sea, bearing with them their booty, and such of their captives as had been spared from the slaughter, long ere the ineffectual aid of the neighbouring garrisons could reach the scene of devastation.

✶✶✶✶✶✶

Barbarossa was born in the island of Mitylene. His father, a *Spahi* of Roumelia, had settled there when the island was conquered by Mahomet II. Of four sons, the eldest, Ishak, traded as a merchant in Mitylene; the other three, Elias, Urudsch, and Khizr (afterwards called Khaireddin), practised commerce and piracy conjointly during the reign of Bajazet II. and Selim. Elias fell in a sea-fight with the Knights of Rhodes. Urudsch was taken prisoner, but was released through the influence of Prince Korkoud, then governor of Caramania. Urudsch and Khaireddin next practised as bold and fortunate sea-rovers, under Mohammed the Sultan of Tunis. They saw, however, the feebleness of the Mahometan Princes of the North African seaports, and they knew the strength of the Ottoman Empire, especially under such a ruler as Selim. They paid court therefore to the Sublime Porte, by sending one of their richest prizes to Constantinople, and received in return two galleys and robes of honour.

They now made themselves masters of some small towns on the

African coast; and being joined by their brother, Ishak, the merchant of Mitylene, they increased their squadron, and succeeded in taking possession by force or by stratagem of Tennes and Telmessan, and also of the strong city of Algiers. Ishak and Urudsch soon after this fell in battle with the Spaniards, and Khaireddin was left sole master of their conquests. He formally recognised the sovereignty of the Turkish *Sultan*, and received from Selim the regular insignia of office, a sabre, a horse, and a banner, as *beyler bey* of Algiers.

Khaireddin carried on active war against the Spaniards, and the independent Arab tribes of North Africa. He took from the Spaniards the little island in front of the port of Algiers, which had for fourteen years been in their occupation; and he defeated and captured a Spanish squadron which was sent to succour the garrison. Acting steadily up to his policy of professing allegiance to the Sublime Porte, Barbarossa sent regular reports of his operations to Constantinople, and desisted, in obedience to orders received thence, from attacking the ships or coasts of France, when that country became connected by treaty with Turkey.

The red-bearded Sea-King of Algiers was now required by Sultan Solyman to measure himself with a formidable opponent in the Genoese Doria, Charles V.'s favourite admiral. Barbarossa repulsed Doria's attack on the island of Djerbel; and then joining his galleys with those of the *corsair*, Sinan, he sailed in triumph along the Genoese coast, which he swept with fire and devastation. He next conveyed 70,000 of the persecuted Moors of Spain from Andalusia to strengthen his own Algerine dominions. In the meanwhile, Doria had captured from the Turks the city of Koron, in the Morea; and Solyman, who recognised in Barbarossa the only Mahometan admiral that could compete with the Genoese hero, sent for Khaireddin to Constantinople to consult with him as to the best mode of carrying on the war by sea against the Spaniards.

Khaireddin set sail from Algiers (1533) in obedience to his *padischah's* commands, with eighteen vessels, five of which belonged to pirates, who had volunteered into the *Sultan's* service; and he captured on the voyage two of Doria's galleys. He was received by the Sublime Porte with the highest honours; and under his personal direction the arsenals of Constantinople were busy throughout that winter with the equipment of a powerful fleet of eighty-four vessels (including the Algerine squadron), with which Barbarossa sailed for Italy in the spring of 1534, while Solyman was commencing his campaign against Persia. Barbarossa (now Khaireddin Pacha), sacked Reggio, Citraro, Sperlonga, and Fondi. His attack on the last-mentioned place was made principally in the hope of surprising and carrying off the celebrated beauty of the age, Giulia Gonzaga, the wife of Vespasian Gonzaga.

Barbarossa wished to present her as a courtly offering to Solyman, and he designed that the flower of the fair of Christendom should shine in his *Sultan's harem*. Barbarossa's crews landed stealthily in the night, and assailed Fondi so vigorously, that the beautiful Giulia was only roused from sleep by the alarm that the Turks were in her palace. Evading their hot pursuit with the greatest difficulty and danger, she was set on horseback in her nightdress by an Italian cavalier, who rescued and rode off with her alone to a place of safety. The sensitive beauty afterwards caused her preserver and companion to be assassinated, whether it was, says the German historian, that he had dared too much on that night, or that he had only seen too much. (Von Hammer, vol. ii. Giulia was the sister of "the divine" Joanna of Aragon, whose portraits are to be seen at Borne, Paris, and Warwick Castle).

After plundering the Neapolitan coasts, Barbarossa stood across to Africa, and captured Tunis, which had long been the object of his ambition. He did not, however, retain this prize more than five months. The Moorish prince, whom he expelled, implored the assistance of Charles V.; and the emperor led to Tunis an army and fleet of such strength, that Barbarossa, after a brave and skilful defence, was obliged to abandon the city. The coldblooded and unsparing cruelty with which, after Barbarossa's retreat, the unresisting and unoffending city was sacked by the Christian forces which had come thither as the nominal allies of its rightful king, equalled the worst atrocities that have ever been imputed to the Turks.

Though driven from Tunis, Khaireddin was still strong at Algiers, and, sailing from that port with seventeen galleys, he took revenge on Spain by plundering Minorca, and he then repaired to Constantinople, where the Sultan conferred on him the highest naval dignity, that of Capitan Pacha. In 1537, he again desolated the shores of Italy; and when Venice took part in the war against the Sublime Porte, Barbarossa captured from her nearly all the islands that she had possessed in the Archipelago, and the cities of Napoli di Romania, and Castel Nuovo. He recovered Koron from the Spaniards; and on the 28th September, 1538, he engaged the combined fleets of the Pope, Venice, and the Emperor in a great battle off Prevesa.

Barbarossa on this occasion practised the bold manoeuvre of cutting the line, which Rodney, St. Vincent, and Nelson made afterwards so celebrated in the English navy. The Turkish admiral's force was inferior to the enemy in number and size of vessels and in weight of metal; but by seamanship and daring, Barbarossa gained a complete and glorious victory, though the coming on of night enabled the defeated Christians to escape without very heavy loss.

The disastrous reverse which Charles V. sustained when he attacked Algiers in 1541, was chiefly the work of the elements. Barbarossa commanded the Turkish fleet sent by Solyman to protect Algiers, but he was detained in harbour by the same tempest that shattered the ships of Spain. The last great service in which Khaireddin was employed by the *Sultan*, was in 1543, when he was sent with the Turkish fleet to assist Francis I., and acted in conjunction with the French squadron in the Mediterranean. He captured the city of Nice, though the castle held out against him; and he is said to have roughly reproved the French officers for their negligence, and for the defective state of their ships as to equipment and necessary stores. The allies, whom he came to protect, were obliged to listen submissively to his rebukes; and it was only by the earnest entreaties and apologies of the French admiral, the Duc d'Enghien, that the choler of the old Turkish veteran was appeased.

During the latter years of Barbarossa's life, he was, when not employed at sea, a regular attendant, as Capitan Pacha, at the *Divan* of the Sublime Porte, where the counsels of the old admiral were always listened to with respect. He died in 1546; and his tomb on the side of the Bosphorus near Beschiktasch still invites attention by the romantic beauty of its site, and by the recollection of the bold *corsair*, who sleeps there by the side of the sounding sea, which so long he ruled. His wealth had been principally devoted by him to the foundation of a college: a striking tribute to the general respect for literature and science which prevailed in Solyman's court, and which exercised its influence over even the rugged temper of Barbarossa, who, from the circumstances of his early life, could not possibly have been a Turkish Raleigh.

******

The true biography of Barbarossa has been little known in western Europe before the German Von Hammer narrated it from the full and indisputable authorities which are found in the Ottoman literature. Barbarossa himself had, by Sultan Solyman's order, dictated an account of his life and adventures to a writer named Sinan, which is still extant; and it is also epitomised and embodied in the *History of the Naval Wars of the Turks*, written by Hadji Khalssa.

******

Some, however, of the Ottoman admirals were themselves eminent for their scientific attainments, and for their contributions to the literature of the country. Such were Piri Reis, and Sidi Ali, two of the commanders of the squadrons which by Solyman's orders were equipped in the ports of the Red Sea, and which, issuing thence, conquered for the Sultan of Constantinople the port of Aden, which England now possesses, and justly values for its important position in the line of European commerce with India by the Red Sea and Egypt.

******

I had the advantage in 1868 of going over the lines round Aden in company with a distinguished engineer officer in the Indian Military Service. The traces and remnants of the old Turkish fortifications were clearly discernible; and my companion eulogised highly the scientific skill with which they had been designed, and the judicious labour bestowed on them, as well as upon the vast reservoirs of water, which have been restored and improved since Aden has been a British possession.

******

Many other cities and districts on the coasts of Arabia, Persia, and the north-west of India were added to the Ottoman Empire; and many gallant contests were sustained with the Portuguese, as well as with the native rulers, by the Turkish admirals, the octogenarian Solyman Pacha and Mourad, and the two whose names have been already mentioned. Piri Reis was the author of two geographical works, one on the Ægean, and one on the Mediterranean Sea, in which their currents, their soundings, their harbours, and their best landing-places were described from personal surveys. Sidi Ali was a poet as well as a sailor; and besides his productions in verse, he wrote a description of his travel overland to Constantinople from Goojerat, where his fleet had been damaged by tempests so as to be no longer able to cope with the Portuguese.

Sidi Ali was also the author of several mathematical and nautical treatises, and of a work called *Mouhit*, on the navigation of the Indian Sea, which he drew from the best Arabian and Persian authorities of his time on the subject of India. (Von Hammer states that copies of the work of Piri Reis on the Archipelago and Mediterranean are to be found in the Royal Libraries at Berlin and Dresden, in the Vatican, and at Bologna. The only known copy of Sidi Ali's *Mouhit* is at Naples).

Two other Turkish admirals of this reign must not be omitted, Dragut (more correctly called Torghoud) and Pialé. Pialé was a Croatian by birth, Dragut was born a subject of the *Sultan*, but of Christian parentage. He, early in life, joined the crew of a Turkish galley, and was chosen captain of a band of thirty sea rovers. He collected a force of thirty vessels, and attacked the Island of Corsica, but was defeated by Doria, who took him prisoner, and chained him to the bench of his galley, where Dragut toiled at the victor's oar for many a weary month.

At last Barbarossa rescued him by threatening to lay Genoa waste if Dragut was not set free; and under the patronage of Khaireddin, Dragut soon reappeared on the waves, chief of a squadron of twenty galleys, that spread terror along the coasts of Italy and Spain. He made himself master of Mehdijé and Tripoli; and, following the example of Barbarossa, he acknowledged himself to be the *Sultan's* vassal, and received in return high rank and substantial aid from Constantinople. The Spaniards took Mehdijé from him; but Dragut had more than once the advantage of Doria in their encounters, and was almost as much dreaded in the Mediterranean as Barbarossa himself. His boldness of spirit was shown even towards the Sultan. He had on one occasion been tempted by the sight of a rich fleet of Venetian *argosies*, and had captured them, though there was peace at that time between the Republic of St. Mark and the Porte.

Dragut was ordered to Constantinople to answer for this outrage, and, as the Grand Vizier Roostem was his enemy, his head was in serious peril. But Dragut, instead of obeying the order of recall, sailed out of the Straits of Gibraltar, and took service under the Emperor of Morocco, until Solyman, after Barbarossa's death, recalled him by pledge of pardon and ample promises of promotion. We shall soon have occasion to notice his final services and death at the siege of Malta.

Pialé Pacha was chiefly signalised during the reign of Solyman by the capture of Oran, and by the great defeat which he gave in 1560 to the combined Christian fleets that were destined for Tripoli and the isle of Djerbé. Two hundred vessels were prepared for this expedition by the Pope, and by the rulers of Genoa, Florence, Malta, Sicily, and Naples. Doria was high admiral of the fleet, and Don Alvaro de Sandi commanded the army which it conveyed. The fleet effected the passage to Djerbé in safety; the troops were landed; the island nearly subdued, and a fortress erected. But before the Christian galleys left the waters of Djerbé, Pialé had heard of the attack, and had left the Dardanelles with a fleet which was reinforced at Modon by the squadrons of the governors of Rhodes and Mitylene.

On the 14th May, 1560, he attacked Doria's fleet, and completely defeated it. Twenty galleys and twenty-seven transports of the Christians were destroyed; seven galleys ran for shelter up the channel of Djerbé, where they were subsequently captured; the rest fled to Italy, leaving their comrades of the land forces to be besieged and captured in their new fortress by the troops, whom the active Pialé soon brought together against them. On the 27th of September Pialé re-entered the harbour of Constantinople in triumph. He had previously sent a vessel to announce his victory, which appeared in the Golden Horn with the captured high standard of Spain trailing in the sea behind her stern.

On the day of the arrival of Pialé Solyman went to the kiosk of his palace, at the water's edge, to honour with his presence the triumphal procession of his Capitan Pacha. Don Alvaro and other Christian prisoners of high rank were placed conspicuous on the poop of the Ottoman admiral's galley, and the captured vessels were towed along rudderless and dismasted. Those who were near Sultan Solyman observed that his aspect on this proud day of triumph bore the same grave and severely calm expression, which was its usual characteristic. The ambassador of King Ferdinand, who was present, attributed this stoical composure to magnanimity, and admired "the great heart of that old sire," which received unmoved anything that fortune could bring.

★★★★★★

"*Eadem erat frontis severitas et tristitis, ac si nihil ad eum haec victoria pertineret, nihil novum aut inexpectatum contigisset. Tam capax in illo sene quantaevis fortunae pectus, tam confidens animus, ut tantam gratulationem velut immotus acciperet.*"—Busbequius. Old Knolles translates this nobly: "I myself saw him with the same countenance that he had always; with the same severity and gravity; as if the victory had nothing concerned him, nor anything chanced strange or unexpected; so capable was the great heart of that old sire of any fortune, were it never so great, and his mind so settled as to receive so great applause and rejoicing without moving."

★★★★★★

The modern German historian of the House of Othman points out that this unexulting austerity of the great *Sultan* may have been caused by the domestic affliction, which by this time he had sustained, and which may have steeled while it saddened his heart. (Von Hammer, vol. ii.).

Glorious, indeed, and prosperous as had been the reign of Solyman the Magnificent, he had, as a man, drunken deeply of sorrow and remorse; and the *Erinnys* of family bloodshed, that for so many centuries has haunted the House of Othman, was fatally active in his generation. To be friendless is the common penalty of despotic power; and Solyman must have felt it the more severely, inasmuch as he appears naturally to have had a capacity for friendship, and to have sought earnestly for it in the early part of his reign. His celebrated *grand vizier*, Ibrahim, was for many years not only his most trusted councillor and general, but the companion of his pleasures and his studies. Yet his suspicions were at last raised against the over-powerful and incautious favourite; and a *vizier*, whom a *Sultan* begins to dread, has not long to live.

Ibrahim was married to Solyman's sister, but not even this close affinity could save him. Ibrahim came to the palace at Constantinople on the 5th March, 1536, to dine with the *Sultan*, as was his custom; and when on the next morning messengers from his home came to seek him, they found him strangled. The state of his body showed that he had struggled hard for life; and, a hundred years afterwards, the traces of his blood on the palace walls were pointed out; fearful warnings of the lot that awaited those who sought to win their entrance there as royal favourites. Von Hammer gives a long list of other high officers whom Solyman once honoured and trusted, but whom he ultimately gave to the fatal bowstring.

******

Von Hammer remarks as an occurrence without parallel in Turkish history, the suicide of one of Solyman's officers, Khosrew Pacha, who starved himself to death, on being deprived of the government of Bosnia. The profound feeling of submission to the Divine Will, which characterises the Mussulmans, makes suicide almost unknown in Mahometan countries. Another high officer of Solyman's, Loutfi Pacha, who was cashiered by the *Sultan* about the same time, acted much more wisely than Khosrew. He employed his involuntary leisure in writing a history of the Ottoman Empire down to his own times.

******

But these acts of severity seem slight, compared with the deaths of the princes of his own race, who perished by his orders. Having been an only son, Solyman was spared the guilt of fratricide on his accession to the throne; but he showed repeatedly in the course of his reign, that when state necessity called for blood, the holiest feelings of humanity interposed in vain. His cousin, the descendant of the unfortunate Prince Djem, who came into his power when Rhodes was taken, was put to death with all his family by Solyman's command, and there was still nearer and dearer blood upon his hands.

While Solyman was still young, a Russian girl in his *harem*, named Khourrem, (which means "the joyous one"), had gained an almost unbounded influence over him by her beauty and liveliness; and such was the fascination of her manners—so attractive and soothing to the weary spirit of royalty were the animated graces of her conversation; her skill was so subtle in reading the thoughts of her lord, and in selecting the most favourable times for the exercise of her power in guiding them, that she preserved her ascendancy in his affections long after they both had outlived the season of youth, and until the day of her death, in 1558. She had persuaded Solyman to enfranchise her, and to make her his wife, according to the Mahometan ritual.

And the honours paid by him to her memory proved the constancy and fervour of his passion even after death. Her domed mausoleum was raised by him close to the magnificent mosque, the Suliemaniye, which he had constructed, and which he appointed as his own place of sepulture. The tomb of the Sultana Khourrem still attests the fatal fondness which the Russian beauty inspired in the greatest of the Turkish *Sultans*, and which transferred the succession to the throne of Othman from a martial and accomplished hero to a ferocious but imbecile drunkard.

★★★★★★

The French writers erroneously claim Solyman's favourite *Sultana* as a Frenchwoman. Von Hammer says that Khourrem was frequently spoken of by the contemporaneous Imperial and Venetian ambassadors as "La Rossa," *i.e.,* "The Russian woman." This was subsequently euphonised into Roxalana, and supposed to have been the personal name of the French fair one. The Italians also laid claim to Roxalana.

★★★★★★

Solyman had a son, Prince Mustapha, born to him by a Circassian, who had been the favourite *Sultana* before the Muscovite slave Khourrem enslaved her master. Khourrem also bore children to Solyman; and all her address was employed to secure the succession to the throne for her son Prince Selim. As a necessary step towards that object, she sought the destruction of Prince Mustapha, who, as the elder born, was regarded as the natural heir. A daughter of the Sultana Khourrem was married to Roostem Pacha, who, by her influence, was raised successively to the dignities of *Beyler Bey* of Diarbekir, and of Second *Vizier*; and, finally, to the highest station in the empire below the throne, to the office of *Grand Vizier*. Roostem Pacha employed all his power and influence as his mother-in-law directed him; and she thus acquired a ready and efficient instrument for the ruin of the devoted Mustapha.

This unhappy prince was distinguished for personal grace and activity, and for high spirit and intelligence. In the various governments which were entrusted to him by Solyman, as he advanced towards manhood, he gave proof of such abilities, both civil and military, that he was looked on as likely to surpass his father in glory, and to become the most eminent of all the House of Othman. The malignant artifices of Khourrem and Roostem awakened in Solyman's mind, first jealousy, and then dread of his over-popular and over-praised son.

As Solyman advanced in years, the poisonous whisperings of the stepmother grew more and more effective. The old *Sultan* was studiously reminded how his own father, Selim, had dethroned Bajazet II.; and the vision was kept before him of a renewal of that scene; of a young and vigorous prince, the favourite of the soldiery, seizing the reins of empire, and of an aged father retiring to Demotika and death. It was at last, in 1553, when Solyman was preparing for the second war with Persia, that he was fully wrought up to the conviction that Prince Mustapha was plotting against him, and that it was necessary, before he marched against the foreign enemy, to crush the germs of treason at home.

In the autumn of that year, Solyman placed himself at the head of the troops which had been collected in Asia Minor, and with which it was designed to invade Persia. The season was then too far advanced for such military operations, and the army was to winter at Aleppo, and to open the campaign in the following spring. But Solyman had been persuaded that it was not safe for him to tarry at Constantinople. He was told by his *grand vizier* that the soldiers in Asia Minor were murmuring, and plotting among themselves in favour of Prince Mustapha, and that the prince encouraged their preparations for a military revolution against the old Padischah Solyman.

He repaired, therefore, to the army; and Khourrem's son. Prince

Selim, at his mother's instigation, sought, and obtained, the *Sultan's* permission to accompany him. When the army reached Eregli (the ancient Archelais), Prince Mustapha arrived at headquarters, and his tents were pitched with great pomp in the vicinity of those of the *Sultan*. On the next day, the *viziers* paid their visits of compliment to the prince, and received presents of sumptuous robes of honour.

On the following morning, Prince Mustapha mounted a stately and richly-caparisoned charger, and was conducted by the *viziers* and *Janissaries*, amid the loud acclamations of the soldiery, to the royal tent, where he dismounted in expectation of having an audience of his father. His attendants remained at the entrance of the tent; Prince Mustapha passed into the interior; but he found there, not the *Sultan*, not any of the officers of the Court, but the seven Mutes, the well-known grim ministers of the blood-orders of the Imperial Man-Slayer.

They sprang upon him, and fastened the fatal bow-string round his throat, while he vainly called for mercy to his father, who was in an inner apartment of the tent. According to some accounts, Solyman, impatient at the long-continued struggle between the Mutes and his victim, looked in upon the horrible scene, and with threatening arm and angry brow urged his executioners to complete the work of death. While the prince thus perished within the tent, his master of the horse, and a favourite *aga*, who had accompanied him to the entrance, were cut down on the outside.

The tidings of this execution soon spread through the camp; and the troops, especially the *Janissaries*, gathered together in tumultuous indignation, and called for the punishment of the *grand vizier*, to whose intrigues they imputed the death of their favourite prince. To appease their fury, the obnoxious Roostem was deprived of his office, and Ahmed Pacha, who had distinguished himself in the Hungarian wars, was made *grand vizier* in his stead. But after the lapse of two years, the son-in-law of the all-powerful *Sultana* was restored to his former dignity, and Ahmed Pacha was put to death on frivolous charges of misconduct and disloyalty.

★★★★★★

Von Hammer (vol. ii.) disputes the accuracy of many of the pathetic details with which Robertson and others, after Busbequius, have narrated the death of Prince Mustapha. But he states that all the Ottoman historians agree with the Christian writers, in representing Roostem as having caused the prince's death, at the instigation of the *Sultana*, his stepmother. In a letter written 23rd Dec, 1553, by Dr. Wotton, our English envoy at Paris, he says: "The Great Turk, going towards Aleppo, sent for his eldest son to come to him; who, trusting to be well received of his father, was most cruelly murdered in his father's presence, and by his commandment. Men, that have seen the said son, say that of all the Ottoman's posterity, there was never none so like to attempt great enterprises, and to achieve them with honour, as he was. The cause hereof is taken to be the favour and love which the Turk beareth to the children he hath by another woman, not mother to him that is slain. But his other sons are nothing of that towardness and activity that this man was of."— (Tytler's *Reigns of Edward VI. and Mary*, vol. ii.)

When the close intimacy which was maintained between the Turkish and French courts at this period is remembered, this testimony as to the high expectations that were formed of Prince Mustapha, and also as to the manner of his death, is remarkably strong.

★★★★★★

The tragedy of the death of Prince Bajazet, another son; whom Solyman, at a later period of his reign, caused to be put to death, was attended with even more melancholy circumstances. After the death of the Sultana Khourrem, but while her son-in-law, the Vizier Roostem, yet lived, a deadly rivalry arose between her two sons, Selim and Bajazet. The tutor of the princes, Lala Mustapha Pacha, had originally favoured Prince Bajazet; but, finding: that his prospects of promotion would be greater if he sided with. Prince Selim, he made himself the unscrupulous partisan of the latter, and, by a series of the darkest intrigues, by suggesting false hopes, and unreal dangers, by intercepting and suppressing, some letters, and procuring others to be written and read, he drove Bajazet into rebellion against his father, the result of which was the overthrow and death of the unhappy prince. (Von Hammer, vol. ii. relates the intrigues at length, on the authority of the Ottoman writer, Ali, who had been Lala Mustapha's secretary).

Solyman believed that Prince Bajazet was an unnatural son, towards whom his fatherly remonstrances and warnings had been vainly employed; and Bajazet was led by the arts of the tutor to regard his father as a morose tyrant, who rejected his child's filial submission and entreaties for pardon, and who was resolved to exercise again the same cruel severity which he had shown towards Prince Mustapha. Bajazet was far more popular with the soldiery and people than Prince Selim, whose drunken and dissolute habits made him an object of general contempt, and whose unpopularity was increased by his personal resemblance to his hated mother, the Sultana Khourrem.

Bajazet's features and demeanour resembled those of his father; his habits of life were blameless; his intellectual powers and literary accomplishments were high; and his capacity for civil government and military command, though not equal to those of the lamented Mustapha, were such as to gain favour and command respect. Thus, even after his defeat at Koniah (8th May, 1559) by his father's Third *Vizier*, Sokolli, a considerable force adhered to Prince Bajazet in his fallen fortunes, and followed him into Persia, where he took refuge, together with his four infant sons, at the court of Shah Tahmasp. He was at first treated there with princely honours, and the *Shah* pledged a solemn oath never to give the royal refugee up to his father. But Solyman sternly and imperatively required the extradition or the execution of the rebel and the rebel's children.

Prince Selim also sent letters and messengers to Persia, to procure the death of his brother and nephews, and he gave liberal quotations of misapplied verses of the *Koran*, and copied passages from eminent writers, to overcome the conscientious scruples of the *Shah*, who long hesitated at the treacherous breach of hospitality which he was urged to commit.

★★★★★★

One of these passages was a sentence from Saadi, worthy to be paralleled with the famous epigraph from Publius Syrus, "*Judex damnatur*," &c. It is this: "Kindness to the Undeserving is injury to the Good."

★★★★★★

Fear at lasct prevailed over honour. Persia's "cicatrice yet looked too raw and red after the Turkish sword," for the "sovereign process" of the *Sultan* to be disregarded; and the present death of Bajazet and his children was resolved on. Tahmasp thought that he evaded the obligation of his oath by giving up his guests, not to the immediate officers of Solyman, but to emissaries sent specially by Selim to receive and slay them. It was the period of the solemn fast which the Schii Mahometans kept annually, in memory of Hossein, when the Turkish princes were delivered up to the executioners. Such was the sympathy which their fate inspired among the Persians, that they interrupted their lamentations for the murdered son of Ali, to sorrow over the royal victims then perishing before them; and instead of the curses on the slayers of Hossein which the Schiis are then accustomed to pour forth, imprecations resounded throughout Tabreez against the executioners of the innocent grandchildren of Sultan Solyman. (The reader will remember the vivid description which Lord Macaulay, in his *Essay on Clive*, gives of the effect produced on the Schii Mahometans by this annual commemoration of the death of Hossein).

CHAPTER 13

The Siege of Malta Continued

Besides the domestic sorrows which clouded the last years of Solyman, his military glory and imperial ambition sustained, in the year 1565 (the year before his death), the heaviest blow and most humiliating disappointment, that had befallen them since the memorable retreat from Vienna. This second great check was caused by the complete failure of the expedition against Malta, which was led by the admirals Mustapha and Pialé, and nobly and victoriously encountered by the Knights of St. John of Jerusalem, under their heroic Grand Master, La Valette. After the Knights had been driven from Rhodes, on Solyman's conquest of that island in the beginning of his reign, they had established their Order at Malta, which, together with the neighbouring island of Goza, was given to them by the Emperor Charles V., who compassionated their misfortunes, admired their valour, and appreciated the importance of the services which they rendered to Christendom, as a barrier against the advancing power of the Ottomans.

When the Knights took possession of Malta, it was little more than a shelterless rock; but they discerned the natural advantages of the place, and immediately commenced fortifying the remarkable system of harbours on the south-eastern side of the island, where the city of Malta now rears its grim ranges of batteries and bastions beneath the British flag. The squadrons of the Knights, issuing from the Maltese havens, co-operated actively with the fleets of Spain, and of every foe of the Crescent; and an incessant warfare was carried on under the Maltese Cross against the Turks, in which deeds of chivalrous enterprise were often performed, but in which a piratical love of plunder and a brutal spirit of cruelty too often disgraced the Christian as well as the Mahometan belligerents.

The attention of Solyman was soon fixed on Malta, as the new nest of the revived hornets, who intercepted the commerce and assailed the coasts of his empire; and at last the capture by five Maltese galleys of a rich Turkish galleon, belonging partly to some of the ladies of the *seraglio*, exasperated the *Sultan*, who regarded it as an insult to his household. He was further urged to an attack upon the Order by the *mufti*, who represented to him how sacred a duty it was to rescue the numerous Moslem slaves who were held in cruel bondage by the Knights. Nor can we suppose him to have been indifferent to the military and political importance of the possession of Malta. If the Ottoman arms had once been securely established in that island, it would have served as a basis for operations against Sicily and South Italy, which hardly could have failed of success.

Accordingly, a mighty armament was prepared in the port of Constantinople, during the winter of 1564. The troops amounted to upwards of 30,000, including 4500 *Janissaries*, and the fleet comprised 181 vessels. The Fifth *Vizier*, Mustapha Pacha, was appointed *seraskier*, or commander-in-chief of the expedition, and under him was the renowned Pialé, the hero of Djerbé. The equally celebrated Dragut was to join them at Malta, with the naval and military forces of Tripoli; and all the stores and munitions of war that the skilful engineers and well-stocked arsenals of Constantinople could supply, were shipped in liberal provision for a difficult siege and long campaign. The fleet sailed from the Golden Horn on the 1st of April, 1565. The *Grand Vizier*, Ali, accompanied the *seraskier* and Capitan Pacha to the place of embarkation; and it was long remembered that, at parting, he said laughingly:

> There go two brisk companions, of an exquisite relish for coffee and opium, on a voyage of pleasure among the islands. Their fleet must be all laden with the Arabian bean and essence of henbane.

Von Hammer recounts this pleasantry, not for its humour, but on account of the characteristic comments made on it by the principal Ottoman historians. They blame it as unworthy of the *grand vizier's* dignity, and say that such levity from such a personage was a bad omen at the commencement of a serious and important enterprise. The remarks which they add, that the *grand vizier* was on bad terms with the two officers at whom he thus jested, and that the *seraskier* and admiral were unfriendly towards each other, and both jealous of Dragut, with whom they were to co-operate, show better causes for the failure of the expedition, than the ill-timed jest which they gravely criticise.

The Knights knew well what a storm was about to break upon Malta, and they exerted themselves to the utmost to improve the -defences of their island home. The old city, as it then existed, occupied the central of the three spits of land which project into the Great Harbour on the eastern side. The innermost of these projecting peninsulas, called Isle de la Sangle, was also occupied and fortified. Mount Sceberras, the ridge of land which runs out to the open sea, dividing the great eastern harbour from the western harbour, called Port Muscet, and on which the modern city of La Valletta stands, was not at this time built upon; except at the extremity, where an important castle, called the Fort of St Elmo, had been raised to command the entrances of both harbours.

On a muster of the forces of the defenders of Malta, they were found to consist of 700 Knights, besides serving brothers, and about 8500 soldiers, comprising the crews of the galleys, hired troops, and the militia of the island. Spain sent a small auxiliary force, and promised that her Viceroy of Sicily should bring ample succour. The Pope gave a sum of 10,000 crowns; but from no other Christian power did the Knights receive aid. Their means of safety consisted in their strong and well-armed walls, their own skill and courage, and, above all, the genius and heroism of their Grand Master, John de la Vallette, who had been elected, providentially for Malta, about seven years before its memorable siege. When the approach of the Ottoman armament was announced. La Vallette assembled his Knights and addressed them:—

> A formidable enemy is coming like a thunderstorm upon us; and, if the banner of the Cross must sink before the misbelievers, let us see in this a signal that Heaven demands from us those lives which we have solemnly devoted to its service. He who dies in this cause, dies a happy death; and, to render ourselves worthy to meet it, let us renew at the altar those vows, which ought to make us not only fearless, but invincible in the fight.

The brotherhood devoutly obeyed their Master's exhortation. They renewed the vows of their religious knighthood; and after this solemn ceremonial, and after partaking together of the Holy Sacrament, they swore to give up all feuds among themselves, to renounce all temporal objects and pleasures until their deliverance should be effected, and to stand between the Cross and profanation to the last drop of their blood.

The Ottoman fleet appeared off Malta on the 19th May, 1565. Pialé wished to wait for the arrival of Dragut before they commenced operations; but the *seraskier* on the next day disembarked the troops and began the attack upon St. Elmo. The rocky nature of the ground on Mount Sceberras made it impossible for the Turkish engineers to work trenches; and, as substitutes, they pushed forward movable breastworks of timber, which were thickly coated on the outside with clay and rushes kneaded together. Five days after the commencement of the siege, the Turkish Sea-Captain Ouloudj Ali (called by the Christians Ochiale), who was destined to acquire such celebrity in the next reign, arrived with six galleys from Alexandria; and at last, on the 2nd June, Dragut appeared with the squadron of Tripoli. The old admiral disapproved of the attack on St. Elmo, saying that the fort must have fallen of itself when the city was taken; but he declared that as the operation had been commenced, it ought to be persevered with.

Fresh batteries were placed by his directions against the fort; and in particular he established one upon the opposite or western side of Port Muscet—on the cape that still bears his name. The Turkish ships plied the seaward defences of the fort with their artillery; on the land side thirty-six heavy guns battered it in breach, and the balls of Dragut's battery from across Port Muscet swept the ravelin with a raking fire. The little garrison did their duty nobly; and aided by occasional reinforcements from the main body of their comrades who held the Bourg and the Isle de La Sangle, they repulsed repeated attempts made by the Turks to escalade their walls; and they impeded the advance of the enemy's works by bold and frequent sorties.

The Viceroy of Sicily had promised La Vallette to send a relieving force to the island by the middle of June; and every day that the defence of St. Elmo could be prolonged, was considered by the Knights to be of vital importance for the safety of the island. When some of the Knights posted in the fort represented to La Vallette the ruined state of its defences, and the rapidly increasing destructiveness of the Ottoman fire, he told them that they must die in discharge of their duty; and the noble band of martyrs remained in St Elmo to die accordingly. Dragut ordered a general assault on the fort on the 16th of June. The landward walls had now been shattered and rent, and the Turkish stormers advanced without difficulty through the yawning breaches; but behind these the Knights, arrayed in steady phalanx, and armed with long pikes, formed a living wall, against which the bravest

Turks rushed with their *scimetars* in vain.

Meanwhile, the Christian cannon from St Angelo and St Michael, the forts at the extremities of the Bourg and the Isle de la Sangle, played with terrible effect on the flanks of the huge columns of the assailants. After six hours' conflict the Ottomans retreated, leaving two thousand of their comrades slain. Dragut himself received his death-wound during the assault. A cannon-ball from the Castle of St Angelo splintered a rock near which he was standing, and the fragments of stone struck the old seaman's head. The *seraskier*, with whom he had been conversing respecting the construction of a new battery to reply to St Angelo, ordered a cloak to be flung over the corpse, and remained calmly on the spot while he completed the requisite instructions to the engineers.

Seven days afterwards, the death of Dragut was avenged by the fall of St Elmo, after a furious and long-continued assault, in which every man of the defenders "was slain in valiant fight," (Knolles). In the siege of this outwork, 300 Knights and 1300 soldiers of the Order, and 8000 of the Turks, perished. Mustapha Pacha, when he looked from the ruins of this small castle across to the massive towers of the Bourg, which was now to be attacked, could not help exclaiming, "If the child has cost us so much, what shall we have to pay for the father?"

He sent a Christian slave to summon the Grand Master to surrender. La Vallette led the messenger round the lofty ramparts, and pointing down to the deep ditches beneath them, he said, "Tell the *seraskier* that this is the only land I can give him. Let him and his *Janissaries* come and take possession." Mustapha commenced the attack with ardour, and both the Bourg and the Isle de la Sangle were closely invested and cannonaded from the mainland; while also a row of formidable Turkish batteries thundered on them from St Elmo and Mount Sceberras. This great siege was prolonged until the 11th of September, by the obstinate vehemence of the besiegers, and the truly chivalrous gallantry of the besieged. During the continuance of the operations, the Turks were reinforced by a flotilla from Algiers, commanded by the Beyler Bey Hassan, the son of the great Barbarossa, and son-in-law of Dragut. Hassan demanded leave to sustain the honour of these illustrious names by leading an assault upon the Isle de la Sangle.

The *seraskier* placed 5000 men at his disposal, and with these Hassan attacked the works from the mainland, while Candelissa, a Greek renegade, who had grown grey in piracy and war, led the Algerine galleys to an attack on the inner part of the harbour. Hassan brought back only 500 men out of his 5000; nor was Candelissa more successful. No less than ten general assaults were made and repulsed before the siege was raised; and innumerable minor engagements took place, in which each side showed such valour as to earn its enemy's praise, and each side also unhappily too often stained its glory by the exhibition of ferocious cruelty. In one of these encounters, the *seraskier* had sent a band of able swimmers across part of the harbour with axes to destroy a stockade which the Knights had erected.

La Vallette opposed these assailants by calling for volunteer swimmers from among the Maltese. The islanders came forward readily for this service; and stripping themselves naked, and armed only with short swords, a band of them swam to the stockade, and after a short but desperate struggle in the water, they completely routed the Turkish hatchet-men, and saved the works. (Constable's *History of the Knights of Malta*, vol. ii.).

The long repetition of defeat and bootless carnage by degrees wore out the energies of the Turks. And at last, at the beginning of September, the news arrived that the long-expected fleet of the Sicilian viceroy was on the sea. The succours thus tardily sent to La Vallette and his brave comrades amounted to less than 8000 men; but rumour magnified their numbers, and the weary and dispirited besiegers on the 11th of September abandoned their heavy ordnance, and left the island, which had been crimsoned with so much slaughter, and had been made the theatre of such unrivalled heroism. This memorable siege is said to have cost the lives of 25,000 Turks, and of 5000 of the brave defenders. So reduced, indeed, was the garrison at the time of its rescue, that when they marched out to take possession of the guns which the Turks had abandoned. La Vallette could only muster six hundred men fit for service.

******

Constable, vol. ii. The writer well quotes Knolles's eulogy on the defenders: "If a man do well consider the difficulties and dangers the besieged passed through in this five months' siege, the manifold labours and perils they endured in so many and terrible assaults, the small relief to them sent in so great distress, with the desperate obstinacy of so puissant an enemy, he shall hardly find any place these many years more mightily impugned, or with greater valour and resolution defended."

******

At the time when the tidings that the siege of Malta was raised, reached Constantinople, Solyman was preparing for a new struggle with Austria. The disputes between the rival parties in Hungary had again brought on hostilities. Maximilian II. (who had succeeded Ferdinand) had in person attacked and captured Tokay and Serenez, and the Turkish Pacha, Mustapha Sokolli, had invaded Croatia. Solyman determined to conduct the campaign against the young German Emperor in person; and there can be little doubt that this Austrian war saved the Knights of Malta from a renewed attack in 1566, which must, in all human probability, have been fatal.

Solyman was now seventy-six years old, and so enfeebled by age and illness, that he was no longer able to sit on horseback, but was borne in a litter at the head of his army, which commenced its march from Constantinople to Hungary on the 1st of May, 1566. Before he left his capita for the last time, Solyman had the satisfaction of seeing the great aqueducts completed, which had been built by his orders for the supply of the city.

The *Sultan* arrived at Semlin, in Hungary, the 27th of June, and received the solemn homage of young Sigismund Zapolya, the titular King of Hungary and Transylvania under Ottoman protection. Solyman especially desired to capture in this campaign the two strong places of Erlau and Szigeth, which had on former occasions baffled the attacks of the Turks. A bold exploit of Count Zriny, the Governor of Szigeth, who surprised and cut off a detachment of Bosnian troops while on their march to reinforce the *Sultan's* army, determined Solyman to make Szigeth the first object of his arms; and on the 5th of August the Ottoman forces encamped round that city. It was destined to be the death-place both of the Turkish sovereign and the Christian chief.

Zriny himself burnt the lower, or new town, as indefensible; but great reliance was placed on the strength of the citadel, which was protected by a deep fen, that lay between it and the old or upper town. The Turks carried the town in five days, though not without severe fighting and heavy loss; and Zriny and his garrison of 3200 men then retired to the citadel, where they hoisted the black flag, and took an oath never to surrender, but to fight to the last man and the last gasp. The Turkish engineers formed causeways across the marsh; and they established breastworks near the walls, where the *Janissaries* were posted, who kept down the fire of the artillery of the besieged by an incessant discharge of musketry upon the embrasures, and at every living object that appeared above the parapet.

******

Knolles describes these works with his usual graphic, though quaint vigour. "Then might a man have seen all the fields full of camels, horses, and of the Turks themselves, like emmets, carrying wood, earth, stone, or one thing or another, to fill up the marsh; so was there with wonderful labour two plain ways made through the deep fen from the town to the castle, where the *Janissaries*, defended from the great shot with sacks of wool and such like things, did with the multitude of their small shot so overwhelm the defenders, that they could not against those places, without most manifest danger, show themselves upon the walls."

******

The heavy cannons of the Ottomans were placed in battery, and the walls began to crumble beneath their salvoes. Solyman was impatient of the delay which the resistance of so small a place as this citadel now caused him, and he summoned Zriny to surrender, and sought to win him over to the Ottoman service by offering to make him ruler of all Croatia. Zriny, whom his countrymen have not unworthily named the Leonidas of Hungary, was resolute to die in defence of his post, and he inspired all his men with his own spirit of unflinching courage. Three assaults were given by the Turks in August and September, all of which Zriny repelled with great loss to the besiegers. The Turkish engineers now ran a mine under the principal bastion, and the attacking columns were kept back until the effect of the explosion could be ascertained. The mine was fired early in the morning of the 5th of September, and the bright streak of fire, that shot up into the sky from the shattered bastion, might have been thought to be the death-light of the great *Sultan*, who had died in his tent during the preceding night.

A few hours before his death, he had written to his *grand vizier* complaining that "the drum of victory had not yet beat." He was not destined to witness Szigeth's fall; though his army continued the siege as if by his command, and all except his *grand vizier*, Sokolli, believed that he still lived and reigned. Sokolli is said to have killed the *Sultan's* physicians lest the important secret should transpire, and to have issued orders in Solyman's name, while the messengers conveyed the despatches to Prince Selim which summoned him to the throne. The fire of the Turkish batteries upon Szigeth was continued for four days after the explosion of the great mine, until all the exterior defences of the citadel were destroyed, and of the inner works only a single tower was left standing. In that tower were Zriny and 600 of his men; the rest of the garrison had perished.

On the 8th of September the *Janissaries* advanced in a dense column along a narrow bridge, that led to this last shelter of the defenders; and Zriny, feeling that his hour was come, resolved to anticipate the charge. The gallant Magyar prepared himself for death as for a marriage feast. He wore his most splendid apparel, and a diamond of high price glittered in the clasp of his crest of the heron's plumes. He fastened to his girdle a purse containing the keys of the tower, and a hundred *ducats* carefully chosen of Hungarian coinage, he said:

> The man who lays me out shall not complain that he found nothing on me for his trouble. These keys I keep while this arm can move. When it is stiff, let him who pleases take both keys and *ducats*. But I have sworn never to be the living finger-post of Turkish scorn.

Then from among four richly-ornamented sabres, which had been presented to him at some of the most brilliant epochs of his military career, he chose the oldest one, he exclaimed:

> With this good sword, gained I my first honours, and with this will I pass forth to hear my doom before the judgment-seat of God.

He then, with the banner of the empire borne before him by his standard-bearer, went down into the court of the tower, where his 600 were drawn up in readiness to die with him. He addressed them in a few words of encouragement, which he ended by thrice invoking the name of Jesus. The Turks were now close to the tower gate. Zriny had caused a large mortar to be brought down and placed in the doorway, and trained point-blank against the entrance. He had loaded this with broken iron and musket balls. At the instant when the foremost *janissary* raised his axe to break in the door, it was thrown open. Zriny fired the mortar; the deadly shower poured through the mass of the assailants, destroying hundreds of them in an instant; and amid the smoke, the din, and the terror of this unexpected carnage, Zriny sprang forth sword in hand against the Turks, followed by his devoted troop. There was not one of those 600 Magyar sabres but drank its fill on that day of self-immolation, before the gallant men who wielded them were overpowered.

******

It is said that some were spared in the conflict by the *Janissaries*, who, admiring their courage, placed their own caps on their heads, for the purpose of saving them.—*Two Sieges of Vienna.*

******

Zriny met the death he sought, from two musket-balls through the body, and an arrow wound in the head. The Ottomans thrice raised the shout of "*Allah*" when they saw him fall, and they then poured into the citadel, which they fired and began to plunder; but Zriny, even after death, smote his foes. He had caused all his remaining stores of powder to be placed beneath the tower, and, according to some accounts, a slow match was applied to it by his orders immediately before the Magyars made their sally. Either from this, or from the flames, which the Turks had themselves kindled, the magazine exploded while the tower was filled with Ottoman soldiery; and together with the last battlements of Szigeth, 3000 of its destroyers were destroyed

Solyman the Conqueror lay stark in his tent before the reeking and smouldering rums. The drum of victory beat unheeded by him who had so longed for its sound. He was insensible to all the roar of the assault, and to the "deadly earthshock" of the fired magazine of Szigeth. Nor could the tidings which now reached the camp of the surrender of the city of Gyula to Pertaw Pacha "soothe the dull cold ear of death." The secret of the decease of the *Sultan* was long well guarded. For more than seven weeks the great Turkish Army of 150,000 soldiers, went, and came, and fought, and took towns and cities in the name of the dead man.

The Vizier Sokolli had caused the body to be partly embalmed before the royal tent was removed from before Szigeth; and, when the camp was struck, the corpse was placed in the covered litter in which Solyman had travelled during the campaign, and which was now borne alone among the troops, surrounded by the customary guards, and with all the ceremonies and homage which had been shown to the living monarch. Sokolli and the other high officers, who knew the truth, after the siege and capture of Babocsa, and some other operations which employed the attention of the troops, gradually drew them towards the Turkish frontier. Solyman's signature was adroitly counterfeited; written orders were issued in his name, and the report was sedulously spread among the soldiers, that a severe attack of gout prevented the *Sultan* from appearing in public.

At last Sokolli received intelligence that Prince Selim had been enthroned at Constantinople; and he then took measures for revealing to the soldiery the death of the great *padischah*. The army was now (24th of October, 1566) four marches distant from Belgrade, and had halted for the night in the outskirts of a forest. Sokolli sent for the readers of the *Koran*, who accompanied the troops, and ordered them to assemble round the *Sultan's* litter in the night, and at the fourth hour before daybreak (the hour at which Solyman had expired forty-eight days before), to read the appointed service for the dead from the *Koran*, and call upon the name of God. At the chosen time, amid the stillness of the night, the army was roused from sleep by the loud clear voices of the *Muezzins*, that rose in solemn chant from around the royal tent, and were echoed back from the sepulchral gloom of the forest.

Those who stood on the right of the corpse called aloud, "All dominion perishes, and the last hour awaits all mankind!"

Those on the left answered, "The ever-living God alone is untouched by time or death."

The soldiers, who heard the well-known announcement of death, gathered together in tumultuous groups, with wild cries of lamentation. When the day began to break, the *grand vizier* went through the camp addressing the assemblages of troops, and exhorting them to resume their ranks and march. He told them how much the *padischah*, who was now at rest and in the bosom of God, had done for Islam, and how he had been the soldier's friend; and he exhorted them to show their respect for his memory not by lamentations, which should be left to the priests, but by loyal obedience to his son, the glorious Sultan Selim Khan, who now was reigning in his stead. Soothed by these addresses, and the promise of a liberal donative from the new *Sultan*, the army returned to military order, and escorted the remains of their monarch and general back to Belgrade. Solyman's body was finally deposited in the great mosque at Constantinople, the Soleimaniye, which is the architectural glory of his reign.

Sultan Solyman I. left to his successors an empire, to the extent of which few important permanent additions were ever made, except the islands of Cyprus and Candia; and which under no subsequent **Sultan** maintained or recovered the wealth, power, and prosperity which it enjoyed under the great lawgiver of the House of Othman. The Turkish dominions in his time comprised all the most celebrated cities of biblical and classical history, except Rome, Syracuse, and Persepolis. The sites of Carthage, Memphis, Tyre, Nineveh, Babylon, and Palmyra were Ottoman ground; and the cities of Alexandria, Jerusalem, Damascus, Smyrna, Nice, Prusa, Athens, Philippi, and Adrianople, besides many of later but scarcely inferior celebrity, such as Algiers, Cairo, Mecca, Medina, Bassorah, Bagdad, and Belgrade, obeyed the Sultan of Constantinople. The Nile, the Jordan, the Orontes, the Euphrates, the Tigris, the Tanais, the Borysthenes, the Danube, the Hebrus, and the Ilyssus, rolled their waters "within the shadow of the Horsetails."

The eastern recess of the Mediterranean, the Propontis, the Palus Maeotis, the Euxine, and the Red Sea, were Turkish lakes. The Ottoman Crescent touched the Atlas and the Caucasus; it was supreme over Athos, Sinai, Ararat, Mount Carmel, Mount Taurus, Ida, Olympus, Pelion, Hoemus, the Carpathian and the Acroceraunian heights. An empire of more than forty thousand square miles, embracing many of the richest and most beautiful regions of the world, had been acquired by the descendants of Ertoghrul, in three centuries from the time when their forefather wandered a homeless adventurer at the head of less than five hundred fighting men.

Solyman divided this empire into twenty-one governments, which were again subdivided into 250 *Sanjaks*. The governments were, 1st, Roumelia, under which term were then comprised all the Ottoman continental possessions in Europe south of the Danube: these included Ancient Greece, Macedonia, Thrace, Epirus, Illyria, Dalmatia, and Moesia; 2. The islands of the Archipelago: this government was vested in the Capitan Pacha; 3, Algiers and its territory; 4. Tripoli in Africa; 5. Ofen, comprising the conquered portions of Western Hungary; 6. Temeswar, combining the Bannat, Transylvania, and the eastern part of Hungary; 7. Anatolia, a title commonly given to the whole of Asia Minor, but here applied to the north-western part of the Peninsula, which includes the ancient Paphlagonia, Bithynia, Mysia, Lydia, Caria, Lycia, Pisidia, and the greater part of Phrygia and Galatia; 8. Caramania, which contains the residue of the last-mentioned ancient countries, and also Lycaonia, Cilicia, and the larger part of Cappadocia; 9. Roum, called also the government of Siwas, and sometimes the government of Amasia: it comprehended part of Cappadocia, and nearly the whole of the ancient Pontus that lay in Asia Minor; 10. Soulkadr: this embraced the cities of Malatea, Samosata, Elbostan, and the neighbouring districts, and the important passes of the eastern ridges of Mount Taurus; 11. Trebizond: the governor of this city commanded the coasts round the south-eastern extremity of the Black Sea; 12. Diarbekir, 13. Van: these two governments included the greater part of Armenia and Kourdistan; 14. Aleppo, 15. Damascus: these two embraced Syria and

Palestine; 16. Egypt; 17. Mecca and Medina, and the country of Arabia Petraea; 18. Yemen and Aden: this government extended over Arabia Felix and a considerable tract along the coast of the Persian Gulf and North-western India; 19. Bagdad; 20. Mosul; 21. Bassorah: these three last contained the conquests which Selim and Solyman had made from the Persians in Mesopotamia and the adjacent southern regions: the Tigris and the Euphrates (after its confluence with the other river) formed their eastern limit, and at the same time were the boundaries between the Turkish and the Persian dominions.

Besides the countries that were portioned out in these twenty-one governments, the *Sultan* was also sovereign over the vassal states of Wallachia, Moldavia, Ragusa, and Crim Tartary. They paid him tribute, which in the cases of the two former were considerable; and the last-named feudatories of the Porte, the Crim Tartars, furnished large and valuable contingents to the Turkish armies. It is not easy to define the territory then belonging to the vassal *khans* of the Crimea beyond that peninsula. They and their kinsman, the Tartar *khans* of Astrakhan, were chiefs of numerous and martial tribes that roved amid the *steppes* to the north of the Euxine, and round the Sea of Azof; but the fluctuation of their almost perpetual wars with the Cossacks, the Muscovites, and each other, prevents the fixing of any territorial boundaries in those regions for any specified epoch.

At least twenty different races of mankind inhabited the vast realms ruled by the great Solyman. The Ottomans themselves, who are now calculated to amount to about thirteen millions, (Ubicini), are believed to have declined in number during the last three centuries; and we may take fifteen millions as an approximate enumeration of them in the 16th century, distributed then, as now, very unequally over the empire; Asia containing four-fifths of them, and Asia Minor being especially their chosen home. Three millions of Greeks (the name and the language continue, whatever we may think as to the predominance of the Sclavonic over the Hellenic element in the modern Greek nation), dwelt in the southern portion of European Turkey; a million more were in Asia Minor.

The Armenian race, little extended in Europe, was numerous in Asia; and may have formerly amounted, as now, to between two and three millions. The Sclavonic part of the population was the largest. Bulgaria, Servia, Bosnia, Montenegro, the Herzegovine, were chiefly peopled by Sclaves; who were also numerous in Moldavia and Wallachia, and there were many thousands of them in Transylvania and

Albania. They may be estimated at six millions and a half at the epoch which we are particularly examining. The race called Rumanys, and supposed to have sprung from the Roman conquerors of the Dacians, and from the conquered Dacians themselves, dwelt principally in Wallachia and Moldavia; their number may then, as now, have been four millions.

The Albanians, who term themselves Skipetars, and are termed by the Turks Arnauts, were and are a nation of mountaineers—bold, hardy, and unscrupulous; fond of robbery at home, and warfare abroad. Their number is now estimated at one million and a half, and is likely to have varied but little. The Tartar race formed the population of the Dobruska and of the Crimea, and the countries round the coast of the continent connected with it, Judging from the amount of soldiery supplied by the Crim Tartars to the Ottoman armies, and other circumstances, I should reckon a million and a half as their probable number in the reign of Solyman.

The Arabic race was extensively spread through Syria, Arabia, Egypt, and the whole North African coast; and the Arabian subjects of Solyman must have been nearly six millions. The Maronites, the Chaldeans, and the Druses of Syria were together under a million. The Kurds, a race of close affinity to the Persians, can be only guessed to have numbered the like amount; and the Turkomans of Diarbekir and the neighbourhood cannot be numbered at more than 100,000. We have yet to add the Magyars of that part of Hungary which obeyed the *Sultan*; the Germans of Transylvania, the Berbers of Algeria and the other African provinces, the Copts of Egypt, the Jews, the Tsiganés (who were and are numerous in Moldavia), and the remnants of the Mamelukes. In speaking of an age and of nations in which the numbering of the people was not practised, it is vain to take a retrospective census with any pretensions to minute accuracy; but probably our calculation would not be very erroneous if we considered that from forty-five to fifty millions of subjects obeyed the commands and were guided by the laws of Solyman Kanounni.

✶✶✶✶✶✶

In making this estimate, I have used the calculations of Ubicini and others, as to the present state of the population of the Turkish empire. I have added the probable amounts of those provinces which the Porte has lost since Solyman's time; and I have generally set off against the natural tendency to increase, the checks which war, revolt, and other depopulating causes are known to have exercised in the empire during its decline. It is certain that the progress of depopulation in the beginning of the seventeenth century was very rapid.

Sir Thomas Roe, who was ambassador at Constantinople for James I., in a letter written by him in 1622, says, "I will tell you a wonder. About sixteen years past, there was a view made of all the villages inhabited in the dominion of the *Grand Signior*, and the lists were 553,000, and odd; and now this last year before the war of Poland, another being made, they are found to be decreased to 75,000 in all, which is a strange depopulation."—(Sir Thomas Roe's *Embassy*). The first enumeration mentioned by Sir T. Roe would have included the provinces conquered from Persia in the reign of Amurath III., but lost again before 1622.

And the smaller number would exclude all those, and also many other former Turkish possessions in Asia, which the Persians then occupied. Probably also every "*Esnaf*," and rural commune, was reckoned separately. Still, after all allowances, I cannot help suspecting the accuracy of the figures of either Sir Thomas or his printers. If we take the first figures to be correct, they would indicate (after allowing for the provinces acquired subsequently to Solyman's death) an aggregate of about five millions of guilds and communes in Solyman's time; and we must then rate the population at more than double the number which I have assigned to it.

※※※※※※

Of the various races which we have enumerated, the Ottomans, the Tartars, the Arabs, the Kurds, the Turkomans, the Mamelukes, and the Berbers held the Mahometan creed, which had been adopted also by large numbers of the Bosnians, Bulgarians, and Albanians. The rest, except the Jews and the Tsiganés, belonged to different branches of the Christian religion, the adherents of the Greek Church being by far the most numerous.

The regular military force of the empire, in the year of the capture of Szigeth, the sunset glory of Solyman's reign, was double that which he found at his accession. He raised the number of the *Janissaries* to 20,000; and the whole paid and permanent army, including the Royal horse-guards and other troops, amounted under him to 48,000 men. Solyman bestowed the greatest attention upon his *Janissaries*. He formed from among them a corps of invalids, into which only veteran soldiers of high merit, who had grown grey in the service, or had been disabled by wounds, were admitted. Solyman also complimented these formidable troops (and his successors continued the custom) by being himself nominally enrolled in their first regiment, and coming among them at the pay day, and receiving a soldier's pay from the colonel.

He honoured another distinguished regiment of the *Janissaries* by accepting a cup of sherbet from their commander, when he inspected the barrack. This incident also gave rise to a custom for each *Sultan*, on his accession, to receive a cup of sherbet from the *aga* or commander-in-chief of the *Janissaries*, which he returned to that warlike functionary with the words, (significant of Ottoman pride and ambition) "We shall see each other again at the Red Apple," the name which the Turks commonly give to the city of Rome. The number of the feudatory troops, and the irregular levies, at the time of the campaign of Szigeth, exceeded 200,000. The park of artillery contained 300 cannons, and the fleet amounted to 300 sail.

Notwithstanding the improvement in the armies of Western Christendom, to which we have referred when speaking of the epoch of the accession of Solyman, the Ottoman troops were still far superior to them in discipline, and in general equipment. We have already mentioned the pre-eminence of the Turks of that age in the numerical force and efficiency of their artillery; and the same remark applies to their skill in fortification, and in all the branches of military engineering. The difference between the care that was paid to the physical and moral well-being of Solyman's troops, and the neglect of "the miserable fate of the poor soldier" in his rivals' camps, is still more striking.

There are some well-known passages in the writings of Busbequius, the Austrian ambassador at the Ottoman court, who accompanied the Turkish forces in some of their expeditions, in which he contrasts the cleanliness, and the good order of a Turkish camp, the absence of all gambling, and the sobriety and temperance of the men, with the tumult, the drunkenness, the licence, the brawling, and the offensive pollution that reeked in and around Christian tents in that age. It were difficulty even for the most experienced commissary-general of modern times, to suggest improvements on the arrangements and preparations for the good condition and comfort of the Ottoman soldiers, that may be read of in the narratives of Solyman's campaigns. We may mention as one of many beneficial regulations, the establishment of a corps of *sakkas*, or water-carriers, who attended in the field and on the march to supply water to the weary and wounded soldiers. Compare this with the condition of the Black Bands who followed Bourbon under the banner of the Emperor Charles.

An ample revenue judiciously collected, and prudently though liberally employed, was one decisive advantage which Solyman possessed over his contemporary monarchs. The crown lands of the *Sultan* at that time produced the large sum of 5,000,000 of *ducats*. The tithe or land-tax, the capitation tax on the *rayas*, the customs, and the other regular taxes raised this to between 7,000,000 and 8,000,000. The burden of taxation on the subject was light, and it was only twice in his reign that Solyman levied an additional impost. The necessity caused by the sieges of Belgrade and Rhodes, in the beginning of his reign, and the cost of armaments in the year of the Battle of Mohacz, compelled him to impose a poll-tax on all his subjects, without distinction of creed or fortune. But the amount was small on each occasion; and never was a similar measure again necessary.

The victorious campaigns of the *Sultan* were soon made to reimburse their outlays, and still further to enrich the Porte. Large contributions were drawn from Hungary and Transylvania; and Ragusa, Moldavia and Wallachia poured tribute into the treasury of the Porte. Another less glorious source of revenue was found in the confiscated goods of the numerous high officers of state, who were executed during this reign. By invariable usage the property of those who die thus, is forfeited to the Crown; and the riches of the Grand Vizier Ibrahim, and other unhappy statesmen of this age were no unimportant accessions to the ways and means of the years in which they perished.

We examined the general principles of the Ottoman government when reviewing the institutes of Mahomet the Conqueror. Every branch of the administration of the empire received improvement from Solyman Kanouni; and, like another great conqueror and ruler, he has come down to posterity with his legislative works in his hand. He organised with especial care the Turkish feudal system of the *ziamets* and *timars*, reforming the abuses which had then already begun to prevail. He ordained that no *timar* (small *fief*) should be allowed to exist if below a certain value. A number of the smaller *fiefs* might be united so as to form a *ziamet* (a grand *fief*), but it was never lawful to subdivide a *ziamet* into *timars*, except in the case of a feudatory who was killed in battle and left more than one son.

By permission of the supreme government several persons might hold a *fief* as joint tenants; but it was still reckoned a single *fief*; and any partition and subdivision not especially authorised by the Sublime

Porte itself was severely punished. The reader who is familiar with the workings of the feudal system in Western Europe will perceive how admirably these provisions were adapted to check the growth of evils, like those, which the practice of subinfeudation produced in mediaeval Christendom. The Turkish *fiefs* descended from father to son, like our fees in tail male.

There was no power of devise or alienation: and in default of male issue of the deceased holder, the *timar* or *ziamet* reverted to the Crown. It had been usual before Solyman's time to allow the *viziers* and governors of provinces to make grants of the lapsed *fiefs* within, their jurisdiction, but Solyman restricted tins to the case of the minor fiefs. None but the *Sultan* could make a new grant of a lapsed *ziamet*, and in no instance did the feudatory who received the investiture of a *timar* from a subject pay any homage, or enter into any relation of feudal duty to the person who invested him. There was no *mesne* lordship. The *Spahi* was the feudal vassal of his *Sultan* and of his *Sultan* alone.

The number of the larger *fiefs*, or *ziamets*, in Solyman's time was 3192; that of the smaller *fiefs*, or *timars*, was 50,160, (Thornton). It will be remembered, that each *Spahi* (or holder of a military *fief*) was not only bound to render military service himself in person, but, if the value of his *fief* exceeded a certain specified amount, he was required to furnish and maintain an armed horseman for every multiple of that sum; or (to adopt the phraseology of our own early institutions), the estate was bound to supply the Crown in tune of war with a man-at-arms for each knight's fee. The total feudal array of the empire in the reign of Solyman amounted to 150,000 cavalry, who, when summoned by the *beyler beys*, and *sanjak beys*, joined the army at the appointed place of muster, and served throughout the campaign without pay. We must not only add this number to the 48,000 regularly paid and permanent troops, when we estimate the military force of the Turkish empire in its meridian, but we must also bear in mind the numerous squadrons of Tartar cavalry, which the vassal *khans* of the Crimea sent to swell the Turkish armies; and we must remember the swarms of irregular troops, both horse and foot, the *Akindji* and the *Azabs*, which the *Sultan's* own dominions poured forth to every campaign.

There is no surer proof of the true greatness of Solyman as a ruler, than the care, which, at the same time that he reformed the Turkish feudal system, so as to make it more efficient as an instrument of military force, he bestowed on the condition of those Rayas, who, like the serfs of mediaeval Europe, cultivated the lands assigned to the *Spahis*. The "*Kanouni Raya*," or "Code of the *Rayas*," of Solyman, limited and defined the rents and services which the *Raya* who occupied the ground was to pay to his feudal lord. It is impossible to give any description of this part of the Turkish law which shall apply with uniform correctness to all parts of the *Sultan's* dominions. But the general effect of Solyman's legislation may be stated to have been that of recognising in the *Raya* rights of property in the land which he tilled, subject to the payment of certain rents and dues, and the performance of certain services for his feudal superior.

★★★★★★

Ranke's *History of Servia*, gives the "Outlines of the Turkish institutions in Servia." That learned writer informs us that in Servia, "the *Spahis* received a tithe of all that the field, vineyard, or beehive produced; and also a small tax on each head of cattle. Moreover, they had a right to demand for themselves a tax, called Glawnitza, of two *piastres* from every married couple. To avoid unpleasant inquiries into the extent of their income, many persons added a portion of the tithe to the Glawnitza. In some parts of the country the people agreed to pay the *Spahis* for each married couple, whether rich or poor, ten *piastres* a year in full of all dues.

This was at once accepted, as it enabled the *Spahis* to ascertain the amount on which they might annually reckon. But the *Spahis* cannot properly be considered as a class of nobles. In the villages they had neither estates nor dwellings of their own: they had no right to jurisdiction; they were not allowed to eject the tenantry by force, nor could they even forbid them from moving and settling elsewhere. What they had to demand, was what might be termed a hereditary stipend, in return for which the duty of serving in war remained unaltered. No real rights of property were ever bestowed on them; for a specific service a certain revenue was granted to them."

There would, however, be need of caution in applying this description to other parts of the Ottoman Empire; for instance, to Asia Minor, where the number of the *Rayas* was far less than in Europe, and where the *Spahis* seem to have generally occupied some part, at least, of their fiefs. Probably the analogy suggested in the text, of our lords of manor and copyhold tenants, will give the clearest and least deceptive idea of the relative positions of the Turkish *Spahi* and his *Raya*; especially as it involves the supposition of a great variety of local customs.

In Egypt, the Ottoman conquerors retained the system which they found established there by the Mameluke sovereigns; that of granting, or rather of farming out lands to military tenants, who took possession of the lands, and paid the State a certain fixed rent for them; and then they, and their sub-tenants, the *Fellahs*, who tilled the ground, took the residue of the profits, in such proportion as the military lords thought fit. Of course, the position of an Egyptian *Fellah* was far worse than that of the *Raya* of an Anatolian or Roumelian *Spahi*.

✶✶✶✶✶✶

The Englishman, who understands the difference between the position of a modern copy-holder and that of a mediaeval villain towards the lord of his manor, will well understand the important boon which the enlightened wisdom of the Turkish lawgiver secured, if he did not originate. And when the difference of creed between the lawgiver and the *Rayas* is remembered, and we also bear in mind the fact that Solyman, though not a persecutor like his father, was a very sincere and devout Mahometan, we cannot help feeling that the great Turkish *Sultan* of the sixteenth century deserves a degree of admiration, which we can accord to none of his crowned contemporaries in that age of melancholy injustice and persecution between Roman Catholic and Protestant throughout the Christian world.

✶✶✶✶✶✶

There might be Mussulman tenants under the *Spahis*, but in the immense majority of cases, the tillers of Turkish feudal lands were Christians. The name of Solyman's Code on the subject, "*Kanouni Raya*," itself proves this. And it is observable that the number and value of the *fiefs* in Turkish Europe, where the number of the Ottoman population has always been very small in comparison with that of the Christian, exceeded the number and value of the *fiefs* in Asia, where the numerical proportion of the followers of the two religions is reversed.

✶✶✶✶✶✶

The difference between the lot of the *Rayas* under their Turkish masters and that of the serfs of Christendom, under their fellow-Christians and fellow-countrymen, who were their lords, was practically shown by the anxiety which the inhabitants of the countries near the Turkish frontier showed to escape from their homes, and live under that Turkish yoke which is frequently represented as having always been so tyrannical. A writer, who was Solyman's contemporary, says:

> I have seen multitudes of Hungarian rustics set fire to their cottages, and fly with their wives and children, their cattle and instruments of labour, to the Turkish territories, where they knew that, besides the payment of the tenths, they would be subject to no imposts or vexations.

✶✶✶✶✶✶

Leunclavius, apud Elzevir, cited in Thornton and other writers. At a later period, the beginning of the seventeenth century, we learn from Sandys that the inhabitants of the Morea sought eagerly to return to the Turkish from the Venetian rule. Dr. Clarke's *Travels* inform us how bitterly the natives of the Crimea regretted the change of masters when the Russians succeeded the Turks in the dominion of that country.

✶✶✶✶✶✶

Besides the important branches of law and government that have been mentioned, the ceremonial law (a far more serious subject in the East than in Western Europe), the regulations of police, and the criminal law, received the personal attention of the great *Sultan*, and were modified and remodelled by his edicts. Every subject-matter of legislation is comprised in the great code of Ottoman law, compiled by Solyman's Molla, Ibrahim of Aleppo, which has been in authority down to the present age in the Turkish Empire. (Its author fancifully named it *Multeka-ul-ubhur, the Confluence of the Seas*, from its oceanic comprehensiveness of the contents of multitudinous libraries).

Solyman mitigated the severity of the punishments which had previously been appointed for many offences. The extreme slightness of the penalties with which crimes of sensuality were visited by him, is justly blamed as a concession to the favourite vices of the Turkish nation; (Von Hammer, vol. ii.), but, in general, his diminution of the frequency with which the punishments of death and mutilation were inflicted, entitles him to the praise of the modern jurist.

The minuteness of the laws, by which he strove to regulate rates of prices and wages, and to prescribe the mode in which articles of food should be prepared and sold, may raise a smile in our more enlightened age; but we should remember how full our own statute book is of similar enactments, and how far our own excise laws still maintain the spirit of vexatious and mischievous interference. Some of the more noticeable laws of Sultan Solyman are those by which slanderers and tale-bearers are required to make compensation for the mischief caused by their evil-speaking; false witnesses, forgers, and passers of bad money are to have the right hand struck off; interest is not to be taken at a higher rate than eleven *per cent.*; a fine is imposed for three consecutive omissions of a Mussulman's daily prayer, or a breach of the solemn fasts; kindness to beasts of burden is enjoined.

Whatever the political economists of the present time may think of the legislation of Solyman Kanouni as to wages, manufactures, and retail trade, their highest praises are due to the enlightened liberality with which the foreign merchant was welcomed in his empire. The earliest of the contracts, called capitulations, which guarantee to the foreign merchant in Turkey full protection for person and property, the free exercise of his religion, and the safeguard of his own laws, administered by functionaries of his own nation, was granted by Solyman to France in 1535.

★★★★★★

There is a remarkable State paper published by the Ottoman government, 1832, in the *Moniteur Ottoman,* justly claiming credit for their nation on this important subject. Mr. Urquhart cites, in his *Turkey and her Resources,* the following passages from this official declaration of Turkish commercial principles:

> It has often been repeated, that the Turks are encamped in Europe; it is certainly not their treatment of strangers that has given rise to this idea of precarious occupancy; the hospitality they offer their guest is not that of the tent, nor is it that of the Turkish laws; for the Mussulman code, in its double civil and religious character, is inapplicable to those professing another religion; but they have done more, they have granted to the stranger the safeguard of his own laws, exercised by functionaries of his own nation. In this privilege, so vast in benefits and in consequences, shines forth the admirable spirit of true and lofty hospitality.
>
> In Turkey, and there alone, does hospitality present itself, great, noble, and worthy of its honourable name; not the shelter of a stormy day, but that hospitality which, elevating itself from a simple movement of humanity to the dignity of a political reception, combines the future with the present. When the stranger has placed his foot on the

land of the *Sultan*, he is saluted guest (*mussafir*). To the children of the West who have confided themselves to the care of the Mussulman, hospitality has been granted, with those two companions, civil liberty according to the laws, commercial liberty according to the laws of nature and of reason.

Good sense, tolerance, and hospitality, have long ago done for the Ottoman Empire what the other states of Europe are endeavouring to effect by more or less happy political combinations. Since the throne of the *Sultans* has been elevated at Constantinople, commercial prohibitions have been unknown; they opened all the ports of their empire to the commerce, to the manufactures, to the territorial produce of the Occident, or, to say better of the whole world. Liberty of commerce has reigned here without limits, as large, as extended, as it was possible to be.

Never has the *divan* dreamed, under any pretext of national interest, or even of reciprocity, of restricting that facility, which has been exercised, and is to this day in the most unlimited sense, by all the nations who wish to furnish a portion of the consumption of this vast empire, and to share in the produce of its territory.

Here every object of exchange is admitted and circulates without meeting other obstacle than the payment of an infinitely small portion of the value to the Customhouse.

The extreme moderation of the duties is the complement of this *régime* of commercial liberty; and in no portion of the globe are the officers charged with the collection of more confiding facility for the valuations, and of so decidedly conciliatory a spirit in every transaction regarding commerce.

Away with the supposition that these facilities granted to strangers are concessions extorted from weakness! The dates of the contracts termed capitulations, which establish the rights actually enjoyed by foreign merchants, recall periods at which the Mussulman power was altogether predominant in Europe. The first capitulation which France obtained was in 1535, from Solyman the

Canonist (the Magnificent).

The dispositions of these contracts have become antiquated, the fundamental principles remain. Thus, three hundred years ago, the *Sultans*, by an act of munificence and of reason, anticipated the most ardent desires of civilised Europe, and proclaimed unlimited freedom of commerce.

The remarks of Ubicini (vol. i.) on this subject, are also well worth consulting.

★★★★★★

An extremely moderate custom duty was the only impost on foreign merchandise; and the costly and vexatious system of prohibitive and protective duties has been utterly unknown among the Ottomans. No stipulation for reciprocity ever clogged the wise liberality of Turkey in her treatment of the foreign merchant who became her resident, or in her admission of his ships and his goods.

We have already observed, in referring to the institutes of Mahomet II., the authority which the *Ulema*, or educators and men learned in the law, possess in Turkey, and the liberal provisions made there for national education. Solyman was a munificent founder of schools and colleges; and he introduced many improvements into the educational discipline and rank of the *Ulema*.

But the great boon conferred by him on this order, and the peculiar homage paid by him to the dignity of learning, consisted in establishing, as rules of the Ottoman Government, the exemption of all the *Ulema* from taxation, and the secure descent of their estates from father to son; the property of a member of this body being in all cases privileged from confiscation. Hence it has arisen, that the only class among the Turks in which hereditary wealth is accumulated in families, is furnished by the educational and legal professions; and the only aristocracy that can be said to exist there, is an aristocracy of the brain.

The splendour of the buildings, with which Solyman adorned Constantinople, suggests a point of comparison between the great Turkish legislator and the Roman Emperor who ruled ten centuries before him, in addition to that which their codes naturally bring before the mind. It would be dishonouring to Solyman to carry the parallel between him and Justinian further than as regards architecture and legislation; nor can there be any balancing of the courage and magnanimity of the victor of Mohacz, with the cowardice and meanness of the unworthy master of Belisarius and personal ringleader of the factions of the Circus.

But the long list, in which the Oriental historians enumerate the sumptuous edifices raised by Solyman in the seven-hilled city of the Bosphorus, recalls the similar enumeration which Procopius has made of the architectural splendours of Justinian. And it was not only in the capital, but at Bagdad, Koniah, Kaffa, Damascus, and other cities that the taste and grandeur of Solyman were displayed Besides the numerous mosques which were founded or restored by his private liberality, he decorated his empire and provided for the temporal welfare of his subjects by numerous works of practical utility. Among them the great aqueduct of Constantinople, the bridge of Tschekmedji, and the restored aqueducts of Mecca are mentioned as the most beneficial and magnificent.

The names of the poets, the historians, the legal and scientific writers who flourished under Solyman, would fill an ample page; but it would be one of little interest to us, while Turkish literature remains so generally unknown in Western Europe, even through the medium of translations. (Von Hammer's work on Ottoman literature is an honourable exception; and a series of very valuable letters, on the same subject, by Von Hammer, appeared in the English *Athenaeum* some years ago).

But, because unknown, it must not be assumed to be unreal; and Solyman was as generous and discerning a patron of literary merit, as any of those sovereigns of Western Europe who have acquired for their ages and courts the much-coveted epithet of "Augustan."

Solyman's own writings are considered to hold an honourable station, though not among the highest in his nation's literature. His poems are said to be dignified in sentiment and correct in expression; and his journals, in which he noted the chief events of each day during his campaigns, are highly serviceable to the investigator of history. They prove the *Sultan's* possession of qualities, which are of far more value in a sovereign than are the accomplishments of a successful author. They show his sense of duty, his industry, and his orderly and unremitting personal attention to the civil as well as the military affairs of the vast empire that had been committed to his charge. Faults, deplorable faults, are unquestionably to be traced in his reign. The excessive influence which he allowed his favourite *Sultana* to acquire; the cruel deaths of his children, and of so many statesmen, whom he gave over to the executioner, are heavy stains on his memory. His own countrymen have pointed out the defects in his government.

Kotchi Bey, who wrote in the reign of Amurath IV. (1623), and who is termed by Von Hammer the Turkish Montesquieu, assigns in his work on the *Decline of the Ottoman Empire*, which he traces up to the reign of the first Solyman, among the causes of that decline—1st, the cessation in Solyman's time of the regular attendance of the *Sultan* at the meetings of the *divan*; 2nd, the habit then introduced of appointing men to high stations who had not previously passed through a gradation of lower offices; 3rd, the venality and corruption first practised by Solyman's son-in-law and *Grand Vizier,* Roostem, who sold to people of the lowest character and capacity the very highest civil offices, though the appointment to all military ranks, high or low, was still untainted by bribery or other dishonest influence.

The fourth censure passed by Kotchi Bey on Solyman is for his evil example in exceeding the limits of wise liberality by heaping wealth upon the same favourite *vizier*, and allowing him not only to acquire enormous riches, but to make them, by an abuse of the Turkish mortmain law, inalienable in his family. This was done by transforming his estates into *vaks* or *vakoufs*; that is to say, by settling his property on some mosque or other religious foundation, which took from it a small quit-rent, and held the rest in trust for the donor and his family.

While admitting the justice of these charges of the Oriental historian. Von Hammer exposes the groundlessness of the censure, which European writers have passed upon Solyman, when accusing him of having introduced the custom of shutting up the young princes of the House of Othman in the *seraglio*, instead of training them to lead armies and govern provinces. He points out that all the sons of Solyman, who grew up to manhood, administered *pachalics* under him, and that one of his last acts before his death was to appoint Amurath, his grandson, to the government of Magnesia.

In the same spirit in which Arrian sums up the character of Alexander the Great, the German historian rightly warns us, when estimating that of Solyman the Great, not to fix our attention exclusively on the blameable actions of his life, but to remember also the bright and noble qualities which adorned him. As a man, he was warm-hearted and sincere, and honourably pure from the depraved sensuality which has disgraced too many of his nation. We must remember his princely courage, his military genius, his high and enterprising spirit, his strict observance of the laws of his religion without any taint of bigoted persecution, the order and economy which he combined with so much grandeur and munificence, his liberal encouragement of art and literature, his zeal for the diffusion of education, the conquests by which he extended his empire, and the wise and comprehensive legislation with which he provided for the good government of all his subjects; let him be thus taken for all in all, and we shall feel his incontestable right to the title of a great sovereign, which now for three centuries he has maintained.

CHAPTER 14

Battle of Lepanto

Solyman the Great, the Magnificent, the Lawgiver, the Lord of his Age, was succeeded by a prince to whom his own national historians give the epithet of "Selim the Sot." The ignoble vices of this prince (to secure whose accession so much and such dear blood had been shed) had attracted the sorrowful notice and drawn down the indignant reprimand of the old *Sultan* in his latter years; but there was now no brother to compete for the throne with Selim; and on the 25th of September, 1566, the sabre of Othman was girt for the first time on a sovereign, who shrank from leading in person the armies of Islam, and wasted in low debauchery the hours which his predecessors had consecrated to the duties of the state.

The effects of this fatal degeneracy were not immediately visible. The perfect organisation, civil and military, in which Solyman had left the empire, cohered for a time after the strong hand, which had fashioned and knit it together for nearly half a century, was withdrawn. There was a numerous body of statesmen and generals who had been trained under the great *Sultan*: and thus somewhat of his spirit was preserved in the realm, until they had passed away, and another generation arisen, which knew not Solyman. Foremost of these was the Grand Vizier Mohammed Sokolli, who had victoriously concluded the campaign of Szigeth after Solyman's death; and who, fortunately for Selim and his kingdom, acquired and maintained an ascendency over the weak mind of the young *Sultan*, which was not indeed always strong enough to prevent the adoption of evil measures, or to curb the personal excesses of Selim's private life, but which checked the progress of anarchy, and maintained the air of grandeur in enterprise and of vigour in execution, by which the Sublime Porte had hitherto been distinguished.

An armistice was concluded with the Emperor Maximilian in 1568, on the terms that each party should retain, possession of what it then occupied; and there was now for many years an unusual pause in the war between the Houses of Hapsburg and Othman. The great foreign events of Selim's reign are the attempts to conquer Astrakhan, and unite the Don and the Volga; the conquest of Cyprus; and the naval war of the Battle of Lepanto. The first of these is peculiarly interesting, because the Turks were then for the first time brought into armed collision with the Russians.

In the middle of the sixteenth century, while the Ottoman Empire, then at the meridian of its glory, was the terror and admiration of the world; the Russian was slowly and painfully struggling out of the degradation and ruin, with which it had been afflicted by two centuries and a half of Tartar conquest. The craft and courage of Ivan III. and Vasili Ivanovich had, between 1480 and 1533, emancipated Moscow from paying tribute to the *Khans* of Kipchakh; and, by annexing other Russian principalities to that of Muscovy, these princes had formed an united Russia, which extended from Kief to Kasan, and as far as Siberia and Norwegian Lapland. Even thus early the Grand Dukes, or, as they began to style themselves, the *Czars* of Muscovy, seem to have cherished ambitious projects of reigning at Constantinople.

★★★★★★

This title is not a corruption of the word *Caesar*, as many have supposed, but is an old Oriental word which the Russians acquired through the Slavonic translation of the Bible, and which they bestowed at first on the Greek emperors, and afterwards on the Tartar *khans*. In Persia it signifies *throne, supreme authority*; and we find it in the termination of the names of the kings of Assyria and Babylon, such as Phalassar, Nabonassar," &c.—Kelly, *Hist. Russia*, citing Karamsin. Von Hammer, in his last note to his 31st book, says, "The title *Czar* or *Tzar*, is an ancient title of Asiatic sovereigns. We find an instance of it in the title 'The *Schar*,' of the sovereign of Gurdistan; and in that of *Tzarina* (*Zapivn*) of the Scythians."

★★★★★★

Ivan III. sought out and married Sophia, the last princess of the Greek Imperial family, from which the conquering Ottomans had wrested Byzantium. From that time forth, the two-headed eagle, which had been the imperial cognisance of the Emperors of Constantinople, has been assumed by the Russian sovereigns as their symbol of dominion.

******

Until after the marriage of Ivan III. with Sophia, the cognisance of the grand princes of Moscow had always been a figure of St. George killing the dragon.—Kelly's *Hist. Russia.*

******

During the minority of Ivan the Terrible (who succeeded in 1533) a period of anarchy ensued in Russia, but on that prince assuming the government, the vigour of the state was restored; the Khanates of Astrakhan and Kasan were conquered and finally annexed to Russia; the Don Cossacks were united with the empire, and Yermak, one of their chiefs, invaded and acquired for Ivan the vast regions of Siberia. The extent of Russia at Ivan's accession, was 37,000 German square miles: at his death, it was 144,000. But so little was Russia then heeded or known in Western Europe, that the charter given by Philip and Mary to the first company of English merchants trading thither purports to be granted "upon the discovery of the said country;" likening it to some region of savages which civilised man might then tread for the first time amid the American wilderness.

Yet even at that period, those who watched the immense extent of the crude materials for warlike power, which the Czar of Muscovy possessed, the numbers, the rugged hardihood of his people, their implicit obedience to their autocrat, their endurance of privations, and the nature of the country so difficult for an invader, expressed their forebodings of the peril to which the independence of other states might be exposed by Muscovite ambition, if once those rude masses acquired the arms and the discipline of civilised war.

******

Richard Chancellor, who sailed with Sir Hugh Willoughby in search of a North-East Passage, and who travelled from Archangel up to Moscow, and afterwards resided at Ivan's court, in his curious account of the Russians (published in *Hakluyt's Voyages*, vol. i.), after mentioning the immense number of troops which the Muscovite duke raised for war, and their endurance of hard fare and cold, graphically describes their want of discipline. He says: "They are men without all order in the field, for *they run hurling on heaps.*"

He afterwards says: "Now, what might be made of these men, if they were broken to order, and knowledge of civil warres? If this prince had within his country such men as could make them understand the thing aforesaid, I do believe that two of the best or greatest princes in Christendom were not well able to match with him, considering the greatness of his power, and the hardiness of his people, and straite living both of man and horse, and the small charges which his warres stand him in." In another page, Chancellor says of the Russians: "If they knew their strength, no man were able to make match with them; nor they that dwell near them should have any rest of them. But I think it is not God's will. For I may compare them to a horse, that knoweth not his strength, whom a little child ruleth and guideth with a bridle, for all his great strength; that if he did know it neither man nor child could rule him."

✶✶✶✶✶✶

It is melancholy to recognise in the fate of Poland and so many other countries the truth of the words used by the Polish King, Sigismund, nearly three centuries ago, when, in remonstrating with England for supplying the *Czar* with military engineers and stores, he called him "the Muscovite, the hereditary enemy of all free nations."

✶✶✶✶✶✶

"*Hostem non modo regni nostri temporarium sed etiam omnium nationum liberarum hsereditarium Moscum.*" The letter of Sigismund to Queen Elizabeth is cited in the recent work of the Russian Dr. Hamel on *England and Russia*. In another letter of Sigismund's, translated by Hakluyt (Hamel), the Polish king says of the *Czar*: "We seemed hitherto to vanquish him only in this, that he was rude of arts and ignorant of policies. If so be that this navigation to the Narva continue, what shall be unknowen to him? The Moscovite, made more perfect in warlike affaires with engines of warre and shippes, will slay or make bound all that shall withstand him, which God defend."

✶✶✶✶✶✶

The Russians, at the time of Selim's accession, had been involved in fierce and frequent wars with the *Sultan's* vassals, the Crim Tartars; but the Porte had taken no part in these contests. But the bold genius of the Vizier Sokolli now attempted the realisation of a project, which, if successful, would have barred the southern progress of Russia, by firmly planting the Ottoman power on the banks of the Don and the Volga, and along the shores of the Caspian Sea. The Turkish armies, in their invasions of Persia, had always suffered severely during their marches along the sterile and mountainous regions of Upper Armenia and Mazerbijan. Some disputes with Persia had arisen soon after Selim's accession, which made a war with that kingdom seem probable; and Sokolli proposed to unite the rivers Don and Volga by a canal, and then send a Turkish armament up the sea of Azoph and the Don, thence across by the intended channel to the Volga, and then down the latter river into the Casjiian; from the southern shores of which sea the Ottomans might strike at Tabriz and the heart of the Persian power.

Those two mighty rivers, the Don and the Volga, run towards each other, the one from the north-west, the other from the north-east, for many hundred leagues, until they are within thirty miles of junction. They then diverge; and the Don (the "*extremus Tanais*" of the ancients), pours its waters into the sea of Azoph, near the city of that name; the Volga blends with the Caspian, at a little distance from the city of Astrakhan, which is built on the principal branch of the Delta of that river. The project of uniting them by a canal is said to have been one entertained by Seleucus Nicator, one of the ablest of the successors of Alexander the Great. It was now revived by the *grand vizier* of Selim II.; and though the cloud of hostility with Persia passed over, Sokolli determined to persevere with the scheme: the immense commercial and political advantages of which, if completed, to the Ottoman Empire, were evident to the old statesman of Solyman the Great.

Azoph already belonged to the Turks, but in order to realise the great project entertained, it was necessary to occupy Astrakhan also. Accordingly, 3000 *Janissaries* and 20,000 horse were sent to besiege Astrakhan, and a co-operative force of 30,000 Tartars was ordered to join them, and to aid in making the canal. 5000 *Janissaries* and 3000 pioneers were at the same time sent to Azoph to commence and secure the great work at its western extremity.

But the generals of Ivan the Terrible did their duty to their stern master ably in this emergency. The Russian garrison of Astrakhan sallied on its besiegers, and repulsed them with considerable loss. And a Russian Army, 15,000 strong, under Prince Serebinoff, came suddenly on the workmen and *Janissaries* near Azoph, and put them to headlong flight. It was upon this occasion that the first trophies won from the Turks came into Russian hands. An army of Tartars, which marched to succour the Turks, was also entirely defeated by Ivan's forces; and the Ottomans, dispirited by their losses and reverses, withdrew altogether from the enterprise.

Their Tartar allies, who knew that the close neighbourhood of the

Turks would ensure their own entire subjection to the Sultan, eagerly promoted the distaste, which the Ottomans had acquired for Sokolli's project, by enlarging on the horrors of the climate of Muscovy, and especially on the peril, in which the short summer nights of those northern regions placed either the soul or the body of the true believer. As the Mahometan law requires the evening prayer to be said two hours after sunset, and the morning prayer to be repeated at the dawn of day, it was necessary that a Moslem should, in a night of only three hours long (according to the Tartars), either lose his natural rest, or violate the commands of his Prophet. The Turks gladly re-embarked, and left the unpropitious soil; but a tempest assailed their flotilla on its homeward voyage, and only 7000 of their whole force ever returned to Constantinople.

Russia was yet far too weak to enter on a war of retaliation with the Turks. She had subdued the Tartar Khanates of Kasan and Astrakhan; but their kinsmen of the Crimea were still formidable enemies to the Russians, even without Turkish aid. It was only two years after the Ottoman expedition to the Don and Volga, that the *Khan* of the Crimea made a victorious inroad into Russia, took Moscow by storm, and sacked the city (1571). The Czar Ivan had, in 1570, sent an ambassador, named Nossolitof, to Constantinople, to complain of the Turkish attack on Astrakhan, and to propose that there should be peace, friendship, and alliance between the two empires.

Nossolitof, in addressing the *viziers*, dwelt much on the toleration which his master showed to Mahometans in his dominions, as a proof that the *Czar* was no enemy to the faith of Islam. The Russian ambassador was favourably received at the Sublime Porte, and no further hostilities between the Turks and Russians took place for nearly a century. But the Ottoman pride and contempt for Russia were shown by the *Sultan* omitting to make the customary inquiry of Nossolitof respecting his royal master's health, and by the *Czar's* representative not receiving the invitation to a dinner before audience, which was usually sent to ambassadors.

Besides his project for uniting the Volga and the Don, the Grand Vizier Sokolli had revived the oft-formed project of opening a communication between the Red Sea and the Mediterranean. Sokolli grandly designed to make such a channel through the Isthmus of Suez, as would enable the Ottoman fleets to sail from sea to sea. His schemes in this quarter were delayed by a revolt which broke out in Arabia, and was not quelled without a difficult and sanguinary war. And when that important province was brought back to submission, the self-willed cupidity and violence of Sultan Selim himself involved the Porte in a war with Venice and other Christian states, for the sake of acquiring the island of Cyprus, which he had coveted while he was governor of Kutahia in his father's lifetime.

✶✶✶✶✶✶

It seems that Selim, like Cassio, found the attraction of Cyprus wine irresistible. A Jew, named Joseph Nassy, had been Selim's boon companion, and persuaded him that he ought to be master of the isle in which the juice of the grape was so delicious. See Von Hammer, vol. ii.

✶✶✶✶✶✶

There was a treaty of peace between Venice and the Porte; but Selim obtained from his Mufti Ebousououd a *fetva* authorising him to attack Cyprus, in open violation of the treaty. Cyprus had at one time been under Mahometan rulers; and the Turkish authorities now proclaimed and acted on the principle, that the sovereign of Islam may at any time break a treaty, for the sake of reconquering from the misbelievers a country, which has formerly belonged to the territory of Islam.

✶✶✶✶✶✶

The case laid by Selim before the *mufti*, and the answer of that functionary, are given at length by Von Hammer, vol. ii. The reader will observe now utterly opposed this principle is to the doctrine laid down in the Turkish military code.

✶✶✶✶✶✶

The Grand Vizier Sokolli earnestly, but vainly, opposed the war with Venice. His influence was counteracted by that of the infamous Lala Mustapha, who had in Solyman's reign been Selim's instrument in the foul practices by which Prince Bajazet and his family were destroyed. Lala Mustapha obtained the command of the expedition against Cyprus; and the island was subdued by the Turks (1570-71), though fifty thousand of them perished to effect its conquest The conduct of the war of Cyprus was as disgracefully treacherous and cruel on the part of the Turks, as its inception had been flagrantly unjust. The Venetian *commandant*, Bragadino, who had defended Famagosta, the chief stronghold of the island, with heroic valour and constancy, was subjected to the grossest indignities, and at last flayed alive, though he had surrendered on the faith of a capitulation, by which the garrison were to march out with all their arms and property, and to be transported in Turkish vessels to Candia.

The charges which Lala Mustapha made against the Venetian general of personal insolence to himself in an interview after the capitulation, of cruelty to the Turkish prisoners during the siege, and of having formerly put Mahometan pilgrims to death, could, even if true, be no justification for the treacherous and inhuman treatment, of which Bragadino was made the victim. But the modern German historian, who narrates with just horror and initiation the crime of the Turkish commander, observes that such an act was too much in the spirit of the age. Selim II. was the contemporary of Charles IX. and Ivan the Cruel The massacre of St. Bartholomew took place not a year before the murder of Bragadino; and scarcely another year had passed away when, at the capture of the fortress of Wittenstein, in Finland, the garrison was cut in pieces by the Russians, and the commandant tied to a spear and roasted alive.

If this took place in France and Finland, what was to be expected in Turkey under the government of a young prince who had been the murderer of his own brother, and who, in direct violation of the law of Mahomet, was an open drunkard, and gave free scope to every vice? We might (if crimes could excuse each other), in addition to the instances of contemporaneous cruelty cited by Von Hammer, refer to the horrors practised by the Spaniards under Don Ferdinand of Toledo, at Naarden, in 1572, in insolent defiance of the terms of a treaty of surrender. (Vol. i. Mrs. Davies's *History of Holland*). But it is both unprofitable and revolting to enter at length on a retrospective study of comparative cruelty. Such deeds bring shame, not only upon particular nations of mankind, but upon human nature in general.

The fall of Cyprus, the unscrupulous violence with which it had been attacked, and the immense preparations in the Turkish seaports and arsenals, now raised anxious alarm, not only at Venice, but all along the Christian shores of the Mediterranean. The Pope Pius V. succeeded in forming a maritime league, of which the Spaniards, the Venetians, and the Knights of Malta were the principal members; and at the head of it was placed Don John of Austria, the natural son of Charles V., and one of the most renowned commanders of the age.

The confederate fleets mustered at Messina early in the autumn of 1571. The force led thither by Don John consisted of seventy Spanish galleys, six Maltese, and three of Savoy. The Papal squadron, under Marc Colonna, added twelve galleys. The Venetian Admiral Veniero brought 108 galleys, and six huge *galeasses*, or *mahons*, of a larger size and carrying a heavier weight of metal than had yet been known in Mediterranean warfare. Great care had been paid by all the confederates to the proper selection of their crews and the equipment of their vessels. Nobly born volunteers from all parts of Roman Catholic Christendom had flocked together to serve under so celebrated a chief as Don John, and in such an honourable enterprise: and the Christian fleet sailed across to seek its enemies eastward of the Ionian Gulf, in the highest state of efficiency.

The Turkish naval forces were assembled in the Gulf of Corinth. The Capitan Pacha, Mouezinzade Ali, was commander-in-chief; and under him were the well-known Ouloudj Ali, Beyler Bey of Algiers; Djaffer Pacha, Beyler Bey of Tripoli; Hassan Pacha, the son of Khaireddin Barbarossa, and fifteen other *beys* of maritime *sanjaks*, each of whom was entitled to hoist his banner on his galley, as a Prince of the Sea. The troops embarked on board the fleet were commanded by Pertew Pacha. The fleet amounted to 240 galleys, and sixty vessels of smaller size. Ouloudj Ali and Pertew Pacha represented to the commander-in-chief that the fleet was hastily and imperfectly manned, and that it was imprudent to fight a general battle until it was in a better state of equipment. But Mouezinzade's courage prevailed over his discretion, and the destruction of his fleet was the result.

On the 7th October, 1571, a little after noon, the Christian fleet appeared near the entrance of the Gulf of Patras, off the little islands of Curzolari (the ancient Echinades), which lie at the mouth of the Aspro Potamo (the Achelous), on the Albanian shore. The Ottoman fleet sailed out of the Gulf of Lepanto to encounter them, and formed in line of battle, Ouloudj. All commanding the left wing; Mohammed Schaoulah, Bey of Negropont, heading the right wing; and the Capitan Pacha, aided by Pertew Pacha, being in the centre. Don John drew up his chief force in the centre in the form of a crescent The Prince of Parma (afterwards so well known in Holland, and the intended conqueror of England), the Admiral of Savoy, Caraccioli, the Neapolitan admiral, and other illustrious leaders were in command of it.

The Marquis of Santa Croce commanded a squadron that was stationed in the rear of the main line as a reserve. A division of fifty-three galleys, under the Venetian *proveditor*, Barbarigo, formed the right wing; and the left wing consisted of fifty-four galleys, under Jean André Doria, nephew of the great admiral of the Emperor Charles. Don John took his own station in advance of the centre line, and the other two admirals of the fleet, Colonna and Veniero, were at his sides. The

Turkish Capitan Pacha seeing this, brought forward his own galley and those of Pertew Pacha and His treasurer, to answer the challenge of the three admiral galleys of the Christians, that thus stood forward between the battles, like the Promachi in the conflicts of the Homeric heroes.

Don John showed his gallantry by thus taking the post of danger; but he also showed his skill by placing the six great Venetian *galeasses* like redoubts at intervals in front of the confederate fleet. The Turks had less fear of these huge vessels than might have been justified by the event of the day; but there was a pause before they began the attack, and each fleet lay motionless for a time, regarding with admiration and secret awe the strength and the splendour of its adversary's array. At length the Turkish admiral fired a gun, charged with powder only, as a challenge to begin the action. A ball from one of Don John's heaviest cannon whistled through the Ottoman rigging in answer; the Turks rowed forward with loud shouts amid the clangour of their drums and fifes to the attack; and the action, commencing on the Christian left, soon became general along the line.

The large Venetian *galeasses* now proved of the utmost service to the Christian fleet. The Turkish galleys in passing them were obliged to break their order; and the fire kept up by the Venetian artillery-men from the heavy ordnance of the *galeasses* was more destructive than ever yet had been witnessed in naval gunnery. Still the Turks pressed forward and engaged the Christian left and centre with obstinate courage. The two high admirals of the conflicting fleets, Don John and Mouezinzade Ali, encountered each other with equal gallantry. Their vessels clashed together, and then lay closely locked for upwards of two hours, during which time the 300 *janissaries* and 100 arquebusiers of the Turk, and the 400 chosen arquebusiers who served on board Don John's ship, fought with the most determined bravery.

The two other admiral galleys of the Christians had come to the support of Don John, and the Capitan Pacha's galley was similarly aided by her *consorts*; so that these six ships formed a compact mass in the midst of the battle, like that which was grouped round Nelson in the *Victory*, by the *Temeraire*, the *Redoubtable*, and the *Neptune* at the Battle of Trafalgar. The death of Mouezinzade, who fell, shot dead by a musket ball, decided the memorable contest. The Turkish admiral galley was carried by boarding; and when Santa Croce came on to support the first line with the reserve, the whole Ottoman centre was broken, and the defeat soon extended to the right wing. In their left

Ouloudj Ali was more successful. He outmanoeuvred Doria; turned his wing; and, attacking his ships when disordered and separated one from another, Ouloudj Ali captured fifteen Maltese and Venetian galleys, and with his own hand struck off the head of the *commandant* of Messina.

But seeing that the day was irreparably lost for Turkey, Ouloudj collected forty of his best galleys, pushed with them through the Christian vessels that tried to intercept him, and stood safely out to sea. They were the only Turkish vessels that escaped. The Ottomans lost in this great battle 260 ships; of which ninety-four were sunk, burnt, or run aground and destroyed upon the coast, the rest were captured and divided among the allies. Thirty thousand Turks were slain; and 16,000 Christians, who had served as galley slaves in the Ottoman fleet, were rescued from captivity. The confederates lost fifteen galleys and 8000 men. Many princely and noble names are recorded in the lists of the killed and wounded of that day; but there is none which we read with more interest than that of Cervantes.

The author of *Don Quixote* served at Lepanto, as a volunteer in the regiment of Moncada, which was distributed among part of the fleet. On the day of the battle Cervantes was stationed on board the galley *Marquesa*, and though suffering severely with illness, he distinguished himself greatly in the action, during which he received two arquebuss wounds, one of which maimed his left hand for life. He often referred with just pride to the loss of his hand, and ever rejoiced at having been present at the glorious action at Lepanto; "on that day so fortunate to Christendom, when" (in his own words) "all nations were undeceived of their error in believing that the Turks were invincible at sea." (*Don Quixote,* book iv.)

The glories of the "Fight of Lepanto " thrilled Christendom with rapture; and they have for centuries been the favourite themes of literature and art. But the modern German historian well observes, that we ought to think with sadness of the nullity of the results of such a battle. After occupying three weeks in dividing the spoils of Lepanto, and nearly coming to blows over them, the Christian squadrons returned to their respective ports, to be thanked, lauded, and dismissed. Meanwhile, the indefatigable Ouloudj Ali, with the squadron which he had saved from Lepanto, gleaned together the Turkish galleys that lay in the different ports of the Archipelago; and, at the end of December, sailed proudly into the port of Constantinople at the head of a fleet of eighty-seven sail. In recompense of his zeal, he received the rank of Capitan Pacha; and the *Sultan* changed his name of Ouloudj into Kilidj, which means "The Sword."

The veteran admiral, Pialé, the hero of Djerbé, was yet alive; and under his and Kilidj Ali's vigorous and skilful directions, a new fleet was constructed and launched before the winter was past While the rejoicing Christians built churches, the resolute Turks built docks. The effect was, that before June, a Turkish fleet of 250 sail, comprising eight *galeasses* or *mahons* of the largest size, sailed forth to assert the dominion of the seas. The confederate Christian powers, after long delays, collected a force numerically superior to the Ottoman; but, though two indecisive encounters took place, they were unable to chase Kilidj Ali from the western coasts of Greece, nor could the Duke of Parma undertake the siege of Modon, which had been designed as the chief operation for that year. It was evident, that though the Christian confederates could win a battle, the Turk was still their superior in a war.

★★★★★★

The Venetian envoy, Barbaro, endeavoured to open negotiations at Constantinople in the winter after the Battle of Lepanto. The *vizier*, in reference to the loss of the Turkish fleet, and the conquest of Cyprus, said to him: "There is a great difference between our loss and yours. You have shaved our chin; but our beard is growing again. We have lopped off your arm; and you can never replace it."

★★★★★★

The Venetians sought peace in 1573, and in order to obtain it, consented not only that the *Sultan* should retain Cyprus, but that Venice should pay him his expenses of the conquest. It was not unnaturally remarked by those, who heard the terms of the treaty, that it sounded as if the Turks had gained the Battle of Lepanto.

After Venice had made peace with the Porte, Don John undertook an expedition with the Spanish fleet against Tunis, which Ouloudj Ah had conquered during the year in which Cyprus was attacked. Don John succeeded in capturing the city, which was the more easy, inasmuch as the citadel had continued in the power of the Spaniards. Don John built a new fortress and left a powerful garrison in Tunis; but, eighteen months after his departure, his old enemy Kilidj Ali reappeared there; and after a sharp siege, made the *Sultan* again master of the city and citadel, and stormed Don John's new castle.

Tunis now, like Algiers and Tripoli, became an Ottoman government. The effectual authority which the Porte exercised over these piratical states of 'North Africa (which are often called the Barbaresque Regencies) grew weaker in course of time; but the tie of allegiance was not entirely broken: and though the French have in our own time seized Algiers, the *Sultan* is still sovereign of Tripoli and Tunis, the scenes of the successful valour of Dragut and Kilidj Ali.

Selim the Sot died not long after the recovery of Tunis; and the manner of his death befitted the manner of his life. He had drunk off a bottle of Cyprus wine at a draught, and on entering the bathroom with the fumes of his favourite beverage in his head, he slipped and fell on the marble floor, receiving an injury of the skull which brought on a fatal fever (1574). He showed once a spark of the true Othman, by the zeal with which he aided his officers in restoring the Turkish navy after Lepanto. He then contributed his private treasure liberally, and gave up part of the pleasure-gardens of the Serail for the site of the new docks. Except this brief flash of patriotism or pride, his whole career, both as prince and sultan, is unrelieved by a single merit; and it is blackened by mean treachery, by gross injustice and cruelty, and by grovelling servitude to the coarsest appetites of our nature.

CHAPTER 15

War with Austria

There is an Eastern Legend, that when the great King and Prophet Solomon died, he was sitting on his lion-throne, clad in the royal robes, and with all the insignia of dominion round him. The lifeless form remained in the monarch's usual attitude; and the races of men and beasts, of *genii* and demons, who watched at respectful distance, knew not of the change, but long with accustomed awe, paid homage, and made obeisance before the form that sat upon the throne; until the staff on which Solomon had leaned, holding it in both hands towards the mouth, and on which the body had continued propped, was gnawed by worms and gave way, letting the corpse fall to the ground. Then and not till then the truth was known; and the world was filled with sorrow and alarm.

This fable well images the manner in which the empire of Sultan Solyman remained propped on the staff of the *vizierate*, and retained its majesty after his death and during the reign of Selim, so long as the power of Solyman's Grand Vizier Sokolli remained unimpaired. When Sokolli's authority was weakened and broken by the corrupt influence of favourites and women at the court of Selim's successor, Amurath III., the shock of falling empire was felt throughout the Ottoman world, (Von Hammer vol. ii.), spreading from the court to the capital, from the capital to the provinces, and at last becoming sensible even to foreign powers.

Amurath III. was summoned at the age of twenty-eight from his government at Magnesia to succeed his father at Constantinople. He arrived at the capital on the night of the 21st of December, 1574, and his first act was to order the execution of his five brothers. In the morning the high officers of state were assembled to greet their master, and the first words of the new *Sultan* were anxiously watched for, as ominous of the coming events of his reign. Amurath, who had retired to rest fatigued with his voyage, and literally fasting from all but sin, turned to the *aga* of the eunuchs and said, "I am hungry; bring me something to eat." These words were considered to be prophetic of scarcity during his reign; and the actual occurrence of a famine at Constantinople in the following year did much to confirm the popular superstition.

Sokolli retained the *grand vizierate* until his death in 1578, but the effeminate heart of Amurath was ruled by courtiers, who amused his listless melancholy; and by four women, one of whom was his mother, the dowager *Sultana*, or (as the Turks term her) the *Sultana Validé*, Nour Banou: the next was Amurath's first favourite *Sultana*, a Venetian lady of the noble House of Baffo, who had been captured by a Turkish corsair in her early years. The fair Venetian so enchanted Amurath, that he was long strictly constant to her, slighting the other varied attractions of his *harem*, and neglecting the polygamous privileges of his creed. The *Sultana Validé*, alarmed at the ascendency which the Sultana Safiye (as the Venetian lady was termed) was acquiring over Amurath, succeeded in placing such temptation in her son's way, as induced him to make his Venetian love no longer his only love; and he thenceforth rushed into the opposite extreme of licentious indulgence even for a Mahometan prince.

Such was the demand created for the supply of the imperial *harem*, that it is said to have raised the price of beautiful girls in the slave-market of Constantinople. One of this multitude of favoured fair, a Hungarian by birth, obtained considerable influence over her lord; but his first love, Safiye, though no longer able to monopolise Amurath's affections, never lost her hold on them; and it was her will that chiefly directed the Ottoman fleets and armies during his reign; fortunately for her native country Venice, which she prevented Turkey from attacking, even under circumstances of great provocation, caused by the outrages and insolence of some of the cruisers of the Republic of St. Mark. The fourth lady who had sway in Amurath's councils, did not owe it to her own charms, but to the adroitness with which she placed before him the charms of others. This was Djanfeda, who was *kiaya* (or grand mistress) of the *harem*. These were the chief ladies who interposed and debated on all questions how the power bequeathed by the great Solyman should be wielded, and with whom the House of Othman should have peace or war.

Generals and admirals trained in the camps and fleets of Solyman still survived; and the hostilities, in which the Turkish Empire was engaged during the reign of Amurath III., were marked by more than one victory, and were productive of several valuable acquisitions of territory. War between Turkey and Persia broke out again soon after Amurath's accession, and was continued for seven years. The death of the Shah Tahmasp, and the tyranny and misgovernment of his successors had thrown Persia into a state of anarchy and weakness, which greatly favoured the progress of the Ottoman arms; though the fortune of the war was often chequered, and the losses of the Turks by the sword, and by fatigue and privation were numerous and severe.

In this war the Turkish armies attacked and conquered Georgia, which had been in alliance with Persia, and they penetrated as far as Daghestan and the shores of the Caspian Sea. The Turkish troops from the Crimea and their Tartar auxiliaries took an important part in those campaigns in the regions of the Caucasus. The Bey of Azoph was, in 1578, rewarded for the alacrity with which he had led the vanguard of an army round the north of the Euxine, with the sounding title of Capitan Pacha of the Caspian Sea. The most remarkable episode in the war was the march in 1583 of Osman Pacha, surnamed Ozdemir or Osman of the Iron Nerves, the commander of the Turkish forces in Georgia, who led an army in the depth of winter through the defiles of the Caucasus, through Circassia, and across the frozen plains of the Kuban to Azoph, and thence to the Crimea, where his unexpected appearance crushed an incipient revolt against the Sultan.

Osman carried the head of the rebel *khan* from the Crimea to Constantinople, where he was received with rapturous honours by the *Sultan*, who took the jewels from his own turban, and the richly adorned *yataghan* from his own belt to deck the veteran hero, the recital of whose exploits and sufferings had excited interest and animated attention in the jaded spirit of the imperial voluptuary. A peace was at last made between Turkey and Persia in 1590, by which the Ottomans obtained Georgia, the city of Tabriz, and also Azerbijan, Schirwan, Loristan, and Scherhezol. A clause was inserted in the treaty, which required the Persians not to curse any longer the three first *caliphs*. As this implied the conversion of the Persian nation from Schiism to Sunnism, which was impracticable the stipulation could only be regarded as a mere form to gratify the religious pride of the *Sultan*, or as designed to furnish pretexts for renewing the war, when the Porte might judge it convenient.

Except the collisions, that from time to time took place near the boundary line in Hungary between the Turkish *pachas* and Christian *commandants* of the respective border countries, the Ottoman Empire preserved peace with the powers of Christian Europe during the reign of Amurath III. until two years before his death, when war was declared against Austria. Commercial and diplomatic relations were established under Amurath with the greater part of Western Europe; the Ottomans ever showing the same wise liberality in all that relates to international traffic, that has been already mentioned. England, which, until the time of Amurath III., had been a stranger to Turkey, sent in 1579 three merchants, William Harebone, Edward Ellis, and Richard Stapel, to Constantinople, who sought and obtained from the Porte the same favour to English commerce, and the same privileges for English commercial residents in Turkey, that other foreign nations enjoyed.

In 1583, William Harebone was accredited to Constantinople as the ambassador of our Queen Elizabeth, who was then the especial object of the hatred of Philip II. of Spain, and sought anxiously to induce the *Sultan* to make common cause with her against the Spanish king, and his great confederate the Pope of Rome. In her state papers to the Ottoman court, the Protestant Queen takes advantage of the well-known horror with which the Mahometans regard anything approaching to image-worship, and styles herself:

The unconquered and most puissant defender of the true faith against the idolaters who falsely profess the name of Christ.

And there is a letter addressed by her agent at the Porte to the *Sultan* in November, 1687, at the time when Spain was threatening England with the Great Armada, in which the *Sultan* is implored to send, if not the whole tremendous force of his empire, at least sixty or eighty galleys:

.... against that idolater, the King of Spain, who, relying on the help of the Pope and all idolatrous princes, designs to crush the Queen of England, and then to turn his whole power to the destruction of the *Sultan*, and make himself universal monarch.

The English advocate urges on the Ottoman sovereign, that if he and Elizabeth join promptly and vigorously in maritime warfare against Spain, the "proud Spaniard and the lying Pope with all their followers will be struck down;" that God will protect His own, and punish the idolaters of the earth by the arms of England and Turkey.

✶✶✶✶✶✶

The letters are given at length by Von Hammer, in his notes to his 39th book. They are in Latin. The first is from Elizabeth to the Vizier Mohammed dated at Windsor, November 15, 1582. The second letter, laid by Elizabeth's ambassador before the *Sultan*, is dated November 9, 1587. There are two more: one, in 1587, requesting the release of some English subjects from Algiers; the other, which is dated on the last day of .November, 1588, announces the victory of the English, and still urges the *Sultan* to attack Spain. Henry III. of France had sent an envoy to Constantinople, in April, 1588, for the same purpose; and to warn the *Sultan* that if Philip conquered England he would soon overpower Turkey. (See Mignet's *Mary Queen of Scots*, vol. ii.)

The Turks seem to have met these applications with fair promises; but they certainly did no more. The English are said to have given considerable sums to the Turkish historian, Seadeddin, to employ in their favour the influence which that learned writer possessed, or was supposed to possess with the *Sultan*, who inherited the family fondness for literature. Some of the Ottoman *grandees* were much impressed by the distinction between the Roman Catholic image-worshippers and the Protestant English.

Sinan Pacha is reported to have told the Austrian Ambassador Pezzen, "That there was nothing needed to make the English into genuine Mussulmans, save a lifting of the finger and a recital of the *Eschdad*" (the formula of confession of faith). But Seadeddin does not seem to have been worth his pay. Perhaps, if Sultana Safiye, or the matron Djanfeda, had been well bribed by our Virgin Queen, the result might have been different. A Turkish squadron in the Channel, co-operating with Drake and Raleigh, would have formed a curious episode in the great epic of the Spanish Armada. I may add that Professor Ranke also, in his recent *History of England* (vol. i.), speaks of "the advances made by the English Government to the Turks in the time of Elizabeth."

✶✶✶✶✶✶

The evils, which the general prevalence of venality and the force of feminine intrigue at the *Sultan's* court had brought upon the Ottoman Empire, were not yet apparent to foreigners, who only saw its numerous fleets and armies, and only heard of its far-extended conquests; but before the close of Amurath's reign, the inevitable fruits of corruption and favouritism were unmistakeably manifest Every appointment, civil, military, judicial, or administrative, was now determined by court influence or money. The *Sultan*, who squandered large sums on the musicians, the parasites, and buffoons, by whom he loved to be surrounded, was often personally in need of money, and at last stooped to the degradation of taking part of the bribes, which petitioners for office gave to his courtiers. One of his principal favourites was Schemsi Pacha, who traced his pedigree up to a branch of those Seljukian princes, whom the House of Othman had superseded in the sovereignty of the East.

The historian Ali, who afterwards wrote Schemsi Pacha's biography, relates, that one day he himself was in that favourite's apartments, when Schemsi came thither from the *Sultan's* presence, and said with a joyous air to one of his domestics, "At last I have avenged my house on the House of Othman. For, if the Ottoman dynasty caused our downfall, I have now made it prepare its own."

"How has that been done?" cried the old domestic gravely.

"I have done it,' said Schemsi, "by persuading the *Sultan* to share in the sale of his own favours. It is true I placed a tempting bait before him; 40,000 *ducats* make no trifling sum. Henceforth the *Sultan* will himself set the example of corruption; and corruption will destroy the empire,"

The armies and military organisation of the Porte now began to show the workings of this taint, not only through the effect of incompetent men receiving rank as generals and as officers, but through the abuses with which its feudal system was overrun, and the sale of *ziamets* and *timars* to traffickers of every description: even to Jews and Jewesses, who either sold them again to the best, bidders, or received the profits of the feudal lauds, in defiance both of the spirit and letter of the law. An alarming relaxation of discipline among the troops, and increasing turbulence and insubordination accompanied those scandals; and at last, in 1589, the *Janissaries* openly attacked the *serail* of the *Sultan* where the *divan* was assembled, and demanded the head of Mohammed Pacha, Beyler Bey of Roumelia, surnamed "the Falcon" for his rapacity.

Their anger against this royal favourite was not causeless, for it was at his instigation that the pay of the troops had been given in grossly debased coinage. They now attacked the palace, and cried, "Give us up the *beyler bey*, or we shall know how to find our way even to the *Sultan*." Amurath ordered that the soldiery should receive satisfaction; and accordingly the heads of the guilty pacha, and of an innocent treasurer whom they had involved in their angry accusations, were laid before these military sovereigns of the sovereign.

It has been truly said that the government which once has bowed the knee to force, must expect that force will thenceforth be its master. Within four years the *Janissaries* revolted twice again, and on each occasion compelled the *Sultan* to depose and change his *vizier*. In 1591 these haughty *praetorians* coerced their sovereign into placing on the vassal throne of Moldavia the competitor who had obtained their favour by bribes. While these, and many other tumults, in some of which the *Spahis* and *Janissaries* waged a civil war against each other in the streets, convulsed the capital, the provinces were afflicted by the rapacious tyranny of their governors and the other officers of state, and by its natural results.

The garrisons of Pesth and Tabriz mutinied on account of their pay being kept back. The warlike tribes of the Druses in Lebanon took arms against their provincial oppressors. The revolt of Transylvania, Moldavia, and Wallachia was a still more formidable symptom of the wretched condition of the empire. The risings in these provinces were encouraged by the war with Austria, which broke out in 1593. And in 1594 the war with Persia was renewed, and marked by little success on the Turkish side.

While his realm was in this distracted state, Sultan Amurath sickened and died (16th January, 1595). Weak both in mind and body, he had long been perplexed by dreams and signs, which he believed to be forebodings of death. On the morning of the last day of his life he had gone to a magnificent kiosk lately built by Sinan Pacha on the shore of the Bosphorus, which commanded an extensive prospect; and he lay there watching the ships that sailed to and from the Propontis and the Euxine. His musicians, as usual, were in attendance, and they played an air which recalled to Amurath's memory the melancholy words of the song to which it belonged. He murmured to himself the first line:

Come and keep watch by me tonight, Oh Death!

And it chanced that at that very time two Egyptian galleys saluted the Porte, and the concussion caused by the guns' fire shattered the glazed dome of the kiosk. As the fragments fell around the *Sultan*, he exclaimed:

At another time the salute of a whole fleet would not have broken that glass; and now it is shivered by the noise of the cannon of these galleys. I see the fate of the kiosk of my life.

Saying so he wept bitterly, and was led by his attendants back to his palace, where he expired that very night.

The multitudinous *seraglio* of Amurath III. had produced to him 103 children, of whom twenty sons, and twenty-seven daughters, were living at the time of his decease. The eldest son, Prince Mahomet, whom his mother, the Venetian Sultana Safiye, promptly summoned from his government in Asia Minor, instantly put his nineteen brothers to death—the largest sacrifice to the Cain-spirit of Mahomet, the Conqueror's law, that the Ottoman histories record. Seven female slaves, who were in a condition from which heirs to the empire might be expected, were at the same time sewn in sacks and thrown into the sea. Safiye had kept the death of Amurath secret until the successor arrived to secure the throne. This was the last time that this precautionary measure was needed on a Turkish sovereign's death; for Mahomet III., who now succeeded to Amurath, was the last hereditary prince who was trusted with liberty and the government of provinces during his predecessor's lifetime.

Thenceforth the Ottoman princes of the blood royal were kept secluded and immured in a particular part of the palace called the *Kaweh* (cage), from which they passed to die or to reign, without any of the minor employments of the state being placed in their hands. The fear lest they should head revolts was the cause of this new system; the effect of which on the character and capacity of the rulers of Turkey was inevitably debasing and pernicious.

Mahomet III. was twenty-three years of age when he came to the throne. On the eighth day after his accession, he went in state to public prayer at the mosque of St. Sophia, a ceremony that had not taken place for two years, on account of Amurath's fear of being insulted by the troops as he passed along the streets. A donative of unprecedented extravagance was now lavished on the soldiery, in order to buy their favour to their new *Sultan*; and anxious exertions were then made to send reinforcements to the armies in Hungary, where the war went hard with the Turks. While these preparations were being made, two regiments that were dissatisfied with the share which they had received of the imperial bounty, surrounded the *grand vizier*, Ferhad Pacha, and with angry cries demanded that more should be paid to them. Ferhad replied by bidding them march to the frontiers, where they should receive their due. They redoubled their murmurs and menaces at this, and Ferhad then said to them, "Know you not that the men who refuse obedience to their chiefs are *infidels*, and that their wives are barren!"

Indignant at this taunt, the mutineers repaired to the *mufti*, and repeating to him Ferhad's words, asked him to issue a *fetva* condemning the *grand vizier*: but the *mufti's* answer to their reply was, "My friends, let the *grand vizier* say all he can, he cannot make you *infidels*, and he cannot make your wives barren."

Being but indifferently satisfied with this legal opinion, the mutineers sought their comrades' aid in getting up an insurrection, saying that the *mufti* would only give his *fetvas* for money, and not for justice. The *Spahis* (the horse-guards of the capital) took up the supposed grievance of the malcontents, and clamoured for the head of Ferhad. A tumult ensued, in which several of the high officers of state, who vainly endeavoured to pacify the rioters, were wounded; but the *Janissaries* were prevailed on to charge their rivals the *Spahis*, and the mutiny was thus suppressed.

Safiye, now Sultana Validé, ruled generally in the court and councils of her son Mahomet, with even more predominant sway than she had exercised in the time of the late *Sultan*. Mahomet was a weak-minded prince, but capable of occasional outburst of energy, or rather of violence. The disasters which the Turkish arms were now experiencing in Wallachia and Hungary, made the *Sultan's* best statesmen anxious that the sovereign should, after the manner of his great ancestors, head his troops in person, and endeavour to give an auspicious change to the fortune of the war. Safiye, who feared that her son when absent from Constantinople would be less submissive to her influence, opposed this project; and for a long time detained the *Sultan* among the inglorious pleasures of his seraglio, while the Imperialists, under the Archduke Maximilian and the Hungarian Count Pfalfy, aided by the revolted princes of the Danubian Principalities, dealt defeat and discouragement among the Ottoman ranks, and wrung numerous fortresses and districts from the empire.

The cities of Gran, Wissgrad, and Babocsa, had fallen; and messengers in speedy succession announced the loss of Ibrail, Varna, Kilic, Ismail, Silistria, Rustchuk, Bucharest, and Akerman. These tidings at last roused the monarch in his *harem*; and he sent for the *mufti*, who, fortunately for Turkey, was a man of sense and patriotic spirit. Adopting a characteristic mode of advising an Ottoman prince, the *mufti* took an opportunity of placing in Mahomet's hands a poem of Ali-Tchelabi, one of the most eminent writers of the time, in whose verses the misfortunes of the empire, and the calamitous progress of the Hungarian war, were painted in the strongest colours.

The *Sultan* was sensibly affected by its perusal, and ordered that the solemn service of prayer and of humiliation should be read, which requires the Mussulman to pray and weep, and do acts of contrition and penitence for three days. The *Sultan* and all his officers of state, and all the Mahometan population of the city, attended, and humbled themselves at these prayers, which were read by the Scheik Mohizedden in the place of the Okmeidan, behind the arsenal Eight days afterwards, an earthquake shook Constantinople, and overthrew many towns and villages in Anatolia. The consternation and excitement of the Ottomans now were excessive. All classes called on the *padischah* to go forth to the holy war against the unbelievers; and the formidable *Janissaries* refused to march to the frontier unless the *Sultan* marched with them.

The historian Seadeddin, who held the high dignity of *Khodja*, or tutor to Mahomet, the *mufti*, and the *grand vizier*, urged on their sovereign that the only hope of retrieving the prosperity and even of assuring the safety, of the empire, lay in his appearing at the head of his armies. Their exhortations, aided by the pressure from without, prevailed over the influence of the Sultana Validé. In her anger and irritation at this decision, and hoping perhaps to cause a tumult during which the current of popular opinion might be changed, or the ministers who opposed her might be killed, the daughter of Venice forgot all the ties which had once bound her to Christendom, and proposed that there should be a massacre of all the Giaours in Constantinople. The fanatics in the *divan* approved of this proposal of a most atrocious and most useless crime; but the authority of wiser statesmen prevailed, and a banishment of all unmarried Greeks in the capital was the only result of the infuriated *Sultana's* design.

Mahomet III. left his capital for the frontier in the June of 1596, with pomp and state which recalled to some spectators the campaigns of the great Solyman. The *Sultan's* resolution to head his armies had revived the martial spirit of the Ottomans; and the display of the sacred standard of the Prophet, which now for the first time was unfurled over a Turkish Army, excited still more the zeal of the True Believers to combat the enemies of Islam. This holy relic had been left at Damascus by Sultan Selim I. after he obtained it from the last titular

Caliph of the Abassides, on his conquest of Egypt. During the reign of Amurath III. it was conveyed from Damascus to Constantinople; and it has since that time been preserved by the *Sultans* as a treasure for extreme need, to be displayed only on great emergencies, when it has become necessary to employ some extraordinary means to rouse the military spirit of the Ottomans, or to recall them to their religious, allegiance to their *Sultan*, as the *caliph*, and the successor of the Prophet Mahomet, whose holy hands once bore that standard in. battle.

The historian Seadeddin accompanied his imperial pupil in this campaign; and his presence proved of value for the purpose of gaining victories, as well as for that of recording them. The *grand vizier*, Ibrahim Pacha, Hassan Sokolli Pacha, and Cicala Pacha, were the principal commanders under the *Sultan*. The biography of the last-mentioned Pacha (whom the Oriental writers call Dzigalizadé) furnishes so striking an example of the career of a renegade of that age, that it may claim a short space in these pages. Cicala was, as his name denotes, an Italian by birth. His father, the Vicomte di Cicala, head of a noble Genoese family that had settled in Sicily, commanded a force of privateers (or, as the Turks would have termed them, pirates), and he cruised against the Mahometan coasts and commerce with as little heed to truce or treaty as any Algerine *reis* ever showed in his enterprises against Christians.

The Knights of Malta sought the co-operation of this daring maritime partisan in many of their adventures; and his galleys joined those of the Order when they attacked Modon in the Morea, in 1531. Though unable to storm the citadel, the *chevaliers* sacked the town, and showed the most savage and sordid rapacity for plunder of every description.

Among other spoils, they carried off 800 Turkish ladies, one of whom, a girl of remarkable beauty, fell to the share of Count Cicala; who was so enraptured with his prize, that on his return to Sicily he married her, having first had her baptised under the name of Lucretia. There were several sons of this marriage. The youngest of them, Scipio, at the age of eighteen, accompanied his father in the expedition against Djerbé, which terminated so disastrously for the Christian confederates. Both the Cicalas were among the captives whom the victorious Turkish Admiral, Pialé, led in triumph to Constantinople. The elder one died in prison; but the youth and beauty of young Scipio Cicala attracted the pitying notice of Sultan Solyman.

The boyish sea-rover was half a Turk by birth, and he had little scruple about becoming one entirely in religion. Sinan Pacha, an old officer high in rank and influence, took the juvenile Mahometan under his especial patronage; and Cicala entered eagerly on the field of distinction and promotion which was opened to him in the *Sultan's* service. He rose to the high office of *Aga* of the *Janissaries*; and though his extreme oppression of the Christians of Constantinople caused him to be removed from that dignity, he obtained an important command in the Persian war, where he greatly signalised himself in several engagements, especially in a nocturnal victory gained by the Turks in 1583, called the "Battle of the Torches."

He had married the granddaughter of Sultan Solyman, and thus obtained influence in the *seraglio*, which even more than his victories and abilities favoured his promotion during the reign of Amurath III., and protected him from the effects of prejudice caused by his occasional defeats, and the unpopularity into which he brought himself by his excessive severity to his own men, and by his cruelty to the *Rayas* of Turkey as well as to the natives of the foreign countries where he commanded. He more than once held the rank of Capitan Pacha, and twice he availed himself of his command of the Turkish Navy for the purpose of sailing to Messina, and demanding an interview with his mother and sister, who resided there.

On the first of these occasions the Spanish Viceroy of Sicily refused his request, and Cicala revenged himself by ravaging the whole coast of the island. This had its effect. Cicala returned in a subsequent year and sent a flag of truce to the Viceroy, urging that he should at least be allowed to have an interview with his mother, whom he had not seen since he was first carried to Constantinople. The viceroy now thought it prudent to send the Countess Cicala to her son's galley, covenanting that she should be sent back at sunset. Strange reminiscences must have been awakened at that interview between the mother, who in her youth had been torn from a Turkish home, and forcibly converted into a Christian matron, and the son, who had begun his life and career in a Christian court and under the flag of the Cross, but now had so long been one of the most dreaded champions of the Crescent.

Cicala kept his word, and sent his mother back on shore at the stipulated time; he then sailed away, leaving for once a Christian shore unvisited by fire or slaughter. The conclusion of Cicala's career after many vicissitudes of fortune was disastrous. He was routed by Shah Abbas in Persia, and died during the hurried retreat of his discontented and mutinous troops, of a fever brought on by anxiety and fatigue. But in 1596, when Mahomet III. marched into Hungary, Cicala, though disliked by the Sultana Validé, was high in favour with the *Sultan*, and his most brilliant exploit was performed during this campaign.

The Archduke Maximilian, who commanded the Imperialists, retired at first before the superior numbers of the great Ottoman Army; and the *Sultan* besieged and captured Erlau. The Imperialists now having effected a junction with the Transylvanian troops under Prince Sigismund, advanced again, though too late to save Erlau; and on October 23rd, 1596, the two armies were in presence of each other on the marshy plain of Cerestes, through which the waters of the Cincia ooze towards the River Theiss.

There were three days of battle at Cerestes. On the first day part of the Turkish force under Djaffer Pacha passed the Cincia, and after fighting bravely against superior numbers, was obliged to retreat with the loss of 1000 *Janissaries*, 100 *Spahis*, and forty-three cannon. The *Sultan* now wished for a general retreat of the army, or at least that he should himself retire. A council of war was summoned in the Ottoman camp, at which the historian Seadeddin was present, and advocated vigorously a more manly policy. "It has never been seen or heard of," said he, "that a *tadischah* of the Ottomans turned his back upon the enemy without the direst necessity." Some of those present recommended that the Pacha Hassan Sokolli should lead the troops against the enemy. Seadeddin answered, "This is no affair for *pachas*: the personal presence of the *padischah* is absolutely indispensable here."

It was finally resolved to fight; and the *Sultan* was with difficulty persuaded to stay with the troops. On the 24th there was another action; and the Turks secured some passages through the marsh. Each side now concentrated its strength, and on the 26th October, the decisive encounter took place. At first the Christians seemed completely victorious. They drove back the leading divisions of the Turks and Tartars; attacked the Ottoman batteries in flank, captured the whole of the guns, forced the *Janissaries* to give way, and drove the Asiatic feudal cavalry in headlong rout from the field. The *Sultan*, who beheld the engagement from an elevated seat on a camel's back, wished to fly, but Seadeddin exhorted him to be firm, and quoted the verse of the *Koran* that says, "*It is patience that brings victory, and joy succeeds to sorrow.*"

Mahomet clasped the sacred standard, and kept his station, protected by his bodyguard and his pages from the victorious Imperialists, who now broke their ranks, and rushed to plunder the Ottoman camp. At this critical moment. Cicala, who had hitherto sate inactive in command of a large body of irregular Turkish cavalry, gave the word to his men, and the spur to his steed, and down came the wild horsemen galloping over friend and foe, and sweeping the panic-stricken Christians by thousands into the swamps of the Cincia. Terror and flight spread through every division of the Imperialists; and in less than half an hour from the time when Cicala began his charge, Maximilian and Sigismund were flying for their lives, without a single Christian regiment keeping their ranks, or making an endeavour to rally and cover the retreat. 50,000 Germans and Transylvanians perished in the marshes or beneath the Ottoman sabre. Ninety-five cannons, of very beautiful workmanship, were captured by the Turks, who, at the beginning of the battle, had lost all their own; and the whole camp, and treasure of the Archduke, and all his material of war were among the fruits of this victory, one of the most remarkable that the Ottomans ever obtained.

The principal credit of the day was fairly ascribed to Seadeddin, and Cicala. (It is but just to the Turkish historian to remark that his reputation for these military services does not rest merely on his own testimony. Naima and other writers are his witnesses). Cicala was promoted after the battle to the rank of *grand vizier;* but was speedily deprived of it by the jealous interference of the Sultana Validé. He held it, however, long enough to be the cause of infinite evil to the empire, by his ill-judged and excessive severity to the troops, that had given way at die beginning of the battle. It was found that 30,000 Ottoman soldiers, principally belonging to the Asiatic feudal force, had fled before the Giaours.

Cicala stigmatised them as *firaris,* or runaways. He ordered that their pay should be stopped, and their *fiefs* forfeited. He publicly beheaded many of these unfortunate soldiers who came into his power; but by far the greater number, when they heard of the new *vizier's* severity, dispersed, and returned to their homes. The attempts made to apprehend and punish them there, naturally caused armed resistance; and the *firaris* of Cerestes were among the foremost and most formidable supporters of the rebellion, which soon afterwards broke out in Asia Minor, and desolated that country for many years.

Mahomet III. eagerly returned after the battle to Constantinople, to receive felicitations and adulation for his victory, and to resume his usual life of voluptuous indolence. The war in Hungary was prolonged for several years, until the peace of Sitvatorok in the reign of Mahomet's successor. But neither the Imperialists nor the Turks carried on operations with any vigour in the intermediate campaigns; and the chiefs of the revolted principalities of Moldavia, Wallachia, and Transylvania, after disputes with each other, sought and obtained terms of reconciliation with the Porte.

During the inglorious remainder of Mahomet III.'s reign, the evils of military insubordination, and the tyranny of the provincial rulers, continued to increase. In 1599 a chief of the military feudatories in Asia Minor, named Abdoulhamid, but better known by the title of Karazaridji, which means "The Black Scribe," availed himself of the universal disorder and discontent to organise a wide-spread revolt against the Porte, and to assume the rank of an independent prince. He formed an army of Koords, Turcomans, and the fugitive *Spahis* of Cerestes; and, aided by his brother, Delhi Housin, the Governor of Bagdad, he gave repeated defeats to the Ottoman armies sent against him.

In 1601, the Persian monarch, Shah Abbas, took advantage of the weakness of the ancient enemy of his nation, to make war upon Turkey; and began rapidly to recover the provinces which Persia had lost in the last reign. In the June of 1603 Sultan Mahomet put to death his eldest son, Mahmoud, a prince of high abilities and courage, and of whose reign great expectation had been formed. Mahmoud had requested his father to give him the command of the armies employed against the rebels in Asia Minor. This show of spirit alarmed the weak and jealous mind of Mahomet; and on being informed that a holy man had predicted to the prince that a new *Sultan* would soon ascend the throne, he ordered his son to be seized and strangled. The *Sultana* who had borne the prince to him, and all Mahmoud's favourite companions, were at the same time thrown into prison, and at the end of a month were all put to death.

Mahomet III. did not long survive this act of cruelty. On the 27th of October a *dervise* met him in the palace-gate, and prophesied to him that in fifty-five days he would meet with some great calamity. The prediction weighed heavily on the superstitious mind of the sickly voluptuary: and, like many other predictions of the same kind, tended powerfully to work its own fulfilment. On the fifty-fifth day (22nd December, 1603), Mahomet III. died, and was succeeded by Sultan Achmet I., the elder of his two surviving sons.

Achmet I. was fourteen years of age when he commenced his reign. By his humanity, or the humanity of his councillors, his brother, Prince Mustapha, was spared from being put to death according to established usage. The mental imbecility of Prince Mustapha may also have been a reason for saving his life, partly out of contempt, and partly out of the superstitious reverence with which all lunatics are regarded in the East. In the beginning of young Achmet's reign he showed some flashes of imperious decision, which might have been thought to be the dawnings of a vigorous and successful reign.

His *grand vizier*, who was to lead a fresh army into Hungary, made some exorbitant demands on the treasury, and threatened not to march unless they were complied with. Achmet sent him the laconic and effective answer, "If thou valuest thy head thou wilt march at once." But the promise of Achmet's boyhood was belied by weakness and selfishness as he approached maturer years. The Turkish historian, Naima, relates a scene which took place in Achmet's *divan* in 1606, when the *Sultan* had attained the age of seventeen, which illustrates his character as compared with that of the great sovereign who had ruled Turkey only forty years before, and which shows the influence for good or for bad which the personal example of the monarch must exercise.

It was May. The horsetails had been planted on the Asiatic side of the Bosphorus, announcing a campaign in that continent, and an army was now being assembled at Scutari, which the young *Sultan* was expected to lead to the Persian war. The *divan* was assembled at the *grand vizier's* palace, and the *Sultan* presided there in person. Achmet addressed his councillors, "It is now too late for a campaign. Provisions are scarce and dear. Is it not better to put off the expedition till next year."

The astonished assembly was silent, until the *mufti*, who vainly wished that Achmet would follow the example of the great Solyman, said, "Would it, then, be fitting to carry back the horsetails, that have been planted in the sight of so many foreign ambassadors? Let the troops at least be marched to Aleppo, to winter there, and to collect stores of provisions."

The *Sultan* interposed, "What is the use of a march to Aleppo?"

"It is of use," answered the *mufti*, firmly, "to save the honour of our tents that have been pitched. Even so Sultan Solyman in the campaign against. Nachdshivan wintered at Aleppo, and then attacked the enemy at the opening of the following spring."

Then said the *Sultan*, "Let Ferhad Pacha go forward with part of the army, so that the camp be not brought back."

"Will he receive the money necessary for the purchase of provisions?" asked the *mufti*.

The *Sultan* replied, "The public treasury is empty. Whence am I to draw the money?"

"From the treasury of Egypt."

"That," said the *Sultan*, "belongs to my private purse."

"Sire," was the rejoinder, "your great ancestor. Sultan Solyman, before the campaign of Szigeth, sent all his own treasures of gold and silver to the public mint."

Sultan Achmet knit his brows, and said, "*Effendi*, thou understandest not. Times are changed. What was fitting then is not convenient now."

So saying, he dismissed the council. The result was, that Ferhad Pacha, who seems to have been rightly called Delhi Ferhad, or Ferhad the Foolhardy, did set forth with a part of the army without pay or supplies. The troops mutinied on their march, and were routed by the first bands of rebels whom they encountered in Asia Minor.

Negotiations for a peace between Austria and the Porte had long been pending, and a treaty was finally concluded on the 11th November, 1606, at Sitvatorok. No change of importance was made in the territorial possessions of either party, except that the Prince of Transylvania was admitted as party to the treaty, and that province became to some extent, though not entirely independent of the Ottoman Empire. But the peace of Sitvatorok is important as marking an era in the diplomatic relations of Turkey with the states of Christendom.

Hitherto the Ottoman *Sultans*, in their pacifications with Christian princes, had affected to grant short truces as favours from a superior to inferiors. They generally exacted annual contributions of money, which Oriental pride considered to be tributes; and they displayed, both in the style of their state papers, and by the low rank of the persons employed by them to conduct the negotiations, the most haughty and offensive arrogance.

But at Sitvatorok the Turks acknowledged and observed the general principles and courtesies of international law. Their commissioners had full powers signed by the *Sultan* and the *grand vizie*r; and they gave the Austrian sovereign the title of *Padischah*, or Emperor, instead of terming him, as had been usual with their predecessors, merely "the King of Vienna." The peace was to be a permanent one; the annual payment of the 30,000 *ducats* by Austria to the Porte was abolished; presents were to be made by the Turks to the Imperialists, as well as by the Imperialists to the Turks; and in future, all ambassadors sent by the *Sultan* to Vienna were not to be as formerly, chosen from among the menial officers of his court or camp, but were to be at least of the rank of *Sanjak Bey*.

It was fortunate for the Ottoman power that the religious dissensions in Germany soon after this period caused the outbreak of the great war which devastated that country for thirty years, and kept the House of Austria fully occupied in struggling for empire and safety against Bohemians, Saxons, Danes, Swedes, and French, instead of availing itself of the weakness of the Turks, and entering upon a career of conquest along the Saave and the Danube. The Spanish monarchy, the other great enemy of the Porte, after the death of Philip II. decayed even more rapidly and uniformly than the Turkish Empire after the death of Solyman. France and England were friendly towards the Turks; and even if they had been hostile, were too much engaged each with its own domestic dissensions during the first half of the seventeenth century for any formidable projects of conquest in the East.

Russia had declined during the last years of the reign of Ivan the Terrible; and she was, long after his death, rent by revolts and civil wars, which were terminated by the accession of the House of Romanoff (1613); but the reign of the first *Czar* of that dynasty (1613-1645) was fully occupied with endeavours to restore the Russian nation from the misery and anarchy into which it had fallen, and in recovering provinces which had been seized by the Swedes and Poles. No first-class European power was in a condition to attack Turkey during that crisis of her extreme misery and feebleness, which lasted through the first thirty years of the seventeenth century, which was checked by the stern hand of Amurath IV. during the last seven years of his reign, but was renewed under the reigns of his imbecile successors, until the ministry of the first *Kiuprili* in 1656.

The Poles and the Venetians were the chief European foes of Turkey throughout this time. Poland was too much torn by domestic faction to accomplish aught worthy of the chivalrous valour of her armies; and Venice, never a sufficient adversary to cope single-handed with a great empire, was in a state of skilfully disguised, but incurable, and increasing decrepitude. Persia was the most dangerous foreign enemy of Turkey during the first half of the seventeenth century; but though the Asiatic possessions of the Porte beyond the Taurus were often in imminent peril, there was little risk of Persian armies advancing so far westward as to strike at the vital parts of the Ottoman dominions.

Achmet I. reigned for eleven years after the peace of Sitvatorok, During this time, his *grand vizier*, Mourad, gained advantages over the rebels in Asia Minor, which partially suppressed the spirit of revolt in that quarter. The war with Persia was continued, but almost uniformly to the disadvantage of the Turks; and the weakness of the empire was signally proved by the ravages which the fleets of the Cossacks perpetrated with impunity along the southern coasts of the Black Sea. In 1613, a flotilla of these marauders surprised the city of Sinope, which is described as having been then one of the richest and best fortified ports of Asia Minor. The Cossacks of the seventeenth century subjected Sinope to the same rapacious and cruel devastation, which it was

to experience from their descendants under Russian guidance in 1853. In both cases the city was taken by surprise; and in both cases, the fleets, which should have encountered the attacking squadron, or at least have taken vengeance on it while retiring with its plunder, were absent from the proper scene of operations.

Sultan Achmet died 22nd November, 1617.

******

The second year of the reign of Achmet I. is marked by the Turkish writers as the date of the introduction of tobacco into the empire. The Ottomans became such enthusiastic and inveterate smokers that within fifty years a pipe was looked on as the national emblem of a Turk. The use of coffee had been introduced into Constantinople in the reign of the great Solyman. The severer expounders of the Mahometan law censure the use of these luxuries. On the other hand the Oriental poets say, that coffee, tobacco, opium, and wine are "the four cushions of the sofa of pleasure," and "the four elements of the world of enjoyment." But the strict legists call them "the four pillars of the tent of debauchery," and "the four, ministers of the devil."

******

He left seven sons, three of whom, in course of time, ascended the throne, but his immediate successor was his brother Mustapha. Hitherto there had been an uninterrupted transmission of the empire from father to son for fourteen generations. According to Von Hammer, the law of succession, which gives the throne to the elder surviving male relation of the deceased sovereign, had been adopted by the House of Othman from the House of Zenghis Khan; but so long as the practice of royal fratricide continued, it was impossible for any dispute to arise between the son of a *Sultan* and that son's uncle.

In consequence of the life of his brother Mustapha having been spared by Achmet I., that prince now became *Sultan*, to the temporary exclusion of his young nephew Prince Othman. But the idiocy of Mustapha, as soon as he was drawn from his place of confinement and enthroned, was so apparent, that in less than three months the high officers of state concurred in deposing him, and summoning Prince Othman, then aged fourteen, to reign in his stead (26th February, 1618). The soldiery acquiesced in this measure the more willingly, that it brought them a new donative. His public treasury was drained of 6,000,000 *ducats* by this renewed claim of the military within a quarter of a year.

The short and unhappy reign of Othman II. was marked by the signature of a peace with Persia, on conditions agreed to during the preceding reign, and rendered necessary by the repeated defeats of the Turks. The Ottomans restored all the conquests that had been made during the reigns of Amurath III and Mahomet III., and the eastern boundary of the empire receded to its line in the reign of Selim II. Relieved from the burden of the Persian war, Othman devoted all his thoughts to the overthrow of his domestic enemies, the *Janissaries* and *Spahis*, whom he not unjustly regarded as the chief curses of the empire, of which they had formerly been the chief support.

The *Janissaries*, in particular, were now regarded as the tyrants over both sovereign and people; and the long feud between the throne and the barrack of the troops of Hadji Bektasch now commenced, which was only terminated in our own century by the ruthless energy of Mahmoud II. Othman II. had sufficient hardness of heart for the task which he undertook. A prince, who kept himself in practice as an archer by using prisoners of war as his marks, or, if they were not at hand, by putting one of his own pages up as a living target, vas not likely to be deterred by the scruples of humanity from using the most efficacious measures against military malignants.

Othman made war on Poland in 1621, chiefly with the view of weakening the *Janissary* regiments by loss in battle and the hardships of the campaign. The losses which the whole army sustained in that war, and the calamitous retreat with which the operations of the *Sultan* (though partially victorious) were concluded, made Othman unpopular with all ranks. And by ill-considered changes in laws and customs, by personal affronts to leading statesmen, and by the exercise of vexatious severity in trifling regulations of police he alienated all classes of his subjects from his throne.

In the spring of 1622, he announced an intention of performing the pilgrimage to Mecca. It was well known that his real design was to proceed to Damascus, and place himself at the head of an army of Koords and other troops, which his favourite *grand vizier*, Dilawer Pacha, was to collect near that city. With this army, when disciplined on a new model, the *Sultan* was to march upon Constantinople, destroy the *Janissaries* and *Spahis*, and completely re-organise the government Sir Thomas Roe, our ambassador, then resident at the Turkish capital, whose letters graphically describe the tragical career of Othman, says of this scheme, that:

> Certainly this was a brave and well-grounded design, and of great consequence for the recovery of this decayed empire, languishing under the insolence of lazy slaves, if God had not destroyed it.

But, in truth, Othman utterly lacked the secrecy and the vigour, with which alone actions of such depth and danger can be performed. When the *Janissaries* rose in furious tumult (May, 1622) to forbid the pilgrimage to Mecca, and to demand the heads of Othman's ministers, the *Sultan* had neither troops ready to defend him, nor was there any party in his favour among the people, to which he could appeal. Instigated by the traitor Daoud Pacha, who hated Othman for having raised a rival to the *grand vizierate*, and by the mother of Sultan Mustapha, who knew that, if this revolt were quelled, Othman would seek to secure himself by putting all his kin to death, the insurgent soldiery proceeded from violence against the ministers to an attack upon the person of the *Sultan*, which had hitherto been held sacred amidst the wildest commotions. Othman was dragged off to the Seven Towers, while the lunatic Mustapha was a second time carried from his cell, and installed on the throne. Daoud Pacha, now *grand vizier*, was determined not to leave his traitorous enterprise incomplete; and with three comrades he proceeded to Othman's prison, and strangled him, with circumstances of gross and insolent cruelty.

★★★★★★

Von Hammer, vol. ii., gives a painfully curious parallel between the death of Othman and that of Andronicus, who built the grand reservoir "Pyrgus" or "Burgas" at Constantinople, which Othman restored.

★★★★★★

The atrocity of this murder before long caused remorse among the *Janissaries* themselves. Among the few glimmerings of intellect which Sultan Mustapha showed during his second reign, were an expression of grief for the death of Othman, and a *hattischerif*, commanding that his murderers should be punished. Generally, Mustapha continued to be as incapable of governing an empire, or of common self-government, as he had been found at his first accession. His mother, the Sultana Validé, exercised the principal power in his name; and the high offices of state were intrigued, or fought for, by competitors, who relied on the bought swords of the *Janissaries* and *Spahis*, as their best means of promotion.

So fearful at length became the anarchy and misery at Constantinople, that even the very soldiers were touched by it. Some instinctive spirit of military discipline still survived among them; and their proud attachment to the Ottoman Empire, which the valour of their predecessors had raised to such power and splendour, had not become wholly inoperative. They assented to the urgent entreaties of the chief ministers that they would forego their customary donative if a new *Sultan* was invested with power; and in August, 1623, the lunatic Mustapha was a second time deposed; and Prince Amurath, the elder surviving brother of Sultan Othman, a child of only eleven years of age, was placed on the throne.

Mustapha's second reign had lasted little more than a year, but it had been productive of infinite misery to the empire. The Persian war had been renewed. Bagdad and Bassorah fell into the hands of enemies. All Asia Minor was desolated by the revolt of Abaza, who had been governor of Merasch, and who was said to have aided the Sultan Othman in concerting that sovereign's project for destroying the *Janissaries*. It is certain, that after Othman's murder, Abaza proclaimed himself as that prince's avenger, and the sworn foe of the *Janissaries*, whom he pursued with implacable ferocity.

In the general dissolution of all bonds of government, and in the absence of all protection to industry or property, the empire seemed to be sinking into the mere state of a wilderness of beasts of prey. Nothing can exceed the strength of the expressions which an eye-witness. Sir Thomas Roe, employs in his correspondence with our King James I. and other persons in England, respecting the misery of the inhabitants of the Turkish dominions, and the symptoms of decay and ruin which he witnessed all around him. (*Sir Thomas Roe's Embassy*).

And it is to be remembered, that there was no wish among Englishmen for the downfall of Turkey. This country sympathised strongly with James's son-in-law, the Prince Palatine, and the other Protestant antagonists of the House of Austria in Germany; and any prospect of the arms of Austria being disturbed by a Turkish war, would have been gladly hailed by our statesmen. But the graphic despatches of Roe describe vividly and repeatedly a state of fallen grandeur, which he regarded as irretrievable. He employs almost the same metaphor which, in our time, has been applied to the Turkish power by one "whose wish was father to the thought," and who has spoken of it "as a sick man about to die upon one's hands." Roe says: "It has become, like an old body, crazed through many vices, which remain when the youth and strength is decayed."

He gives in a letter, written in the year of Sultan Othman's death, some calculations as to the extent to which depopulation had lately taken place, which may possibly be exaggerated; but his testimony as to the general nature of what he actually beheld, is unimpeachable. He says:

> The ruined houses in many places remain; but the injustice and cruelty of the government hath made all the people abandon them. All the territory of the *grand seignior* is dispeopled for want of justice, or rather, by reason of violent oppression; so much so, that in his best parts of Greece and Natolia, a man may ride three, four, and sometimes six days, and not find a village able to feed him and his horse; whereby the revenue is so lessened, that there is not wherewithal to pay the soldiers, and to maintain the court. It may be patched up for a while out of the treasury, and by exactions, which now are grievous upon the merchant and labouring man, to satisfy the harpies; but when those means fail, which cannot long endure, either the soldiery must want their pay, or the number must be reduced; neither of which will they suffer: and whosoever shall attempt either remedy, shall follow Othman to his grave. This is the true estate of this so much feared greatness; and the wisest men in the country foresee it, and retyre their estates as fast as they can, fearing that no haste can prevent their danger. (*Sir T. Roe's Embassy*).

These seemingly well-founded prognostications of the speedy dissolution of the Ottoman Empire were written in 1622. Since then, that empire has endured already for two centuries and a half. Our attention will now be directed to one of those rulers, who have been mainly instrumental in falsifying these and similar predictions.

Chapter 16
Military Revolts

Amurath IV., at the time of his accession (10th September, 1623), was under twelve years of age. But even thus early, he gave indications of a resolute and vengeful character, and showed that a prince, animated by the spirit of the first Selim, was once more on the Ottoman throne. The Turkish historian, Evliya, relates of him:

> When Sultan Amurath entered the treasury after his accession, my father, Dervish Mohammed, was with him. There were no gold or silver vessels remaining—only 30,000 *piastres* in money, and some coral and porcelain in chests. '*Inshallah*' (please God), said the *Sultan*, after prostrating himself in prayer, 'I will replenish this treasury fifty-fold with the property of those who have plundered it.'—Hulme.

The young *Sultan*, during the first year of his reign, acted principally under the directions of his mother, the Sultana Mahpeiker, who, providentially for the Ottoman Empire, was a woman of remarkable talent and energy, which were taxed to the uttermost to meet the dangers and disasters that clouded round the dawn of her child's sovereignty. From every part of the empire messengers arrived with evil tidings. The Persians were victorious on the frontier. The rebel Abaza was lord and tyrant over Asia Minor. The tribes of the Lebanon were in open insurrection. The governors of Egypt and other provinces were wavering in their allegiance. The Barbaresque regencies assumed the station of independent powers, and made treaties with European nations on their own account. The fleets of the Cossack marauders not only continued their depredations along the Black Sea, but even appeared in the Bosphorus, and plundered the immediate vicinity of the capital.

In Constantinople itself there was an empty treasury, a dismantled arsenal, a debased coinage, exhausted magazines, a starving population, and a licentious soldiery. Yet the semblance of authority was preserved, and by degrees some of its substance was recovered by those who ruled in the young prince's name; and, though amid tumult and bloodshed, and daily peril to both throne and life, young Amurath, observing all things, forgetting nothing, and forgiving nothing, grew up towards man's estate.

There is a wearisome monotony in the oft-repeated tale of military insurrections; but the formidable mutiny of the *Spahis*, which convulsed Constantinople in the ninth year of Amurath's reign, deserves notice on account of the traits of the Turkish character, which its chief hero and victim remarkably displayed; and also because it explains and partly palliates the hard-heartedness which grew upon Amurath, and the almost wolfish appetite for bloodshed, which was shown by him in the remainder of his reign. In the beginning of that year, a largo number of mutinous *Spahis*, who had disgraced themselves by gross misconduct in the late unsuccessful campaign against Bagdad, had straggled to Constantinople, and joined the European *Spahis*, already collected in that capital. They were secretly instigated by Redjib Pacha, who wished by their means to effect the ruin of the Grand Vizier Hafiz, a gallant though not fortunate general, to whom the young *Sultan* was much attached, and who had interchanged poetical communications with his sovereign, when employed against the Persians. (The poems or *gazelles* of the *Sultan* and *vizier* are given in German by Von Hammer in his note to his 47th book. They are full of fanciful imagery drawn from the game of chess).

The *Spahis* gathered together in the hippodrome, on three successive days (February, 1632) and called for the heads of the Grand Vizier Hafiz, the Mufti Jania, the Defterdar Mustapha, and other favourites of the *Sultan*, seventeen in all. The shops were closed, and the city and the *serail* were in terror. On the second day the mutineers came to the gate of the palace, but withdrew on being promised that they should have redress on the morrow. On the third day, when the morning broke, the outer court of the *seraglio* was filled with raging rebels. As the Grand Vizier Hafiz was on his way thither to attend the *divan*, he received a message from a friend, who warned him to conceal himself until the crowd had dispersed. Hafiz answered with a smile, "I have already this day seen my fate in a dream: I am not afraid to die."

As he rode into the *seraglio*, the multitude made a lane for him, as if out of respect, but as he passed along they cast stones at him: he was struck from his horse, and borne by his attendants into the inner part of the palace. One of his followers was murdered, and one grievously wounded by the *Spahis*. The *Sultan* ordered Hafiz to make his escape, and the *grand vizier* took a boat at the water-gate of the Serail, and crossed over to Scutari Meanwhile the rebels forced their way into the second court of the *seraglio*, which was the usual hall of the *divan*, and they clamoured for the *Sultan* to come forth and hold a *divan* among them. The *Sultan* appeared and held a divan standing. He spoke to the mutineers, "What is your will, my servants?"

Loudly and insolently they answered, "Give us the seventeen heads. Give these men up to us, that we may tear them in pieces, or it shall fare worse with thee." They pressed close upon the *Sultan*, and were near upon laying hands on him.

"You give no hearing to my words; why have you called me hither?" said Amurath. He drew back, surrounded by his pages, into the inner court. The rebels came after him like a raging flood. Fortunately the pages barred the gate. But the alarm and the outcry became the greater. They shouted aloud, "The seventeen heads, or abdicate."

Redjib Pacha, the secret promoter of the whole tumult, now approached the young *Sultan*, and urged on him that it was necessary to still the tumult by granting what was demanded. He said that it had become a custom for the chiefs to be given up to the soldiery. "The Unchained Slave must take what he pleases; better the head of the *vizier* than that of the *Sultan*." Amurath sorrowfully gave way, and sent a summons to Hafiz to return and die. The *vizier* hesitated not; and, as he came back, the *Sultan* met him at the water-gate. The gate of the inner court was then opened. The *Sultan* ascended the throne of state; and four deputies from the insurgents, two *Spahis* and two *Janissaries*, came before him. He implored them not to profane the honour of the *Caliphate*; but he pleaded in vain; the cry was still "The Seventeen Heads."

Meanwhile Hafiz Pacha had made the ablution preparatory to death, which the Mahometan law requires, and he now stood forth and addressed Amurath.

> My Padischah, let a thousand slaves, such as Hafiz, perish for thy sake. I only entreat that thou do not thyself put me to death, but give me up to these men, that I may die a martyr, and that my innocent blood may come upon their heads. Let my body be buried at Scutari.

He then kissed the earth, and exclaimed;

> In the name of God, the All-merciful, the All-good. There is no power or might save with God, the most High, the Almighty. His we are, and unto Him we return.

Hafiz then strode forth a hero into the fatal court. The *Sultan* sobbed aloud, the pages wept bitterly, the *viziers* gazed with tearful eyes. The rebels rushed to meet him as he advanced. To sell his life as a martyr, he struck the foremost to the ground with a well-aimed buffet, on which the rest sprang on him with their daggers, and pierced him with seventeen mortal wounds. A *Janissary* knelt on his breast, and struck off his head. The pages of the *seraglio* came forward and spread a robe over the corpse. Then said the *Sultan*:

> God's will be done! But in His appointed time ye shall meet with vengeance, ye men of blood, who have neither the fear of God before your eyes, nor respect for the law of the Prophet.

The threat was little heeded at the time, but it was uttered by one who never menaced in vain.

Within two months after this scene fresh victims had fallen before the bloodthirsty rabble that now disgraced the name of Turkish troops. The deposition of Amurath was openly discussed in their barracks; and the young *Sultan* saw that the terrible alternative, "Kill, or be killed," was no longer to be evaded. Some better spirits in the army, shamed and heart-sick at the spirit of brigandage that was so insolently dominant over court and camp, placed their swords at their sovereign's disposal; and a small but brave force, that could be relied on in the hour of need, was gradually and quietly organised. The dissensions also among the mutinous troops themselves, and especially the ancient jealousy between the *Spahis* and the *Janissaries*, offered means for repressing them all, of which Amurath availed himself with boldness and skill His first act was to put the arch-traitor, Redjib Pacha, suddenly and secretly to death. He then proceeded to the more difficult one of reducing the army to submission.

This was done on the 29th day of May, 1632, the day on which the *Sultan* emancipated himself from his military tyrants, and commenced also his own reign of terror. Amurath held a public divan on the shore of the sea near the Kiosch of Sinan. The *mufti*, the *viziers*, the chief members of the *Ulema* were there, and the two military chiefs, who had devoted themselves to the cause of the *Sultan* against the mutinous troops, Koesè Mohammed and Roum Mohammed. Six squadrons of horse-guards, whose loyalty could be trusted, were also in attendance, and ready for immediate action. Amurath seated himself on the throne, and sent a message to the *Spahis*, who were assembled in the hippodrome, requiring the attendance of a deputation of their officers. Amurath then summoned the *Janissaries* before him and addressed them as faithful troops who were enemies to the rebels in the other corps. The *Janissaries* shouted out that the *padischah's* enemies were their enemies also, and took with zealous readiness an oath of implicit obedience, which was suggested at the moment.

Copies of the *Koran* were ready, and were handed through the ranks. The *Janissaries* swore on the sacred book, "By God, with God, and through God." Their oath was formally registered; and Amurath then turned to the deputies of the *Spahis*, who had by this time arrived, and had witnessed the loyal fervour of the *Janissaries*. The *Sultan* reproached them for the rapacity and lawlessness of their body. They answered humbly that the *Sultan's* charges were true, but that they were personally loyal, though unable to make their men obey them.

"If ye are loyal," said Amurath, "take the oath which your brethren the *Janissaries* have taken, and deliver up to me the ringleaders of rebellion from your ranks." Surrounded by the royal horse-guards and *Janissaries*, the *Spahi* officers obeyed in fear and trembling. Amurath then ordered the judges to stand forward. He said to them, "Ye are accused of selling your judgments for gold, and of destroying my people. What answer have you to give?"

"God is our witness," said they, "that we seek not to make a traffic of justice, or to oppress the poor; but we have no freedom or independence; and if we protect thy subjects against the violence of the *Spahis* and the tax-gatherers, we are accused of corruption, our tribunals are assailed by armed men, and our houses are pillaged."

"I have heard of these things," said the *Sultan*.

Then arose in the *divan* a valiant judge of Asia, an Arab by birth, and he drew his sabre, and cried "My *Padischah*, the only cure for all these things is the edge of the sword."

At these words the *Sultan* and the whole assembly fixed their eyes on the Arabian judge, who stood before them with flashing eyes and weapon, but said no more. The declaration of the judge was registered; and then all present, the *Sultan*, the *viziers*, the *mufti*, and the chief officers, signed a written manifesto, by which they bound themselves to suppress abuses and maintain public order, under the penalty of bringing on their heads the curses of God, of the Prophet, of all angels, and of all true believers.

Amurath had need of acts as well as of words; and the work of death speedily began. Energetic and trusty emissaries were sent through Constantinople, who slew the leaders of the late insurrection, and all whom Amurath marked for destruction. The troops, deprived of their chiefs, and suspicious of each other, trembled and obeyed. The same measures were taken in the provinces, and for many months the sword and the bowstring were incessantly active. But it was in the capital, and under Amurath's own eye, that the revenge of royalty for its long humiliation reaped the bloodiest harvest.

Every morning the Bosphorus threw up on its shores the corpses of those who had been executed during the preceding night; and in them the anxious spectators recognised *Janissaries* and *Spahis*, whom they had lately seen parading the streets in all the haughtiness of military licence. The personal appearance and courage of Amurath, his bold and martial demeanour, confirmed the respect and awe which this strenuous ferocity inspired. He was in the twentieth year of his age; and though but little above the middle stature, his bodily frame united strength and activity in a remarkable degree. His features were regular and handsome. His aquiline nose, and the jet-black beard which had begun to grace his chin, gave dignity to his aspect: but the imperious lustre of his full dark eyes was marred by an habitual frown; which, however, suited well the sternness of his character.

Every day he displayed his horsemanship in the hippodrome: and he won the involuntary admiration of the soldiery by his strength and skill as a cavalier and swordsman, and by his unrivalled force and dexterity in the use of the bow. He patrolled the streets in disguise at night; and often, with his own hand, struck dead the offenders against his numerous, edicts in matters of police. If any menacing assemblage began to form in any of the streets, the *Sultan* received speedy tidings from his numerous spies; and, before revolt could be matured, Amurath was on the spot, well armed, and with a trusty guard of choice troops. He rode fearlessly in among the groups of *Spahis* or *Janissaries*, who slunk in savage silence from before their *Sultan*, each dreading lest that keen eye should recognise and mark him, and that unforgiving lip pronounce his doom.

The insurrection in Asia Minor had been quelled in 1630, by the defeat and submission of Abaza, whom Amurath had spared, principally out of sympathy with his hatred towards the *Janissaries*, and had made Pacha of Bosnia. He now employed that able and ruthless chief in Constantinople, and appointed him *Aga* of his old enemies the *Janissaries*. Abaza served his stern master well in that perilous station; but he at last incurred the displeasure of Amurath, and was executed in 1634. The habit of blood-shedding had now grown into a second nature with the *Sultan*. All faults, small or great, were visited by him with the same short, sharp, and final sentence; and the least shade of suspicion that crossed his restless mind was sufficient to ensure its victim's doom. He struck before he censured: and, at last, the terror with which he was regarded was so general and profound, that men who were summoned to the *Sultan's* presence, commonly made the death-ablution before they entered the palace.

The career of Amurath is a memorable proof of how perilously the possession of unlimited power tempts, first to excessive severity for real wrongs—next to ruthless haste in punishing for imaginary offences—and, finally, to the practice of inhuman cruelty on the slightest suspicion or vexation. The earliest executions which Amurath ordered, when he assumed independent power, were those of traitors and mutineers, whose guilt was as heinous as it was unquestionable. His slaughters grew more sweeping; but still, for a long time, his cruelty was seldom or never awakened out of mere wantonness or caprice. It was against real or suspected state offenders that the Imperial Manslayer exercised his terrible prerogative during the first two years of his actual sovereignty. But by degrees his temper grew more moody, and human life became as nothing in his eyes. When he rode forth, any unfortunate wretch who displeased him by crossing or impeding the road, was instantly put to death, and frequently fell pierced by an arrow from the gloomy despot's own bow.

He once caused a party of women, whom he saw dancing in a meadow, to be seized and drowned, because their noisy merriment disturbed him. At another time, a boat, with many females on board, passed along the Bosphorus nearer to the walls of the *seraglio* than he thought proper. He ordered the batteries to open on them, and they were sent to the bottom before his eyes. He beheaded his chief musician for singing a Persian air, which he said was doing honour to the enemies of the empire. Many other acts of equal atrocity are recorded of him; and the number of those who died by his command is reckoned at 100,000. Among them were three of his brothers, and, as was generally believed, his deposed uncle Mustapha. One of his sayings is preserved by an Italian writer, who asserts that Amurath's favourite book was *The Prince* of Machiavelli, which had been translated into Turkish.

The *Sultan's* own maxim is certainly worthy of such inspiration. It is this:

"Vengeance never grows decrepit, though she may grow grey."

In the last years of Amurath's life, his ferocity of temper was fearfully aggravated by the habits of intoxication which he acquired. In one of his nocturnal perambulations of the capital, he met a drunkard, named Mustapha Bekir, who entered into conversation with him, and boasted that he possessed that which would purchase all Constantinople, and "the son of a slave" himself. ("The son of a slave" is a term by which the Turkish people often speak of the *Sultan*.) In the morning, Amurath sent for the man, and reminded him of his words. Nothing daunted, Bekir drew a flask of wine from his robe, and held it out to the *Sultan*, saying:

"Here is the liquid gold, which outweighs all the treasures of the universe, which makes a beggar more glorious than a king, and turns the mendicant *fakir* into a horned Alexander." (So Horace says to the wine-flask: "*Addis cornua pauperi.*")

Struck with the confidence and joyous spirit of the bold bacchanal, Amurath drained the flask, and thenceforth Mustapha Bekir and the *Sultan* were boon companions. When the plague was in 1637 carrying off 500 victims daily at Constantinople Amurath often passed his nights in revels with his favourite. "This summer," he said, "God is punishing the rogues. Perhaps by winter He will come to the honest men."

Never, however, did Amurath wholly lose in habits of indulgence the vigour of either mind or body. When civil or military duty required his vigilance, none could surpass him in austere abstemiousness, or in the capacity for labour. And, with all his misdeeds, he saved his country. He tolerated no crimes, but his own. The worst of evils, the sway of petty local tyrants, ceased under his dominion. He was unremittingly and unrelentingly watchful in visiting the offences of all who were in authority under him, as well as those of the mass of his subjects; and the worst tyranny of the single despot was a far less grievous curse to the empire than had been the military anarchy which he quelled. Order and subordination were restored under his iron sway. There was discipline in the camps; there was pure justice on the tribunals. The revenues were fairly raised, and honestly administered. The abuses of the feudal system of the *ziamets* and *timars* were extirpated; and, if Amurath was dreaded at home, he made himself still more feared by the foe abroad.

It was at first highly perilous for him to leave the central seat of empire. He commenced an expedition into the troubled parts of his Asiatic dominions in the end of the year 1633; but when he had marched a little beyond Nicomedia, he hanged the chief judge of that city, because he found the roads in bad repair. This, excited great indignation among the *Ulema*, and the leaders of that formidable body in the capital began to hold language little favourable to the *Sultan's* authority.

Warned by his mother, the Sultana Validé, of these discontents, Amurath returned suddenly to Constantinople, and put the chief *mufti* to death. This is said to be a solitary instance of the death of a *mufti* by a *Sultan's* order. It effectually curbed the tongues and pens of the men of the law during the remainder of Amurath's reign. In the spring of 1635, he again marched forth from his capital with the avowed intention of not only inspecting his Asiatic provinces, but of expelling the Persian heretics from the cities within the ancient limits of the Ottoman Empire, which they still occupied. In the campaign of this year he conquered the city of Eriwan, and showed the true spirit of the ancient Ottoman *Sultans* in the care with which his troops were provided for, as well as in the strict discipline which he maintained, and the personal valour and generalship which he displayed!

When it was necessary to undergo privations, the *Sultan* shared them with his men; and the English writer, Rycaut, says of him, that:

> For several months he made use of no other pillow for his head than his saddle, no other blanket or quilt than the covering or foot-cloth of his horse.

The recovery of the city and territory of Eriwan was an important exploit; but the march of Amurath through Asia Minor and back, was also a royal visitation of terrible severity to all the provincial governors, whom he convicted or suspected of the slightest disaffection or neglect. In 1638 he made his final and greatest expedition against the Persians, to re-annex to the Ottoman Empire the great city of Bagdad, which had been in the power of those enemies of the House of Othman and of the Sunnite creed for fifteen years, and had been repeatedly besieged in vain by Turkish armies.

There is a tradition in the East that Bagdad, the ancient city of the *Caliphate*, can only be taken by a sovereign in person. The Great Solyman had first won it for Turkey; and now, at the end of a century after that conquest, Amurath IV. prepared his armies for its recovery. The imperial standard of the Seven Horsetails was planted on the heights of Scutari on the 9th March, 1638, and a week afterwards Amurath joined the army. A proclamation was made by which the march from Scutari to Bagdad was divided into 110 days' journey, with fixed periods for halts; and on the 8th of May the vast host moved steadily forward in unmurmuring obedience to its leader's will.

Throughout this second progress of Amurath (the last ever made by an Ottoman sovereign in person through any of the Asiatic provinces not immediately adjacent to Constantinople; Hulme), he showed the same inquisitorial strictness and merciless severity in examining the conduct of all the provincial authorities, that had been felt on his former march to Eriwan. *Pashas*, judges, *Imams*, and tax-collectors thronged to kiss the *Sultan's* stirrup; and, if there was the slightest taint of suspicion on the character of any functionary for probity, activity, or loyalty, the head of the unhappy homager rolled in the dust beneath the imperial charger's hoofs.

On the 15th November, 1638, after the pre-appointed 110 days of march, and eighty-six days of halt, the Ottoman standards appeared before Bagdad, and the last siege of this great city commenced. The fortifications were strong; the garrison amounted to 30,000 men, 1200 of whom were regularly trained musketeers; and the Persian Governor, Bektish Khan, was an officer of proved ability and bravery.

A desperate resistance was expected, and was encountered by the Turks: but their numbers, their discipline, and the resolute skill of their *Sultan*, prevailed over all. Amurath gave his men an example of patient toil, as well as active courage. He laboured in the trenches, and pointed the cannon with his own hands. And, when in one of the numerous sorties made by the garrison, a Persian soldier, of gigantic size and strength, challenged the best and boldest Turk to single combat, Amurath stood forth in person, and after a long and doubtful conflict clove his foe from skull to chin with a sabre stroke. On the 22nd December, the Turkish artillery had made a breach of 80 yards, along which the defences were so completely levelled, that, in the words of an Ottoman writer, "a blind man might have galloped over them with loose bridle without his horse stumbling," (Hulme).

The ditch had been heaped up with fascines; and the Turks rushed forward to an assault, which was for two days baffled by the number and valour of the besieged. On the evening of the second day Amurath bitterly reproached his *grand vizier*, Tayar Mohammed Pacha, for the repulse of the troops, and accused him of want of courage. The *vizier* replied:

> Would to God, my *Padischah*, that it were half as easy to ensure for thee the winning of Bagdad, as it will be for me to lay down my life in the breach tomorrow in thy service.

On the third day (Christmas Eve, 1638) Tayar Mohammed led the forlorn hope in person, and was shot dead through the throat by a volley from the Persian musketeers. But the Turks poured on with unremitted impetuosity, and at length the city was carried. Part of the garrison, which had retired to some inner defences, asked for quarter, which was at first granted; but a conflict having accidentally recommenced in the streets between some Persian musketeers and a Turkish detachment, Amurath ordered a general slaughter of the Persians, and after a whole day of butchery, scarcely 300 out of the garrison, which had originally consisted of 30,000 men, were left alive. A few days afterwards, Amurath was exasperated by the accidental or designed explosion of a powder magazine, by which 800 *Janissaries* were killed and wounded; and he commanded a massacre of the inhabitants of the city, in which 30,000 are computed by the Ottoman historian to have perished.

In February Amurath commenced his homeward march, after having repaired the city walls, and left one of his best generals with 12,000 troops to occupy Bagdad, which has never since been wrested from the Turks. The *Sultan* reached Constantinople on the 10th June, 1638, and made a triumphal entry into his capital; which is memorable, not only on account of its splendour, and of the importance of the conquest which it celebrated, but because it was then that Constantinople beheld for the last time the once familiar spectacle of the return of her monarch victorious from a campaign, which he had conducted in person. The Ottoman writer, (cited by Hulme), who witnessed and described the scene, says that:

> The *Sultan* repaired to his palace with splendour and magnificence which no tongue can tell, and no pen adequately illustrate. The balconies and roofs of the houses were everywhere thronged with people, who exclaimed with enthusiasm, 'The blessing of God be on thee, Conqueror! Welcome, Amurath! May thy victories be fortunate!' The *Sultan* was sheathed in resplendent armour of polished steel, with a leopard-skin over

his shoulders, and wore in his turban a triple aigrette, placed obliquely, in the Persian mode. He rode a Nogai charger, and was followed by seven led Arab horses with jewelled caparisons, while trumpets and cymbals resounded before him, and twenty-two Persian Khans were led captives at the imperial stirrups. As he passed along he looked proudly on each side, like a lion who has seized his prey, and saluted the people, who shouted '*Barik-Allah!*' and threw themselves on the ground. All the vessels of war fired constant salutes, so that the sea seemed in a blaze; and seven days and nights were devoted to constant rejoicings.

A peace with Persia, on the basis of that which Solyman the Great had granted in 1555, was the speedy result of Amurath's victories (15th September, 1639). Eriwan was restored by the Porte; but the possession of Bagdad, and the adjacent territory by the Ottomans, was solemnly sanctioned and confirmed. Eighty years passed away before Turkey was again obliged to struggle against her old and obstinate enemy on the line of the Euphrates. For this long cessation of exhausting hostilities, and this enduring acknowledgment of superiority by Persia, Turkey owes a deep debt of gratitude to the memory of Amurath IV.

Amurath died at the age of twenty-eight, on the 9th of February, 1640. In the interval between his return from Bagdad and his last illness, he had endeavoured to restore the fallen naval power of his empire, he had quelled the spirit of insurrection that had been rife in Albania and the neighbouring districts during his absence in Asia, and he was believed to be preparing for a war with Venice. A fever, aggravated by his habits of intemperance, and by his superstitious alarm at an eclipse of the sun, proved fatal to him after an illness of fifteen days. One of his last acts was to command the execution of his sole surviving brother Ibrahim. It may be doubted whether this mark of "the ruling spirit strong in death" was caused by the delirium of fever, or from a desire that his favourite the Silihdar *Pacha* should succeed to the throne on the extinction of the race of Othman, or whether Amurath IV. wished for the gloomy satisfaction of knowing that his House and Dynasty would descend to the grave with him.

The Sultana Validé preserved Ibrahim's life, and used the pious fraud of a false message to the *Sultan* that his command had been fulfilled. Amurath, then almost in the pangs of death, "grinned horrible a ghastly smile" in the belief that his brother was slain, and tried to rise from his bed to behold the supposed dead body. His attendants, who trembled for their own lives should the deception be detected, forcibly held him back on the couch. The *Iman*, who had been waiting in an adjoining room, but had hitherto feared to approach the terrible dying man, was now brought forward by the pages; and, while the priest commenced his words of prayer, the "*effera vis animi*" of Amurath IV. departed from the world.

CHAPTER 17

War with the Cossacks

We have now traced the fortunes of the House of Othman during a period of nearly four hundred years. A further space of rather more than two centuries remains to be examined, which comprises the reigns of fifteen princes. But, with the exception of the great though unsuccessful Mahmoud II., perhaps with the exceptions also of Mustapha II. and Selim III., the Turkish princes whom we are proceeding to contemplate form figures of but languid interest on the historic page. The decay of the State accords with the degeneracy of its rulers; and minute descriptions of the troubles and calamities of declining empire are generally monotonous and unattractive. We shall indeed still have our attention drawn to fierce and eventful wars; and we shall still meet with names, that must ever live high in martial renown; but they are wars in which the Crescent has generally, though not invariably, gone back; they are principally the names of commanders, who have grown great, not in the advancement, but at the expense of the House of Othman: such names as Montecuculi, Sobieski, Eugene, and Suwarrow.

Yet gleams of glory and success on the Turkish side will not be found altogether wanting, and there have been truly great men in the councils and the armies of Turkey. She has had her Kiuprilis, and others, whose names have long deserved and commanded more than merely Oriental celebrity. We may remark, also, that these last two centuries of Ottoman history, though less picturesque and spirit-stirring than its earlier periods, are more practically instructive and valuable for us to study, with reference to the great problems which the states of Central and Western Europe are now called on to solve.

When Sultan Amurath IV. expired, his brother Ibrahim, whom he had vainly doomed with his own dying breath to die, was the sole surviving representative in male descent of the House of Othman. Ibrahim had during Amurath's reign been a prisoner in the royal palace; and for the last eight years had trembled in the daily expectation of death. When the *grandees* of the empire hastened to his apartment with the tidings that Sultan Amurath was no more, and with congratulations to their new sovereign, Ibrahim in his terror thought that the executioners were approaching, and barred the door against them. He long refused to believe their assurances of Amurath's decease; and was only convinced when the *Sultana*-mother ordered the body of her dead son to be carried within sight of the living one.

Then Ibrahim came forth, and mounted the Turkish throne, which received in him a selfish voluptuary, in whom long imprisonment and protracted terror had debased whatever spirit nature might have originally bestowed, and who was as rapacious and bloodthirsty, as he was cowardly and mean. Under Ibrahim the worst evils that had prevailed in the time of Amurath's weakest predecessors were speedily revived; while the spirit of cruelty, in which Amurath had governed, continued to rage with even greater enormity.

For a short period Ibrahim's first *grand vizier*, Kara-Moustafa, laboured to check the excesses and supply the deficiencies of his sovereign. The Christian subjects of the Porte received from Kara-Moustafa impartial justice; and he attempted with some degree of temporary success to keep down the growth of abuses in the financial administration of the empire. He had the perilous honesty to speak with frankness to the dissolute tyrant whom he served, to oppose Ibrahim's mad caprices, and to strive against the pernicious influence of the favourite *sultanas* and buffoons, who trafficked in the sale of posts and dignities. The offence which the *vizier* thus gave, and the reputation of having amassed much wealth, were sure causes of ruin to one who served a moody and avaricious master like Ibrahim.

At the same time the *vizier's* character was far from faultless; and his errors and his merits co-operated to effect his destruction. Moustafa was violent and implacable in his enmity towards all who rivalled or seemed likely to rival him in power; and he was unscrupulous as to the means which he employed in order to overthrow an adversary. But his deadliest foes were those whose inferiority of sex and station screened them from reprisals; and the immediate cause of the *grand vizier's* fall was an affront which he gave to the lady who held the office of governess of the *harem*. This female functionary of Ibrahim's State, the *Kiaya-Khatoum*, had sent a requisition to the *grand vizier* for an instant supply of 500 carts of wood for the use of the *harem*. At this very time grave tidings of troubles in the provinces and on the frontiers had reached Constantinople.

Intent on these matters, Kara-Moustafa neglected to send the faggots for the ladies. A few days afterwards, while he was presiding in the *divan*, he received, two hours before the usual time of the council's rising, a message from Ibrahim commanding him immediately to dismiss the *divan* and appear before the *Sultan*. The *vizier* obeyed, and hastened before his royal master. Ibrahim instantly demanded of him, "Why have not the 600 loads of wood for the *harem* been supplied?"

"They shall be sent," replied the *vizier*. Then, with more courage than prudence, he added:

"My *Padischah*, is it wise or proper for thee to call on me to break up the *divan*, and to concise and delay the weightiest affairs of State, for the sake of attending to 500 loads of wood, the whole value of which does not amount to 500 *aspres*? Why, when I am before thee, dost thou question me about firewood, but sayest not a word about the petitions of thy subjects, the state of the frontier, and of the finances?"

The Mufti Yahya, who was informed of this conversation by Husein Effendi, who was present, advised the *grand vizier* to be more guarded in his words, and to treat nothing as of trifling importance in which the *Sultan* took an interest. Kara-Moustafa replied, "Is it not doing the *Sultan* good service to tell him the truth? Am I to turn flatterer? I had rather speak freely and die, than live in servile falsehood." (The Turkish historian, Naima, who narrates this speech, states that he heard it related by Husein Effendi Von Hammer, vol. iii.).

Resolved, however, not to die without an effort to overthrow his enemies, Kara-Moustafa formed a device to ruin Youssouf Pacha, who had lately risen rapidly in favour with the *Sultan*, and who was the *vizier's* mortal foe. Kara-Moustafa caused money to be distributed among the *Janissaries* of the capital, to induce them to refuse their rations, and to allege the undue influence of Youssouf Pacha as the cause of their discontent But the scheme was soon disclosed to the *Sultan*, who summoned Kara-Moustafa before him, and ordered his instant execution. Kara-Moustafa escaped from the royal presence to his own house; and, when pursued thither by the executioners, instead of exhibiting the passive submission, which Oriental statesmen have generally shown in such circumstances, he drew his sabre and fought desperately, till he was overpowered by numbers, disarmed, and strangled.

★★★★★★

When Kara-Moustafa's palace was searched by the *Sultan's* officers, five pictures, being portraits of Kara-Moustafa and four other ministers of state, were found in a place of concealment. It was supposed that the late *vizier* had used them in magical rites; and a Moor, who was said to have been his tutor in sorcery, was burnt alive. Von Hammer remarks that probably Kara-Moustafa was fond of paintings, but kept them as forbidden treasures in a secret part of his house. The strict followers of the Mahometan law consider all representations of the human form, either in statuary or painting, to be impious: both as encouragements to idolatry and as profanations of God's chief workmanship. They say, that at the Last Day pictures and statues will rise round the artists who produced them, and call on the unhappy makers to supply their creatures with souls.

******

The successor of Kara-Moustafa in the *grand vizier*ate was Sultanzadé Pacha. He was determined not to incur his predecessor's fate by uncourtly frankness towards his sovereign. He flattered every caprice, and was the ready instrument of every passion of the *Sultan*, whose immoderate appetite for sensual pleasures, and savage fondness of ordering and of witnessing acts of cruelty now raged without stint or shame. Ibrahim, who remembered the check which Kara-Moustafa used to impose on him, could not help feeling some degree of surprise at the universal obsequiousness of his new *grand vizier*; and asked one day of Sultanzadé, "How is it that thou art able always to approve of my actions, whether good or evil?"

"My *Padischah*," replied the shameless minister of despotism, "thou art *caliph*; thou art God's shadow upon earth. Every idea, which thy spirit entertains, is a revelation from Heaven. Thy orders, even when they appear unreasonable, have an innate reasonableness, which thy slave ever reveres, though he may not always understand."

Ibrahim accepted these assurances of infallibility and impeccability; and thenceforth spoke of himself as a divinely inspired agent in the midst of the most disgraceful scenes of folly, vice, and crime. So gross were these, that the very inmates of his *harem* sometimes murmured; and the *Sultan's* mother remonstrated with him against the corruption and frivolity of his conduct; but in vain. Ibrahim replied by quoting the words of his *grand vizier*; and let loose his absolute power in the gratification of every frivolous vanity and caprice, of every depraved appetite, of every feverish fit of irritable passion, and every gloomy desire of suspicious malignity.

The treasures, which the stern prudence of Amurath had accumulated, were soon squandered by the effeminate prodigality of his successor. In order to obtain fresh supplies of gold for his worthless favourites, and for the realisation of his wild fancies, Ibrahim sold every office of state, and every step in the honours both of Pen and Sword, to the highest bidder. The burdens of the old taxes were inordinately increased, and new imposts were added; the very names of which showed the frivolous causes for which the *Sultan* drained the resources of his subjects, thus adding the sense of insult to that of oppression.

One of Ibrahim's passions was a morbid craving for perfumes, especially for amber. Another was an excessive fondness, not only of wearing, but of seeing around him, furs of the most rare and costly description. To meet these desires, Ibrahim created two new taxes; one called the Fur Tax, and the other called the Amber Tax. The madness of the *Sultan's* love for furs was worked up to the utmost by hearing a legend told by an old woman, who used to amuse the ladies of the *harem* by narrating stories to them at night.

This legend described a certain king of the olden time, who was dressed in sable-skins, whose sofas and couches were covered, and whose palace was carpeted and tapestried also with the fur of the sable. Ibrahim instantly set his heart on being similarly arrayed, and on decking the *serail* in like manner. He dreamed all night of sables; and in the morning he commanded in the *divan* that letters should be sent to all the governors and great men of the empire, enjoining each of them to collect and forward to Constantinople a certain number of sable-skins.

A similar requisition was made on all the *Ulema*, and all the civil and military officers in the capital. Some of them were driven to desperation by this mad tyranny, and openly gave vent to the indignation which it inspired. Mohammed Tchelibi, the judge of Galata, appeared before the *grand vizier* clad in the gown of a common *dervise*, and reproached him bitterly for the folly and wickedness of the government. He demanded an audience of the *Sultan*, and added:

> There can but happen to me one of three things. You may kill me; and, in that case, I shall think myself fortunate in being made a martyr. Or, you may banish me from Constantinople; which will not be unpleasant, as there have been several shocks of earthquake here lately. Or, perhaps, you will deprive me of

my employments. But in that I have saved you the trouble. I have appointed my deputy, and have changed my judge's robe and turban for the *dervise's* gown and cap.

The *vizier*, alarmed at such boldness, heard him in silence, and concealed his resentment. A colonel of the *Janissaries*, named Black Mourad, to whom the 500 men of his regiment were devotedly attached, at this time returned from the Candian wars, and was met on landing by a treasury officer, who, in conformity with the resolution of the *divan*, demanded of him so many sable-skins, so many ounces of amber, and a certain sum of money. Rolling his eyes, bloodshot with wrath, on the tax-gatherer. Black Mourad growled out:

I have brought nothing back from Candia but gunpowder and lead. Sables and amber are things that I know only by name. Money I have none; and, if I am to give it you, I must first beg or borrow it."

Not satisfied with the produce of these exactions, the *Sultan* arbitrarily confiscated and sold a large mass of heritable property. The capricious fancies of his favourite ladies were as costly to the empire as his own. Ibrahim permitted them to take what they pleased from the shops and bazaars without payment. One of these fair plunderers complained to the sovereign that she disliked shopping by daylight; and forthwith appeared a mandate from the *Sultan* requiring all the merchants and shop-keepers of the capital to keep their establishments open all night, and to provide sufficient torchlight for their wares to be seen clearly. Another lady told Ibrahim that she wished to see him with his beard adorned with jewels. Ibrahim decked himself accordingly, and appeared in public thus bedizened.

The Turks looked on this as an evil omen; because, according to Oriental traditions, the only sovereign who had adopted such embellishment was King Pharaoh of the Red Sea. Enormous treasures were squandered on the construction of a chariot, incrusted with precious stones, for the use of another *Celoeno* of the *harem*; and 25,000 *piastres* were expended, that an equally splendid skiff should bear the *Sultan* along the Bosphorus. The disasters of the Venetian wars during the year 1648 irritated more and more the Ottoman nation against their imbecile but oppressive ruler; and a formidable conspiracy was organised to deprive him of the power which he abused.

Foremost among the conspirators were the chief officers of the *Janissaries*; and the most active of these was Black Mourad, the colonel who had spoken with such rough frankness of the royal requisition for amber and sable. He knew that his head was in hourly peril; and it was indeed only by a timely warning from a private friend in the *seraglio* that he escaped death. The *Sultan* and his *vizier* celebrated with great splendour on the 6th of August, 1648, the marriage of one of Ibrahim's daughters, a child of eight years old, with the *vizier's* son. Mourad and three other *Janissary* colonels, named Moussliheddin, Begtasch, and Kara-Tschaoush, were bidden to the royal marriage feast, at which it was intended to secure and slay them. But the doomed men avoided their sovereign's snare, and summoned, the same night, their comrades to the mosque of the *Janissaries*.

It was there resolved to depose the *grand vizier*. This was the first avowed object of the conspirators, but they were fully prepared to strike further. The birth of several princes since Ibrahim's accession, the eldest of whom, named Mahomet, was now seven years old, had deprived the *Sultan* of the protection, which, in the early part of his reign, he derived from being the sole representative of the House of Othman. The whole body of the *Ulema* co-operated with the soldiery; and no one was more active or determined in promoting the revolution than the chief *mufti*, whose deadly enmity Ibrahim had earned by a gross insult offered to his daughter.

Ibrahim heard the demand of the insurgents respecting his *vizier*, and took away from him the seals of office; but with a gleam of friendship and humanity, feelings of which at other times he seemed destitute, he strove to protect his fallen favourite's life. The soldiery and the *Ulema* made Sofi Mohammed Grand Vizier, and sent him to the *Sultan* to make known their will that the evil minister should be given up to them for punishment. Ibrahim had the imprudence to strike the chosen *vizier* of the army and the people, and to threaten him that his own turn for punishment should soon arrive.

The insurgents now surrounded the palace, and their words grew more and more menacing. The *Sultan* sent his master of the horse to bid them disperse. The veteran Moussliheddin harangued him in the hearing of the *Janissaries*, the *Spahis*, and the civil officers, who were now all joined in the revolt, saying:

> The *padischah* has ruined the Ottoman world by pillage and tyranny. Women wield the sovereignty. The treasury cannot satiate their caprices. The subjects are ruined. The armies of the *infidels* are winning towns on the frontiers: their fleets blockade

the Dardanelles. Hast thou not been an eye-witness of the state of affairs? and why hast thou not told the *padischah* the truth?

Answered the envoy:

The *padischah* knows nought of this. The guilt is mine: for I feared to speak the truth to the *padischah* in the presence of the late *vizier*. But now tell me what ye desire, and I will faithfully repeat your words before the throne.

Moussliheddin, in the name of the assembly, demanded three things: first, the abolition of the sale of offices; secondly, the banishment of the favourite *sultanas* from the court; thirdly, the death of the *grand vizier*. The master of the horse took back this message to the *Sultan*, who made feeble preparations for resistance by arming the gardeners and pages of the palace. It was now night, and the chiefs of the *Ulema* among the insurgents wished to retire to their homes. But the men of the sword were wiser than the men of the law; and the colonels of the *Janissaries* said to their judicial comrades, "If we separate tonight, we may be unable to assemble again in the morning. Let us keep together till we have re-established order in the world; and let us in a mass pass this night in the mosque."

The *Ulema* obeyed, and in the morning the united revolutionists began their work of vengeance. The obnoxious *vizier* was discovered in his hiding-place and slain, as was the grand judge of Roumelia, who was hated by the people for his debauchery and venality. A message was now sent into the *serail*, requiring the *Sultan* to come forth to the troops. As Ibrahim complied not with this desire, two of the chief *Ulema* were commissioned to wait upon Ibrahim's mother, the Sultana Validé, and to inform her that it was resolved to depose the *Sultan*, and to enthrone her grandson Mahomet in his stead. It has been mentioned that this princess had vainly expostulated with Ibrahim respecting his career of insane profligacy and tyranny.

The only effect of her remonstrances had been to draw on her the *Sultan's* hatred; and Ibrahim had treated her and the princesses, his sisters, with gross indignity, and was justly suspected of meditating their destruction. But the aged *Sultana* now strove hard to avert the wrath of the people from her unworthy son. It was known that the force of armed attendants in the *serail* was utterly inadequate to protect Ibrahim against an assault by the insurgents; and this slight guard was evidently indisposed to peril their lives for an odious and despised master.

The Sultana Validé consented to receive a deputation from the army and people, consisting of the *mufti*, the *cadiaskers*, and of Moussliheddin, Begtasch, and Black Mourad, the *Janissary* colonels. They found her apparelled in the deepest mourning, and only a negro eunuch attended to fan her. They stood before her in respected silence, and she said to them, "Is it a just thing thus to raise revolts? Are ye not all slaves, whom the bounty of this House has fed?"

The old veteran, Moussliheddin, moved to tears by these words, replied:

> Gracious mistress, thou art right. We have all known the benefactions of this House; no one more than myself for these eighty years. It is because we are not thankless men, that we can no longer stand idly by, and witness the ruin of this illustrious House and of this realm. Oh, would that I had not lived on to see these days! What is there that I can covet further for myself? Neither gold nor rank could profit me. But oh; most gracious lady, the foolishness and the wickedness of the *Padischah* are bringing irreparable ruin upon the land. The unbelievers hate captured forty strong places on the Bosnian frontier, and eighty of their ships cruise before the Dardanelles, while the *Padischah* thinks of nothing but of his lusts and his sports, of squandering and of corruption. Your wise men, learned in the law, have met together, and have issued a *fetva* for a change in the occupation of the throne. Until this be accomplished, ruin cannot be averted. Be gracious, oh lady! oppose this not. You would not strive against us, but against the holy law.

The *Sultana* begged hard that they would leave her son in possession of the sovereignty, under the guardianship of the *Ulema* and the *grand vizier*. Some of the deputies seemed disposed to yield; but the aged grand judge of Anatolia, Hanefizadé, took up the discourse, and said:

> Oh, royal lady, we have come hither, fully relying on your grace, and on your compassionate solicitude for the servants of God. You are not only the mother of the *Sultan*; you are the mother also of all true believers. Put an end to this state of trouble; the sooner the better. The enemy has the upper hand in battle. At home, the traffic in places and ranks has no bounds. The *Padischah*, absorbed in satisfying his passions, removes himself farther and farther from the path of the laws. The call to prayers from the minarets of the Mosque of Aya Sofia is drowned in the

noise of fifes, and flutes, and cymbals from the palace. No one can speak counsel without peril to the speaker: you have yourself proved it. The markets are plundered. The innocent are put to death. Favourite slaves govern the world.

The *Validé* made one more effort, and said, "All this is the doing of wicked ministers. They shall be removed; and only good and wise men shall be set in their stead."

"What will that avail?" replied Hanefizadé. "Has not the *Sultan* put to death good and gallant men who served him, such as were Kara-Moustafa Pacha, and Youssouf Pacha, the conqueror of Canea?"

"But how," urged the *Sultana*, "is it possible to place a child of seven years upon the throne?"

Hanefizadé answered:

In the opinion of our wise men of the law a madman ought not to reign, whatever be his age; but rather let a child, that is gifted with reason be upon the throne. If the sovereign be a rational being, though an infant, a wise *vizier* may restore order to the world; but a grown-up *Sultan*, who is without sense, ruins all things by murder, by abomination, by corruption, and prodigality.

"So be it, then," said the *Sultana*; " I will fetch my grandson, Mahomet, and place the turban on his head."

The little prince was led forth amid the enthusiastic acclamations of the military and legal chiefs. All the attendants of Ibrahim had now abandoned hm. A throne was raised near the Gate of Happiness of the *serail*; and three hours before sunset, on the 8th of August, 1648,. the principal dignitaries of the empire paid homage to Sultan Mahomet IV. Only a few were admitted at a time, lest a crowd should frighten the child. The Sultana Validé placed her grandson in charge of a trusty guard; and the *viziers* and the *Ulema*. proceeded to announce to Ibrahim the sentence of deposition.

"My *padischah*," said Abdul-aziz-Effendi, "according to the judgment of the *Ulema*, and the chief dignitaries of the empire, you must retire from the throne."

"Traitor," cried Ibrahim, "Am I not your *padischah*? What means this?"

"No," answered Abdul-aziz-Effendi, "thou art not *padischah*, for as much as thou hast set justice and holiness at nought, and hast ruined the world. Thou hast squandered thy years in folly and debauchery;

the treasures of the realm in vanities: and corruption and cruelty have governed the world in thy place."

Ibrahim still remonstrated with the *mufti*, saying repeatedly, "Am I not *padischah?* What means all this?"

A *Janissary* colonel said to him, "Yes, you are *Padischah*; you are only required to repose yourself for a few days."

"But why then," said Ibrahim, "must I descend from the throne?"

"Because," answered Aziz Effendi, "you have made yourself unworthy of it, by leaving the path in which your ancestors walked."

Ibrahim reviled them bitterly as traitors; and then, lowering his hand towards the ground, he said, "Is it a child so high, that you are going to make *Padischah?* How can such a child reign? And is it not my child, my own son?"

At last the fallen *Sultan* yielded to his destiny, and suffered them to lead him to prison, repeating, as he went, "This was written on my forehead; God has ordered it"

He was kept in sure, but not rigorous captivity for ten days, when a tumult among the *Spahis*—some of whom raised a cry in his favour, decided his fate. The chiefs of the late revolution resolved to secure themselves against a reaction in behalf of Ibrahim, by putting him to death. They laid a formal case before the *mufti*, and demanded his opinion on the following question:

> If it lawful to depose and put to death a sovereign, who confers the dignities of the pen and of the sword not on those who are worthy of them, but on those who buy them for money?

The laconic answer of the *mufti* was, "Yes." The ministers of death were accordingly sent to Ibrahim's prison, whither the *mufti*, the new Grand Vizier Sofi Mohammed, and their principal colleagues also repaired, to witness and to ensure the fulfilment of the sentence. Ibrahim was reading the *Koran* when they entered. Seeing them accompanied by the executioners, whom he himself had so often employed to do their deadly work in his presence, he knew his hour was come; and he exclaimed, "Is there no one of all those who have eaten my bread, that will pity and protect me? These men of blood have come to kill me! Oh, mercy! mercy!" The trembling executioners were sternly commanded by the *mufti* and the *vizier* to do their duty. Seized in their fatal grasp, the wretched Ibrahim broke out into blasphemies and curses; and died, invoking the vengeance of God upon the Turkish nation for their disloyalty to their sovereigns.

The *mufti* justified his regicidal *fetva* by the authority of the sentence in the law, which says:

> *If there are two caliphs, let one of them be put to death.*

A sentence which Von Hammer, (vol. iii.), terms:

> A proposition to shudder at in the law of Islam. A proposition, which, arbitrarily applied and extended, sanctions the execution not only of all deposed sovereigns, but also of all princes whose existence seems to menace the master of the throne with rivalry. It is the bloody authorisation of the state-maxim of the Ottomans for the murder of kings' brothers, sons, and fathers.

The principal foreign events of the reign of Ibrahim, were the siege of Azoph, and the commencement of the long war with the Venetians, called the war of Candia. The important city of Azoph, which commands the navigation of the sea of that name, and gives to its occupiers great advantages for warlike operations in the Crimea, and along all the coasts of the Euxine, had, at the time of Ibrahim's accession, been for four years in the possession of the Cossacks of the vicinity, who were nominal subjects of the Russian *Czar*. Ibrahim's first *vizier*, Kara-Moustafa, was well aware the necessity of maintaining the Turkish power northward of the Black Sea; and in 1641, a strong army and fleet left Constantinople for the recovery of Azoph.

This expedition was aided by a Tartar force, under the Khan of the Crimea. The Cossacks defended the place bravely; and after a siege of three months, the Turks were obliged to retire with a loss of 7000 *Janissaries*, and of a multitude of auxiliary Wallachians, Moldavians, and Tartars, whom the Ottoman historians do not enumerate. A fresh expedition was sent in the next year; and on this occasion Mohammed Ghirai, the Crimean Khan, led no less than 100,000 Tartars to Azoph, to co-operate with the regular Turkish troops. The Cossacks found themselves unable to resist such a force. The *Czar* refused to aid them; and sent an embassy from Moscow to Ibrahim, renouncing all concern with Azoph, and desiring to renew the old amity between Russia and the Porte. (Rycaut, book ii.)

In this emergency the Cossack garrison, with the same ferocious energy which their race has often displayed, set fire to the city which they could no longer defend, and left a heap of ruins for the Turks and Tartars to occupy. The Ottoman general rebuilt the city and fortified it anew with care commensurate with the importance of the post. A garrison of 26,000 men, including twenty companies of *Janissaries*, with a numerous train of artillery, was left under Islam Pacha, to protect the Turkish interest in these regions.

The incessant attacks of the Cossacks on the Turkish, and of the Tartars on the Russian territories, were the subjects of frequent complaints between the courts of Moscow and Constantinople during Ibrahim's reign. Each sovereign required the other to keep his lawless vassals in check. The Czar Alexis Michaelowicz protested against being held responsible for the acts of the Cossacks, whom, in a letter to the *Sultan*, he termed:

> A horde of malefactors who had withdrawn as far as possible from the reach of their sovereign's power, in order to escape the punishment due to their crimes.

The *Sultan* and the *vizier*, on the other hand, required that no one on the side of Russia should do the least damage to aught that belonged to a subject of the Sublime Porte, either on the Sea of Azoph or the Black Sea. The pretext of shifting the blame on the Cossacks, and, in general, all excuses were to be inadmissible. On condition of this being done, and of the *Czar* paying the ancient tribute to the Khan of the Crimea, the *Sultan* promised not to aid the Tartars against Moscow. But, whatever the sovereigns might write or desire, still the system of border war between Cossack and Tartar was carried on; and the Turkish and Russian troops more than once came into collision north of the Euxine in Ibrahim's time, while protecting their irregular confederates, or seeking redress for themselves.

In 1646 the Tartars pursued the Cossack into the southern provinces of Russia; and brought away thence 3000 prisoners, whom they sold for slaves at Perekop. A Russian Army advanced against Azoph, to avenge that affront, but was beaten in several actions by Mousa Pacha and the Turkish garrison, who sent 400 prisoners, and 800 Muscovites' heads to Constantinople, as trophies of their success.

The Crimean *khan*, Islam Ghirai, was more bitter against the Russians than was his master the *Sultan*; and boldly refused to obey orders from Constantinople not to molest those whom he regarded as the natural enemies of the Turkish Empire. He had early in 1648 made an incursion into Poland and Russia, and carried off 40,000 subjects of those realms into slavery. The Polish .and Russian sovereigns sent ambassadors to the Sublime Porte to ask redress: and Ibrahim despatched two of his officers to the Crimea with a letter to the *khan*, in which he was commanded to collect the Christian prisoners whom he had seized in violation of all treaties, and to send them to Constantinople, that they might be given up to the representatives of their governments.

Khan Ghirai read the letter, and coldly replied—

> I and all here are the *Sultan's* servants. But the Russians only desire peace in appearance; they only ask for it while they feel the weight of our victorious arms. If we give them breathing time, they ravage the coasts of Anatolia with their squadrons. I have more than once represented to the Divan that there were two neglected strong places in this neighbourhood, which it would be prudent for us to occupy. Now, the Russians have made themselves masters of them; and they have raised more than twenty little fortified posts. If we are to remain inactive this year, they will seize Akkermann, and conquer all Moldavia.

With this answer the *Sultan's* messengers were obliged to return to Constantinople.

The immediate occasion of the war of Candia was the offence given in 1644 to the *Sultan* by the capture of a rich fleet of merchant vessels, which was voyaging from Constantinople to Egypt. The captors were Maltese, not Venetian galleys: but they anchored with their prizes in the roads of Kalisméne on the south coast of Candia, which had now been in the possession of the Venetians since the time of the fourth crusade, when, on partitioning the conquered Greek Empire, they purchased that important island from their fellow-crusader the Marquis of Montserrat, to whom it had first been allotted as his portion of the sacred spoil Sultan Ibrahim was maddened with rage, when he heard of the capture of the Turkish ships, some of which were the property of one of the chief eunuchs of the imperial household.

He threatened destruction to the whole Christian name, and ordered armaments to be instantly despatched against the Maltese knights; but his officers persuaded him not to renew the enterprise, in which the great Solyman had failed so signally, against the barren and strongly fortified rock of Malta; and rather to turn his arms to .the acquisition of the rich and valuable Isle of Candia. They pointed out to him that Candia was most advantageously situated for incorporation with the Ottoman dominions, and that it might be easily wrested by surprise from its Venetian masters, who had given just cause for hostilities by allowing the piratical Maltese to secure their booty on the Cretan coasts. It was resolved accordingly by the Porte to attack Candia. There was at that time peace between Turkey and Venice.

Ibrahim and his ministers determined to aid force by fraud; and they pretended to receive most graciously the excuses which the republic of St Mark offered for the accidental reception of the Maltese galleys at Kalisméne. A large fleet and army left the Dardanelles, on the 30th April, 1645, with the declared object of assailing Malta; but, after the expedition had paused for a time on the south coast of the Morea, the *generalissimo* Youssouf Pacha put to sea again, read to his assembled captains the *Sultan's* orders, which had previously been kept secret; and instead of sailing westward for Malta, stood to the south with a favourable wind, which brought the Turkish squadron to Canea, at the western extremity of the Isle of Candia, on the 24th of June. The suspicions of the Venetian government as to the real object of the expedition, had not been wholly quieted by the protestations of the *Sultan's* ministers.

Orders had been sent from Venice to put the fortresses of the island in a state of defence, and to collect the militia; and reinforcements had been sent to the garrison. But the native population hated the rule of the Venetian oligarchy; and the troops and galleys under the governor's command were inadequate for the defence of so long a line of seaboard as Crete presents to an invader. The Turks landed without opposition; and Canea, the principal city of the western part of the island, was besieged and captured by them before the end of August. In the following year they took Retino, and in the spring of 1648 they began the siege of Candia, the capital of the island. This memorable siege was prolonged for twenty years by the desperate exertions of the Venetians, who strained their utmost resources to rescue Candia.

They frequently inflicted severe and humiliating defeats on the Turkish squadrons; they even captured the islands of Lemnos and Tenedos from the Ottomans, and more than once ravaged the coasts near Constantinople; but they were never able to drive away the besieging army from before Candia; though the operations of the Turks were retarded and often paralysed by the imbecility and corruption of the Sublime Porte throughout the reign of Ibrahim, and the first part of that of his son Mahomet IV., whose elevation to the throne at the age of seven years, when his father was deposed and murdered, has been already narrated. It would be useless to dwell on the internal history of Turkey during Mahomet IV.'s minority, and to recapitulate the ever-recurring incidents of court intrigue, military insubordination and violence, judicial venality, local oppression and provincial revolt.

The strife of factions was aggravated by the deadly rivalry that sprang up between the old Sultana Validé, the *Sultan's* grandmother, and his mother the young Sultana Validé, whose name was Tarkhan—a rivalry which led to the murder of the elder princess. As no stronger foe than Venice attacked the Ottoman Empire, it lingered on through this period of renewed misery and weakness, until at length, in 1656, through the influence of the Sultana Tarkhan, the Grand Vizierate was given to an aged statesman named Mohammed Kiuprili, who deserves to be honoured as the founder of a dynasty of ministers that raised Turkey, in spite of the deficiency of her princes, once more to comparative power, and prosperity, and glory, and who long retarded, if they could not averts the ultimate decline of the Ottoman Empire.

CHAPTER 15

War with Russia and Poland

The court astronomer at Constantinople, on September 15th, 1656, determined that the most favourable time for the investiture of Mohammed Kiuprili with the *Grand Vizierate*, was the hour of the midday prayer, at the instant when the cry of "God is Great" resounds from the heights of the minarets.

According to a prescribed rule of Islam, the noontide prayer is repeated, not at the exact moment when the sun is on the meridian, but a few seconds afterwards; because the tradition of the prophets teaches that at the astronomical noon the devil is wont to take the sun between his two horns, so that he may wear it as the crown of the world's dominion; and the fiend then rears himself as Lord of the Earth, but he lets the sun go directly he hears the words, "God is Great," repeated on high in the summons of the true believers to prayer. The Turkish historian says:

> Thus, the demons of cruelty, debauchery, and sedition, who had reached the meridian in the reigns of Amurath and Ibrahim, and during the minority of Mahomet, were obliged to yield up their crown of domination, when the voice was heard, that proclaimed Kiuprili Grand Vizier of the Empire.—Von Hammer, vol. iii.

Mohammed Kiuprili was the grandson of an Albanian, who had migrated to Asia Minor, and settled in the town of Kiupri, near the mouth of the River Halys. The ruler of the councils of the Ottoman Empire had been, in early youth, a kitchen-boy, from which situation he rose to that of a cook. After twenty-five years of service he became the steward of the Grand Vizier Khosrew; and under Khosrew's successor he was made Master of the Horse. That successor favoured

Kiuprili, as being a native of the same province as himself; and by his influence Kiuprili was made Governor of Damascus, Tripoli, and Jerusalem, and one of the *viziers* of state. Afterwards he accepted the inferior post of Sanjak Bey of Giuztendil in Albania, where he led an armed force against some of the numerous insurgents of that region, but was defeated and taken prisoner.

After he was redeemed from captivity, he retired to his native town; but was persuaded by a *pacha*, called Mohammed with the Wry Neck, to follow him to Constantinople. His new patron became *grand vizier*, but soon began to regard Kiuprili as a dangerous rival for court favour. It does not, however, appear that Kiuprili used any unfair intrigues to obtain the *grand vizierate*. Friends, who knew the firmness of his character, his activity, and his keen common sense, recommended him to the Sultana Validé, as a man who might possibly restore some degree of tranquillity to the suffering empire; and the *Grand Vizierate* was offered to Kiuprili, then in the seventieth year of his age.

He refused to accept it, save upon certain conditions. He required that all his measures should be ratified without examination or discussion; that he should have free hands in the distribution of all offices and preferments, and in dealing out rewards and punishments, without attending to recommendations from any quarter, and without any responsibility; that he should have authority superior to all influence of great men or favourites; that exclusive confidence should be placed in him, and all accusations and insinuations against him should be instantly rejected. The Sultana Validé, on behalf of her son, swore solemnly that all these conditions should be fulfilled, and Mohammed Kiuprili became Grand Vizier of the Ottoman Empire.

His former patron, Mohammed the Wry-Necked, had been dismissed to make room for him; and the court had ordered that the deposed minister should be put to death, and that his goods should be confiscated in the usual manner. Kiuprili interceded, and saved his life, and gave him the revenues of the government of Kanischa. This was the first, and it was almost the last act of humanity that marked Kiuprili's administration. A stern correction of abuses was required; and Kiuprili applied it, not indeed with the ostentatious cruelty of Sultan Amurath IV., but with the same searching and unsparing severity, which had marked that monarch's rule.

Kiuprili took the precaution of compelling the *mufti* to sign a *fetva*, sanctioning by anticipation all the *grand vizier's* measures: and he then employed the most efficacious means for ridding the empire of all who disturbed or threatened public order. A number of fanatical *scheiks* and *dervishes*, who troubled Constantinople by their tumults, and their lawless violence against all who did not comply with their *dogmas*, were seized and banished.

One of them, who murmured against the *vizier*, and who had great influence with the populace, was strangled, and thrown into the Bosphorus. Kiuprili intercepted a letter from the Greek Patriarch to the *Vaivode* of Wallachia, containing a prediction very similar to those which are frequent in our own time. The *patriarch* said:

> The power of Islam is drawing to an end. The Christian faith will soon be supreme. All their lands will speedily be in the possession of the Christians; and the Lords of the Cross and the Church-bell will be the Lords of the empire.

Kiuprili read in this an encouragement to revolt, and hanged the Greek patriarch over one of the city gates. No delinquency past or present, no preparation for plot or mutiny, escaped the *vizier's* vigilance. He planted his spies in every province and town, and secured the agency of trusty and unquestioning executioners of his commands. The impress of a resolute will was felt throughout the empire; and men obeyed without hesitation the man, whom they perceived never to hesitate himself, never to neglect or abandon those who served him, and never to forgive those who thwarted or disobeyed him. Kiuprili dealt his blows against every race, class, profession, and station, where he saw or suspected offence. He never vented his wrath in threats. "His blows outsped his words;" and, while he was biding his time to strike, he was of unrivalled skill in disguising his preparations.

The Turkish historian Naima relates, on the authority of Medschibi, who had been one of the *grand vizier's* confidential servants, that Mohammed Kiuprili had a maxim, that wrath and reproach are always superfluous, and frequently dangerous for the possessor of power; that it is silly for a statesman to fly out into a passion; and that lulling a victim to sleep is the safest way of killing him.

Thirty-six thousand persons are said to have been put to death by Mohammed Kiuprili's command, during the five years of his *Grand Vizierate*. The chief executioner of Constantinople, Soulfikar, confessed afterwards that he himself had strangled more than 4000, and thrown them into the Bosphorus, Von Hammer, who repeats and accredits these numbers, states that the aged despot, who thus marked every month of his ministry by the sacrifice of more than 500 lives, had acquired a reputation for mildness and humanity when he was a provincial governor. It is fair to suppose that he lavished human life when *grand vizier*, not out of any natural cruelty in his disposition, but from the belief that he could not otherwise suppress revolt and anarchy, and maintain complete obedience to his authority.

******

Our English traveller, Wheeler, who visited Turkey a few years after Mohammed Kiuprili's death, relates a legend which he heard respecting him, which proves how terrible his severities must have been, and the impression left by them on the public mind. Wheeler, in describing one of the streets of Constantinople, says of it: "This street is adorned with several of the monuments of the *viziers* and *bashas*, who have highly merited of the emperor either in the wars or government. Among which we observed one with the *Cuppalo* covered only with a grate of wire; of which we had this account:

'That it was the monument of Mahomet Cupriuli, father to the present *vizier*, who settled the government, which during the minority of the present emperor was very near destruction through the discontents and faction of the principal *Hagaes*, and the mutinies of the *Janissaries*. Concerning whom, after his decease, being buried here and having this stately monument of white marble covered with lead erected over his body, the *grand signior* and the *grand vizier* had this dream both in the same night; to wit that Cupriuli came to them and earnestly begged a little water to refresh him, being in a burning heat. Of this the *grand signior* and the *vizier* told each other in the morning, and thereupon thought fit to consult the *mufti* what to do concerning it: who, according to their gross superstition, advised that he should have the roof of his sepulchre uncovered that the rain might descend on his body, thereby to quench the flames tormenting his soul. And this remedy, the people who smarted under his oppression, think he had great need of, supposing him to be tormented in the other world for his tyrannies and cruelties committed by him in this." Wheeler's *Travels*.

******

The price at which the restoration of order was bought under Mohammed Kiuprili, was indeed fearful; but, though excessive, it was not paid in vain. The revolts which had raged in Transylvania and Asia Minor were quelled; the naval strength of the empire was revived;

the Dardanelles were fortified; the Ottoman power beyond the Black Sea was strengthened by the erection of castles on the Dnieper and the Don; and, though the war in Candia still lingered, the islands of Lemnos and Tenedos were recovered from the Venetians. His own authority in the empire was unshaken until the last hour of his life; and he obtained for his still more celebrated son, Ahmed Kiuprili, the succession to the *Grand Vizierate*. It is said that old Kiuprili, when on his death-bed (31st October, 1661), after recommending his son as the future *vizier*, gave the young *Sultan* four especial rules to follow. One was, never to listen to the advice of women: another was, never to let a subject grow over-rich: the third was, to keep the public treasury full by all possible means: and the last, to be continually on horseback, and keep his armies in constant action.

Sultan Mahomet IV. was now advancing towards manhood; but he was of far too weak a character to govern for himself. His great delight was the chase; and to this he devoted all his energies and all his time. Fortunately for his empire, he placed the most implicit confidence in Ahmed Kiuprili, the new *vizier*, and maintained his favourite minister in power against all the numerous intrigues that were directed against him. Ahmed Kiuprili was the real ruler of Turkey from 1661 to his death in 1676; and he is justly eulogised both by Ottoman and Christian historians as the greatest statesman of his country.

He was only twenty-six years of age when he was called on to govern the empire; but his naturally high abilities had been improved by the best education that the *Muderris* of Constantinople could supply; and he had learned practical statesmanship as a provincial governor and general, during the ministry of his father. Ahmed Kiuprili could be as stern as his sire, when duty to the state required severity; and he was equally tenacious in not permitting the least encroachment on his authority. But he was usually humane and generous; and his most earnest endeavours were directed to mitigate the burdens of imperial taxation, and to protect the people from the feudal exactions of the *Spahis*, and from the arbitrary violence of the *pachas* and other local functionaries.

Like his father, Ahmed Kiuprili commenced his administration by securing himself against any *cabals* of the *Ulema*; and he gave at the same time a noble rebuke to the chief of that order, who spoke in the *divan* against the memory of the late *grand vizier*. Ahmed Kiuprili said to him, "Mufti, if my father sentenced men to death, he did so by the sanction of thy *fetva*."

The *mufti* answered, "If I gave him my *fetva*, it was because I feared lest I should myself suffer under his cruelty."

"*Effendi*," rejoined the *grand vizier*, "is it for thee, who art a teacher of the law of the Prophet, to fear God less than His creature?" The *mufti* was silent. In a few days afterwards he was deposed and banished to Rhodes; and his important station given to Sanizadé, a friend on whom Ahmed Kiuprili could rely.

It was in the civil administration of the Turkish Empire that the genius of Ahmed Kiuprili found its best field of exercise; but he was soon called on to fulfil the military duties of the *Grand Vizierate*, and to head the Ottoman armies in the war with Austria, which broke out in 1663. This, like most of the other wars between the two empires, originated in the troubles and dissensions which were chronic for a century and a half in Hungary and Transylvania. After several conflicts of minor importance during 1661 and 1662, between the respective partisans of Austria and the Porte in these provinces, who were aided against each other by the neighbouring *pachas* and *commandants*, an Ottoman Army was collected by the *grand vizier* on a scale of grandeur worthy of the victorious days of Solyman Kanouni: and Kiuprili resolved not only to complete the ascendency of the Turks in Hungary and Transylvania, but to crush entirely and finally the power of Austria. Mahomet IV. marched with his troops from Constantinople to Adrianople; but there he remained behind to resume his favourite hunting while his *grand vizier* led the army against the enemy.

The *Sultan* placed the sacred standard of the Prophet in Kiuprili's hands at parting; and on the 8th June, 1663, that formidable ensign of Turkish war was displayed at Belgrade. Kiuprili had under his command 121,000 men, 123 field-pieces, 12 heavy battering cannon, 60,000 camels, and 10,000 mules. With this imposing force, he overran the open country of Hungary and Transylvania, almost without opposition; and besieged and captured the strong city of Neuhausel in the September of that year, which was the most brilliant achievement that the Turks had effected in Europe, since the Battle of Cerestes, more than fifty years before. The *vizier*, after this siege, did not recommence active operations with his main army until the spring of the following year, but his light troops spread devastation far and wide through Austria.

******

Sir Paul Rycaut says, "The Tartars, every one after the manner of his country leading one or more spare horses, made inroads within five miles of Vienna; destroying and laying waste all places before them. Things there resembling Doomsday, covered with fire; and not as much left as made an appearance of habitation."

******

In May, 1664, Kiuprili advanced and crossed the River Mur; and he besieged and captured the fortress of Serivar, which the Turks dismantled and set fire to, on the 7th July, as a mark of contempt for the reigning Emperor of Austria, by whom it had been founded. From the ruins of Serivar the Ottoman Army marched northward, passing by the western extremity of Lake Balaton. They captured Egervar, Kipornak, and other strong places; and on the 26th July, the Turks reached the right bank of the River Raab, near to the town of Kaermend. Could they cross that river the remainder of the march against Vienna seemed easy; the Imperialist Army which opposed them in this campaign was inferior to them in numbers; but happily for Austria, that army was commanded by one of the ablest generals of the age, who was destined to gain the first great victory of Christendom in a pitched battle in open field against the full force of the Turkish arms.

Count Raymond de Montecuculi was, like many other of the greatest generals known in modern history, an Italian. He was born at Modena, of a noble family of that duchy, in 1608. He entered into the Austrian service; and acquired distinction in the latter part of the Thirty Years' War; and afterwards in hostilities against Poland. In 1664 he was named *generalissimo* of the Imperial forces, and sent to check the menacing progress of the Turks. The Austrian and Hungarian army, which was placed under Montecuculi's command, was weak in numbers; and at the opening of the campaign he was unable to prevent the Vizier Kiuprili from crossing the Mur, and reducing the Christian cities that lay between that river and the Raab.

But, while the Turks were engaged in these operations, Montecuculi effected a junction with the auxiliary troops of the states of the empire, and also with a valuable force of French troops, which had voluntarily marched under the Count of Coligny and other noblemen, to serve in the Hungarian war. With his army thus strengthened, Montecuculi took up a position near Kaermend on the Raab, covering the road to Vienna; and, from the breadth and rapidity of the river in that place, the attempts made by the Ottoman vanguard to force a passage were easily repulsed.

Kiuprili now marched up the Raab, along the right bank towards

Styria, closely followed along the left bank by Montecuculi, who thus turned the enemy farther away from the Austrian capital, and also from the Turkish reserves which were concentrating at Ofen and Stuhweissenburg. Several efforts of the Turks to cross the river were checked by the Imperialists; but at last the armies marched past the point where the Laufritz flows into the Raab, in the vicinity of the village of St. Gothard; and then, the single stream of the Raab wanted depth and breadth sufficient to present a serious obstacle to the Turks. Both armies, therefore, halted and prepared for the battle, which appeared to be inevitable.

Some overtures for negotiation first took place, in which the Turkish officers behaved with the utmost arrogance. When Reningen, the Austrian envoy, spoke of the restoration of Neuhausel to the emperor, the *vizier* and his *pachas* laughed at him, and asked whether anyone had ever heard of the Ottomans voluntarily giving up a conquest to the Christians. They refused to admit the terms of the old treaty of Sitvatorok as a basis for a peace; and said that peace must be granted, if at all, on principles created by the recent successes of the Sublime Porte. Montecuculi continued his preparations for battle: he issued careful directions to his troops, particularising the order of their array, the relative positions of each corps, the depth of the lines, and the disposal of the baggage and stores. The 1st of August, 1664, saw the result of Montecuculi's sage dispositions, and the first great proof that the balance of superiority between the Ottoman and Christian arms had at last been changed.

The convent of St. Gothard, which has given name to this memorable battle, is on the right bank of the Raab, at a little distance above its confluence with the Laufritz. A space of level ground extends along the right bank of the Raab westward from the convent and village of St. Gothard to the village of Windischdorf, also on the right bank of the river. These two villages formed the extreme wings of the Turkish position before the battle. Along the left bank of the river there is an extent of level ground of equal length with that on the right side, but of much greater breadth; and it was here, on the left side, that the conflict took place.

In the centre of the plain, on the left side (that is to say in the centre of the Imperialist position), stands the village of Moggersdorf; and immediately opposite to Moggersdorf the river bends in and describes an arc towards the southern or Turkish side. This greatly facilitated the passage of the river by the *vizier*, as he was enabled to place guns in

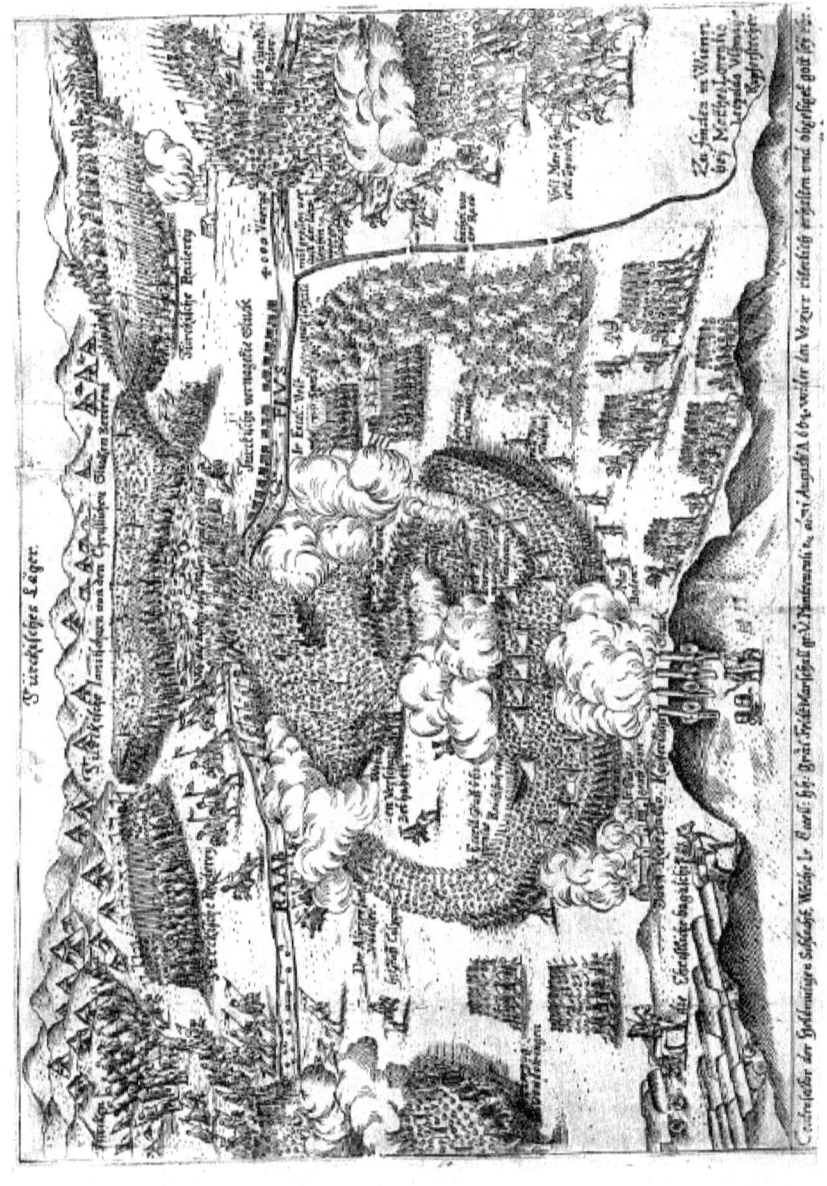

battery on each side of the convex of the stream, and sweep away any troops that disputed the landing-place on the other bank, in the centre of the bend of the river.

Montecuculi placed the auxiliary German troops of the empire in the centre of his line, in and near to the village of Moggersdorf The Austrians and Hungarians were in his right wing; the French auxiliaries formed his left. The Turks had a large superiority in numbers, and in personal courage they were inferior to no possible antagonists. But the military discipline of the Turkish soldiers had become lamentably impaired since the days of Solyman, when it commanded the envious admiration of its Christian foes. It had even declined rapidly since the time when the last great battle between Turk and German was fought at Cerestes (1596). The deterioration in the intelligence and skill of the Ottoman officers was still more conspicuous.

On the opposite side, the German and the other armies of Western Christendom, had acquired many improvements in their weapons, their tactics, and their general military organisation during the Thirty Years' War, which had called into action the genius of such commanders as Tilly, Wallenstein, Gustavus Adolphus, Bernhard, Torstenston, Turenne, and Montecuculi himself. The Turkish artillery, though numerous, was now cumbrous and ill-served, compared with the German. The *Janissaries* had given up the use of the pike (which seems to have been one of their weapons in Solyman's time; Von Hammer, vol. ii.), and the Ottoman Army was entirely deficient in foot brigades of steady spearmen, and also in heavily-armed regular cavalry.

The German infantry was now formed of pikemen and of musqueteers; and part of their horse consisted of heavy *cuirassier* regiments, which, in Montecuculi's judgment, were sure, if a fair opportunity of charging were given them, to ride down Turkish infantry or cavalry, without it being possible for any serious resistance to be offered to them. In that great general's opinion, the want of the pike, which he calls "the queen of weapons," (*Al Turco manca la picca, che h la regina delle armi a piedi*), was the fatal defect in the Turkish military system. We shall find the Chevalier Folard, half a century afterwards, expressing a similar judgment with reference to the negligence of the Turks in not adopting the invention of the bayonet.

Montecuculi's criticisms on the defects in the Turkish armies were written by him after the battle of St. Gothard; but his military sagacity must have divined them, as soon as he observed the *vizier's* troops, and made trial of their tactics and prowess in the early operations of the campaign. But the Turks themselves, before they fought at St. Gothard, knew not their own deficiencies; they were flushed with triumph at the advantages which they had hitherto gained under Ahmed Kiuprili; and with full confidence in their chief and themselves, they advanced, about nine in the morning of the 1st of August, 1664, to the Raab, and began the passage of the eventful stream. Kiuprili had placed his batteries along the sides of the arc of the stream, which has already been described; and his Janissaries, who were drawn up in the Turkish centre, crossed the river without much loss, and attacked and carried the village of Moggersdorf.

The centre of the Christians was thus completely broken, and the Ottomans appeared to be certain of victory, when Montecuculi brought succour from the right wing. Prince Charles of Lorraine, who in this battle gave the prelude of his long and brilliant career, led his regiment of Austrian heavy cavalry to the charge in person, and killed with his own hand the commander of the *grand vizier's* guards. The advanced troops of the Turkish centre, thus taken in flank by the Austrian cavalry, were driven back to the Raab; Moggersdorf was then attacked by the Imperialists, and set on fire; but the *Janissaries*, who had entrenched themselves in the village, refused to retreat or surrender, and kept their post till they perished in the flames, with obstinacy (says Montecuculi) worthy to be reflected on and admired. Kiuprili brought large reinforcements over from the right bank, and Montecuculi now sent word to the Count of Coligny and the French in his left wing, that it was time for them to aid him with all their might.

Coligny sent him instantly 1000 infantry and two squadrons of cavalry, under the Duc de la Feuillade and Beauvezé. When Kiuprili saw the French coming forward with their shaven chins and cheeks, and powdered *perruques*, he asked scornfully of one of his attendants, "Who are these young girls?" But the young girls, as he termed them, without regarding the formidable Turkish battle-cry of "*Allah!*" rushed upon the Turks and cut them down, shouting out on their part, "*Allons! Allons! Tue! Tue!*" Those *Janissaries* who escaped that carnage remembered long afterwards the French cry of "*Allons! Tue!*" and the Duc de la Feuillade was for many years talked of in their barracks as "*Fouladi*," which means " The man of steel."

Kiuprili's first attack had failed, though he still retained some ground on the left bank of the Raab. He now (towards noon) prepared for a combined attack (such as he ought to have made in the first instance) upon both the Christian wings, while he, at the same time, assailed their centre with greater forces. Four large masses of irregular Ottoman cavalry dashed across the Raab at Montecuculi's right wing: three similar bodies attacked the French on the left; Kiuprili led a force of cavalry and infantry upon the centre; and, at the same time, detached squadrons were ordered to pass the river at points a little distant from the field of battle, and gain the flanks and rear of the Imperialists. An obstinate conflict now took place all along the line. Some parts of the Christian army gave ground, and several of its generals advised a retreat; but Montecuculi told them that their only chance of safety, as well as of victory, was to take the offensive with a mass of the best troops, and make a desperate charge on the Ottoman centre.

A strong force of the Christian cavalry was now concentrated for this purpose; and the word was passed along the ranks that they must break the Turks or perish. John Spork, the Imperialist general of cavalry, who was called the Austrian Ajax, prostrated himself bareheaded on the ground in front of his men, and prayed aloud:

> Oh, mighty *Generalissimo*, who art on high, if thou wilt not this day help thy children the Christians, at least do not help these dogs the Turks, and thou shalt soon see some thing that will please thee.

******

> This may remind some readers of the wish of Miltiades before Marathon, not for favour, but merely for fair play, from the gods. Herodotus, lib. vi. sect. 116. The well-known prayer of the American backwoodsman when about to attack the bear, is still more like Spork's devotions. This Austrian Ajax could ill have comprehended the sublime spirit in which his assumed prototype the Homeric Ajax prayed in battle (*Iliad*, book xvii. verse 645). Most probably he had never heard of it. Spork was made a Count by the Austrian emperor in reward for his services, but he always wrote his name (which he did with great difficulty) "Spork, Count," and not "Count Spork." He said he was a Spork, before he was a Count.

******

Having arranged his lines for the decisive charge, Montecuculi gave the word, and the Imperialists rushed forward with a loud shout, which disconcerted the Turks, who, accustomed themselves to terrify their enemy by their battle-cry, and to give the attack, recoiled before the unexpected assault of their opponents. Thrown into utter confusion by the irresistible shock of Montecuculi's *cuirassiers*, which was supported vigorously by the Christian musketeers and pikemen, the Ottomans were driven into the Raab; *Janissary, Spahi*, Albanian, Tartar, going down alike beneath the impetuous rush of the Christian centre, or flying in panic rout before it The Ottoman cavalry in the wings lost courage at seeing the defeat of their centre, where the *vizier* and all their best troops were stationed, and they rode off the field without an effort to retrieve the fortune of the day.

More than 10,000 Turks perished in the battle; and the triumph of Montecuculi was graced by the capture of fifteen pieces of cannon and forty standards. On the morrow, the victor caused a solemn service of thanksgiving to be celebrated on the field of battle. A chapel was founded there, and still attests the scene of this memorable battle, which commenced the compensation for the 300 years of defeat which European Christendom had sustained from Turkey, ever since the day when the confederate forces of Servia and Hungary were crushed by Sultan Amurath I. at Kossova.

It is because the Battle of St. Gothard presents thus to our notice a turning point in the military history of Turkey, that it has been described with a particularity of detail, such as can be given to none of the long list of battles, which yet will come before our notice, while tracing the declining fortunes of the Ottoman Empire. The advantage also of possessing the comments of Montecuculi himself on this campaign, and on Turkish warfare generally, has been an additional reason for giving prominence to his victory at St. Gothard. The defects which he points out in the Turkish military system, have continued to exist, or rather have existed with aggravation, until the reign of the late Sultan Mahmoud. They may be summed up as consisting in the neglect of the Turks to keep pace with the improvements made by other nations in the weapons and in the art of war; and in the appointment of incompetent officers through bribery and other corrupt influences.

The pernicious effects of these vices of the Ottoman war department have been partly counteracted by the remarkable personal valour of the common soldiers among the Turks, their sobriety, and the vigour of their constitutions; and also by the care taken to provide them with good and sufficient provisions both when in barracks and when employed on active duty. These are favourable points in the Ottoman service, which every military critic from Count Montecuculi down to Marshal Marmont has observed; and the more important of them, those which regard the natural soldierly qualities of the Ottoman population, show that Turkey has never lost that element of military greatness, which no artificial means can create or revive, but to which the skill of great statesman and great generals (if the *Sultan's* empire should be blessed with them) may superadd all that has for nearly two centuries been deficient.

The immediate result of the Battle of St. Gothard was a truce for twenty years on the footing of the treaty of Sitvatorok, which the Turks before their defeat had so arrogantly refused. But Neuhausel remained in the possession of the Ottomans; so that Ahmed Kiuprili, notwithstanding his great overthrow by Montecuculi, was able to re-enter Constantinople as a conqueror. His influence over the *Sultan* was undiminished; and the next great military enterprise, that Kiuprili undertook, was one of unchequered success and glory. This was the reduction of the city of Candia, which had now for nearly twenty years been vainly besieged or blockaded by the Turks.

Mahomet IV. at first proposed to lead in person the great armament which Kiuprili collected at Adrianople for this expedition. The imperial tent was raised in the camp; and the *Sultan* caused those parts of the Turkish historians to be read before him, which narrate the capture of Constantinople by Mahomet II., the Battle of Calderan under Selim I., and the sieges of Rhodes and Belgrade by Solyman. But Mahomet IV. appeased the martial ardour, which those recitals produced in him by hunting with redoubled energy. It was only in the chase that he was enterprising and bold: he shrank from the battlefield; and he was not even a hero in his *harem*, where a Greek slave-girl of Retino tyrannised with capricious violence over the over-fond and over-constant *padischdi*.

This favourite *Sultana* was zealously devoted to the interests of Kiuprili, who was thereby rendered so secure in his authority, that he ventured to remain in the island of Candia from the time of his landing there in 1666 to the surrender of the long-besieged capital in 1669. During these three last years of the siege, every possible effort of bravery and all the then available resources of the military art were employed both by assailants and defenders. Morosini (afterwards renowned as the conqueror of the Morea, and surnamed the Peloponnesian) commanded in the city; ably seconded by the Duc de la Feuillade, the hero of St. Gothard, and many other high-born and high-spirited volunteers, who flocked from every country of Christendom to Candia, as the great theatre of military glory.

On the Turkish side, Kiuprili and his generals and admirals urged on the operations of the besiegers by sea and by land with indomitable obstinacy, and with a degree of engineering skill, from which the Turks of more recent times have far degenerated.

★★★★★★

Juchereau says of the Turks of this century, "It is only since the establishment of the school for engineers at Sulitzi, that they have learned under Frank officers, in consulting their military archives and the plans of their ancient engineers, those ways and parallels of trenches, of which they were the inventors, and which so distinguished the siege of Candia."

★★★★★★

It is computed that during the final thirty-four months of the siege, during which Kiuprili commanded, 30,000 Turks and 12,000 Venetians were killed. There were fifty-six assaults, and ninety-six sorties; and the number of mines exploded on both sides was 1364. Several attempts were made by the Venetians to purchase peace without ceding Candia. Put to their offers of large sums of money, Kiuprili replied: "We are not money-dealers; we make war to win Candia, and at no price will we abandon it."

The Ottomans persevered in their enterprise, until Morosini, on the 6th September, 1669, surrendered on honourable terms the city which the incessant mining had converted into a confused mass of gigantic mole-heaps. A peace was made between Venice and the Porte, by which the city and island of Candia became the property of the *Sultan*. Kiuprili remained there several months after the conquest was completed, during which time he was well and wisely employed in organising the local government of Crete under its new sovereign.

The next scene of warlike operations, on which Ahmed Kiuprili entered, deserves especial attention, because it brings us to the rival claims of Poland, Russia, and Turkey to dominion over the Cossacks, and is intimately connected with the long and still enduring chain of hostilities between the Russian and Turkish Empires. The Cossacks of the Don had become subjects of Ivan the Terrible, Czar of Muscovy, in 1549; but the Cossacks of the Dnieper and the Ukraine were long independent; and their first connection was with Poland.

The Poles affected to consider them as vassals, but the wisest Polish rulers were cautious in the amount of authority which they attempted to exercise over these bold and hardy tribes. The imperious tyranny of other less prudent sovereigns of Poland was met by fierce opposition on the part of the Cossacks, who called in their former constant enemies, the. Tartars, to aid them against their new Polish oppressors. Deserted, after some years of warfare, by the Tartars, the Cossacks of the Ukraine appealed to the Russian Czar Alexis. Many years of chequered and sanguinary hostilities followed, and at last the Cossack territory was nominally divided between Russia and Poland at the truce of Androssan, in 1667. But the Cossacks, who dwelt near the mouths of the rivers Boug and Dnieper, and who were called the Zaporofskian Cossacks, refused to be included in the Polish dominions by virtue of that arrangement, and placed themselves under the protection of the *Czar*.

In 1670, the Cossacks of that part of the Ukraine which had been left under Poland, petitioned the Polish Diet for certain privileges, which were refused; and a Polish army under Sobieski was sent into the Ukraine to coerce the Cossack malcontents. The Cossacks, under their Hetman Dorescensko, resisted bravely; but at last they determined to seek the protection of the Sublime Porte; and Dorescensko, in 1672, presented himself at Constantinople, and received a banner with two horse-tails, as Sanjak Bey of the Ukraine, which was immediately enrolled among the Ottoman provinces. (Since the time of Amurath III. the governors of the large provinces, or *eyalets*, received the rank of *vizier*, and were *pachas* with three horsetails. The *sanjak beys*, or governors of the smaller districts, were *pachas*, with two horse-tails).

At the same time, the Khan of the Crimea was ordered to support the Cossacks, and 6000 Turkish troops were marched to the Ukraine. The Poles protested loudly against these measures. The *Czar* added his remonstrances, and threatened to join Poland in a war against Turkey. The *grand vizier* haughtily replied that such threats were empty words and out of place, and that the Porte would preserve its determination with regard to Poland. A short time previously, another Turkish minister had answered similar warnings by boasting:

> God be praised, such is the strength of Islam, that the union of Russians and Poles matters not to us. Our empire has increased in might since its origin; nor have all the Christian kings, that have leagued against us, been able to pluck a hair from our beard. With God's grace it shall ever be so, and our empire shall endure to the day of judgment.

Kiuprili himself, when the Polish ambassador reproached the Turks with injustice in aiding the revolted subjects of Poland, replied in a remarkable letter, written with his own hand; in which he states that:

> The Cossacks, a free people, placed themselves under the Poles, but being unable to endure Polish oppression any longer, they have sought protection elsewhere, and they are now under the Turkish banner and the horse-tails. If the inhabitants of an oppressed country, in order to obtain deliverance, implore the aid of a mighty emperor, is it prudent to pursue them in such an asylum? When the most mighty and most glorious of all emperors is seen to deliver and succour from their enemies those who are oppressed, and who ask him for protection, a wise man will know on which side the blame of breaking peace ought to rest. If, in order to quench the fire of discord, negotiation is wished for, so let it be. But if the solution of differences is referred to that keen and decisive judge, called 'The Sword,' the issue of the strife must be pronounced by the God, who hath poised upon nothing heaven and earth, and by whose aid Islam has for 1000 years triumphed over its foes.

This avowal of the principle of intervention in behalf of an oppressed people was a bold measure for the prime minister of a nation, like the Turkish, which kept so many other nations in severe bondage; it was especially bold in Kiuprili, who at that very time was directing the construction of fortresses in the Morea to curb the reviving spirit of independence, of which the Greeks had given some signs during the recent Venetian war.

In the Polish campaign of 1672, Sultan Mahomet IV. was persuaded to accompany the powerful army which Kiuprili led to the siege of the important city of Kaminiec, in Podolia. Kaminiec fell after nine days' siege (26th August, 1672), and Lemberg shared its fate on the 9th of September. The imbecile King of Poland, Michael, then made the peace of Bucsacs with the Turks, by which Poland was to cede Podolia and the Ukraine, and pay an annual tribute to the Porte of 220,000 *ducats*. The *Sultan* returned in triumph to Adrianople; but the congratulations which were lavished on him as conqueror of the Poles were premature.

Sobieski and the other chiefs of the Polish nobility determined to break the treaty which their king had made. They refused to pay the stipulated tribute; and, in 1673, the *grand vizier* made preparations for renewing the war upon the Poles, and also for attacking the Czar of Russia, from whom they had received assistance. The Turks marched again into Podolia; but, on the 11th of November, 1673, Sobieski, who now led the Poles, surprised the Turkish camp near Khoczim, and routed Kiuprili with immense slaughter.

The princes of Wallachia and Moldavia had deserted from the Turkish to the Polish side with all their contingents; a transfer of strength which aided materially in obtaining Sobieski's victory. But Kiuprili's administrative skill had so re-invigorated the resources of Turkey, that she readily sent fresh forces into the Ukraine in the following year. Sobieski with his Poles and the Russians (who now took an active part in the war) had the advantage in the campaign of 1674; and, in 1675, Sobieski gained one of the most brilliant victories of the age over the Turks at Lemberg.

But the superior strength and steadiness of the Porte and Kiuprili in maintaining the war against the discordant government of Poland, were felt year after year; and, in 1676, the Turkish commander in Podolia, Ibrahim, surnamed Scheitan, that is, "Ibrahim the Devil," made himself completely master of Podolia, and attacked Galicia. Sobieski (who was now King of Poland) fought gallantly with far inferior forces against Ibrahim at Zurawna; but was glad to conclude a peace (27th October, 1676), by which the Turks were to retain Kaminiec and Podolia; and by which the Ukraine, with the exception of a few specified places, was to be under the sovereignty of the *Sultan*.

Three days after the peace of Zurawna, Ahmed Kiuprili died. Though his defeats at St. Gothard and Khoczim had fairly given rise to an opinion among the Ottoman ranks that their *vizier* was not born to be a general, his military services to the empire, for which he won Candia, Neuhausel, and Kaminiec, were considerable; and no minister ever did more than he accomplished in repressing insurrection and disorder, in maintaining justice and good government, and in restoring the financial and military strength of his country. He did all this without oppression or cruelty. He protected all ranks of the *Sultan's* subjects; he was a liberal patron of literature and art; he was a warm friend, and a not implacable enemy; he was honourably true to his plighted word towards friend or foe, towards small or great: and there is far less than the usual amount of Oriental exaggeration in the praises, which the Turkish historians bestow upon him, as:

> The light and splendour of the nation; the conservator and governor of good laws; the vicar of the shadow of God; the thrice learned and all-accomplished *Grand Vizier*.

Chapter 19

The Second Siege of Vienna

The value of such a minister as Ahmed Kiuprili to Turkey was soon proved by the rapid deterioration in her fortunes under his successor in the Vizierate, Kara Mustapha, or Black Mustapha: a man whose character was in every respect the opposite of Kiuprili's; and who to slender abilities united the wildest ambition and almost boundless presumption. He was son-in-law to the *Sultan*; and by the influence which that marriage gave him, he obtained the high office, which he abused to the ruin of his master, and the deep disaster of his country. Kara Mustapha's favourite project was a new war against Austria, in which he hoped to capture Vienna, and to make himself the nominal viceroy, but real sovereign of ample provinces between the Danube and the Rhine.

But the first years of his *vizierate* were occupied in an inglorious war with Russia. That empire had been no party to the late peace of Zurawna; and it supported Dorescensko against the Porte, when that fickle Cossack grew discontented with the *Sultan's* authority. Kara Mustapha led a large army into the Ukraine, and besieged Cehzrym, but was beaten by the Russians, and fled with ignominy across the Danube. In the following year he resumed the war with fresh forces; and after several alternatives of fortune, he stormed Cehzrym on the 21st of August, 1678. But the losses which the Turks sustained both from the Russian sword and the climate, were severe; and it is said, that even at this early period of the wars between the two nations, the Turks entertained an instinctive apprehension of the power of the Muscovites. (Thornton citing Spon, whose travels were published in 1678. "Spon says, 'Of all the princes of Christendom, there was none whom the Turks so much feared as the Czar of Muscovy.'")

A peace was made in 1681, by which the Porte gave up the disputed territory to Russia; and it was stipulated that neither power should raise fortifications between the rivers Boug and Dniester. Five years afterwards, a territorial arrangement was concluded between Poland and Russia, which recognised the sovereignty of the *Czar* over the whole of the Ukraine.

In 1682, Kara Mustapha commenced his fatal enterprise against Vienna. A revolt of the Hungarians under Count Tekeli, against Austria, which had been caused by the bigoted tyranny of the Emperor Leopold, now laid the heart of that empire open to attack; and a force was collected by the *grand vizier*, which, if ably handled, might have given the House of Hapsburg its deathblow. Throughout the autumn of 1682 and the spring of 1683, regular and irregular troops, both horse, foot, artillery, and all kinds of munitions of war, were collected in the camp at Adrianople on a scale of grandeur that attested and almost exhausted the copiousness, which the administration of Kiuprili had given to the Turkish resources.

The strength of the regular forces, which Kara Mustapha led to Vienna, is known from the muster-roll which was found in his tent after the siege. It amounted to 275,000 men. The attendants and camp-followers cannot be reckoned; nor can any but an approximate speculation be made as to the number of the Tartar and other irregular troops that joined the *vizier*. It is probable that not less than half a million of men were set in motion in this last great aggressive effort of the Ottomans against Christendom.

The Emperor Leopold had neither men nor money sufficient to enable him to confront such a deluge of invasion; and, after many abject entreaties, he obtained a promise of help from King Sobieski of Poland, whom he had previously treated with contumely and neglect. Poland was at peace with Turkey, nor had the Porte in any way failed in observance of the recent treaty. But neither Sobieski nor other Christian adversaries of the Turks were very scrupulous as to such obligations; and the Polish king promised to aid the Austrian Emperor with 58,000 men.

The Turkish Army proceeded along the western side of the Danube from Belgrade, and reached Vienna without experiencing any serious check, though a gallant resistance was made by some of the strong places which it besieged during its advance. The city of Vienna was garrisoned by 11,000 men under Count Stahremberg, who proved himself a worthy successor of the Count Salm, who had fulfilled the same duty when the city was besieged by Sultan Solyman. The second siege of Vienna lasted from the 15th July to the 12th September, 1683, during which the most devoted heroism was displayed by both the garrison and the inhabitants. The numerous artillery of the Turks shattered the walls and bastions, and the indefatigable labours of their miners were still more effective. The garrison was gradually wasted by the numerous assaults which it was called on to repulse, and in the frequent sorties, by which the Austrian commander sought to impede the progress of the besiegers.

Kara Mustapha, at the end of August, had it in his power to carry the city by storm, if he had thought fit to employ his vast forces in a general assault, and to continue it from day to day, as Amurath IV. had done when Bagdad fell. But the *vizier* kept the Turkish troops back out of avarice, in the hope that the city would come into his power by capitulation; in which case he would himself be enriched by the wealth of Vienna, which, if the city were taken by storm, would become the booty of the soldiery. The Turkish Army murmured loudly at the incompetency, the selfishness, and the vain confidence of their chief, who took no measures for checking the approach of the relieving army that was known to be on its march; though the passage of the Danube might easily have been guarded against Sobieski by a detachment from the immense forces which were at the *grand vizier's* command.

Sobieski had been unable to assemble his troops before the end of August; and, even then, they only amounted to 20,000 men. But he was joined by the Duke of Lorraine and some of the German commanders, who were at the head of a considerable army, and the Polish king crossed the Danube at Tulm, above Vienna, with about 70,000 men. He then wheeled round behind the Kalemberg Mountains to the north-west of Vienna, with the design of taking the besiegers in the rear. The *vizier* took no heed of him; nor was any opposition made to the progress of the relieving army through the difficult country which it was obliged to traverse. On the 11th of September the Poles were on the summit of the Mount Kalemberg; and the biographer of Sobieski, (Coyer, *Memoir of Sobieski*), says:

"From this hill, the Christians were presented with one of the finest and most dreadful prospects of the greatness of human power; an immense plain and all the islands of the Danube covered with pavilions, whose magnificence seemed rather calculated for an encampment of pleasure than the hardships of war; an innumerable multitude of horses, camels, and buffaloes; 2,000,000 men all in motion, swarms

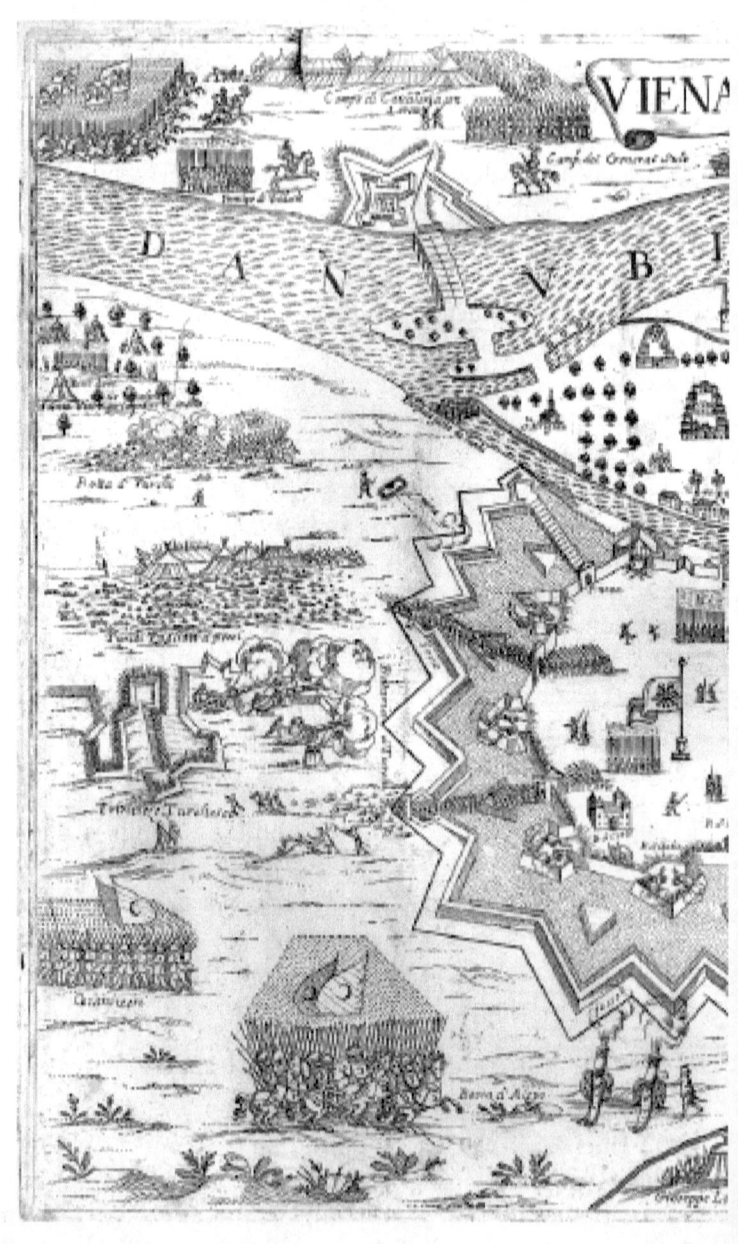

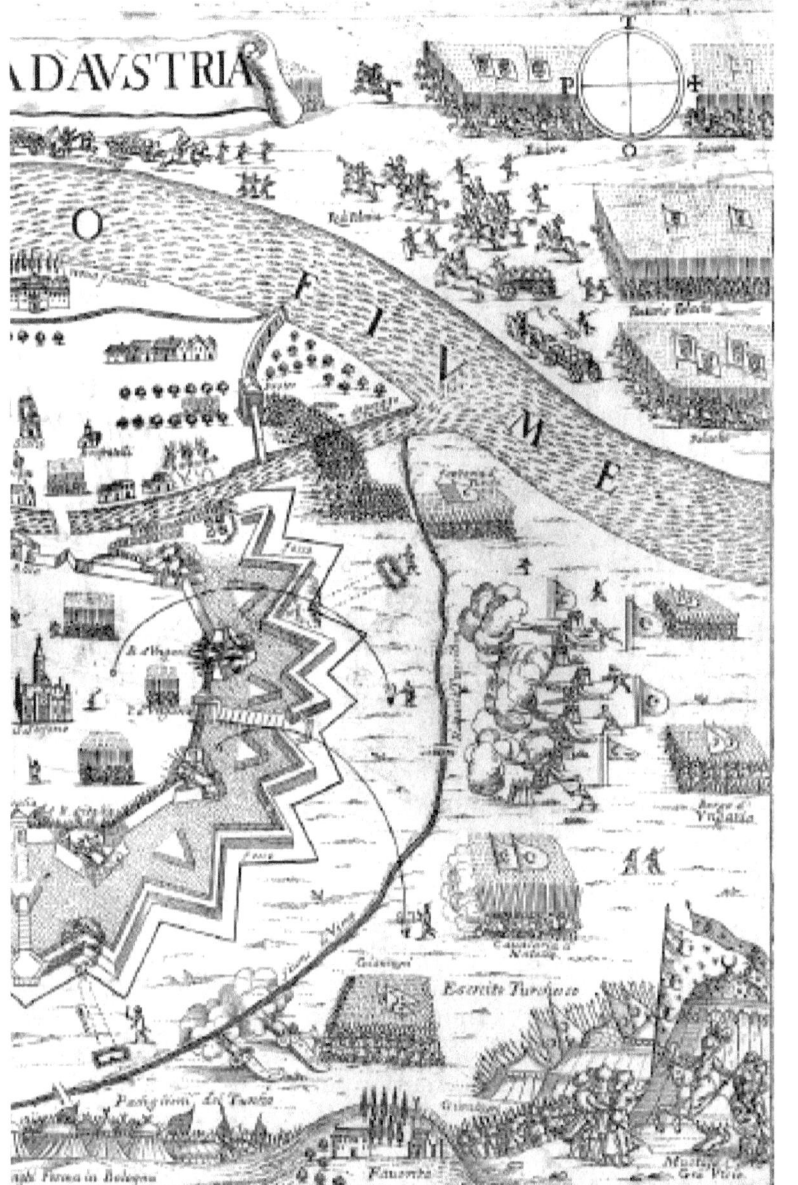

of Tartars dispersed along the foot of the mountain in their usual confusion; the fire of the besiegers incessant and terrible, and that of the besieged such as they could contrive to make; in fine, a great city, distinguishable only by the tops of the steeples and the fire and smoke that covered it."

But Sobieski was well accustomed to the menacing aspect of Turkish armies; his eagle glance saw instantly the *vizier's* want of military skill, and the exposure of the long lines of the Ottoman, camp to a sudden and fatal attack. "This man," said he, "is badly encamped: he knows nothing of war; we shall certainly beat him." And in a letter, sent by him to the Queen of Poland on the night before the battle, he wrote these words:

> We can. easily see that the general of an army, who has neither thought of entrenching himself nor concentrating his forces, but lies encamped as if we were 100 miles from him, is predestined to be beaten.

The ground through which Sobieski had to move down from the Kalemberg, was broken by ravines; and was so difficult for the passage of the troops, that Kara Mustapha might, by an able disposition of part of his forces, have long kept the Poles in check, especially as Sobieski, in his hasty march, had brought but a small part of his artillery to the scene of action. But the *vizier* displayed the same infatuation and imbecility that had marked his conduct throughout the campaign. He at first refused to believe that Sobieski and any considerable number of Polish, troops were on the Kalemberg; and, when at last convinced that an attack would be made upon his lines, he long delayed the necessary order for the occupation of the hollow ways, through, which alone the Poles could debouch from the slopes of the high, ground which they had gained.

Unwilling to resign Vienna, Mustapha left the chief part of his *Janissary* force in the trenches before the city, and led the rest of his army towards the hills, down which Sobieski and his troops were advancing. In some parts of the field, where the Turks had partially entrenched the roads, their resistance to the Christians was obstinate; but Sobieski led on his best troops in person in a direct line for the Ottoman centre, where the *vizier's* tent was conspicuous; and the terrible presence of the victor of Khoczim was soon recognised.

"By *Allah!* the King is really among us," exclaimed the Khan of the Crimea, Selim Ghirai; and turned his horse's head for flight. The mass of the Ottoman army broke and fled in hopeless rout, hurrying Kara Mustapha with them from the field. The *Janissaries*, who had been left in the trenches before the city, were now attacked both by the garrison and the Poles, and were cut to pieces.

The camp, the whole artillery, and the military stores of the Ottomans became the spoil of the conquerors; and never was there a victory more complete, or signalised by more splendid trophies. The Turks continued their panic flight as far as Raab. There Kara Mustapha collected round him some of the wrecks of the magnificent army which had followed him to Vienna. He sought to vent his fury by executing some of the best Turkish officers, who had differed from him during the campaign. His own fate, when he was executed by the *Sultan's* orders a few weeks afterwards at Belgrade, excited neither surprise nor pity.

The great destruction of the Turks before Vienna was rapturously hailed throughout Christendom as the announcement of the approaching downfall of the Mahometan Empire in Europe. The Russians and the Venetians declared war against the Porte; and Turkey was now assailed on almost every point of her European frontiers. The new Grand Vizier Ibrahim strove hard to recruit the armies, and supply the deficiency in the magazines, which the fatal campaign of his predecessor had occasioned. But city after city was now rent rapidly away from Islam by the exulting and advancing Christians.

The Imperialist armies, led by the Duke of Lorraine, captured Gran, Neuhausel, Ofen, Szegedin, and nearly all the strong places which the Turks had held in Hungary. The Venetians were almost equally successful on the Dalmatian frontier; and the Republic of St. Mark now landed its troops in Greece, under Morosini, who rapidly made himself master of Coron, Navarino, Nauplia, Corinth, Athens, and other chief cities of that important part of the Turkish Empire. In Poland the war was waged less vigorously; nor did the Turks yet relinquish their hold on Kaminiec.

But a great defeat which the main Ottoman Army sustained on the 12th August, 1687, at Mohacz (on the very scene of Solyman's ancient glory), excited the discontents of the soldiery into insurrection against the *Sultan*, and on the 8th of November, in that year, Mahomet IV. was deposed, in the forty-sixth year of his age, and thirty-eighth of his reign.

It had been the good fortune of this prince to have able *grand viziers* during a considerable part of his reign; but he chose his ministers

from female influence or personal favouritism, not from discernment of merit, as was proved when he entrusted power to Kara Mustapha, who did more to ruin the Ottoman Empire than any other individual that is mentioned in its history. Mahomet IV. reigned, without ruling. His mind was entirely absorbed by his infatuation for the chase; and the common people believed that he was under a curse, laid on him by his father, Sultan Ibrahim, who had been put to death when Mahomet was placed on the throne, and who was said to have prayed in his last moments that his son might lead the wandering life of a beast of prey.

Though not personally cruel, Mahomet IV. as soon as heirs were born to him, sought anxiously to secure himself on the throne by the customary murder of his brothers. They were saved from him by the exertions of the Sultana Validé and his ministers; but he often resumed the unnatural design. His mother, the Sultana Validé Tarkhan, was determined at even the risk of her own life to shelter her two younger sons from being slaughtered for the further security of the elder; and she took at last the precaution of placing the two young princes in an inner room of the palace, which could only be reached by passing through her own apartments. Even there one night the *Sultan* himself entered with a dagger in his hand, and was gliding through to the chamber where his brothers lay.

Two pages watched near the Sultana Validé; they dared not speak in the presence of the imperial man-slayer, but one of them touched her and awakened her. The mother sprang from sleep, and, clinging round the *Sultan*, implored him to strike her dead before he raised his hand to shed his brothers' blood. Mahomet, accustomed to yield to the superior spirit of the Validé, renounced for the time his scheme of fratricide, and retired to his apartment; but on the morrow he put to death the two slaves who had hindered him from effecting the murderous project which he wished to have accomplished, but which he wanted nerve to renew.

Timidly vindictive, and selfishly rather than constitutionally cruel, Mahomet continued to long for the death of his brothers, though he hesitated to strike. And when he was at last deposed to make room for his brother Solyman on the throne, he may have regretted that his infirmity of purpose had spared the fated rival, whom an adherence to me old fratricidal canon of the House of Othman would have removed for ever from his path.

In the reign of Mahomet IV. another innovation on the ancient stem institutions of the empire was completed, which also was probably caused as much by weakness as by humanity. It was in 1675, in the last year of the *vizierate* of Ahmed Kiuprili, that the final levy of 3000 boys for the recruiting of the Turkish Army was made on the Christian population of the Ottoman Empire in Europe. The old system of filling the ranks of the *Janissaries* exclusively with compulsory conscripts and converts from among the children of the Rayas, had been less rigidly enforced since the time of Amurath IV.

******

> There is some difficulty in reconciling the various dates assigned to the discontinuance of the recruiting the *Janissaries* by enrolments of Christian children. The change was most probably gradual. See Von Hammer, vol. i. & vol. iii..

******

Admission into the corps of *Janissaries* now conferred many civil as well as military advantages; so that it was eagerly sought by men who were of Turkish origin, and born to the Mahometan faith. The first measure of relaxation of the old rule was to treat those, who were the children of *janissaries*, as eligible candidates for enrolment Other Mussulman volunteers were soon received; and the levies of the tribute of children from the Christians grew less frequent and less severe; though they were still occasionally resorted to in order to supply the thousands of pages, who were required to people the vast chambers of the *serail*, and who were in case of emergency drafted into the army of the state. But ever since the year 1675, the *Rayas* of the empire have been entirely free from the terrible tax of flesh and blood, by which the Ottoman military force was sustained during its early centuries of conquest With this change in the constitution of the corps of *Janissaries*, the numbers of that force were greatly increased: large bodies of them were now settled with their families in the chief cities of the empire, where they engaged in different trades and occupations.

Though still able to contend at sea with such an enemy as Venice, the Sublime Porte had seen a still greater decline take place in its naval power than in its military, compared with the state of its fleets and armies in the days of the great Solyman. This was principally caused by the progress of carelessness and corruption in the navy-boards and arsenals at Constantinople; but much of it was due to the *Sultan's* losing that firm hold on the resources of the Mahometan powers of North Africa, which his great ancestor possessed, when Barbarossa and Dragut executed his bidding with the fleets of Tripoli, Tunis, and Algiers.

The Barbaresque Regencies had in the middle of the seventeenth century become practically independent states. They sometimes sent naval succour to the Porte in its wars; but this was done rather in a spirit of voluntary goodwill and recognition of community of creed and origin, similar to that which formerly made Carthage give occasional aid to Tyre, than out of the obedient subordination of provincial governments to central authority. The strength and audacity of these piratical states, especially of Algiers, had so increased, that not only did their squadrons ravage the Christian coasts of the Mediterranean, but their cruisers carried on their depredations beyond the Straits of Gibraltar, both northward and southward in the Atlantic.

They pillaged the island of Madeira; they infested the western parts of the English Channel and the Irish Sea for many years; and the Algerine rovers more than once landed in Ireland, and sacked towns and villages, and carried off captives into slavery. They even ventured as far as Iceland and Scandinavia, as if in retaliation for the exploits of the old Norse Sea-Kings in the Mediterranean seven centuries before. Algiers had a marine force comprising, besides light galleys, more than forty well-built and well-equipped ships, each manned by from 300 to 400 *corsairs*, and mounting from forty to fifty guns.

The number of Christians who toiled in slavery in the dockyards and arsenals at Algiers or at the oar in her fleets, fluctuated from between 10,000 to 20,000. Tunis and Tripoli had their fleets and their slaves, though on a smaller scale. Our Admiral Blake tamed the savage pride of these barbarians in 1655. He awed the Dey of Algiers into the surrender of all his English prisoners; and when the Dey of Tunis refused to do the same, Blake burnt the pirate fleet under the guns of the town, destroyed the forts, and compelled obedience to his demands. The Dutch admiral De Ruyter, and the French admiral De Beaufort also at different times punished the insolence of the Barbary *corsairs*; but their outrages and cruelties were never entirely quelled till Lord Exmouth's bombardment of Algiers in the present century.

In 1663 England concluded a treaty with Algiers and the Porte, by which she was to be at liberty to chastise the Algerines when they broke their engagements, without its being considered a breach of amity between England and Turkey. The rulers of the Barbaresque States styled themselves *Dahis* or *Deys*. According to some authorities, the Algerine chiefs termed themselves *Deys* as delegates of the *Sultan*. According to others, the title came from the old Asiatic word *Dahi*, which signified a superior, even at the time of the ancient republic of

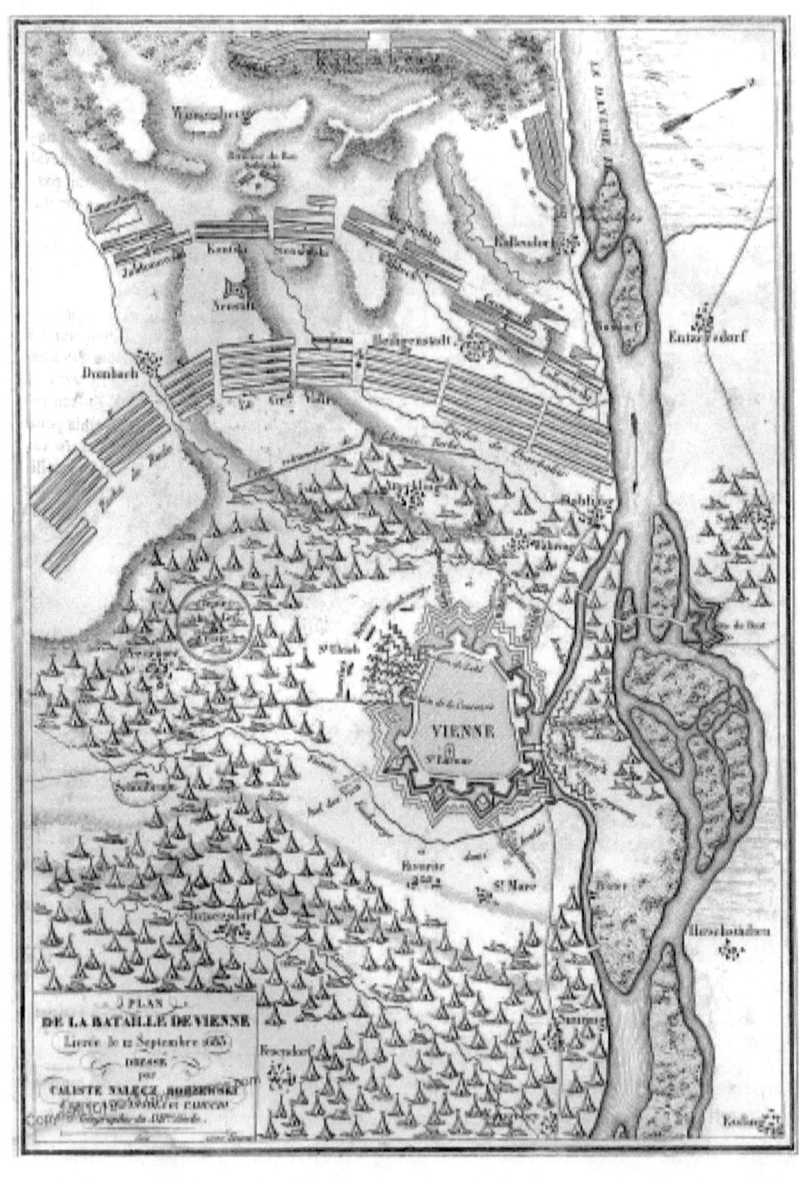

Mecca, and afterwards among the Ishmaelites. They were elected by the military body, consisting of the descendants of the *Janissaries* and others of Turkish race.

They used to apply to the *Sultan* for his firman appointing them *pachas*, and confirming their election; but this soon became a mere formality. The contests between the Greeks and the Christians of the Latin Church in Jerusalem raged furiously during Mahomet IV's reign. But the Ottomans of that age watched with far stronger interest the agitation caused among the Jewish nation by the celebrated *Sabbathai Levi*, who in 1666 came forward at Jerusalem, and asserted that he was the Messiah. Under that title he sent circular letters to all the Jewish synagogues of the Ottoman Empire; and such was his dexterous audacity in imposition, so eagerly were the legends respecting his miraculous powers received, that thousands of his countrymen flocked together at his bidding, not only from Constantinople, Smyrna, and other Turkish cities, but from Germany, Leghorn, Venice, and Amsterdam.

Some of the *rabbis* opposed him; and the most violent tumults were raised at Jerusalem, Cairo, Smyrna, and other cities of the East, where Sabbathai proclaimed his pretended mission. The Ottomans observed his progress with religious anxiety; not from any belief in his alleged character, but on the contrary, from the fear that he was the *Dedjal* or Antichrist, who, according to the Mahometan creed, is to appear among mankind in the last days of the world. They believe also that the speedy advent of the Day of Judgment is to be announced by the reappearance on earth of the prophet Mehdi. And, as at the same time at which Sabbathai came forward in Palestine, another religious impostor arose in Kurdistan, who called himself the prophet Mehdi, and excited thousands of Kurds to follow him, the alarm of many orthodox Moslems at these combined signs of the end of the world was extreme.

The Vizier Ahmed Kiuprili, in order to check the troubles caused by Sabbathai, seized and imprisoned him: but his fanatic followers only saw in this the certain prelude to their Messiah's triumph. They said that according to an ancient prophecy Messiah was to disappear for nine months, and was then to return mounted on a lioness, which he was to guide with a bridle made of seven-headed serpents; and then he was to be lord of the world. But one of Sabbathai's countrymen, who was jealous of his influence, denounced him before the *Sultan's* ministers as endeavouring to raise a revolt among the people.

Sabbathai was brought before the *Sultan* for examination; and Mahomet then made him the characteristic offer of an opportunity of proving by a miracle his right to be acknowledged the Messiah.

One of the *Sultan's* best archers was called forward, and Sabbathai was invited to stand steady as a mark for the arrows, which of course could do no harm to a personage gifted with miraculous powers; only the *Sultan* wished to see them bound back from off his body. At these words, and the sight of the bended bow, Sabbathai's courage failed him. He fell prostrate, and owned that he was nothing but a poor *rabbi*, and no whit different from other men. The *Sultan* then offered to allow him to embrace the Mahometan faith, and so make some amends for the scandal which he had caused, and for the crime of high treason which he had committed by assuming the title of Messiah of Palestine, which was one of the *Sanjaks* of the Sublime Porte.

Sabbathai eagerly accepted the proposal. He became a Moslem; and instead of being worshipped as Messiah or dreaded as Antichrist, he filled for ten years the respectable but prosaic station of a doorkeeper in the *Sultan's* palace. He, however, still made himself conspicuous by his religious zeal; but that zeal was now directed to winning converts from Judaism to Mahometanism, in which he was singularly successful. He was ultimately banished to the Morea, where he died.

******

According to the graphic sketch of the career of Sabbathai by the late Dean of St. Paul's, some of the Jews continued to believe in him notwithstanding his apostasy and death, and "Sabbathaism still exists as a sect of Judaism."—Milman's *History of the Jews*, vol.iii.

******

The Kurdish spiritual pretender, the self-styled *mehdi*, was captured by the Governor of Moussul and sent before the *Sultan*, a few months after Sabbathai had owned his imposture in the royal presence. The young Kurd abandoned the character of Precursor of the Last Judgment, as soon as he was led before his *sovereign*. He answered his interrogators with sense and spirit; and his life also was spared. The Jewish Antichrist was serving the *Sultan* as a doorkeeper, and the Kurdish *mehdi* was made his fellow-servant, in the capacity of one of the pages of the treasure-chamber of the palace.

Although his immoderate fondness for hunting made Mahomet IV. habitually neglect the duties of government, he was never indifferent to literary pursuits; and he showed an hereditary fondness for the society of learned men. His patronage of the chase and his patronage of letters were sometimes strangely blended. He was liberal in his encouragement of historical writers, especially of such as professed to record the current history of his own reign. He loved to see them at his court; he corrected their works with his own pen; but he expected that each royal hunting should be chronicled by them with sportsmanlike minuteness, and that the death of each wild beast, which was slain by the *Sultan's* hand, should be portrayed with poetic fervour. A despotic patron is dangerous to the life of the author, as well as to the vitality of his works.

The Turkish historian Abdi was one whom. Sultan Mahomet IV. delighted to honour. The *Sultan* kept him always near his person, and charged him with the special duty of writing the annals of his reign. One evening Mahomet asked of him, "What hast thou written to-day?"

Abdi incautiously answered that nothing sufficiently remarkable to write about had happened that day. The *Sultan* darted a hunting-spear at the unobservant companion of royalty, wounded him sharply, and exclaimed, "*Now* thou hast something to write about." (Von Hammer, vol. iii., cites this from Abdi's own book).

CHAPTER 20

Negotiations for Peace

Solyman II. when raised to the throne of the Ottoman Empire in 1687, had lived for forty-five years in compulsory seclusion, and in almost daily peril of death. Yet, as sovereign, he showed more capacity and courage than the brother whom he succeeded; and, perhaps, if he had been made *Sultan* at an earlier period, Turkey might have escaped that shipwreck of her state, which came on her after the death of her great minister Ahmed Kiuprili, through the weakness of Sultan Mahomet IV. and the misconduct of his favourite Vizier Kara Mustapha, the originator of the fatal march upon Vienna. Solyman despised the idle sports and debasing sensuality of his predecessors, and earnestly devoted himself to the task of re-organising the military power of his empire, and of stemming, if possible, the progress of defeat and disaster.

But he was unable to control the excesses of the mutinous *Janissaries*, who, throughout the winter which followed Solyman's accession, filled Constantinople with riot and slaughter, and compelled the appointment and displacement of ministers according to their lawless will. At length this savage soldiery resolved to pillage the palaces of the *grand vizier* and the other chief dignitaries. The *vizier*, Siavoush Pacha, defended his house bravely against the brigands, who were joined by the worst rabble of the capital, Jewish and Christian, as well as Mahometan.

On the second day of the insurrection they forced the gate of the house, and rushed in, slaying and spoiling all that they met with Siavoush Pacha, with a few of his surviving servants round him, made a last attempt to defend the entrance to the *harem*, that sanctuary of Moslems, which the rebels now assailed, regardless alike of every restraint of law, of creed, of national and of private honour. More than a hundred of the wretches were slain before the resistance of the brave man of the house was overcome, and Siavoush fell dead on the threshold of his *harem*, fighting bravely to the last gasp.

The worst outrages and abominations were now practised by the rebels; and the sister of the slain *vizier*, and his wife (the daughter of Mohammed Kiuprili), were cruelly mutilated and dragged naked through the streets of Constantinople. The horror and indignation which these atrocities inspired, and the instinct of self-preservation, roused the mass of the inhabitants to resist the brigands, who were proceeding to the sack of other mansions, and to the plunder of the shops and bazaars. The chief Preacher of the Mosque of the Great Solyman, and other members of the *Ulema*, exerted themselves with energy and success to animate the well-affected citizens, and to raise a feeling of shame among the ranks of the *Janissaries*; many of whom had been led away by temporary excitement and the evil example of the ruffians, who had joined them from out of the very dregs of the populace.

The Sacred Standard of the Prophet was displayed over the centre gate of the *Sultan's* palace, and the true believers hastened to rally round the holy symbol of loyalty to their Prophet's Vicar on earth. The chief pillagers and assassins in the late riot were seized and executed. The *mufti* and three other principal *Ulema*, who had shown a disposition to obey the mutinous *Janissaries*, were deposed; and men of more integrity and spirit were appointed in their places. Some degree of order was thus restored to the capital; but the spirit of insubordination and violence was ever ready to break out; and the provinces were convulsed with revolt and tumult. It was not until the end of June, 1688, that the *Sultan* was able to complete the equipment of an army, which then marched towards the Hungarian frontier.

The Austrians and their allies had profited vigorously by the disorders of the Turkish state, and had continued to deal blow after blow with fatal effect. Three generals of the highest military renown, Charles of Lorraine, Louis of Baden, and Prince Eugene, now directed the Imperialist armies against the discouraged and discordant Ottomans. The important city of Erlau in Hungary surrendered on the 14th of December, 1687, and came again into the dominion of its ancient rulers, after having been for a century under Mahometan sway. Gradiska, on the Bosnian frontier, was captured by Prince Louis of Baden. Stuhweissenberg was invested; and, as the Turks had abandoned Illock and Peterwaradin, the route to Belgrade lay open to the Austrian armies.

A Turkish general named Yegen Osman was ordered to protect

Belgrade; but he was cowardly or treacherous; and, as the Imperialists advanced, he retreated from Belgrade, after setting fire to the city. The Austrian troops, following close upon the retiring Turks, extinguished the flames, and laid siege to the citadel, which surrendered after a bombardment of twenty-one days, on the 20th of August, 1688. Stuhweissenberg was stormed on the 6th of September; and Yegen Osman fired Semendra, and abandoned it to the advancing Christians. Prince Louis destroyed a Turkish Army in Bosnia; and city after city yielded to the various Austrian generals who commanded in that province and in Transylvania, and to the Venetian leaders in Dalmatia.

The campaign of the next year in these regions was almost equally disastrous to Turkey. The *Sultan* announced his intention of leading the Ottoman armies in person; and proceeded as far as the city of Sofia. Part of the Turkish forces were posted in advance at the city of Nissa, and were attacked there and utterly defeated by the Imperialists under Prince Louis of Baden. Nissa, evacuated by the Turks, was occupied by the conquerors. On the tidings of this defeat reaching the Turkish headquarters at Sofia, the *Sultan*, in alarm, retreated within the mountain range of the Balkan to the city of Philippopolis. Florentin, Fethislam, and Widdin, next fell into the power of the Imperialists; and before the close of the year 1689, Great Waradein and Temeswar were all that the Ottomans retained of their late extensive provinces north of the Danube; while even to the south of that river the best portions of Bosnia and Servia were occupied by the victorious Austrians.

In the southern parts of European Turkey, the fortune of the war was equally unfavourable to Sultan Solyman. Morosini, one of the greatest generals that the Republic of St. Mark ever produced, completed the conquest of the Morea, which he divided into four Venetian provinces. It was only against the Poles and the Russians that the Turks and their Tartar allies obtained any advantages. A large Tartar force from the Crimea, led by Azmet Ghirai, overran part of Poland in 1688; reinforced the Tartar garrison in Kaminiec, and defeated the Poles on the Sireth.

The Russian general Galitzin attempted to invade the Crimea. He obtained some advantages over part of the Tartar forces, but when be advanced towards the Isthmus of Perekop, in the autumn of 1688, he found that the retreating Tartars had set fire to the dry grass of the steppes, and reduced the country to a desert, from which he was obliged to retire. And, in 1689, when the Russians again advanced to the Isthmus, they were completely defeated by the Ottoman troops, that had taken post there to guard the Crimea. But these gleams of success could not dissipate the terror which the disasters in Hungary and Greece had spread among the Turkish nation.

Only seven years had passed away since weir magnificent host, under the fatal guidance of Kara Mustapha, had marched forth across the then far-extended north-western frontier, with the proud boast that it would sack Vienna and blot out Austria from among the kingdoms of the earth. Now, the Austrians, and their confederates the lately despised Venetians, the conquered of Candia, held victorious possession of half the European Empire of the House of Othman. For the first time since the days of Hunyades, the Balkan was menaced by Christian invaders; and at sea the Turkish flag, the flag of Khaireddin, Pialé, and Kilidj Ali, was now swept from the Mediterranean.

Seldom had there been a war, in which the effect that can be produced on the destinies of nations by the appearance or the absence of individual great men, was more signally proved. On the Christian side, Sobieski, Eugene, Louis of Baden, the Prince of Lorraine, and Morosini had commanded fortune; while among the Turks, no single man of mark had either headed armies, or directed councils. Yet the Ottoman nation was not exhausted of brave and able spirits: and at length adversity cleared the path of dignity for merit.

In the November of 1689, the *Sultan* convened an extraordinary Divan at Adrianople, and besought his councillors to advise him as to what hands he should entrust with the management of the state. In the hour of extreme peril the jealous spirit of intrigue and self-advancement was silent; and all around Solyman II. advised him to send for Kiuprili-Zadé-Mustapha, brother of the great Ahmed Kiuprili, and to give the seals of office to him as Grand Vizier of the Empire.

Kiuprili-Zadé-Mustapha, at the time when he assumed this high dignity, was fifty-two years of age. He had been trained in statesmanship during the *vizierates* of his father and brother, Mohammed and Ahmed Kiuprili: and it was expected and hoped, on the death of Ahmed in 1676, that Sultan Mahomet IV. would place the seals in the hands of Kiuprili-Zadé. Unhappily for the Ottoman nation, that *Sultan's* partiality for his own son-in-law prevailed; nor was it until after thirteen years of misgovernment and calamity had nearly destroyed the empire, that the third Kiuprili succeeded his father and brother, as director of the councils, and leader of the armies of Turkey.

His authority was greatly increased by the deserved reputation which he enjoyed of being a strict observer of the Mahometan law, and an uncompromising enemy to profligacy and corruption. After having paid homage to the *Sultan* on his appointment, he summoned to the *Divan* all the great dignitaries of the empire, and addressed them on the state of the country. He reminded them in severe terms of their duties as Moslems, of their sins; and he told them that they were now undergoing the deserved chastisement of God. He described to them the extreme peril in which the empire was placed.

"If we go on thus," said he, "another campaign will see the enemy encamped beneath the walls of Constantinople."

He then pointed out to them how they ought to act as true believers; and bade them take heart, and be courageous in the defence of their country, however hardly they might find themselves pressed. Kiuprili abolished some imposts introduced by his predecessor, which produced little to the state, while they were peculiarly vexatious to the subject; but he sought to fill the exhausted treasury by exacting heavy contributions from all the late officials who had enriched themselves at the public expense. All the superfluous gold and silver vessels of the palace were sent to the mint to be coined into money for the military chest. And Kiuprili set the example to the other chief men of the state of aiding the public cause by similar contributions.

He gave up the whole of his plate; and the *grand vizier*'s table was served thenceforth with vessels of copper. Funds for the immediate prosecution of the war were thus obtained; and the belief of the Turks in the ability and in the holiness of the new *vizier* brought recruits rapidly to the army, which was collected near the capital. Kiuprili called out all the veterans who had been discharged and pensioned, and he distributed them among the new levies. He placed governors, on whom he could rely, in the most important *pachalics*. He sought also fit men and measures for the revival of the Turkish marine. Mizirli-Zadé-Ibrahim, who had distinguished himself in the defence of Negropont against the Venetians, was raised to the chief naval command in the Mediterranean; and another bold and skilful officer, Mezzomorto, was commissioned to form and lead a flotilla on the Danube.

But the highest merit of Kiuprili-Zadé-Mustapha is, that he had the wisdom to recognise the necessity of the Sublime Porte strengthening itself by winning the loyal affections of its Christian subjects. Although he was so earnest a believer in Islam, and so exemplary in his obedience to its precepts, that he was venerated by his contemporaries as a saint, he did not suffer bigotry to blind him to the fact, that cruelty to the *Rayas* must hasten the downfall of the Ottoman Empire. He saw that the Christian invaders of Turkey found everywhere sympathy and recruits among the populations of the land.

The Christian Albanians were enrolling themselves under the banner of Venice; the Servians were rising to aid the Emperor of Austria; and in Greece the victorious progress of Morosini had been aided by the readiness with which the village municipalities and the mountain tribes placed themselves under his authority, and by the strenuous support which bands of Christian volunteers gave him, in beleaguering the fortresses held by the Turks. (Von Hammer, vol. iii., Emerson Tennant's *Greece*, vol. i.).

Kiuprili-Zadé was not content with judging correctly: he took prompt practical measures to check the evils which he was swift to discern. One of the first acts of his *vizierate* was to despatch the most explicit and imperative orders to all the *pachas*, that no Turkish officer should exercise or permit any kind of oppression towards the *Rayas*: and that no payment should be required of them except the Capitation Tax. For the purposes of this tax, Kiuprili divided the *Rayas* into three classes, according to their incomes. The first or wealthiest paid four *ducats*, the middle class two *ducats*, and the lowest one *ducat* a head.

This institution was called the Nizami Djidid, the New Order. Kiuprili also took the bold and sagacious step of making a Mainote Greek Bey of Maina. This was Liberius Geratschari, who had passed seven years as a Turkish galley-slave. He was now set at liberty, and sent to the Morea to support the Turkish interest among his countrymen against that of the Venetians, who had begun to alienate the Greek Rayas from their side by impolitic government. Von Hammer remarks that Kiuprili-Zadé showed himself in this measure to be superior as a politician, both to his brother Ahmed, who had sought, in the former Venetian war, to curb the rising disaffection in the Morea by fortified posts and garrisons; and also to the subsequent *grand viziers*, who, when it was proposed to make the Morea a principality like Moldavia and Wallachia, and govern it by native Christians, rejected the scheme as derogatory to the dignity of the Sublime Porte. (Von Hammer, vol. iii.)

Kiuprili had even the enlightened spirit to despise the old *dogmas* of Turkish *muftis* and judges, according to which the *Rayas* were followed only such churches as they already possessed, but were strictly forbidden to enlarge them, or to build new places of worship. Kiuprili sanctioned the foundation of a Greek Church wherever it was desired; and thereby became the founder of thriving villages, which sprang up in districts where there had been previously only scanty bands of suffering and disaffected outcasts. Once, in passing through part of Servia, Kiuprili halted for the night in a wretched hamlet of *Rayas*, who had neither edifice nor minister of religion. Kiuprili ordered that a church should be built there, and that a Christian priest should be sent for to serve it.

In return for this boon, which filled the poor peasants with rapturous gratitude, Kiuprili required of them, that each head of a family should bring him a fowl, whenever he passed through the village. Fifty-three fowls were immediately brought to him; that being the number of families. In the next (and, unhappily for the *Rayas*, the last) year of his *vizierate*, Kiuprili passed through the same place. He received a hundred and twenty-five fowls from the heads of the happy population, which flocked together with their Greek priest at their head to welcome the benevolent *vizier*.

"Look," said Kiuprili to the staff of Turkish officers round him, "Look at the fruits of toleration. I have increased the *Sultan's* power; and I have brought blessings on his government from those who were wont to curse it." (Ubicini, vol. ii.)

The Greeks of the empire used to say that Kiuprili founded more churches than Justinian. Had subsequent Turkish ministers imitated Kiuprili-Zadé Mustafa in their policy towards the Christian population of Turkey, the Ottoman Empire would now command far ampler resources, than it can derive from the unaided valour and loyalty of its Moslem inhabitants; and the most serious sources of its internal weakness would long ago have been removed.

Besides the glory of having, while sincerely religious, practised religious toleration, the third Kiuprili deserves honourable mention for his recognition of the great principle of political economy, that (with very few and very peculiar exceptions) trade between man and man ought to be free from all state interference. When pressed by one of his advisers to frame regulations for purchases and sales, Kiuprili-Zadé replied:

> The *Koran* prescribes nothing on the subject. Purchase and sale ought to be left to the free will of the contracting parties.—Von Hammer, vol. iii.

Kiuprili-Zadé Mustapha is termed by Ottoman historians Kiuprili Fazyl, which means "Kiuprili the Virtuous." They say of him, as his highest praise, that he never committed a crime, and that he never used an unnecessary word. They record as an instance of his eminence in taciturnity, that once, while *grand vizier*, he received a ceremonial visit from three of the *Ulema*, who had formerly held the offices of army judges. Kiuprili let them depart without having addressed a syllable to them. His old Master of Requests, Nigahi Effendi, said to him, "My gracious lord, you should have spoken something to them."

"I am not a hypocrite," answered Kiuprili. He was austerely simple in all his habits. In his campaigns he generally marched on foot, like the rank and file of the infantry. He disliked military music. He seldom moved his quarters before sunset. Amid the pomp and splendour of the Turkish court and camp the *grand vizier* was distinguishable by the plainness of his dress. He was an indefatigable student, and read diligently in his tent, when on active service, as well as in his palace when at Constantinople.

Such are some of the praises by which his country's historians signalise Kiuprili-Zadé Mustapha. The renown for statesmanship acquired by him, and which Christian writers have concurred with Mahometan in bestowing, is the more remarkable, by reason of the shortness of the period permitted to him for the display of his administrative genius. He was killed in battle within two years from the time when the seals of office were placed in his hands. His contemporaries judged of him, as of his brother Ahmed, that he shone more in the council than in the field. But the military career of Kiuprili-Zadé was highly honourable to his abilities as well as to his courage; and, though ultimately defeated, he gained a respite of infinite importance for the Ottoman Empire, by the successes which he at first obtained.

When he was made *grand vizier*, one of the invading armies of the enemy had advanced as far as Ouskoup, in northern Macedonia, where it was actively aided by the Christian Albanians and their Patriarch. A chieftain of those regions, named Karpos, had accepted a diploma of investiture from the Austrian emperor, and, assuming the old title of *Kral*, had fortified himself in Egri-Palanka. It was indispensable to relieve Turkey at once from the foes, who thus struck at the very heart of her power in Europe. Kiuprili held a council of war at Adrianople, at which Selim Ghirai, the Khan of the Crimea, and Tekeli, the Hungarian refugee, were present Khodja Khalid Pacha, the *Seraskier* of the Morea, a native of Ouskoup, was sent with all the regular Turkish troops that could be collected, against that place.

The Crimean *khan*, at the head of a large Tartar force, co-operated with him. They gained two victories over the combined bodies of

Germans, Hungarians, and Albanians, who had assumed the old mediaeval badge of the cross. The chieftain Karpos was seized by the Tartars and executed on the bridge of Ouskoup. Nearly all the important posts which the invaders and their insurgent confederates had occupied in those districts, were recovered by the *Sultan's* troops, and the pressure on this vital part of the empire was almost entirely removed. Encouraged by these successes, Kiuprili pushed forward with the greatest vigour his armaments for the next campaign. Louis XIV., who was at war with the German Empire, sent in the winter of 1680 a new ambassador, the Marquis de Chateunef, to Constantinople, to encourage the Turks to persevere in hostilities against Austria.

Chateunef was also ordered to negotiate, if possible, a peace between Turkey and Poland, to prevent the recognition of William of Orange as King of England by the Sublime Porte, and to regain for the Catholics in Palestine the custody of the Holy Sepulchre, which the Greek Patriarch had lately won from them. Chateunef obtained the last object, and he found in the new *vizier* a zealous ally against Austria. But the Turks refused to suspend hostilities with Poland; and with regard to the Prince of Orange and the English crown, Kiuprili answered that he should recognise the king whom the English people had proclaimed. He added that it would ill become the Turks, who had so often dethroned their own sovereigns, to dispute the rights of other nations to change their masters.

In August, 1690, Kiuprili-Zadé Mustapha took in person the command of the Ottoman armies that advanced from Bulgaria and Upper Albania through Servia, against the Imperialists. After a murderous fight of two days, Kiuprili drove the Austrian general, Schenkendorf, from his lines at Dragoman, between the cities of Sofia and Nissa. The *vizier* then formed the siege of Nissa, which capitulated in three weeks. The Austrian generals were prevented from concentrating their forces for its relief, by a well-planned irruption into Transylvania, by the Hungarian refugee Tekeli at the head of a Turkish Army.

Tekeli defeated the Imperialists in that province, and proclaimed the *Sultan* as sovereign lord, and himself as Prince of Transylvania. After the capture of Nissa, the Grand Vizier marched upon Semendra, which was stormed after resisting desperately for four days. Widdin was also regained; and Kiuprili then undertook the recovery of Belgrade. On the twelfth day of the siege a shell from the Turkish batteries pierced the roof of the principal powder magazine of the city; and a destructive explosion ensued, which gave the Turks an easy conquest.

Having placed a strong garrison in this important city, and completed the expulsion of the Austrians from Servia, Kiuprili returned to Constantinople. He was received there with deserved honours after his short, but brilliant campaign, in which he had compelled the invading Giaours to recede from the banks of the Morava and the Nissa to those of the Danube and the Saave.

On the 10th of May, 1691, Kiuprili the Virtuous received a second time the Sacred Standard from the hands of his sovereign, Sultan Solyman, who died before the campaign was opened. Solyman II. was succeeded by his brother Achmet II., who was girt with the sabre of Othman on the 13th July, 1691. The new *Sultan* confirmed Kiuprili in his dignity; and the *vizier* proceeded to concentrate his forces at Belgrade, and to throw a bridge over the Saave. He then marched up the right bank of the Danube to encounter the Imperialists, who, under the command of Louis of Baden, descended from Peterwaradin. The two hosts approached each other on the 19th of August, near Salankemen.

At the same time, the Christian and Mussulman flotillas, which accompanied their respective armies along the Danube, encountered on the river. The Turkish flotilla was victorious; but, on the land, the day proved a disastrous one for the House of Kiuprili and for the House of Othman. Contrary to the advice of the oldest *pachas* in the army, the *vizier* refused to await behind the lines the attack of the Imperialists. The veteran warrior Khodja Khalid censured this impetuosity.

Kiuprili said to him, "I invited thee to follow me that thou mightest figure as a man, and not as a phantom."

Khalid, touching the thin hairs of his grey beard, replied, "I have but a few days to live. It matters little whether I die today, or tomorrow; but I would fain not have been present at a scene in which the empire can meet with nought but calamity and shame."

"Advance the cannon!" cried Kiuprili; and himself formed the *Spahis* for the fight.

Kemankesh Pacha began the battle by rushing, with 6000 Kurdish and Turcoman irregular cavalry, upon the Christian lines.

"Courage, my heroes," cried Kemankesh, "the *Houris* are waiting for you!"

They galloped forward with shouts of "*Allah!*" but were received by the Christians with a steady fire, which drove them back in discomfited and diminished masses. Again they charged impetuously; again they broke, fell or fled. The Austrians now pressed forward to where the Sacred Standard was reared in the Mahometan ranks. Ismael, the Pacha of Caramania, dashed against them with the troops of Asia. His squadrons were entangled in an abattis of felled trees, by which the Prince of Baden had protected his right wing. The Asiatics wavered and were repulsed. Kiuprili saw his best men shot down round him by the superior musketry of the Imperialists.

"What is to be done?" he cried to the officers of his guards.

They answered, "Let us close, and fight sword in hand."

Kiuprili, arrayed in a black vest, invoked the name of God, and threw himself, with drawn sabre, against the enemy. His guards rushed onward with him. An obstinate and sanguinary struggle followed, which was decided against Turkey by the bullet that struck Kiuprili, while cleaving his way desperately through the Austrian ranks. His guards lost courage when they saw him fall; and the fatal tidings that their great *vizier* was slain, soon spread disorder and panic throughout the Ottoman Army. The Prince of Baden's triumph was complete; and the Turkish camp with 150 cannon fell into the conqueror's power. But the victory was dearly purchased, and the Austrian loss in men and officers was almost equal to that of the Turks.

The Battle of Salankeman drove the Ottomans again from Hungary; Tekeli was defeated by the Imperialists and expelled from Transylvania; and throughout the four years of the disastrous reign of Achmet II. the current of defeat was unabated. Besides the curse of the victorious sword of the foreigners, and the usual miseries of domestic insurrection, the fearful visitations of pestilence and famine came upon the devoted empire. A great earthquake threw down part of Smyrna; and a still more destructive conflagration ravaged Constantinople in September, 1693. Heartbroken at the sufferings and shame of the State, and worn by disease, Achmet II. expired on the 6th February, 1695.

Mustapha II., the son of the deposed Mahomet IV., now came to the throne, and showed himself worthy of having reigned in happier times. On the third day after his accession, he issued a *hatti-scherif,* in which he threw the blame of the recent misfortunes upon the *Sultans,* and announced his intention of restoring the ancient usages, and of heading his armies in person. As the German historian observes, (Von Hammer, vol. iii.), this document is too remarkable not to deserve citation. Sultan Mustapha II. thus announced his royal will.

> God, the supreme distributor of all good, has granted unto us, miserable sinner, the *Caliphate* of the entire world. Under monarchs, who are the slaves of pleasure, or who resign themselves

to indolent slumber, never do the servants of God enjoy peace or repose. Henceforth, voluptuousness, idle pastime, and sloth are banished from this court. While the *Padischas*, who have ruled since the death of our sublime father Mahomet, have heeded nought but their fondness for pleasure and for ease, the Unbelievers, the unclean beings, have invaded with their armies the four frontiers of Islam They have subdued our provinces. They have pillaged the goods of the people of Mahomet. They have dragged away into slavery the faithful, with their wives and little ones. This is known to all, as it is known to us.

I therefore have resolved, with the help of the Lord, to take a signal revenge upon the Unbelievers, that brood of Hell; and I will myself begin the holy war against them. Our noble ancestor the Sultan Solyman (May his tomb exhale unceasingly the odour of incense!) during the forty-eight years of his reign, not only sent his *viziers* against the unclean Christians, but placed himself at the head of the Champions of the Holy War, and so took upon the *infidels* the vengeance which God commands. I also, I, have resolved to combat them in person. Do thou, my *grand vizier*, and ye others, my *viziers*, my *Ulema*, my lieutenants and *agas* of my armies, do ye all of you assemble round my person, and meditate well on this my imperial *hatti-scherif*.

Take counsel; and inform me if I ought to open hostilities in person against the emperor, or to remain at Adrianople. Of these two measures choose that which will be most profitable to the Faith, to the empire, and to the servants of God. Let your answer be the truth; and let it be submitted to me before the imperial stirrup. I wish you Health.

The deliberation of the *divan* on this summons lasted for three days. Many thought that the presence of the *Sultan* in the camp was undesirable. Others feared that he had only addressed them with a view of learning their thoughts. Finally, they all resolved that the departure of the *Padischah* to assume the command-in-chief of the army, would not only expose the sacred person to too much risk and fatigue, but would involve excessive expense. Consequently, the *divan* represented to the *Sultan* that his Majesty ought not to commit his imperial person to the chances of a campaign, but ought to leave the care of war to the *grand vizier*.

To this address the *Sultan* returned a laconic *hatti-scherif*, "I persist in marching." The most active measures then were taken to hasten the preparations for the campaign; and the gallantry of the young *Sultan* was at first rewarded by important success. He advanced in the summer of 1695, from Belgrade to Temesvar, and recaptured the important fortresses of Karansebes, Lipna, and Lugos. On the 22nd of September, he encountered near Lugos the Austrian Army under General Veterani. Sultan Mustapha gained a complete victory, and Veterani and half his troops were left dead on the field.

During the winter, which followed this victory, Mustapha and his councillors toiled unremittingly to repair the finances of the empire, and to increase the number and improve the discipline of the troops. Heavy taxes were laid on tobacco, on black eunuchs, and other articles of luxury. Many of the chief men of the empire seconded their sovereign's zeal, and raised bodies of troops at their own expense, of which they took the command. Mustapha had formed a corps of 3000 infantry from the royal gardeners, or Bostandjis, of Adrianople and Constantinople. He now divided those into three regiments, which were equipped in peculiar uniform, and trained with especial care.

The *Sultan* opened the campaign of 1696 at the head of a numerous and well-appointed army. He defeated the Austrians under the Duke de Saxe near Temesvar, and raised the siege of that place. Mustapha strengthened the garrisons of the fortresses which the Turks still held in Hungary, and then returned to Adrianople, not unjustly proud of his achievements; though the great Solyman, whom he chose as his model, would probably have pushed his advantages further. The hopes and pride of Turkey now began to revive; but in 1697, Prince Eugene took the command of the Imperialist armies in Hungary; and the Crescent soon went down before him.

Sultan Mustapha collected his army for this fatal campaign at Sofia, and marched thence to Belgrade, where he halted and held repeated councils of war. Some enterprises of minor importance, the sending forward a detachment to reinforce the garrison of Temesvar, and the occupation of several posts along the Danube were successfully attempted; but there was discord among the Ottoman officers, and there was oscillation in the *Sultan's* will as to the main line of operations that ought to be followed. The *Grand Vizier*, Elwas Mohammed, was unpopular with the other *pachas*, who leagued together to oppose his projects, and thwart his tactics. The *vizier* himself was depressed by a dream, which he saddened his equally credulous comrades also by narrating.

He dreamed that the late *grand vizier*, Kiuprili-Zadé Mustapha, the martyr of Salankeman, had entered his tent and given him a cup of sherbet, which the Apparition had first tasted. "God knows," cried the *grand vizier*, when he told his dream, "that this was the cup of martyrdom, which I, too, am destined to drink in this campaign." He wished to keep the army on the right bank of the Danube, and crossing the Saave to march upon Peterwaradin, and attempt the recovery of that important fortress. The other officers proposed to cross the Danube and the Theiss, and to endeavour to surprise Eugene's army, which was camped on the banks of the Bacska.

After much angry discussion this last project was adopted. The army crossed the Danube and the Theiss; but it was found that all hope of surprising Eugene was idle, and the Austrians and Turks both endeavoured to gain the fort of Zitel, which is situate at the junction of the Theiss with the Danube. The Ottomans obtained some advantage over a detachment of Eugene's army, and sacked Zitel. They then reverted to the scheme of besieging Peterwaradin, and marched to Valova; where they began to construct bridges to enable them to pass to the right bank of the Danube and attack Peterwaradin; the old bridges having been occupied or destroyed by the Austrians. Finding that Eugene had secured Peterwaradin against attack, they held another council of war, and resolved to march northwards up the right or eastern bank of the Theiss and attack Szegedin.

The activity of Eugene disconcerted this project also. He threw a strong division into Szegedin; and with the rest of his army followed the Turks, watching for a favourable opportunity of attacking them. This was soon obtained. The Austrian hussars captured one of the *pachas*, named Djafer; who, finding his life threatened, confessed to the Austrians that the *Sultan* had given up his project of attacking Szegedin, and now designed to cross the Theiss near Zenta, with the intention of marching upon upper Hungary and Transylvania. Eugene instantly moved with all possible speed towards Zenta, in the hopes of assailing the Ottoman Army while in the act of passing the river.

It was on the 11th of September, about two in the afternoon, that the *Sultan* saw his great enemy approach. The Turks had formed a temporary bridge across the river; and the *Sultan*, the cavalry, and the greater part of the artillery of his army, had passed over to the left or eastern bank; but the infantry was still on the western side. The *Sultan* and his officers had taken the precaution of forming a strong entrenchment to protect their rear during the passage of the bridge, and seventy guns had been kept in position on the right bank for that purpose.

Undaunted by these preparations, Eugene formed his columns, as they came up, into line for the attack; and although at this critical time a courier arrived from Vienna with peremptory orders to Eugene not to risk a battle, he determined to disobey his emperor's orders, and continued his preparations for a decisive engagement, (Coxe's *History of the House of Austria* vol. ii.). If the Ottomans had anticipated him by a resolute advance against the Austrian centre, before Eugene's troops had all arrived, and before his artillery had been brought into position, it is probable that they would have crushed the Imperialists. But discord and disorder were rife in the *Sultan's* camp. The *grand vizier* summoned the *pachas* and *Spahis*, most of whom had passed over to the eastern bank, back to the menaced side; but he did not move beyond his entrenchments, and the *Sultan* himself did not recross the river to share in and conduct the conflict.

Only two hours of daylight were left when Eugene had completed his dispositions for action. He formed his army into a half-moon, so as to assail the whole semicircle of the Turkish entrenchments, and he posted his cannon where they commanded the bridge. He then made a simultaneous attack on every part of the Turkish lines, which was everywhere successful. The Turks fought without concert or confidence; and a large body of *Janissaries* mutinied, and began to massacre their own officers in the very heat of the action. The Christians gave no quarter; more than 20,000 Turks were slain, including the *grand vizier* and a large number of *pachas*; and more than 10,000 were drowned in endeavouring to pass the river. The battle was lost and won before the close of the day; and in the words of Eugene in his despatch to Vienna:

> The sun seemed to linger on the horizon to gild with his last rays the victorious standards of Austria."

The *Sultan*, from the eastern bank of the Theiss, witnessed the destruction of his host, and fled with the remnants of his cavalry in dismay to Temesvar. Thence he retired to Constantinople, and never appeared again at the head of an army. In the extreme distress to which the defeat at Zenta had once more reduced the Ottoman Empire, resort was again had to the House of Kiuprili, and again that illustrious family supplied a minister who could prop, if he could not restore, the falling state.

Housein Kiuprili had in the time of the *vizierate* of Ahmed Kiuprili, received the name of Amoud-schah-zadé, which means "Son of the Uncle." He was so called because he was the son of Hassan, who was the younger brother of Mohammed Kiuprili, and the uncle of Ahmed Kiuprili. Amoud-schah-zadé Housein Kiuprili had in early life been an idle voluptuary; but the disasters which befell Turkey after the expedition against Vienna roused him to a sense of what he owed to the honour of his House and to his country. He filled many important offices with zeal and ability; and when raised to the *grand vizierate* in 1697, he gave proofs of his possessing in ample degree that genius for finance and for administrative reform, which was the eminent characteristic of his family. Every possible effort was made by him to collect the means of opposing further resistance to the enemies of the empire.

A tax was laid upon coffee: a contribution in the nature of an income tax was required from all the principal officers of the state: and Housein Kiuprili even ventured to appropriate to the urgent necessities of the country a large sum from the revenues of the religious foundations. He succeeded in collecting and equipping an army of 50,000 foot and 48,000 horse for the defence of the European provinces. A Turkish fleet was sent into the Black Sea, and another into the Mediterranean.

******

Von Hammer cites, in a note to his 60th book, an official list, which a Turkish writer gives of the Ottoman forces on land and sea, as augmented by Housein Kiuprili. It specifies the number of troops supplied by each province, and their character.

******

But while the *vizier* thus prepared war, it was with the wish for peace. He knew too well the exhaustion of the empire, and felt the impossibility of preventing further disasters if hostilities were continued. It was not only in the Danubian provinces that the war went hard with Turkey. The Venetians were making further progress in Dalmatia; and in Greece they were advancing beyond the isthmus of Corinth; though Negropont had been bravely and successfully defended against them, and seasonable relief had been obtained for the Ottoman forces that were employed along the coasts and in the islands of the Archipelago, through the gallantry of the Turkish Admiral Mezzomorto, who gained two victories over the Venetian fleets. Poland was an inactive antagonist; but Russia had become a truly formidable enemy.

Peter the Great was now sovereign of that vast empire, and was teaching the lately rude and barbarous Muscovy to know her own gigantic strength, and also to use it like a giant. He had already drawn around him skilful officers and engineers from Western Europe; and he had formed a body of troops on the models of the Imperialist and French armies. But ships, harbours, and maritime power were the dearest objects of his heart; and one of the earliest marks of his ambition (never lost sight of by himself or any of his successors) was to obtain the mastery of the Black Sea. With this view he prosecuted the war against Turkey with a vigour and skill very different from the conduct of Galitzin and other former Russian commanders. Peter resolved first to conquer the strong city of Azoph, which, as has been mentioned, had been fortified by the Turks with peculiar care, and was justly regarded as a position of the greatest importance.

He led an army of 60,000 men (including his new-modelled regiments) against Azoph, in 1695. He also formed a large flotilla of vessels, drawing but little water, which co-operated with his army in the siege. His first attempt was unsuccessful; and he sustained a repulse, which was severe, enough to discourage a spirit of ordinary firmness. The Russians were driven back from Azoph, in 1695, with a loss of 30,000 men. But in the following spring the *Czar* renewed the siege with fresh forces. His flotilla defeated a squadron of light Turkish vessels, that attempted to relieve the city; and he kept in check the Ottoman *Pachas*, who advanced from the Crimea with troops along the coast as far as the village of Akkoumin. Azoph surrendered to the *Czar* on the 28th July, 1696; and he immediately began to improve the fortifications and harbour, and to fit out vessels of war, on a scale, which showed for what important ulterior projects the possession of Azoph had been sought by Russia.

Thus menaced from many quarters, the Ottoman court listened willingly to the English ambassador. Lord Paget, who urged on the Turkish statesmen the necessity of peace, and offered the mediation of England to obtain it. Similar proposals had been, made by the representatives of Holland and England at earlier periods of the war, and negotiations had once been opened at Vienna, but no salutary result had followed. But now both Turkey and her chief antagonist Austria were sincerely desirous of peace. The Emperor Leopold had indeed seen his armies obtain triumphs, which might have filled many monarchs with ambitious visions of ampler conquests, and might have led to a march upon Constantinople, as the fit retribution for the repeated siege of Vienna. But Leopold was of a wiser or a colder spirit. He was anxious for sure and peaceful possession of the valuable provinces that had already been re-conquered from the Turks in the war; and, though Austria had been generally victorious, she had suffered severely in men and in treasure.

Above all, the prospect that the succession to the Spanish throne would soon become vacant, made the German emperor anxious to terminate hostilities in Eastern Europe, and prepare for the great struggle in the West, which was already foreseen as inevitable.

Lord Paget proposed to the Porte that England should intervene to effect a pacification on the footing of the "*Uti Possidetis*;" that is to say, on the principle that each of the contending parties should keep what it possessed at the time of commencing negotiations. Sultan Mustapha could ill brook the cession of such broad and fair territories, as a treaty, framed on this rule, would assign to his adversaries; and he endeavoured to introduce some important modifications. He placed before Lord Paget a counter-project, written in his own hand (an unprecedented act for a Turkish *Sultan*), and which was accompanied by a letter from the *grand vizier* to the King of England.

The mediation of England was requested, in order that a peace might be concluded generally on the foundation of the "*Uti Possidetis*," but with stipulations that the Austrians should abandon Transylvania, that the city of Peterwaradin should be razed, that the Austrians should evacuate all the fortified places on the Turkish side of the River Unna, and with other exceptions of a similar nature. Lord Paget's secretary was sent by him with the *grand vizier's* letter to Vienna; and the Austrian Government was informed of the readiness of England to mediate between the belligerents. In reply to this, a communication was made to the Porte that the Emperor Leopold was willing to treat for peace, but on condition that each party was to keep all that it then possessed, and on condition also that Russia was comprised in the treaty.

Venice and Poland were added; and Holland co-operated with England as a mediating power. The Czar Peter, though not desirous of continuing the war, single-handed, against Turkey, was disinclined for peace, and dissatisfied with the proposed principle for negotiation. He passed through Vienna in 1698; and, while in that capital, he had an interview with the Emperor Leopold on the subject of the treaty with the Ottoman. Peter questioned the Austrian sovereign about the causes of his desire for peace with Turkey. Leopold replied that he had not sought for peace, but that England had, in the first instance, offered her mediation; and that each of the allied Christian sovereigns was to keep the conquests which he had made. But the Russian was anxious, not only to secure Azoph, but to obtain the important city of Kertch in the Crimea; and he insisted that the cession of this place should be made a term of the treaty, and that in the event of Turkey declining to give it up, Russia and Austria should form a fresh league against her.

He was answered by a promise to endeavour to obtain Kertch for him; but he was told that it was not fit to renew an offensive alliance on the eve of assembling a congress for pacification. In another conversation, which Peter had with the Austrian minister, Count Kinsky, he asked what power it was that insisted on a peace.

The Austrian replied, "Our Holy Roman Empire insists on it; Spain insists on it; it is required by England and Holland; and, in a word, by all Christendom."

"Beware!" replied the *Czar*, "how you trust to what the Dutch and the English say. They are looking only to the benefit of their commerce; they care nothing about the interests of their allies."

The Polish sovereign also objected to recognise the "*Uti Possidetis*" principle. He complained that a treaty on this footing would leave the Ottomans in possession of Kaminiec, which was the key to Poland. At length, after many difficulties and delays, the five belligerent, and the two mediating powers sent their plenipotentiaries to the place appointed for that congress, which was the town of Carlowitz, on the right bank of the Danube, a little below Peterwaradin (24th October, 1698).

The German historian, Von Hammer, (vol. iii.), says truly of the Peace of Carlowitz, that it is one of those treaties which ought to be considered with particular care, even as there are certain battles which demand and receive the special attention of the historical student. The treaty of Carlowitz is memorable, not only on account of the magnitude of the territorial change which it ratified; not only because it marks the period when men ceased to dread the Ottoman Empire as an aggressive power; but, also, because it was then that the Porte and Russia took part, for the first time, in a general European Congress; and because, by admitting to that congress the representatives of England and Holland, neither of which states was a party to the war, both the *Sultan* and the *Czar* thus admitted the principle of intervention of the European powers, one with another, for the sake of the general good.

The negotiations at Carlowitz were long; and the representatives of the mediating powers had, more than once, great difficulty in preventing an angry rupture. Besides disputes as to ceremonials and titles, the congress was required to arrange many serious claims and objections, and each of the belligerents, except Austria and Venice, desired some deviations in its own favour from the general principle of "*Uti Possidetis.*" The Russian envoy long and fiercely insisted on the cession of Kertch. The Ottomans wished Austria to give up Transylvania, or to pay an annual sum for retaining it. They also desired Venice to restore many of her conquests beyond the Morea, and that the Russians should evacuate Azoph.

The Poles asked for the restoration of Kaminiec; and the Imperialists, though generally loyal to the fundamental principle of the congress, introduced new matters of dissension, by demanding that the custody of the Holy Sepulchre should be restored to the Franciscans, that the Jesuits should be confirmed in their possessions in the Isle of Chios, and that the Porte should grant certain privileges to the Trinitarians, a society instituted for the purpose of ransoming Christian captives from slavery. The Greek Mavrocordato, who was the principal diplomatist on behalf of the *Sultan* at the congress, replied to these claims of Austria, that the Sublime Porte knew nothing of Trinitarians, of Franciscans, or of Jesuits. It was, however, agreed that certain articles should be drawn up, by which the *Sultan* promised to continue his protection to the Christians according to the ancient capitulations and *hatti-scherifs*.

On another point the Ottomans were characteristically and honourably firm. Austria required that Count Tekeli, the Hungarian chief, who had taken shelter in Turkey, should be given up as a rebel to the emperor. This was refused; and nothing could be exacted, beyond a promise on the *Sultan's* part, that Tekeli and his partisans should be kept at such a distance from the frontier, as not to be able to foment disturbances in any part of the emperor's dominions. Austria, on the other hand, consented that the confiscated dowry of Helen Zriny, Tekeli's wife, should be restored to her, and that she should be allowed to join her husband.

✯✯✯✯✯✯

In a former negotiation in 1689 between the Turkish and Imperialist envoys, under the mediation of the Dutch ambassador at Vienna (which proved abortive), the Austrians had peremptorily insisted on Tekeli being given up to them to be punished for his treasons. The Turkish envoy, Soulfikar, observed that he himself looked on Tekeli as an enemy to the Porte, and the author of the war. He said that Tekeli was no more than the *Sultan's* dog, and that it mattered little to the *Padischah* whether such a creature lived or died, but that he himself had not travelled so far on that embassy to become Tekeli's assassin. The Dutch ambassador observed on this, that the Turks could not make a serious matter about giving up Tekeli, now that they had themselves treated him as a mere dog. Soulfikar replied, "Ay, Tekeli is indeed a dog; a dog that lies down or rises, that barks or is quiet, according to the *Sultan's* bidding. But this dog is the dog of the *Padischah* of the Ottomans; and at a sign from him the dog may be metamorphosed into a terrible lion."

******

At length, after many weeks of arguments, bickerings, threats and intrigues, the terms of pacification were arranged. Austria and Turkey concluded a treaty for twenty-five years; by which the emperor was acknowledged sovereign of Transylvania, all Hungary north of the Marosch and west of the Theiss, and of Sclavonia, except a small part between the Danube and the Saave. With Venice and Poland treaties without limitation of time were effected. Poland recovered Podolia and Kaminiec. Venice retained her conquests in Dalmatia and the Morea; but restored to the Turks those which she had made to the north of the Isthmus of Corinth. Russia refused to consent to anything more than an armistice for two years, which was afterwards enlarged into a peace for thirty years; as the *Czar's* attention was, in the commencement of the eighteenth century, principally directed to schemes of aggrandisement at the expense of Sweden. By this armistice the Russians kept possession of Azoph, and of the districts which they had conquered to the north of the sea of that name.

It was on the 26th of January, 1699, that the pacification of Carlowitz was completed. It left the two feebler Christian powers, Venice and Poland, restored to temporary importance; the one by the acquisition of the Morea, the other by the recovery of Kaminiec. But it was in the altered state of the three greater belligerents, compared with what they had been in 1682, that men recognised the momentous effects of the seventeen years' war, which was terminated at Carlowitz. Russia had now stretched her arms southward, and grasped the coasts of the Maeotis and the Euxine. At the beginning of the war Austria trembled for the fate of her capital, and saw her very national existence seriously menaced: at the end of the conflict the empire of the House of Hapsburg was left not merely in security, but enlarged: not merely enlarged, but permanently strengthened and consolidated: while the House of Othman saw many of its fairest dominions rent away, and was indebted for the preservation of the remainder from conquest by the invading Christians, to the intervention of two other Christian states.

From that time forth all serious dread of the military power of Turkey has ceased in Europe. The Crescent had reached its zenith and henceforth the waning moon of the Ottomans would endure in the east until its final setting at the close of the First World War.

ALSO FROM LEONAUR
AVAILABLE IN SOFTCOVER OR HARDCOVER WITH DUST JACKET

THE FALL OF THE MOGHUL EMPIRE OF HINDUSTAN by H. G. Keene—By the beginning of the nineteenth century, as British and Indian armies under Lake and Wellesley dominated the scene, a little over half a century of conflict brought the Moghul Empire to its knees.

LADY SALE'S AFGHANISTAN by Florentia Sale—An Indomitable Victorian Lady's Account of the Retreat from Kabul During the First Afghan War.

THE CAMPAIGN OF MAGENTA AND SOLFERINO 1859 by Harold Carmichael Wylly—The Decisive Conflict for the Unification of Italy.

FRENCH'S CAVALRY CAMPAIGN by J. G. Maydon—A Special Correspondent's View of British Army Mounted Troops During the Boer War.

CAVALRY AT WATERLOO by Sir Evelyn Wood—British Mounted Troops During the Campaign of 1815.

THE SUBALTERN by George Robert Gleig—The Experiences of an Officer of the 85th Light Infantry During the Peninsular War.

NAPOLEON AT BAY, 1814 by F. Loraine Petre—The Campaigns to the Fall of the First Empire.

NAPOLEON AND THE CAMPAIGN OF 1806 by Colonel Vachée—The Napoleonic Method of Organisation and Command to the Battles of Jena & Auerstädt.

THE COMPLETE ADVENTURES IN THE CONNAUGHT RANGERS by William Grattan—The 88th Regiment during the Napoleonic Wars by a Serving Officer.

BUGLER AND OFFICER OF THE RIFLES by William Green & Harry Smith—With the 95th (Rifles) during the Peninsular & Waterloo Campaigns of the Napoleonic Wars.

NAPOLEONIC WAR STORIES by Sir Arthur Quiller-Couch—Tales of soldiers, spies, battles & sieges from the Peninsular & Waterloo campaigns.

CAPTAIN OF THE 95TH (RIFLES) by Jonathan Leach—An officer of Wellington's sharpshooters during the Peninsular, South of France and Waterloo campaigns of the Napoleonic wars.

RIFLEMAN COSTELLO by Edward Costello—The adventures of a soldier of the 95th (Rifles) in the Peninsular & Waterloo Campaigns of the Napoleonic wars.

AVAILABLE ONLINE AT **www.leonaur.com**
AND FROM ALL GOOD BOOK STORES

www.ingramcontent.com/pod-product-compliance
Lightning Source LLC
Chambersburg PA
CBHW030217170426
43201CB00006B/117